To Don and Betsy —
The friends of our
youth are the best
of all !
Love,
Leslie

Bets, my rapport with
Benno owed much
to your guiding
presence at our
initial contact. Your
influence is legendary
in the Old North State !

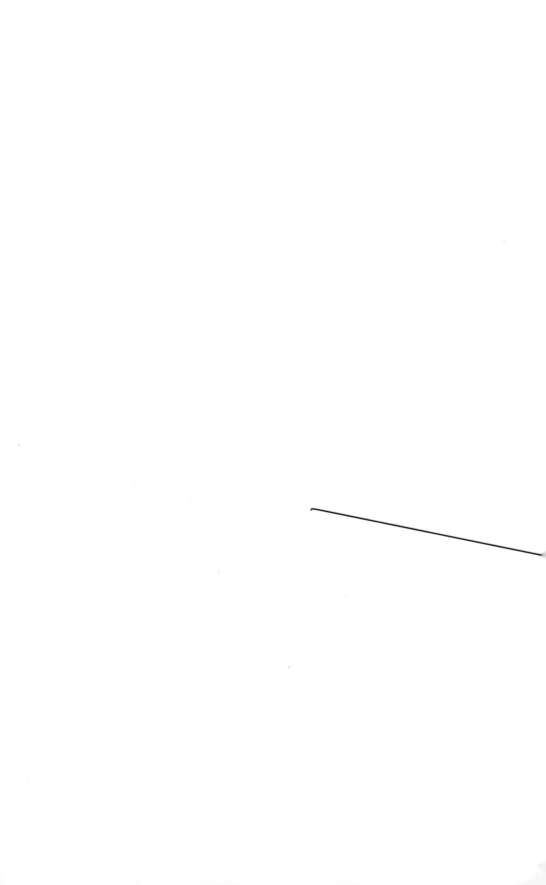

THE RESEARCH UNIVERSITY PRESIDENCY IN THE LATE TWENTIETH CENTURY

THE RESEARCH UNIVERSITY PRESIDENCY IN THE LATE TWENTIETH CENTURY

A Life Cycle/Case History Approach

H. Keith H. Brodie
and Leslie Banner

AMERICAN COUNCIL ON EDUCATION
PRAEGER
Series on Higher Education

Library of Congress Cataloging-in-Publication Data

Brodie, H. Keith H. (Harlow Keith Hammond), 1939–
    The research university presidency in the late twentieth century : a life cycle/case history approach / H. Keith H. Brodie and Leslie Banner.
        p.   cm—(ACE/Praeger series on higher education)
    Includes bibliographical references and index.
    ISBN 0–275–98560–1 (alk. paper)
    1. Universities and colleges—United States—Presidents—Biography.   2. Universities and colleges—United States—Administration.   I. Banner, Leslie.   II. Title.   III. American Council on Education/Praeger series on higher education.
    LB2341.B655   2005
    378.01—dc22   2004028275

British Library Cataloguing in Publication Data is available.

Library of Congress Catalog Card Number: 2004028275
ISBN: 0–275–98560–1

First published in 2005

Praeger Publishers, 88 Post Road West, Westport, CT 06881
An imprint of Greenwood Publishing Group, Inc.
www.praeger.com

Printed in the United States of America

The paper used in this book complies with the Permanent Paper Standard issued by the National Information Standards Organization (Z39.48–1984).

10 9 8 7 6 5 4 3 2 1

For Stephanie, who perseveres

CONTENTS

ACKNOWLEDGMENTS

This book would not exist without the cooperation of our eight subjects and we are deeply grateful not only for their time but also for the seriousness and attention to detail with which they approached both the interviews and the subsequent review of their responses. They generously expended emotional and intellectual energy for this project and we sincerely hope they are pleased with the results. We appreciate as well the various courtesies extended to us by members of their staffs.

Initial background research for this project was ably and enthusiastically pursued by our office assistant Steven A. Kelts and, after his departure for graduate school at Stanford, by his successor Diana Kees. For institutional profiles and for clarification of some details of terms in office, we are indebted to the archivists and special collections librarians of the universities our presidents have served. We also owe thanks to the webmasters, archivists, and librarians at all Research I universities in the United States who have labored to provide historical information on their websites about their institutions' presidents, thus making survey studies such as ours far less onerous.

We are honored to be publishing under the auspices of the American Council on Education and especially appreciate the patient, intelligent guidance and friendship of Susan Slesinger at Praeger Publishers. Essential technical support during the final stages of manuscript preparation was provided by Richard A. Soloway, spouse extraordinaire.

INTRODUCTION
TO THE STUDY

This book is a study of the research university presidency by means of case histories gathered and analyzed using a life cycle approach. The case histories are presented in the form of personal narratives—taped interviews built around questions that address the various stages a presidency passes through, identifying specific tasks and conflicts associated with each stage. While deliberately narrow rather than broad in scope in order to examine specific situations each president faced and how he responded, this work can lay claim nonetheless to being representative because it is restricted to leaders of similar institutions during the same period, or overlapping periods, of time, whose experiences and insights were therefore colored by similar circumstances and expectations.

GENESIS OF THE STUDY

From 1985 to 1993, the authors of this work enjoyed the privilege of observing a research university presidency from the inside. Because one of us, the president, had originally been trained as a psychiatrist, and the other, the writer/editor, in the study of literature, it was natural that when time for reflection on this experience was granted, we would examine it in terms of developmental psychology and personal narrative. What resonated most with the psychiatrist/president was a comparison with the Eriksonian principle of the life cycle, which holds that each stage of human development requires successful engagement with certain basic conflicts if the individual is to reach a full and healthy maturity. Applying this concept to understanding the course of a complex leadership position seemed potentially useful; it would provide a tool for identifying and examining patterns in the presidency and addressing questions of culture, governance, and especially stress, for the issues of burnout and the decreasing average life span of these college and university presidencies have been regularly noted and debated in both the popular press and higher education literature for the past twenty years or more.

A working descriptive hypothesis was therefore developed: that there is an identifiable pattern or life cycle in the research university president's job, including a series of predictable tasks and milestones that must be successfully negotiated if a presidency is to continue on track. To test this hypothesis we decided to collect our case histories not from newspaper accounts or bystanders, but from the presidents themselves, asking for their collaboration in creating texts that would address their tenures in terms of time, task, and conflict, and that would include their own frank, personal evaluations of their experiences. In doing so we hoped also to discover whether the epigenetic principle would hold true, that is, whether one must resolve the conflicts associated with one stage of the presidency before moving on to achieve success in the next.

Working outward from our own experiences at Duke University, we focused our study on a period of time and type of institution we already knew well. More important, however, we realized that by restricting the chronological focus to presidential terms that began in the 1980s, we would be able to draw from a pool of leaders who had left behind at least one presidency about which they could speak freely; and by restricting our selection of participants to former presidents of AAU Research I universities, we could draw meaningful comparisons and generalizations from a relatively small sample.[1] Undeniable, too, in our thinking, was the star power of these institutions, whose standing as the most complex and influential sector of American higher education makes their histories and their leaders inherently interesting to a wide range of readers.

A review of books and articles on the topic of college and university presidencies confirmed our sense that a focused study of the kind we contemplated—a comparative analysis of the experiences of peer presidents in the face of predictable conflicts—would be unusual in the literature of higher education leadership. Few if any of these studies have differentiated among institutions, usually taking together all types and levels from the community college through the largest comprehensive and research universities. Nor have many sought to focus closely on the experiences of individual leaders, typically being more concerned with broader compilations of data as is the case with the ACE (American Council on Education) profile series *The American College President* that has become a fundamental point of reference for leadership studies. Furthermore, where presidents have been asked to speak frankly on the record, they usually have done so anonymously. Important insights are gleaned in this way, of course—witness, for example, excerpts from unattributed interviews in Robert Rosenzweig, *The Political University: Policy, Politics, and Presidential Leadership in the American Research University* (1998)[2]—but there is a loss, too, when the personal and specific cannot be usefully linked with the history of what is otherwise known in a particular context. Presidential memoirs that offer candid assessments of their authors' experiences are sometimes both informative and compelling, as personal narratives often can be, and in this regard the present study may be considered a subcategory of the memoir genre.

DESIGN AND METHODOLOGY

Using our life cycle framework, we created a time line for the university presidency, dividing it into four phases: the prelude or courtship, appointment, and preparation phase; the honeymoon period; the plateau or settled period of an administration; and the exit phase, extending from a president's first thoughts of resignation to actual departure from office. We then described tasks and typical areas of conflict appropriate to each phase and used these and the time line to develop open-ended questions that would focus our subjects' recollections and encourage their creative participation in this way of looking at their presidencies.

Next, we set about identifying former leaders of AAU Research I universities who had been appointed in the 1980s, and here we made a surprising discovery: The only woman who met the criteria for our study was Donna Shalala, who led the University of Wisconsin-Madison from 1988 to 1993. From 1980 through 1989, no other AAU Research I institution had appointed a female president or chancellor, and only one non-AAU Research I university had done so, the University of California-Santa Barbara, where Barbara Uehling became chancellor in 1987 (UC-Santa Barbara did not gain AAU membership until 1995, the year after Uehling stepped down). This decade-long reluctance among the most respected research intensive universities to appoint women to their top leadership position was all the more surprising as the 1970s had seemed to promise a breakthrough when four women were appointed in quick succession: in 1975, Lorene Lane Rogers at the University of Texas-Austin; in 1976, Mary F. Berry at the University of Colorado-Boulder;

xiv   Introduction to the Study

and in 1978, Hanna H. Gray at the University of Chicago and Barbara
Uehling at the University of Missouri-Columbia.[3] Whatever the complex
set of reasons for this sudden open-and-shut-out at the top for women
(and the cluster of appointments in western and midwestern states is geo-
culturally suggestive), the real breakthrough came at last in the 1990s
with seven appointments, followed by thirteen between 2000 and 2004.[4]

We had begun our search for study candidates by eliminating from the
AAU membership list all leaders of non-Research I and Canadian institutions. We then identified presidents or chancellors who had been appointed in the 1980s and eliminated those who had not yet stepped down
and those who had been appointed before their institutions attained AAU
membership. Five institutions had appointed two presidents each during
the 1980s, all of whom had stepped down by the time of our study, and
we decided not to include any university more than once. We ended up
with a pool of thirty possible candidates to whom we began writing selectively, asking that they participate in our study by agreeing to a candid
ninety-minute taped interview directed by the life cycle hypothesis, which
we explained. We also included several sample questions keyed to their
individual experiences, and we offered them the opportunity to review
their interview transcripts and remove material they were uncomfortable
with making public. Eight responded favorably, agreeing to be interviewed
within the framework we described.[5] In order of presidential terms they
were: 1980, Donald Kennedy (Stanford), Harold Shapiro (University of
Michigan), Michael Sovern (Columbia); 1982, James Freedman (University of Iowa); 1985, Robert O'Neil (University of Virginia); 1986,
Benno Schmidt (Yale); 1988, Paul Hardin (University of North Carolina
at Chapel Hill); and 1988/1989, Vartan Gregorian (Brown University).[6]
In addition to the universities where our participants had served as presidents in the 1980s and 1990s and from which they had resigned, three
presidents brought relevant comparative experiences to their interviews:
James Freedman and Harold Shapiro were still serving as president at
Dartmouth and Princeton, respectively, and Robert O'Neil had been
chancellor of Indiana University-Bloomington, 1975–1980, and president
of the University of Wisconsin System, 1980–1985. Thus, our total pool
of presidential experience extended somewhat beyond the study's set pa-
rameters, from 1975 (O'Neil) to the date of interview (Freedman and
Shapiro), and encompassing a total of five public and five private Research
I universities, one private Doctoral II (Dartmouth, which has professional
schools of business, engineering, and medicine in addition to its Ph.D.
programs), and one public university system.

With two exceptions (Paul Hardin and Benno Schmidt), the inter-

views took place in the participants' own offices, and most of these sessions stayed within the suggested ninety-minute limit. Harold Shapiro
and Robert O'Neil agreed to follow-up questions (Shapiro by telephone)
and Benno Schmidt requested a second full-length session in New York
after his initial interview in North Carolina. The project's design apparently struck a chord with our subjects who paid us the compliment of serious intellectual engagement, giving interviews that proved to be not
only thoughtful, but anecdotal, lively, philosophical, personal, and candid in ways a sitting president can seldom be. The interview format
worked especially well in two ways: the time commitment was adequate
for focused reflection without being burdensome to our busy subjects, and
the open nature of the questions allowed for an important element of
narrator choice, that is, each president's story could be told, within the
framework, as he thought best. Thus, the fact that all topics were not addressed equally nor all questions interpreted similarly by all presidents in
itself became of interest.

PRESENTATION

The presidential narratives are presented twice: first, in a comparative
analysis organized according to the life cycle theory, and then in full, with
interview questions edited out or indicated in brackets. Each of the full-
length narratives begins with a brief profile of the president and the institution or institutions he led, and offers readers the opportunity to see
his comments fully and in context and to hear his distinctive narrative
voice, inferring attitude and emotion for themselves. Readers who have
a particular interest in the recent history of one or more of the universities represented may want to turn immediately to this section.

The analysis of the narratives in Part I follows the time line and phases
we established to define the presidential life cycle, beginning with a comparison of the presidents' routes to office, any preparations they made,
their initial attitudes toward the selection of an administrative team, and
their preliminary thoughts on what they hoped to accomplish. We des-
ignated this series of tasks the prelude, the earliest phase of a presidency
when both the university's representatives and the candidate/president-
elect are functioning on assumptions, expectations, and partial knowledge. The prelude begins with the first contact from a search committee
and inaugurates tasks that, while they will continue into later phases of
the presidency, in the beginning especially, have the potential for significant consequences.

In the next phase, the honeymoon, we explored the first months of presidential tenure, asking for examples of conflicts that for better or worse ended the new leader's trial period, and inquiring about considerations of risk, that is, whether the desire to become firmly established as president affected decisions during the first year or so in office. In the section on the plateau, our designation for the settled phase of an administration, we focused on conflict resolution in the course of governance, and in the exit we examined how each president came to leave office, his thought processes leading up to and the events surrounding his decision, the effects on campus of announcing an impending departure, and finally, coming full circle, the president's personal experience as predecessor and successor.

We found that interrupting the flow of our subjects' narratives to set their responses on each topic side-by-side with their colleagues' created almost a whole new text, a tutorial on the research university presidency. Leading similar institutions, they had shared similar experiences; sharing similar experiences, they had pursued similar solutions and yet *personally* had had different reactions and varying outcomes. The life cycle framework imposed an artificial organization and selection process on the presidents' recollections to be sure, but it also encouraged them to describe some of the painful or troubling aspects of their presidencies, to account not only for successes but also for failures, for problems insoluble, only partially soluble, or soluble at a high price. The life cycle approach may have condensed and pruned these presidents' narratives in the telling, but in no way did it serve to obscure the complexity of their experiences.

One final word about the texts: These are the presidents' stories. While we reference information from outside sources in a limited way when providing more context seems useful, here we wanted primarily to grasp the presidents' points of view, to listen to their own evaluations of themselves and of what happened to them. Their strong, at times exuberant, voices come through in the narratives, conveying something of the emotional and psychological elements of university leadership, private information about undertaking a public trust that is well worth hearing.

NOTES

1. Association of American Universities, founded in 1900. We used the 1994 edition of A *Classification of Institutions of Higher Education* (Princeton, NJ: Carnegie Foundation for the Advancement of Teaching) in which Research I universities are defined as institutions that "award 50 or more doctoral degrees" and receive "$40 million or more in federal support" annually (p. xix). This edition is more relevant to our study than the 2000 edition.

2. Robert Rosenzweig, *The Political University: Policy, Politics, and Presidential Leadership in the American Research University* (Baltimore, MD: The Johns Hopkins University Press, 1998). The author identifies the group of presidents involved but not the individual speakers.

3. We do not count acting/interim appointments nor do we include the "acting" year of appointments subsequently made permanent. Lorene Rogers, a member of the chemistry faculty at the University of Texas-Austin, served as acting president from September 1974 to September 1975 when she was named the fifteenth president of the University of Texas at Austin, becoming the first woman to head a Research I university. She stepped down in 1979. Hanna Holborn Gray served as acting president of Yale University from 1977 to 1978, and is now counted by Yale as the eighteenth president, a change of policy instituted after the interim service of Howard Lamar as acting president, 1992–1993 (in the wake of Benno Schmidt's sudden departure) was honored by dropping the "acting" from his title (personal communication, Danelle Moon, Manuscripts and Archives, Yale University Library, August 10, 2004). Although Mary F. Berry served as chancellor of the University of Colordo-Boulder only from 1976 to 1977, hers was not an interim appointment; in fact, the Colorado Regents were greatly disappointed when she left the university to join Jimmy Carter's cabinet as assistant secretary for Health, Education, and Welfare. Berry, who holds history and law degrees from the University of Michigan and is currently a chaired professor of history at the University of Pennsylvania, is both the only woman and the only African American ever appointed to the Boulder chancellorship (personal communication, UC-Boulder archivist David M. Hays, June 21, 2004; Hays also cites Ronald A. James, *Our Own Generation*, Regents of the University of Colorado, 1979).

4. Women appointed to lead Research I universities, 1990s: 1993, Duke University, Nannerl O. Keohane; 1993, University of California-Irvine, Laurel L. Wilkening; 1994, SUNY-Stony Brook (AAU 2001), Shirley Strum Kenny; 1994, University of Iowa, Mary Sue Coleman; 1994, University of Pennsylvania, Judith Rodin; 1997, University of Alabama-Birmingham (non AAU), W. Ann Reynolds; 1998, North Carolina State University (non AAU), Marye Anne Fox. Women appointed to lead Research I universities, 2000–2004: 2000, University of Illinois-Chicago (non AAU), Sylvia Manning; 2001, Brown University, Ruth J. Simmons; 2001, Indiana University-Bloomington, Sharon Stephens Brehm; 2001, Princeton University, Shirley M. Caldwell Tilghman; 2001, University of Illinois Urbana-Champaign, Nancy Cantor; 2001, University of Miami (non AAU), Donna E. Shalala; 2002, Ohio State University, Karen A. Holbrook; 2002, University of Alabama-Birmingham (non AAU), Carol Z. Garrison; 2002, University of Michigan, Mary Sue Coleman; 2003, University of Cincinnati (non AAU), Nancy L. Zimpher; 2004, Massachusetts Institute of Technology, Susan Hockfield; 2004, University of California-San Diego, Marye Anne Fox; 2004, University of Pennsylvania, Amy Gutmann.

5. We especially regret that Donna Shalala felt unable to participate.

6. Although Vartan Gregorian did not arrive on the Brown campus until January 1989, he dates his service as president from his appointment in August 1988, while still heading the New York Public Library (correspondence of August 12, 2004, from Eleanor Lerman, Director of Publications and Public Affairs, Carnegie Corporation of New York).

PART I

The Analysis

CHAPTER 1

Prelude

That period from the first indications of interest on the part of a search committee to the day a new president actually takes office.

We posited the prelude phase of a presidency as consisting of four broadly conceived and overlapping tasks: negotiating candidacy, preparing for office by researching the institution and the job, deciding how to build an administrative team, and setting a preliminary agenda. Most of our presidents recounted errors in judgment, omissions, or misunderstandings during the prelude phase that led to conflicts later in their terms.

CANDIDACY

The first task for a candidate in the early stages of a search is to recognize and resolve, if possible, any ambivalence that might cloud or lead to the premature end of a presidential term, as happened, for example, in February 2000, when Vartan Gregorian's successor at Brown, Gordon Gee, departed for Vanderbilt after only two years, citing a poor "fit."[1] Personal conflicts inherent in contemplating any job change, questions of rapport with the university community, the board of trustees, and, for public institutions, the head of the state university system, as well as questions of career goals and ambitions all must be addressed. We therefore asked each of our presidents to comment on how and why he came to the office.

Candidates Kennedy, Shapiro (at Michigan), and Sovern had followed internal tracks to head their universities and, having served as provosts, were already known quantities to trustees, administrators, colleagues, and faculty who had served on governance committees. Not surprisingly, they recalled no particular conflicts about standing for and then accepting the presidency, especially since, as Harold Shapiro puts it, nobody "had to leave town to do it," i.e., there were no potential family upheavals or questions of institutional culture or other products of emotional and material change to consider. The presidency, for them, was not so much a professional target as a logical sequence; they displayed a relaxed attitude that might be characterized as, "Well, this just happened." Donald Kennedy, for example, takes a low-key approach when he notes simply that he does not think "anybody who takes a provostship ought to have [the presidency] completely out of mind":

> Suppose the president dies? If you have a serious commitment to doing academic administration in an institution that you care about—and [Stanford] has really been my only institution—then you have to consider that as a possibility.

Later in the interview, Kennedy provides further insight into his expectations on being asked to serve as provost:

> At the time, the university had made only internal appointments to the provostship. It had made only one external appointment of a president and that was not successful. Stanford's a place that has always considered that it has a rather special culture, and understanding that culture is important.

Harold Shapiro depicts himself as having been far less savvy than Kennedy about the possibility of a progression from provost to president:

> When I got a call from the president of the University of Michigan that he was interested in my becoming provost, I'm not sure that I knew what a provost was. I know that I didn't know what a president did. I always remind myself that when I first went to the University of Michigan as a faculty member, not only did I not know who the president was, I didn't care who the president was. I thought whoever it was he was doing his job and I was doing my job and the two of us would probably never meet, and we didn't, of course, for many years. That was just fine, I'm sure, with him; it was certainly fine with me. So I had absolutely no concept.

I knew so little about [the provostship] that if I'd had to leave town to do it, if someone else had offered me the same job somewhere else, I never would have done it. It just did not occur to me then that I might be president. However, I had enjoyed being chair of the [economics] department . . . and I didn't have to leave town, and I thought it would be an interesting and exciting experience, so why not? And that's how I became provost. Then it was only two and a half years or so before I was appointed president, and of course, I had begun to understand what the issues were. It was only in that position that I finally began to understand what a president was.

Like Shapiro, Michael Sovern reports "no burning hunger for academic administration," and says that for him, "it really was a series of accidents," beginning with his work in faculty governance, that led to the leadership of Columbia. But when eventually approached about the position of provost, his recollections demonstrate considerable sophistication about where such a promotion should take him. He told a member of the search committee:

"Bob, this is not a job I would want except under the most unusual circumstances." Being a good scholar he said, "What circumstances?" And I said, "Either of two. One, if you can't find anybody good, I would do it for a couple of years as a kind of draftee because this is an important job and we want it done right. The other is, if Bill McGill is going to step down as president, then I might be interested in the provostship with a view to succeeding him." And that was the first time I had ever acknowledged any interest in the presidency even to myself.

Except for Harold Shapiro who discussed his recruitment to Princeton in the context of his exit from Michigan, our external candidates took time to recall the makeup of search committees, questions asked, procedures followed, a level and type of detail internal candidates omitted. These recollections of the search process were more or less positive along a continuum ranging from James Freedman's unreserved praise for the Iowa search to Benno Schmidt's mea culpa for what he regarded as a skewed process at Yale. Between these two extremes, Vartan Gregorian, Paul Hardin, and Robert O'Neil related candidacies that only in retrospect emerged as having missing or perplexing elements with presidential repercussions. At the time, each thought he was participating in an unambiguous and familiar process in circumstances with which he was comfortable. Vartan Gregorian, former provost at Penn, knew the chairman of the Brown trustees[2] personally and found the search to be "thorough" and "professional." Paul Hardin, president of Drew University, was a native North Carolinian "married to a preacher's daughter who had seven hometowns in this state, so we knew the territory and were known widely throughout North Carolina." And Robert O'Neil, president of the University of Wisconsin System, although he had "never been to Charlottesville before . . . came to a relatively unfamiliar institution through a quite familiar channel"—the outgoing president of UVA who, unusually enough, "had been deputized by the search committee of the board of visitors to contact, as I later learned, several candidates whom he had known." Elements of these three searches are examined in more detail under preparation and agenda setting, as is the search that brought James Freedman to Dartmouth—a process almost perverse in its outcome, for Freedman describes an outstanding, even creative search strategy that successfully engaged his own cherished beliefs about higher education while positioning him for immediate conflict as Dartmouth's new president. Here, however, we consider the two extremes that our interviews produced on the topic of the outside search, beginning with Freedman's unblemished experience at Iowa.

Contemplating the leap from dean of the University of Pennsylvania Law School to his first presidency, James Freedman admits he "didn't know at the time how good [the search process] was, how exceptional it was." His enthusiastic description of his recruitment to the University of Iowa is of a process that augured well: The search he remembers as a "model" set up no conflicts for the early days of his presidency and in fact, created a situation of strength through propitious alliances. He lists as influencing factors his prior knowledge of the institution (through friends and having taught at the law school one summer term); the immediate rapport he felt with both the chair of the faculty search committee and the chair of the board of regents; and the honesty and respect with which he felt both the committee and the board treated him—sufficient to persuade him to accept an initial salary at Iowa *less* than he was being paid as dean of Penn Law. In fact, the effectiveness of the role played in the search by the board at Iowa is notable. To defuse somewhat the impact of the state's public records law, they persuaded the press to publish only the names of the final candidates; all nine members of the board (small, it must be said, for a large public university) interviewed the seven finalists and three of the nine had strong political connections, all of which Freedman views positively:

> The board won me over. . . . I had an opportunity to meet the entire board, which is not always common. . . . I was also impressed

with the way they did business. They essentially had a list of about twenty questions which they'd asked every single candidate, so none of us were subject to the whim of the moment and none of us got derailed on some hobbyhorse or other . . . the search process forged a bond between the chairman of the board and me. I don't know if that was by design, but that was what happened.

It was especially interesting because . . . the chairman . . . had been a state senator. One of the other members was a former lieutenant governor under then Governor Ray. . . . Another person on the board . . . was . . . the Republican National Committeeman. . . . The fact of having some politically astute, experienced people had to be a big help.

Finally, it was important to Freedman that the process had given him, in the chair of the search committee, a ready-made faculty ally, "someone . . . whom I had as a friend, someone I could ask during those first few months, 'Is this wise? is this sensible? what's the culture here? I'm doing this kind of thing, what do you think?'"

Although a native New Englander, Ivy League educated and in the midst of a successful Ivy League career, James Freedman was quite sure about his move to the presidency of a large midwestern university, so sure that when the chairman of the board offered him the job, he recalls, "I didn't have to go home and wait and think. He told me all the terms and the like, and I wanted it so much that I said, 'Can I call my wife?' And he said, 'Sure. I'll step out of the room.' And I said, 'You don't have to step out of the room!'" In contrast, Benno Schmidt, also in the midst of a successful Ivy League career in academic law, felt an ambivalence about moving to his first presidency, even to his alma mater, that he now believes may have tainted the search process, one that, in his words, was "smooth . . . perhaps too smooth."

Having begun his term as dean of Columbia University Law School on July 1, 1984, Benno Schmidt found himself being approached only a little over a year later by Cyrus Vance on behalf of the Yale University presidential search committee. Schmidt recalls his enthusiasm about his role at Columbia where he was "off to a terrific start"—prestigious new faculty were signing on, money was coming in, alumni were rallying, and Schmidt was understandably "anxious for the Yale process not to derail that":

So I insisted with Cy Vance on a very expedited procedure . . . that there be no publicity . . . no public discussion. I didn't want anybody to think that I was looking for a different position. I wanted it to be very clear that I had not thrown my hat in the ring, as I had not, they called me. And I said to Mr. Vance that if Yale wanted me to consider being its president I would not do that as part of a short list of possible candidates. I would consider it if they told me I was the one they wanted, and I would give them a quick answer within 48 hours, but I was not going to enter into a process where I was one of several people, where I felt that the word would leak out. . . . I would not [risk] indicating that I wanted to leave Columbia and then having it not happen. I thought that would have been very bad and demoralizing for Columbia, and I didn't want to hurt Columbia in any way, and that's the way it went.

There were a couple of aspects of that process which, looking back on it, were perhaps not ideal. It was in the nature of the process I insisted on that many members of the Yale Corporation had no chance to meet me at all. In fact, I met most members of the Yale Corporation on the day they actually decided formally to offer me the job. That meant the search committee of the Corporation was engaged with me over a period of some weeks and felt that they knew the person they were considering, but many members of the Corporation did not. I later learned that not all [of them] were necessarily of one mind about who should be the next president or indeed the type of person. . . . So, the expeditiousness of [the process] was good in some ways for me but not good in that the entire board was not engaged, and some people felt the selection moved a little bit too quickly to a conclusion. I don't know that for sure, but I have the sense that that was the case. This did not pose any insuperable problem, but I think it might have been a little bit better for me had there been wider discussion, had the process taken a little more time.

Affecting Schmidt's hindsight is his knowledge of the unprecedented degree of institutional change he immediately asked Yale's board to face with him, a degree he acknowledges was "difficult" and "uncomfortable." Although he emphasizes that Yale Corporation members were unstinting in their support throughout his term, it is evident that he also believes a more orthodox search process might have been to his advantage after all, creating a higher level of comfort and confidence among trustees from the very beginning. Schmidt's ambivalence about leaving Columbia so soon had led him to a miscalculation that created unnecessary strain around the search, hardly the ideal way to begin a high-profile presidency. Yet, for all the expeditiousness of the process he insisted on, he did not overlook the importance of negotiating family issues before accepting the presidency. It is ironic, therefore, that his punctiliousness in addressing with the trustees the matter of his wife's career proved ultimately unsuccessful in defusing it as a presidential issue:

I was genuinely surprised (and actually continue to be surprised) by the negative reaction many members of the Yale community had to the fact that my wife Helen felt she needed to be based in New York City to continue her career as a filmmaker. That had been very clearly understood in my discussions with the trustees, with Cy Vance, from the beginning. That was a view that I strongly supported, in fact, and a view that seemed to me both natural and right for Helen's career and for our relationship, and it seemed to be one that the Yale community, as a forward-looking and progressive community by and large, would understand and indeed in many ways celebrate. I thought Helen's career would be something that people at Yale would be excited that she was pursuing. In my naïveté, I thought that if there were to be problems about that view, they would come from the alumni who might be hanging on to the idea of the traditional university president's wife presiding over teas . . . but I thought the faculty and the students would surely find the situation not only understandable, but forward-looking and good. And I guess it turned out to be exactly the opposite.

The trustees understood completely and found it perfectly acceptable. I didn't have much of a problem with the alumni who were generally very supportive of me as president and many of them were enthusiastic about Helen's career. They'd see her films, read about her, and meet her on occasion. . . . But I had a very clear sense that with some faculty and with many of the students, the perennial issue arose of the president of a major university not being around all the time . . . put into the perspective that because Helen was not in New Haven full time as her base and we kept a home in New York as well as the President's House in New Haven, that that somehow represented a lack of commitment by me to New Haven and to Yale. . . . I was surprised when the most effective sign the prodivestment student protesters were carrying around campus was, "Where's Benno?" . . .

. . . Many of [the trustees] had a reaction of surprise similar to my own. There were plenty of things to criticize me about because I was taking lots of controversial positions, but for [Helen's residence in New York] to have been a source of criticism and unhappiness was a big surprise. Still is, still is.

PREPARATION

One of the deceptively obvious tasks of the prelude phase is gathering information about the job and the institution under consideration, not only to make an informed decision but also to avoid unpleasant surprises and unanticipated conflicts in the first year of a presidency. Despite their considerable prior academic and administrative experience, seven of our eight presidents described themselves as unprepared in some crucial area or areas of institutional knowledge as their terms in office began. Either they had chosen to do little or no homework or, believing they were or would be adequately prepared by dint of experience, were caught off guard.

Asked whether there were issues that should have been discussed before he accepted the presidency of Brown University, Vartan Gregorian responded unequivocally:

> There were certain things that were not volunteered and I did not ask, things that did not occur to me to ask. I had not done an exhaustive study; I had not done a great deal of homework. I did not know that Brown was operating under a consent decree as a result of a sex discrimination case. The Lamphere decree governed Brown's entire hiring system; a federal judge had to approve each outside hire. The first inkling I had of that fact—I thought it was a joke until later I discovered it was not—was when I said, well, I would like to be a member of the faculty, I always have been, and [the response was,] "Well, we'll see what the judge will say about that." So, anyway, that was one surprise. The second surprise was again my fault, not theirs; this was the issue of (and something that I recommend every incoming president ask about) the last accrediting committee report. [Brown had just been visited by] an accrediting committee in '87–'88, and I was not given a copy [of the report]. It was a year later, after I had come, that I stumbled onto it. That report had analyzed several strengths and weaknesses of Brown which I should have known about. So, in terms of the search, the committee did not volunteer [this information], it might not have occurred to them [to do so], and it did not occur to me to ask during the search process. Also, I did not know that one of my friends, who happened to be a member of the board of trustees at Brown, was a candidate. It was only later that I discovered this . . . but you can't touch all the bases; it's a very hard period because you're studying your own transfer, your own dislocation, your own uprooting, and more attention sometimes is paid to how you're going to extricate yourself from your current obligations than to what kind of new ones you're going to have [to take on].

Gregorian also concedes that under the circumstances he was "naïve" in his expectations of minimizing the president's role as fund-raiser at Brown:

Because the moment you, as president, discover the financial situation, you have to do something about it. You have to start fundraising. You can always have a balanced budget through deferred maintenance, but deferred maintenance, unless you have plans for it, becomes planned neglect. So I'm never impressed by balanced budgets alone. First, you have to see what kind of shape the campus is in, [what the situation is with] financial aid, all kinds of things. . . . So anytime you have a [potential] president being interviewed, he or she will need not just to see whether the books are balanced, but to see [that] the books aren't balanced at the expense of something important.

At Yale, only after accepting the presidency did Benno Schmidt discover the extent to which the books had been "balanced at the expense of something important":

[Did I realize the financial strains on Yale, the maintenance problems when I accepted the job?] No. I saw the books—oh, I saw the books! It was not at all an issue of anything being hidden from me, not at all. I was given complete access and both the trustees and Bart Giamatti and his colleagues at Yale were absolutely open and very clear about the position of the university. I think the problem was that no one had tried systematically to assess Yale's financial position . . . to give you just one example: There had never been a complete engineering study of Yale's buildings, [a survey] so that people had a sense of what the problems were. . . .

. . . I remember this so well: After I was named president, I wanted to try to meet the faculty in a fairly personal way. . . . I didn't want to be in Bart's way (I moved up to Yale six months before I started), so . . . [t]he librarian was kind enough to [arrange for me to use] a large room up in the stacks that held Yale's world-renowned collection of rare bookplates. So I sat in this bookplate room . . . faculty [came to] see me every half an hour; it was brutal. I began to notice, sitting in this room, that some days (I started this process in January) I would be sitting there and my teeth would be chattering and I would be in my overcoat with my muffler around my neck. Other days it was just stiflingly hot, ninety degrees, having nothing to do with what the weather was outside. When I would get up and go down to find a men's room in the stacks, often I would have to walk through an inch of standing water. I remember asking about this and the librarian telling me that there had really been no work done on the library's heating system since it was built, and it still had the old plumbing system, and she was very much aware and people were very much aware of this, but again, not so much systematically. Then

Henry Turner . . . a great professor of German history and at that time the master of Davenport College, came for his appointment in the library. . . . He said, "I'd like to take you over to Davenport and show you the basement." . . . Standing water, exposed wires, pipes with all the insulation falling off. He would put his finger in the wall and pull off hunks of plaster. . . . the heating didn't work well, the plumbing was a disaster. Then I started asking some of the other masters about the condition of their colleges and what was going on down in their basements. Again, this was not exactly news, everybody knew about these problems, but they just hadn't, for one reason or another, added it all up.

. . . Yale had eleven million square feet of buildings, most of which were over fifty years old. When all of [the information] was assembled in one room and we had a chance to look at it systematically, it was shocking. Seeing it whole was a shock.

Schmidt had not been prepared to discover that Yale, "for all of its phenomenal strengths was living beyond its means," the single fact that played the biggest part in shaping his presidential term. Nor was Harold Shapiro prepared for a similar discovery at Princeton:

One of the things that I learned within months was that, much to my surprise, although the university had just finished a big and successful capital campaign, the operating budget of the university had what I would call a structural deficit. That is, it was actually in deficit and the kind of deficit that would grow over time. So my experience at Michigan had taught me, I thought, that when a problem like this arises nothing is gained by delay. You've just got to address it. It's tough, but you get it over with and you go on to the next stage. Well, when I informed the community here that we had a budget problem, I was met with absolute incredulity. That is, it couldn't be possible, it must be made up, it must be social engineering of some kind. I think people here had begun to believe their own rhetoric, that is, that everything had been so successful, the money was coming in over the transom, and there really couldn't be a problem. Besides which, Princeton was sitting there with a two-and-a-half-billion-dollar endowment. How could anybody be in trouble?

Of course, we weren't in trouble like survival trouble, but we still had a serious deficit in our operating budget and I proceeded to announce that we were going to do what was necessary to get the budget under control. . . . Well, people just thought this was some kind of ridiculous idea that I had.

Why didn't experienced academic administrators like Vartan Gregorian, Benno Schmidt, and Harold Shapiro learn more before accepting these presidencies? Apparently because they were already psychologically committed to the institutions. Like Gregorian, Shapiro had done little or no homework before accepting Princeton's offer:

> I just said to myself, "Well, here's a great university. It's got to have its own problems, but I don't need to know those. Those aren't going to determine whether I do this or not. Here's a university that's so good it must know what it's doing." . . . I told myself that I would go to Princeton and learn and then think about what to do. That was my attitude.

Vartan Gregorian, after spearheading the financial resuscitation of the New York Public Library (1981–1989), was eager to return to what he fantasized would be the more balanced life of the academy:

> Maybe it was wishful thinking, or wistful, but . . . [o]ne of the reasons I chose Brown was that it is small, private, and manageable, and I wanted to do a lot more in terms of intellectual and academic and educational issues, to deal with these rather than with financial issues. But, I tell you, that was unrealistic in retrospect.

And for Benno Schmidt, who describes himself as having been "supremely happy at Columbia Law School," the Yale offer was literally a "call":

> I think that the Yale presidency is almost certainly the only academic job of any kind in any university in the world that would have tempted me to leave. But I did feel that it was something of a call. I mean, sure, Henry Rosovsky turned it down when he was dean at Harvard, but he had nothing to do with Yale. I had two Yale degrees. In many ways I attributed almost everything that I had been able to do to Yale and particularly to Yale Law School, and I felt an immense sense of loyalty.

James Freedman, too, seems to have felt that the invitation to lead Dartmouth College was an irresistible call. A native of Manchester, New Hampshire, born to Jewish intellectuals of modest means for whom the Ivy League represented "the establishment world of higher education [and] the apotheosis of their dreams" for their son,[3] Freedman could both return home and fulfill long-held personal and professional ambitions by leaving Iowa City for Hanover. The way the job resonated with these powerful personal themes may have led him to overlook or fail to consider carefully enough the differences in institutional culture that ultimately played a significant part in his Dartmouth presidency's being "a much rockier, uneven . . . kind of experience" than his presidency at Iowa had been. First, there was the surprising role of alumni at Dartmouth:

> I wasn't [concerned about the Dartmouth alumni] when I came, but boy, I learned soon after. I had no idea of the way in which alumni then felt entitled to run this place and entitled to be heard. They were here constantly; every weekend the place was overrun with class officers and club officers and the alumni council and all these boards of overseers. I just had no idea of the prominence of alumni. It's not that they make a lot of policy and it's not even that they influence academic policy—I don't think they do. But their omnipresence here, and their sense of engagement in the place and entitlement to be engaged in the place was just far greater than anything I'd ever known. I should have taken my cue from the beginning because the difference in the inaugurations at Iowa and Dartmouth said worlds about the difference between the two schools. The Iowa inauguration [included] dozens of university presidents . . . Harold Shapiro spoke on behalf of the Big Ten presidents; Stan Ikenberry . . . spoke on behalf of the AAU. . . . There was a sense of, "Iowa is part of a national academic community and we want that represented here." Dartmouth set up the inauguration for July 19 . . . middle of the summer. Not a single academic was here. Not a single academic was asked to speak. I was allowed to have a speaker, and my speaker was Vartan Gregorian. . . . But the Dartmouth inauguration was set up for the alumni. It wasn't set up for the national academic community, it was set up for the alumni. And no one gave a thought [to this]. It wasn't [that] they made a decision against it, it just never occurred to them that this ought to be an event in the academic life of the college and you ought to have other presidents here, certainly the Ivy presidents, and there ought to be people bringing greetings from the Ivy League, or greetings from some other outfit. It never occurred to anybody. This was an in-house event, this was a bar mitzvah, this was a wedding. And that's when I first should have begun to be quite aware that alumni play a big, big role here.

Then there was the chip-on-the-shoulder attitude with which Dartmouth alumni approached their new president, keeping Freedman on the defensive:

> My ideas upset them. At every alumni dinner I went to those first few years you could always count on people saying, "Are you going to—" the word "Harvardize" became a word here, that I was trying to "Harvardize" because I was the first president who wasn't Dartmouth. "We're not Harvard and who would want to be, and Har-

vard's all nerds." The students had this attitude as much as the
alumni. Harvard was the symbol of everything that was wrong, and
it bespoke such an inferiority complex. . . . The sense of inferiority
here was all focused on my having come from Harvard and sounding as if I had a Harvard agenda, which was intellectual seriousness,
great dignity, aspirations for the faculty, wanting students who were
not every single one well-rounded. . . . Students with an edge to
them. All of those values should be Dartmouth's values, but people
saw that as saying, "You're unhappy with Dartmouth because it isn't
like Harvard, and that's what you're trying to do to us."

And finally, there was the anti-Semitism, oblique, perhaps, on the part
of those who were concerned about "Harvardization," and virulent on the
part of the student staff and outside supporters of *The Dartmouth Review*:

Easterners are different from Iowans. Iowans welcomed us. I mean,
we were strange creatures out there, a little different. But they welcomed us . . . even though I was an outsider. People welcomed us.
The Jewish issue never arose in Iowa. No one said a word to me
about it. The board would have if they had thought it would be an
issue because they were that kind of board. But no one ever did. . . .
It never was an issue there. Here [at Dartmouth], it was, of course,
something of an issue, and all the issues of anti-Semitism were connected with the *Review*—as you know, anti-Semitism was a leitmotif through the history of the *Review* . . . that had to have something
to do with the reaction in alumni land, too. It wasn't against Jews
but "Jewish" was itself a surrogate word for intellectual, for Harvard,
for a set of values that they did not see as Dartmouth. Now, you put
together Jewish, Harvard, intellectual, and you know you're talking
about a creature they thought was not really of the history of Dartmouth.
    [When the *Review* targeted me for anti-Semitic attacks,] I can't
tell you I ever thought about leaving, but I did think a lot about,
"How is this ever going to end? When and how are we going to bring
this to an end?" The board was scared to death I was going to leave.
No one ever said that to me, but they had made a huge investment
in me because I was so different and because the mission was so significant, and were I to have left after a couple of years, it would have
hurt Dartmouth because it would have confirmed in the national
press that this is an ungovernable place, run by the right wing and
a bunch of people like Buckley and Simon and a man named George
Champion, who was the retired chairman of Chase Manhattan
Bank, a Dartmouth graduate. I never really thought of leaving, but
the anti-Semitism was the absolute—you know, when they did that
business of me in a Hitler uniform [Oct. 26, 1988] and the article ti-

tled, "Ein Reich, Ein Volk, Ein Freedmann" [Oct. 19, 1988] that was the bottom. The board was so concerned, their question was, "How do you respond to that? How does the board respond?"—since I couldn't respond because it was about me, but it was so ugly.

For Jim Freedman and his wife, the early years at Dartmouth carried elements of stress that had been largely unanticipated, wear and tear for which their experience at the University of Iowa had not prepared them. One question that naturally arises is whether differences in institutional cultures can ever be discovered and adequately taken into account before one becomes immersed in them. Based on his own experience, Robert O'Neil thinks not:

> I suppose there may have been questions I could have asked [in the interview], but in order to appreciate the differences between Virginia and any place I'd been in the past, one could not find that out by asking questions. The ideal way of knowing what those differences were, I suppose, would have been to be able to come here, say, as a visitor for a year, and then all of a sudden to be engaged in the presidential search. By that time you would know the institution. My experience has been unusual. Four times I have come in as an outsider. . . . At Cincinnati, at Indiana, at Wisconsin, and at Virginia, I was totally an outsider and really knew next to nothing about the institution. Being an outsider has some advantages, but it also has disadvantages in that there are lots of things you just simply don't know and can't know if you come upon one institution from the perspective of another. So I think my answer to the question, were there questions that I should have asked? is that I don't think such differences as later proved to be significant could have been gleaned from simply asking questions.

Like Vartan Gregorian, Robert O'Neil had been looking to return to the academy when he was offered the presidency of the University of Virginia. After five years as head of the huge, multicampus Wisconsin system, he felt "somewhat distanced from the life of a functioning academic institution[,] more closely tied to the state government and less closely tied to faculty and student issues. So I welcomed the opportunity to return, as . . . at Indiana, to a central, single campus role." And like Harold Shapiro and James Freedman, O'Neil brought to a much smaller and decidedly different institution experience gleaned from leading large midwestern universities. But from the beginning he found that these prior administrative experiences did not necessarily translate to Virginia as he had expected, citing such specific differences as a surprising lack of enthusiasm for international programs, an unusual tolerance for classified research, a less cohesive faculty senate than he was used to, the failure of a structure for Afro-American affairs that had worked well at Indiana, and a disappointing outcome for his task force on the status of women. However, the first "inkling" that he was to find the culture of the University of Virginia persistently baffling, came during early talks when the board of visitors expressed their expectations and "among these expectations were things that seemed to me had already been achieved":

> There was always here, and I think to some extent still is, a sense that this university was until quite recently a small, semi-private Southern men's college. For example, many people would say [the University of Virginia] became a research university only since World War II. That is demonstrably untrue. Virginia became an AAU member in 1904 and would have been a charter member in 1900 almost certainly had there been a president.[4] . . . I contrast . . . that fact, with the perception that Virginia has become a research institution only in the last few years. It's a curious kind of under-evaluation. Now that's something that it would take months to understand; you can't ask the question, "How do you see yourselves?"
>
> This is one of the great mysteries to me; there has always been here a certain discontinuity or disparity between the external reality and an internal perception that one could paraphrase as, "We've only just arrived," when that's clearly not true. [While president] I was never clear (nor am I to this day) why it's advantageous to speak in those terms.

Another puzzling cultural artifact O'Neil notes is the relatively high nostalgia quotient that underlay campus turmoil over a legislative mandate for all Virginia universities to plan for expansion:

> This is the smallest save one of the AAU public institutions. . . . As close by as College Park, only two hours up the line, is the only really big state U in this part of the world. College Park is virtually indistinguishable from East Lansing or Champaign-Urbana or Madison, not necessarily in quality or mix, but just in sheer size. So it's not as though you're talking about some exotic place that's a thousand miles away, and most people here, if you asked them, "Were we to expand by 10 percent, would we be larger than the University of Maryland-College Park?" I suppose would have said, "No, that's a much larger institution." Yet there was somehow this feeling that Virginia was already a huge institution where traditions and personal relationships had been strained, and if there were further ex-

pansion, they would be strained beyond the breaking point. . . . I did
have a fair number of discussions [with faculty and others], and I
don't think anyone could ever pinpoint rationally what it was, what
would be lost. . . . Again, it's a dissonance between the perception
and the reality.

In hindsight, while the peculiarities of UVA culture may have caught
Robert O'Neil off guard (and may even have added a level of discomfort
that played a part, however minor, in his decision to announce his resignation after only four years in office), it was probably impossible, as he
says, to anticipate or prepare for them. Differences between institutional
cultures will exist, and it is only prudent to assume that some may prove
to be stumbling blocks at the beginning of a term or land mines later in
a presidential career.

For Paul Hardin and Donald Kennedy, the unanticipated elements at
the beginning of their terms were less institutional than personal. Paul
Hardin, coming from higher education's private sector of small, church-
related colleges, thought that he was at least aware of what he would face
in accepting the chancellorship of a large public university:

I knew I was beginning with a bit of a culture shock. . . . I was the
chief executive officer in an unambiguous way for twenty years, presiding over three privately supported schools. I knew that there was
a system head here who was my boss, and I knew that state systems
in general are fraught with bureaucracies and complexities that I had
not had to deal with. So I did come in with my eyes open to the
fact that I was entering a different culture, but I did not come in
with any sense that I would be in conflict in personal ways with the
president.

Unfortunately, Hardin had not been informed that relations between the
chairman of UNC's board of trustees (and head of the chancellor search
committee) Bob Eubanks and UNC system president C. D. Spangler were
somewhat strained over the matter of a report Eubanks had contracted
for with an outside consultant.[5] Thus, Hardin says, he was "quite innocent" of "an underlying tension" in the search process engendered by the
contents of the study, which was being referred to in the press as a "management audit":

There had been a study of the UNC system by a committee chaired
by James Fisher and a long report had been written. . . . I have
known Jim Fisher [author of *The Effective College President* (1988)

and *The Power of the Presidency* (1984).] slightly for years, but I had nothing to do with that report and did not know of its existence until I was well into the search process. . . . The report (which I read later) took a posture supportive of the flagship campus at Chapel Hill and a little negative with respect to the UNC system. It was fairly understandable that that would've made the system head uneasy; in fact, it made several people uneasy because the Fisher Report was hard-hitting. . . .

. . . In the early months of my relationship with President Spangler I felt something less than full rapport. As I look back on it, I think it had to do with his fear that I had come there to advocate and execute the Fisher Report when the truth is I had come there because I'm a native North Carolinian.

After reading the report, Hardin did indeed adopt some of its points for action, resulting in heated disagreements with President Spangler over Hardin's insistence on the need for financial autonomy and higher tuition at the Chapel Hill campus. But the candidate had received early warning of potential incompatibility both in style and substance during the search process:

[Keith Brodie] said that he thought that President Spangler would not choose me if I made an issue of who attends AAU. . . . I felt then—told Mr. Spangler I felt then—and still feel now, that it's been a mistake for system heads to be the voting members of AAU when it was a single entity in the system that was the member and everybody knows that. . . . I had decided on Keith's advice not to make this a do-or-die issue, but I didn't want to leave it silent. After Mr. Spangler and I had several friendly conversations, I said, "Dick (we'd become first name by then), "talk with me about AAU." "I'm going!" he said—got the hair up on the back of his neck. I said, "Well, let me ask you why?" He said, "Because I'm the Chief Executive Officer of the University of North Carolina." I said, "Well, yes, but I'm the Chief Executive Officer of UNC-Chapel Hill, and it is Chapel Hill that is the member, right?" He said, "Yes, but I'm your superior officer." . . .

. . . There was a time when I knew President Spangler wanted me to resign. He didn't ask me to flat out, but after that financial responsibility thing went through, and there had been some tension with respect to tuition, I went to him one day after a board meeting when some issues had been resolved and said, "I think things are going well." He said, "Well, you may think so, but there are some members of this board that would like to hold my coat while I fire you." I said, "Well, Mr. President, I'm a survivor, and so are you. I

remember you went to Pinehurst once with the board of governors
and the rumor was out that they might be out to get you, and you're
still here, so I think you and I better learn to work together." And
we did. At that same season I told the chairman of the board of governors, "I'm going to tell you something that I won't say to Mr. Spangler because I don't want this to wave a red flag, but I think the
president would like me to be out of the way, would like me to step
aside. It won't happen. I'm too devoted to Carolina to resign in a
temper on some short-term issue, and, frankly, if the president asks
me to resign, I would respectfully decline and just see how it would
work out in the board of governors." I don't know whether that message ever got to President Spangler or not, but I was never asked to
resign, and in fact, the last four years or so, maybe even five, of my
seven-year tenure were quite smooth in terms of my relationship
with President Spangler. I think we set each other down and neither one blinked, and we decided to work together for the good of
the state of North Carolina.

Paul Hardin's conflicted relationship with C. D. Spangler became a re-
curring theme in the first years of his administration, as vividly recounted
in his interview, but even if he had gathered more information about the
personality and governance philosophy of the system head or had known
about differences between Spangler and some trustees, he, too, was already psychologically committed to leading the institution: "If I had
known more than I did, I would still have come."

Certainly Donald Kennedy, on faculty at Stanford since 1960, was too
committed to turn down that institution's presidency. Yet, although immersed for years in the culture of the institution and an internal candidate with administrative experience not only at Stanford but also in
Washington, DC, as Commissioner of the Food and Drug Administration, he nonetheless felt the need for additional preparation and eventually suffered serious consequences for lack of it. In 1979, only eight
months after Kennedy accepted the provostship, President Richard
Lyman announced that he was accepting an offer to head the Rockefeller
Foundation in New York. Kennedy had expected that

> Dick would go for at least a few more years, and that if I ultimately
> became a candidate for the presidency, I would be reasonably well
> prepared. In point of fact, compared with what would have been my
> preference, it all happened too fast. [I would have preferred] more
> time to make some judgments about my fellow vice presidents in a
> collegial setting.

Working with the senior management team as provost, Kennedy became part of a "very collegial unit." Then, suddenly, he was appointed president, "and the question became, would I keep the players from the Lyman administration?"

> We had a team relationship already. I wasn't coming in on a parachute and looking around saying, "Okay, who are the troops?" I'd worked with them, I'd developed some trust in them, they'd developed some trust in me, and that's a very strong incentive to keep a team together. Which is, in fact, what I did, although I now believe that I made a few mistakes in that department. . . . One of the vice presidents had a difficult problem with clinical depression. He reached a point at which it made him much less effective in his job. I kept him on too long, trying out modifications in his position that I thought might allow him to continue. It was a serious mistake. We lost a lot of effectiveness in that job. . . . The vice president for business and finance, although he was very smart and still enjoys a good reputation as a consultant on higher education productivity and policy, turned out not to have terrific judgment about people he was appointing in certain spots—internal audit, for example—and I relied a little more on his judgments about appointments than I should have. In the end, when we had our difficulties with the Dingell subcommittee on indirect costs, he was disappointing in his unwillingness to take personal responsibility and to support the people on his own staff. Now I think I was too tolerant because we had formed a rather strong bond among us when we were all working for Dick, and that made it more difficult for me to make hard evaluations *de novo*.

For Donald Kennedy, the longer apprenticeship he had expected would prepare him for the presidency might have provided important insights about team building and personnel choices that would have placed him in a less vulnerable position years later during the attacks on Stanford led by Congressman John Dingell. On the other hand, of our interviewees who addressed the topic of team building, all expressed a caution and lack of certitude that places Kennedy's choice in perspective.

TEAM BUILDING

Assembling an effective team of senior administrators is, like the need for setting and adjusting goals, a task that begins during the prelude phase and essentially never ends. In the beginning it raises questions of change versus maintaining the status quo, that is, whether to retain the officers of the prior administration or to appoint new ones. Of the five presidents who spoke directly to this issue, three reported that a philosophy of continuity, moderation, and a general reliance on naturally occurring turnover had worked reasonably well for them, while two described their experiences as vexatious, conflictual, and even painful. In the former group were Robert O'Neil, Harold Shapiro, and Benno Schmidt:

> [O'Neil] I have always felt that coming in as an outsider is a situation in which, other things being equal, you are probably well advised to keep as many of the people who are already in place as you can. And on the whole, I think that's been a wise policy everywhere.

> [Shapiro] I've always had the view that it's a mistake to come in and sweep clean unless there's some kind of crisis. . . . You're always in the process of team building because people are always moving on. . . . You make some mistakes. Not every appointment works out. I have made my share of mistakes, but on the whole I like to think of people as long-term colleagues. I don't like to change. I think that people work more effectively the longer they work together.

> [Schmidt] My effort was to try to maintain as much continuity as I could. After all, I was new from the outside, and so only where I felt that a change was required did I try to force change. . . . I maintained about half of the nonacademic top administrative team and replaced the others either as they left or in one or two cases, [made changes] where I felt [they] really had to be made. [Among these] were a couple of personally difficult things, but there was no particular institutional angst about it.

A considerable degree of personal and institutional anxiety, however, apparently surrounded these decisions for Vartan Gregorian and Donald Kennedy, both of whom recalled them in terms of conflict and consequences. While Gregorian approached the question of his administrative team at Brown with the accepted philosophy of continuity and minimal change, he noted in our interview the problems such a course is likely to bring with it:

> If you don't move fast, within the first six months, to build your own team, your decisions appear to be whimsical. If you do it within six months, it's impersonal, no hard feelings, "He always brings his own team," and when displaced people apply for jobs elsewhere, they say,

"He's bringing his own team. Nothing is wrong with us." But after six, seven months, if you let people go, they know they did not meet your expectations. That's the biggest problem.

On the other hand,

> if you enter an institution and make changes wholesale, it may imply that your predecessor did not have good judgment. So, your predecessor naturally does not like that, people who have been with this president [don't like it], trustees won't like it because they will have been in charge for the past eight, ten, twelve years and you're passing judgment on them also. So, how to make those changes in a way that is not judgmental? You have always to say that you are looking to the future rather than to the past, and you're trying to tailor an administration to fit the mission you have articulated. And even that is easier said than done.

Gregorian analyzed at length a series of hiring pitfalls:

> [On following the advice of committees.] In nine years I made some mistakes in my appointments. I followed the recommendations of the faculty-student advisory committees. What search committees sometimes saw as strengths, I saw instead as indecisiveness. People they saw as tough individuals, I sometimes saw as not necessarily tough or knowledgeable. And sometimes their notions about the positions and perceived priorities were not the same as mine. Some of them did not share my notion that administration's role is only to serve faculty and students. . . . Members often saw the university as a strict hierarchy: they were determined to exercise their authority and power, rather than deal with the principle that, "We've been entrusted with the fate of this institution and who is strong enough to lead." There are two different approaches, and if you, as president, are very busy the entire time, fundraising and so forth, you don't necessarily realize this subtle attitude of your colleagues and the consequences of their recommendations.

> [On selecting strong officers.] This also is a very tricky business because while I appreciate strength, outsiders may perceive a vice president or provost or dean as being stronger than you are. That's all right . . . as long as the vice president and others don't . . . expect that you must do what they say. The important thing is that you develop an effective team. Otherwise, your administration will be divided into "Mr. or Mrs. No or Yes," the soft ones and the hard ones.

[People will see] if they want something, they will go to the soft ones. . . . So, [the question is,] how to gather strong people around you for a common mission rather than strong people around you who may be divisive, or who put their personal agendas and ambitions first, trying to impress the trustees—"We're running the show while the president is traveling," or sigh and say, "Oh my God, you should see what I am doing, and he is opposing me." That's where you make some big mistakes, by tolerating them. Strong people sometimes undercut each other. If you bring weak people, they don't serve you well. So how you put the right team together is a major challenge. It worked for me very well at Penn, but I would say at Brown it was not a spectacular success because I had some appointees who saw each other as rivals rather than as team players.

[On backing out of a hiring decision.] That was difficult, putting the administration together. I would say I made four, five big mistakes during my nine years in terms of judging character, and once you make a mistake, you have to realize [you should] cut your losses. Most presidents don't do that; I did not even do it in one or two instances. Yes, [it's very hard to let someone go,] but then you compound the situation by not dealing with it effectively and immediately because you don't want people to think you cannot keep [administrators], or you're indecisive, or you haven't the capacity to judge who's the best person. But by delaying you hurt the institution and yourself, [and] the person, too. It's not the person's fault because that role was thrust on him or her on the basis of interviews. So, if you interview somebody and you're not a good judge of character, you can't blame the person. He did not say, or she did not say, "I'm the greatest." You thought they were. You chose them.

It is interesting to consider the gloss these four presidents' commentaries puts on the situation of Donald Kennedy at Stanford. As we have seen, his decision to retain the existing administrative team, people with whom he had worked closely while provost under the previous president, would lead to difficulties and eventually serious consequences during the Dingell investigation. Second-guessing himself during our interview, Kennedy thought he should have begun his term with an immediate reevaluation of all senior level officers in order to "deflate [their] expectations a little bit" as well as garner the views of others at the university. Yet, the philosophy of continuity expressed by his peers would support his initial instinct not to alter the team, while Vartan Gregorian's exploration of the complexities of these decisions places Kennedy's dilemma further into a context of universal uncertainties when trying to choose administrators wisely.

AGENDA SETTING

No matter how integral to a specific institution an agenda for action may be, and despite support from a variety of constituencies, implementation will inevitably bring conflict. Thus we were interested in what our presidents would say about the origins of their agendas beyond the personal interests, goals, and experiences in higher education they would naturally bring to office. Their responses fell into three general groupings, the early elements of their presidential plans deriving either from gradual internal developments, immediate institutional crises, or the board of trustees.

The internal candidates in our group—Kennedy, Sovern, and Shapiro—described agendas that flowed naturally from initiatives and goals developed while serving as faculty and then as provosts of their institutions. In contrast to external candidates, they did not reference specific trustee involvement at this early stage. Donald Kennedy recalls having "some discussions [with the trustees]" at the time he was appointed and later laying out academic and facilities' needs in his inaugural address. These included the strengthening of the humanities and restoring "some serious attention to undergraduate education," but, he says, that was "as close to an agenda as I had." Similarly, Michael Sovern relates that he had no "master plan." His initial agenda was academically "substantial" but general, the "product of lots of conversations and almost osmotic relationships over the years." Asked whether the trustees had agenda items of their own to discuss with him, Sovern said emphatically that "They did not."

> I [had] shared my views on a number of key issues with both trustees and a number of faculty. . . . But I did not ever lay out a master plan for them for the university as a whole, and I didn't have one. . . . [My agenda] was my own judgment about what was needed, much of it at a level of generalization, it has to be said, that would not have provoked opposition. To say we needed to strengthen our schools and departments, to have better community relations, to keep the university's door open to needy students—these are not controversial ideas, and I really thought we could do them all, so it wasn't a case of having to choose at that point. Later in my tenure we'd make some tough choices, but this was still the beginning.

One very specific agenda item, however, was already on the table: the sale of the land under Rockefeller Center, which Sovern describes as an ongoing negotiation inherited from his predecessor. It finally came to fruition in 1985 and was "the most significant financial event" of his presidency.

While he shared some career similarities with Kennedy and Sovern, Harold Shapiro had served longer as provost (three years versus their one year each) and was preparing to lead a public, not a private, institution. Thus it is not surprising that he did have a master plan ready as he stepped into the presidency, one that he had formulated in response to the university's dependence on state coffers during a time of recession:

> Even though I didn't anticipate the [second] energy crisis, which made the situation more dramatic, I had worked out in my head a strategy for where to take the University of Michigan, with or without an energy crisis. For example, I had decided that . . . the way to strengthen the overall university was to begin on the periphery by strengthening the professional schools—not at all an obvious strategy, I don't think. Most people would say, that's not the core of the university, you've got to start with the arts and sciences. In Michigan's circumstances at the time, I came to exactly the opposite conclusion. . . . It wasn't a matter of philosophy so much as just what was possible at the time, given the way you could generate resources in these professional schools—you weren't quite so dependent on the state. And therefore, rather than just wait until the state's economy improved, what I thought we would do is strengthen the periphery while we had a chance, try to focus on the smaller-but-better strategy in the core until the situation improved. . . . The campus had been prepared, if anybody was listening, because during the time I was provost we were moving in these directions. The energy crisis just made it mandatory that we move more quickly.

Because of the economic circumstances, Shapiro had to move more dramatically and drastically at Michigan in 1980 than either Kennedy or Sovern, who also began their presidencies that year; it is interesting to compare how economic dependence on the state can exert a shaping force on the agenda of a public university at the same time that peer institutions like Stanford and Columbia in the private sector remained relatively insulated. Although most of Shapiro's colleagues at other research universities were not yet facing severe economic pressures, they would do so later in the 1980s and early 1990s (as he himself would at Princeton). Of course, revenue cutbacks are not the only way the state can impact a university's agenda; as Robert O'Neil points out, political mandates can be imposed almost overnight, altering the circumstances a president faces and sending the best laid agendas out the window, for "life is always a bit chancy in the public sector."

Among external candidates, we have already seen that three who came in from the outside—Vartan Gregorian, Benno Schmidt, and Harold Shapiro (at Princeton)—also found their early agendas shaped for them by their institutions' financial exigencies, but exigencies realized only after they had accepted the jobs. Three others—James Freedman, Paul Hardin, and Robert O'Neil—reported that components of their agendas were first introduced by members of the board of trustees during the search process. Freedman notes that whereas at Iowa, the trustees "were very modest people on issues of education" who "obviously approved of what I told them, of why I wanted to be a president, what I wanted to do," at Dartmouth the chairman of the board had taken a more direc- tive role. He insisted that before seeking a new president, the trustees needed to find out "what the rest of the world thinks about Dartmouth":

> And he and members of the search committee interviewed Bart Gi- amatti at Yale, David Riesman, Henry Rosovsky, Hanna Gray, many eminent people. Essentially the message they got back was that the rest of the world doesn't know Dartmouth academically. You're an undergraduate college, you're a nice place, nobody associates educa- tional innovation with you, many people think you barely belong in the Ivy League, you certainly make sense in a football league because there are eight of you clustered up there geographically, but nobody puts Dartmouth in the same breath as Harvard, Yale, Princeton. You're just not a significant intellectual player by comparison with those.

One key to change at Dartmouth, it was decided, would be to break with the tradition of choosing only Dartmouth alumni as presidents:

> That was never announced, but Sandy [the board chairman] will tell you he was very determined that they were going to say, "Dartmouth is part of a larger world of higher education," and that's one way to show it. So they had this national search based upon the sense that, "We really need to do some things academically and intellectually, that's what we need." And clearly, that's why they hired me. I mean, we had very good discussions about it. . . . I could have stayed longer [at Iowa] with perfect ease. So it was easy to be candid in saying to the Dartmouth search committee, "If I come here, what I really want to do is—," what I [later] said in my inaugural address. [I told the

board,] "Everything I know about Dartmouth is, it's too male-dominated, it's too much of a jock school, it's too concerned with well-rounded people," and that speech says well-rounded people may have no point at all.

It is probably unusual for a job candidate to speak at length on the topic of what he does not like about an institution that is looking him over, but James Freedman's educational philosophy and goals were clearly compatible with board chairman Sandy McCollouch's view that "Dartmouth had to become a much more serious place." Further, as part of attaining their goal, the trustees also told Freedman that they wanted the new president of Dartmouth "to be a player, visible on the national scene . . . to find a way to get some attention, and to be one of those people who are taken seriously as a president because of his views on education." As we have seen, this board-and-president-imposed agenda threw Freedman into immediate conflict with the alumni, who "weren't so sure why the place had to be changed," as well as onto a national stage where, describing himself as "naïve," he discovered "you're at the mercy then of the press and of how good your stuff is, and whether it's worthy of respect."

The Dartmouth board seems to have been exceptionally strong in dictating goals for dramatic change at their university, goals that presupposed an outspoken president who could attract national attention and, as it happened, controversy. By contrast, both Paul Hardin and Robert O'Neil describe boards with more generalized and predictable objectives in mind, though in Hardin's case the trustees' agenda was at first not entirely clear. At UNC, to counteract faculty uneasiness over the generosity of the recent contract buyout of the football coach and the expenses associated with the construction of the "Dean Dome," the new home of the Tarheels championship basketball team, trustees were "looking for someone who had a track record of no nonsense in intercollegiate athletics" and who had "the energy and the experience" to lead the university's bicentennial campaign, "the single imposition of an agenda item that was most apparent." Although Hardin states that he "came without an agenda," after reading the Fisher Report he "formed [his] own . . . in part by reference to that report." It is interesting to recall that Hardin says the contentious report was "contracted" by UNC's board chairman, although

> I don't think that Bob [Eubanks] was personally behind any critical comments about the system. I think Jim Fisher was asked to come in and make the report, and he had a certain viewpoint about it that found its way into the report.

By commissioning the so-called "management audit,"[6] trustees on the UNC search committee ultimately did influence the new chancellor's agenda and subsequent conflict with the system head.

Robert O'Neil, as already noted, found himself in the peculiar position of being presented with an agenda by the UVA board which, from his point of view, had long been a done deal. Furthermore, as was the case with James Freedman, O'Neil discovered that his identity as a "national" candidate was a definitive part of this agenda:

> [The board of visitors'] expectations . . . [were] very difficult to define, and they weren't ever explicit. If one had asked, and I certainly made efforts to ascertain from the board of visitors what their expectations were, I don't think they had anything very clearly in mind except this "national presence" notion which to a greater degree than I think they realized, was already achieved and would have continued to be, regardless of whether they had chosen a president from inside or outside. It was not in my interest, I guess, to tell them before the appointment was made that that factor would probably make a whole lot less difference than they may have assumed. In fact, I believed at the time and have continued to believe since then, that more emphasis was placed on origin, experience, background, and so on, of the next president than was really warranted.

NOTES

1. Jodi Wilgoren, "President Stuns Brown U. by Leaving to Be Vanderbilt Chancellor, *New York Times*, February 8, 2000, Late Edition, p. A20; "Gee's Departure Surprises Brown," *The Providence (R.I.) Journal*, February 8, 2000, http://www.projo.com/report/pjb/stories/03145631.htm, accessed 2/8/00; Kit Lively, "Grumbling, Raised Eyebrows, and Worse as Gordon Gee Prepares to Leave Brown," *Chronicle of Higher Education*, February 25, 2000, pp. A44–45.

2. Called chancellor at Brown.

3. James O. Freedman, *Idealism and Liberal Education* (Ann Arbor: The University of Michigan Press, 1996), 25.

4. O'Neil explains: "For the first eighty years there was no president; Thomas Jefferson's theory ('That government is best which governs least') was that the chairman of the faculty, on the European model, should be the senior administrator. So it was not until 1904 that a president was appointed."

5. It is evident from the tone and content of President C. D. Spangler's February 2, 1988, memorandum to all of the UNC system chancellors addressing the issue of "the so-called 'management audit,'" that he felt his leadership had been challenged: "It is not clear what the status of the document is or how the Board of Trustees for whom it was presumably prepared will regard it. The re-

port speaks . . . to basic questions of governance and to questions of policy that are of central concern to the Board of Governors and to me." Spangler considered the report to be "seriously and fundamentally flawed" because the outside consultants who prepared it had not "comprehended" the workings of the UNC system or Chapel Hill's place within it. Furthermore, although the report noted the " 'remarkable presidential leadership of the past,' " it "characterize[d] this past leadership as 'memorable aberrations' . . . one of the most astonishing statements ever made about American higher education or about The [sic] University of North Carolina." Citing the consultants' "profound lack of understanding" of the university's history, Spangler found the report's recommendations "neither original nor apt." He concluded that UNC-Chapel Hill had "flourished" under the governance structure established by the state of North Carolina, and confirmed that the selection of a new chancellor for UNC-Chapel Hill would proceed as "clearly described in the laws of our State and the Code of our University . . . within the framework of that governance structure under which we have all prospered." C. D. Spangler, letter dated February 2, 1988, Chancellor Jane Milley Papers, series 10, University Files, box 3, North Carolina School of the Arts Archives.

6. "A recent 'management audit' of the Chapel Hill campus . . . was commissioned by the chancellor search panel. That report stated, 'If the president is not supportive of the final candidates advanced, the board [of trustees] should not compromise its need for a strong chancellor. . . . If necessary, the board should draw public attention to the problem rather than settle for a lesser person.' " Liz Clarke, "2 'Outsiders' Top List for UNC-CH Chancellor," *Raleigh News and Observer*, March 22, 1988, sec. 1, pp. 1A, 6A.

CHAPTER

Honeymoon

That period from the day a new president actually takes office
until the moment a decision is made that alienates one or more
constituencies.

As they carry forward the tasks of getting to know an unfamiliar institutional culture, developing an agenda, and making judgments about their senior officers, new presidents typically hope for an indeterminate period of calm, optimism, and goodwill within the university community, or at least a time-out, a provisional suspension of harsh judgment and scholastic internecine warfare while institution and leader take stock of one another. We hypothesized, therefore, that true to human nature, such a hoped-for honeymoon phase would be characterized by reluctance on the part of the new president to take any immediate action that would end this pleasant interlude prematurely, i.e., that a new president during the first year may be risk averse. We posited further what we called a defining moment, when the honeymoon has ended and the president takes a stand of some kind that has implications for the remainder of his term.

The questions we asked surrounding the honeymoon phase yielded a range of responses that gave us a much wider window on the presidencies—and the attitudes—of our subjects. In fact, the relatively uncomplicated idea of a honeymoon yielded unexpectedly complex, even strongly felt, commentaries by some of our presidents. Others objected to our admittedly negative definition of the defining moment, reinterpreting the idea in their own, more positive terms. Still others shared not only their accounts of risks taken and honeymoons ended, but also their philosophies of risk as a part of institutional leadership.

HONEYMOONS

Did our participants think they had had such a thing as a presidential honeymoon? Michael Sovern was succinct; for him, life as Columbia's president was a honeymoon that "seemed as though it might never end":

> In fact, I didn't have serious difficulty with a substantial group of faculty until I was in my second decade as president. . . . [My predecessor] Bill McGill had told me, "Don't serve more than ten years," but I didn't listen to him.

Donald Kennedy (who, like Sovern, had become president in 1980 at his home institution) also saw himself as having had an extended honeymoon, but one he elected to analyze for us in detail, viewing the concept very much in terms of personal relationship time rather than chronological breathing space. Asking the pertinent question, "Honeymoon with whom?" and noting that obviously a university president "has a number of constituencies," Kennedy began with Stanford's trustees and "events that . . . attenuated the solidity" of his relationship with them from 1987 on:

> One [such event] was my divorce and remarriage. That's an unusual thing for a president to do in office, and I think some board members said, "What's the matter? Presidents just don't do that. They're not supposed to be like other people and have disruptions in their personal lives." I don't blame the trustees for their reaction.
>
> The second event occurred when, after much internal fussing, we reported to the board a change in housing policy that would have permitted domestic partners to share university housing. Of course, this was widely seen publicly as a "gay" issue. . . . Although I asked [the trustees] for comments, there were none. [But] after they had a chance to see some press reaction, [they] came back in the next meeting and said, in effect, "What did you pull off on us?" That was a second issue on which I lost some board support.
>
> But had it not been for the indirect cost controversy, those would have been vanishing ripples, I think. During the indirect cost controversy . . . the chairman of the board was unfailing in his support, and the board never took any unsupportive public action. But I be-

lieve their feeling would have been, had you asked them to express it, "We've got to have a change."

Kennedy next discussed his "equally important" relationship with the faculty, which he judged had gone well for the first eight years; then,

> various kinds of faculty concerns arose, some about political issues, some about the rate of increase in indirect costs, which involved publicly aired dissatisfactions about the rate. Among the science faculty there was a feeling that I did not respond early enough to their complaints. So in 1988 or 1989 there was a fairly significant drop in my relationship with some faculty.

He reported generally good rapport with students (except during the mid-1980s debate over divestment) and with alumni throughout his presidency:

> Alumni are distant from the president of the university. . . . Their picture is apt to be derived from what they read about the president and what he is doing . . . [seen] through the lens of their own political convictions. Some conservative alumni were unhappy with the degree to which I was committed to increasing minority enrollment, promoting public service, and supporting changes in the Western Culture curriculum—they saw those things as rather left-liberal. But they found that very hard to square with other positions, that I was quite supportive of the athletic program, for example. So they confronted various versions of me which they got through the press or through occasional talks I gave. It's very difficult to generalize about alumni, but the institution was doing well, the fund-raising went very well, and generally Stanford was seen favorably by the world, except during the indirect cost controversy.

In contrast to Donald Kennedy, Benno Schmidt and Vartan Gregorian interpreted the honeymoon as a period of calm for the institution, separate and apart from their own reception as new presidents or their relationship with any constituency. Thus, Schmidt's response, when asked how long he thought his honeymoon period at Yale lasted, was a loud laugh and a description of an institution in turmoil:

> It's natural for people to take a kind of wait-and-see attitude about a lot of things, but I'm not aware that there was any honeymoon. There was a period, a year or so perhaps, when people didn't know me at all, but certainly I had the sense of being thrown right away

into the thick of things and having to deal with some very major institutional issues right away, because of the infrastructure problems,
because of the politics of the campus—there was this terrific blowup
about divestment which started with Bart [Giamatti] and continued
over into my administration and caused a constant sense of frenetic
upheaval—and also because the collective bargaining process was
due to hit my second year and in the very strange character of Yale
collective bargaining, the bitterness and the disputatiousness starts
to warm up a full year ahead of time. . . . So I didn't have any sense
of a quiet period at all. I mean, my own inauguration was one of the
wildest public events in Yale's history. I enjoyed it; it reminded me
a little of Columbia in the old days, with mounted police escorts. . . .
I don't think "honeymoon" is quite the way it felt, although I'm quite
sure that if you ask most people at Yale they'd say, oh no, we didn't
have any view of this guy one way or the other for the first year or
two, or even longer. . . . No one even knew me very well at my inauguration. So it wasn't that that was a response to what I stood for.
No one had the least idea of what I stood for. And yet, it was only
mounted and motorcycle police that got me from the library to
Woolsey Hall.

Similarly, Vartan Gregorian arrived at Brown in institutional medias
res:

I had no honeymoon. My first day [as president], there was already
a [student] sit-in in my office. I went and sat with them and talked
to them. It was about ethnic studies—[the students] had a thousand
signatures [on a petition] they'd been waiting [to give me]. Then in
the first year came the library strike. So there was no honeymoon in
that sense. But I was not held responsible for those [events].

More pertinent to Gregorian and to Schmidt personally was the honeymoon period as a time of crucial first impressions, a characterization
about which they are both explicit. First, Gregorian:

What is going to be my modus operandi? I said up front, the first
day, I don't accept demands. Student demands, staff demands, no
demands. I only accept petitions, letters, complaints, suggestions,
but no demands. The second thing during the honeymoon period is
how you communicate to your constituencies; how you behave
stamps the mark of your presidency. You must set your imprint
within two or three months. Perceptions are important because they
assume a reality of their own. For example, within three or four
months of my presidency—it may have been less than that—there

was a racial incident. Somebody had written racist graffiti. I immediately went to the dormitory where this happened because I knew that this would be used by some for different ends. So I became the main speaker. I asked students to join me, denouncing anti-Semitism and racist slurs against blacks. I even got myself into trouble by saying if I found those who were doing [these things], I would expel them immediately. But the ACLU said, no, you cannot do that, you have to judge, you have to go through a process, who do you think you are? That said, the students were testing me, they were already determining who I was. I said there are many outlets for racism in this nation; Brown is not going to be one of them. Period. No ifs and buts.

[As a rule, I didn't use a spokesperson.] I spoke for myself. I wanted people to hear where I [stood]. Presidents have to have their own style; there is no formula for what presidents should [do]. Circumstances require different solutions and stances.

For Schmidt, the consequences of a personal style not yet calibrated to a new environment were decidedly negative, and he reviewed his difficulty for us at some length:

I had something of a reputation as a civil libertarian which I think was right, and of course, Columbia *had* divested, right? And I was coming from the outside, and a lot of students in particular but also some faculty who saw eye-to-eye with them, thought that I might be coming to Yale with a sympathetic view toward divestment and toward the general notion that political agitation by students ought to cause the university to react sympathetically in all kinds of ways. In fact, I had a principled objection to divestment, but I had never been called upon to [express it publicly]. I had expressed it at Columbia; I told Mike Sovern it was a terrible idea when Columbia did it, that it was unprincipled, that it was not sound to take the position that if 3 percent of the student body started making a lot of noise you'd do what they said. I had an absolute view about freedom of speech on the campus which necessitated my intervening early on in a disciplinary process that had punished a student for a rather puerile effort at satire which was anti-gay, and my view was that speech is sacrosanct. On a university campus freedom of expression is the paramount value, no ifs, ands, or buts. So I took that position and people were at that time, oddly enough, starting to identify as conservatives people who defended freedom of expression on university campuses (bizarre from an historical point of view) because it happened often that the speech that was being protected on the campus was unpopular, was politically incorrect. So when I re-

sisted divestment, when I protected that kind of speech, when I
made clear that Yale would have no speech codes, that there was
not going to be any requirement that speech be nice in order to be
protected, when I came out against what was being done on other
campuses in a very clear and hard way, the students and a lot of the
faculty perceived early on that I was a pretty uncompromising conservative. I plead guilty in part. I certainly was uncompromising. I
am not sympathetic and I have never been sympathetic to the notion that universities ought to be explicit political actors in promoting a certain political agenda. I just don't believe that. Indeed,
I think it's incompatible with the academic mission of the university in the long run. . . .

   . . . [My viewpoint] caused some problems with the students and
with certain of the faculty . . . right away, as soon as I arrived. . . . I
think I alienated a lot of people . . . The style in which I conveyed
[my feelings on] that issue, the uncompromising language of principle, was a style better suited to the law school setting where students are more adult by definition and are engaged in studying the
relative roles of principle and politics and expediency and resolving
different kinds of decisions. In that law school environment a certain rigorous clarity of position and expression is appreciated, and
people who disagree can do so in no uncertain terms without losing
their mutual respect and liking. But in a college setting I'm afraid
that some of that came across as very austere, unsympathetic, and,
among my most extreme critics, even authoritarian. . . .

   . . . [That perception] was a negative when we got over into the
totally different territory of, okay, granted we've got to rebuild the
place and it's falling down, how quickly do we do it? I had people
who thought, gee, this is a character who comes to what he thinks
is right and then doesn't listen and doesn't bend much. I don't think
that was right, but I think that was definitely the feeling that some
people had.

Schmidt believes that the Yale community's early perceptions of him
did not take into account the reality of his willingness always to "participate in a full exchange of views," or the fact that a principled stand
on any particular issue did not necessarily equate with administrative in-
flexibility across the board. It may be that had Schmidt, during his first
year, encountered a different set of issues, less political and more academic, perceptions about him may have been less polarized. James Freedman has pointed out that in his first year at Iowa he was fortunate to
encounter a problem "shaped on the right kind of issue," one of "academic values and quality," institutional turf where he was entirely com-

fortable and held mainstream faculty views. Of course, he, too, had to learn to moderate his style. His original letter to a faculty grievance committee "irritated a lot of people because it sounded too legalistic, and I began to learn that I just could not behave like a law school dean in these settings; that was not the lingua franca of the larger academic community."

James Freedman was one of three of our presidents who invoked telling institutional comparisons in the context of their early days in office. Although he did not comment on the idea of a honeymoon per se, when asked about his overall experience at Iowa, he spontaneously, if implicitly, contrasted it with his introduction to Dartmouth: "[Iowa] was not a place where you had to fear the right-wing crazies or where you had to fear—I mean, the alumni just worshipped the place, and for anyone who was president, it was like being Chief Justice of the United States." As we have already seen, instead of the five-year honeymoon Freedman recalls at the University of Iowa, Dartmouth offered immediate conflict and ultimately the most dramatic of the defining moments elicited in our interviews. For Harold Shapiro, economic woes at both Michigan and Princeton had precluded much in the way of a honeymoon at either institution, but experience at the former did not make things easier during his inaugural year at the latter. The ultimate success of his straight-shooting style at Michigan led to Shapiro's confident assumption that Princeton's unanticipated deficit should be tackled immediately and in the same forthright manner—possibly a mistake, as he now says, for at Princeton the sudden, unvarnished announcement of hard times was met with "a lot of disbelief, a lot of grumpiness, a lot of whining":

> And so that was hard to get over. On reflection, thinking about this now in retrospect, had I thought just a little bit more about it, I may have found some way to hide the problem for a year or two, in order to gain some better sense of the institution—after all, I hadn't been on the faculty here—and then come at the issue afterwards. But I didn't have that perspective then, and so I just went ahead. A lot of unhappiness came out in various ways. . . .
>
>   . . . [By the early 1990s] people grudgingly realized that there really may have been something to being ahead of the curve in the financial area. But getting back to your question, how long did the honeymoon last? It didn't last long because I decided to take that issue on right away.

For Robert O'Neil, the end of his honeymoon at the University of Virginia appears to have turned on an irony of bad luck in a personnel matter, a case of institutional déjà vu going back some twenty years to his experiences as a member of the law school faculty at Berkeley during the mid-1960s. There, Chicano students had objected strongly to the appointment of a Hispanic administrator whom they regarded as a "Clarence Thomas or Ward Connerly [in today's terms], who would be likely to say, 'Well, I got here on my own efforts,' and pull the drawbridge up behind him":

> What the dean agreed to do was to allow the students to interview him [on tape], which probably was a mistake, and then appointed a faculty committee that I chaired. Mike Heyman [later UC-Berkeley chancellor, 1980–1990] was one of the members . . . We ended up listening to the interviews . . . [and Mike said] . . . "He really folds, he's inconsistent. But I still think we ought to back [the dean]" . . . I said, "Mike, we can't. The students—I hate to say it—the students are right." So, although none of us were very happy about it, and even though [the candidate] had been a very good student of mine my first year there and I liked him, I convinced them that this was the right thing to do. Some of our senior colleagues probably to this day are bitter about the fact that we, and myself in particular, capitulated to minority student pressure, and the dean had to withdraw the offer. [Yet] bringing him in under those circumstances would have been as bad for him as for anyone else.

This was, O'Neil points out, "remarkably similar" to events during his first year at UVA when, in April 1986, both undergraduate and graduate African American students protested in what became "a very messy situation":

> If you can imagine the president of the Virginia NAACP coming from Richmond to demand the removal of the person who was then the highest ranking black administrator here, that indicates how difficult a situation it was. I had looked at the structure of the office of Afro-American affairs, and the structure seemed to me fairly familiar. I then discovered that my predecessor had brought in as a consultant Herman Hudson, who had been the dean of Afro-American affairs at Indiana University-Bloomington. He had designed a structure which, as I well knew because I had been close to it, worked perfectly at Indiana. But for some reason which may be partly structural, partly personal, that structure not only did not work here but was in fact the target of a protest which led to the complete revamping of the office. [The students were concerned about] the particular person who was in that job. [They found him] distant,

unresponsive. Whether that was fair, I don't know because this began so soon after I got here that I really never had an adequate opportunity to judge either the structure or the person. He was willing to resign and it seemed to me essential that he leave the office. . . . I think some feeling was expressed [by faculty who were critical] that when an administrator holding faculty rank is attacked by students, then the administration should stick up for him. . . .

. . . [Despite faculty criticism] . . . the last thing you want to do in a situation like that is to persuade the person to stay because it's totally untenable. . . . The irony is that some of those who rallied around this person also had no particular use for him. Somehow, there was an emotional reaction, one I think in some cases of fear, that if a group of angry black students—doesn't matter if they're right or wrong—can do this even to a *black* administrator, then we're in terrible trouble. So I think that was the point at which [the honeymoon ended]. [For me, in terms of angering one or more constituencies,] it was definitely a no-win situation. We didn't realize how bad it was until a few days before [the protest] happened, but with better foresight, the thing to do clearly would have been to head it off earlier.

[The honeymoon] had lasted a fairly long time, three-quarters of the first year, and that's not bad. There really wasn't too much going on . . . up to that point. But from then on, I suspect, there was some skepticism created by [this] incident.

DEFINING MOMENTS

If decision making may be seen as the defining task of a president, so may the defining moment—as we conceived it—be the discernible beginning of alienation within the university community as decisions not universally admired have to be taken by a new president who, at least in the eyes of some, has now drawn the first line in the administrative sand. The defining moment signals that the accumulation of enemies has begun and with it will come a gradual increase in negative pressures. Robert O'Neil's description of a "no-win situation" during his first year at UVA is a clear-cut example, that is, he faced making a controversial choice sure to alienate some faculty and administrators, thereby providing a core group of continuing critics. Another clear example is found in Benno Schmidt's presidency at Yale, as he pointed out in our first interview:

> Banner—At some point in the presidency there comes a moment
>   that you might think of as a *defining moment*, when you realize
>   you are making some choices that are going to forever plague
>   your presidency—

Schmidt—Yeah.

Banner—You're going to alienate a constituency, it's going to be with you to the bitter end—

Schmidt—Yep.

Banner—Can you identify a particular decision or series of decisions where that awareness was coming through to you?

Schmidt—I am afraid I think there were quite a few of them.

Schmidt saw as defining moments his decisions to maintain uncompromising positions on divestment and speech codes early in his tenure at Yale, decisions that alienated many students and faculty (though not trustees) and in his view created serious stumbling blocks later in his administration.

For Harold Shapiro and James Freedman, such critical early decisions also generated negative tensions but with the difference that their ultimate results were successful enough to strengthen rather than erode their presidencies. Considering the question of defining moments at Michigan and Princeton, Shapiro cited his economic strategies as responses to defining *situations*, which necessitated a series of choices that alienated some faculty at Michigan and many at Princeton, but eventually led to widely recognized results that included financial stability at both institutions—positive conclusions despite initially negative beginnings.

The most dramatic example of a single, early defining moment with an ultimately positive rather than negative outcome was offered by James Freedman who, on March 28, 1988, during the first year of his Dartmouth presidency, made a speech to the faculty in which he dared to attack the conservative student-run newspaper *The Dartmouth Review*:

> This place had taken the strategy until then of ignoring the *Review*, of not responding, of not protecting faculty, and I might well have done the same thing those years, but when we had another incident, it was a different point in time and my only point—I hadn't been here the earlier times. So I thought it was necessary to [speak out about the *Review*]. And standing in front of that faculty, I'll tell you, my knees—I was nervous. I mean, this was a big moment. I could have lost everything. That was a far bigger moment than anything at Iowa. I was doing something that had never been done here. It was taking on the *Review*. We had told the newspapers I was going to do this. The *New York Times* was here, and of course there was a story in the *Times* the next day.[1] I knew that I was stepping onto a larger stage and it was a big risk; I was throwing down the gauntlet. So that really was a defining moment. One of the most senior fac-

ulty women here, Marysa Navarro, got up at the meeting and cried, and said, "I have been waiting all these years for a president to do this," and came to the front of the room and gave me a great big hug. And I'll tell you, that was quite a moment, really an emotional moment.

The immediate risks that Freedman faced when he made this speech were not those of offending many faculty or members of the board or even the majority of Dartmouth students. Rather, they had to do with alienating well-to-do, influential conservative alumni and taking continual drubbings in the national press:

> Our great concern was that every time we attacked the *Review* we got more publicity. Nothing is greater than "President Attacks a Bunch of Kids," and "President Attacks His Own Students," and "President Attacks Newspaper." The awkwardness of all this was that it was a bunch of kids, but in fact, they were the cat's-paws for these adults.

Produced off campus and neither supported nor sanctioned by the college, *The Dartmouth Review* has been financed since its inception in 1980 by politically conservative alumni and organizations. At the time of Freedman's speech, Patrick Buchanan and William Rusher, editor of the *National Review*[2] were on the *Review*'s advisory board. Following the speech, attacks on Dartmouth and Freedman in the editorial pages of the *Wall Street Journal* were excoriating, predictably taking the Dartmouth president to task on freedom-of-speech grounds, for the "hilariously bald hypocrisy" and "perfect doublespeak" that had made Freedman the "Bull Connor of academia."[3] But from Freedman's point of view, the results on campus were well worth the off-campus barrage:

> Once I got here I appreciated the agonies that my predecessor had to live through for six years with the *Review*, and I just knew I had to do something, and the speech was the something I had to do. As I say in my book,[4] it is not my nature to confront and to denounce and to invite controversy. But I felt I had absolutely no choice. Sometimes these things just fall into your lap, they are fortuitous, and you have an opportunity to show who you are and what your values are. As it happened, in retrospect, as painful as all of that was and those years were, it was fortuitous that it came early and it did give me an opportunity to say, "I am going to defend this faculty, and I'm not going to allow the *Review* to drag our faculty and the

name of this college in the mud and to make us a constant subject of controversy on the national scene." I have not had a fight with the faculty in ten years, and I think it was in part because they saw I was willing to put myself on the line for their values.

Like Robert O'Neil and Benno Schmidt, in the moment of decision making, Freedman had recognized the degree of alienation he risked, that the right decision could nevertheless result in lasting negative repercussions for his presidency.

Although our concept of the defining moment as adverse resonated immediately with Benno Schmidt, most of our presidents resisted the inherent negativism of the idea, preferring to redefine the "defining moment" along more positive lines, to look for it among successful outcomes or symbolic events of their presidencies, or to see it as a summing up or benchmark rather than as the early warning signal or political demarcation we had proposed. Thus, Robert O'Neil, when asked to select a defining moment, did not respond with the incident of the black administrator at UVA. Rather, he highlighted two "clearly identifiable crises" with public impact that occurred about midway through his chancellorship at Indiana:

One was the largest outbreak of Legionnaires' disease at any college or university, second in numbers only to the Bellevue/Stratford American Legion convention in Philadelphia [1976] and roughly two years later, in the summer of 1978. The other was a coal strike earlier that same year [1978]. Indiana was at that time 97 percent coal dependent for its electric power, so when there was a coal strike in Kentucky and Tennessee it had a drastic impact on Indiana's operation of electricity-dependent facilities. . . . It was hard even to keep the lights on, and finally we did decide, with a little lead time but not much, that we had to close a week before the scheduled spring vacation.

A crisis of that sort really does serve to bring people together under most circumstances, in a way that in my experience then makes easier addressing other issues as they may arise. When I felt we ought to start a freshman seminar program at Indiana—a large public institution with an entering class that is close to six thousand—it seemed to me that if we could get 100 faculty willing to teach a freshman seminar, we could at least provide half the freshmen with some kind of meaningful contact with a senior faculty member. When an appeal of that kind went out to the senior faculty—this may be a year after the coal strike and the Legionnaires' disease which came very close on the heels of one another—I think

some of the contacts that had been developed in the course of working through those two very painful experiences served us well in mobilizing support [for the freshman seminars and] on other issues.

For O'Neil, facing nonacademic public problems that posed threats to
the Indiana University community created a bonding experience that affected and therefore somewhat defined subsequent campus attitudes
toward him, influencing in turn academic decision making in a positive
way.

Interestingly, former law professors Michael Sovern and Paul Hardin,
although leading dissimilar institutions, both shifted the concept of the
defining moment from the restricted academic political canvas we had
proposed to acts of behind-the-scenes, nonacademic executive decision
making. Although Sovern, when urged to select a defining moment,
chose taking Columbia College coed in 1982 as one of the "two most important decisions" during the early years of his presidency, it was the second decision, selling the land under Rockefeller Center in 1985, that he
emphasized as the "transforming event" of his presidency. The decision
to go coed had been a faculty initiative, albeit one that Sovern was rightly
proud to have implemented without damage to Barnard, while the Co-
lumbia/Rockefeller land deal was outside the purview of the faculty—
"confidential." As Sovern explained, "There is no tradition at
Columbia—and it is not unique in this—of faculty participation in management of the university's investment portfolio. The only issue was sell
or not sell":

> The land was subject to a very long-term lease to the Rockefellers.
> Under the terms of that lease we were getting about $10 million a
> year in rent. Columbia was in very bad financial shape at this point,
> and in fact, Rockefeller Center represented roughly half of our total
> endowment and almost all of our unrestricted endowment. And that
> was *not* a desirable state of affairs. So my predecessor had opened ne-
> gotiations for a sale to the Rockefellers, but those negotiations had
> stalled. The Rockefellers offered, finally, $220 million to buy the
> land. At that point U.S. Treasuries were paying about 15 percent,
> so had we accepted the offer, instead of getting the $10 million a
> year in rent, we would have gotten over $30 million a year in in-
> terest. Hard to turn the offer down. But we did, and it took more
> than a year before we got $400 million. And then we sold. But it
> was very difficult—it took that long for the Rockefellers to believe
> that I meant it when I said we would not sell for less than $400 mil-
> lion, and their circumstances made a purchase desirable. With the

$400 million, of course, the $10 million became $60 million a year.[5] . . . It was the single most important financial event of my term, perhaps of any Columbia president's term.

Sifting through possible "defining moments," Paul Hardin made choices much like Sovern's. As Hardin sought redefinition toward the positive and away from the negative idea of a decision that created disaffection within an important constituency, he pointedly rejected early events in his chancellorship that actually fit our criteria:

> I had a lot of defining moments in the sense of important moments for one reason or another, and I'm not going to take as defining moments the early alienation of some members of the board of governors and the tension with Dick Spangler because those moments were survived and we developed a good relationship.

Hardin considered choosing as a defining moment the long controversy over a freestanding black cultural center at UNC, a national news story involving on-campus racial politics[6] that occupied the approximate midpoint of his term (1991–1993), "because I ended up having to offend both sides of that equation. . . . It was a lose-lose situation." However, he rejected it, preferring, like Michael Sovern, to choose moments of executive decision making, "those moments that were private then, can be discussed now, of standing up for Carolina at some risk." Somewhat reversing himself about the significance of "the tension with Dick Spangler," Hardin cited early conflicts with his system president over low tuition (which Hardin wanted to raise), and the budget flexibility bill (for which Hardin publicly lobbied and saw passed in 1991), and face-offs with Republican governor Jim Martin (1989) and Democratic governor Jim Hunt (1995) over proposed budget cuts:

> When all the facts are on the table, I would choose that aggregation of confrontations with my president and with my two governors that had positive outcomes, protecting and strengthening the university. The confrontation about financial responsibility clearly strengthened Chapel Hill, and it would not have taken place if I hadn't taken some risks. The confrontations with two governors resulted in budget turnarounds that you can't say greatly strengthened the university, but they avoided weakening it. The loss of strength would have been obvious.

Finally, Vartan Gregorian redefined the defining moment most radically of all, seeing it not as a public moment with academic ramifications nor as a private moment of executive action, but rather as a personal rev-elation and an end point:

> The defining moment to me always has been, in any job I've had, when you're afraid that you may lose your enthusiasm, your curios-ity, your sense of mission and direction, and when you know the rou-tine is taking over. And then you get apprehensive that maybe you are beginning to love the routine and sit back. That's when I leave.

RISK TAKING

Risk was a naturally occurring subject among our presidents as they considered—and modified—our concept of a defining moment. We had hypothesized that new executives, fearful of going down in institutional history as their university's shortest-term president, would exercise cau-tion during their initial year in office and pursue a policy of little risk taking. However, no one in our sample admitted to delaying a decision or an action because of the risks entailed for the smooth beginning of a presidential term. In fact, as we have already seen, two of our presi-dents—Harold Shapiro and Benno Schmidt—thought they *should* have delayed their decisions, second-guessing their early plunges into risky administrative waters at Princeton and Yale, respectively, while Paul Hardin acknowledged he had not even fully understood he was taking a risk with his system president when he delivered his inaugural address calling for more autonomy for UNC campuses, "I came as an innocent, unawares."

The topic of risk taking elicited both anecdotal material and state-ments of leadership philosophy. Most succinct was Paul Hardin, "You just have to be alert because somebody is going to do you in if you're head of a public institution." Hardin described risks he had taken in his rela-tionships with "superior officers" in the state hierarchy—the university system president and two governors. In fact, he extended to his peer group in the state that same chain-of-command concept of risk taking: "I think other chancellors . . . had private conversations with President Spangler that involved risks taken . . . he hired good chancellors, and he hired chancellors that are not, by and large, obsequious. I expect that I did not have by any means the only confrontations with President Span-gler." We can contrast Paul Hardin's selection of risk experiences, which might also be categorized as externally directed, with the choices of our other public university leaders—James Freedman, Robert O'Neil, and Harold Shapiro—who responded to questions about risk in terms of in-ternal governance. For example, Freedman recalled that during his first year at Iowa he risked alienating many faculty (including the dean of the medical school) when he overruled the faculty grievance committee's decision to award tenure to a candidate voted down by his department:

> I just took the view that . . . you couldn't have a committee of three people from other disciplines, indeed other schools, award someone tenure, although I was perfectly glad to have the [originating] department do it over [to correct procedural flaws]. That was hard for a number of reasons, the first being that in accepting the part that we would do it over, we were obviously going in the face of . . . all the people who had gone through the process of denying tenure. But the more important thing was, I had gone in the face of the faculty. I was called before a meeting of the faculty senate, which was eighty people elected from throughout the university, and had to defend this. . . . I never felt threatened through any of it. I always thought I was right, for better or worse.

Asked whether it was not fairly early in his presidency to be taking a risky stand, Freedman agreed but pointed out the governance issue, that is, if he had not done so he "would have been prey to every other grievance committee down the road." Although exercised on a less perilous scale, Freedman's attitude in his first year at Iowa that some administrative risks are best faced immediately, carried over into his presidency at Dartmouth, a philosophy that in his view left him no choice but to take on *The Dartmouth Review* at whatever cost within a few months of arriving in Hanover.

Robert O'Neil expressed an attitude toward risky decisions similar to Freedman's "for better or worse" stance. Asked whether in his decision making he weighed risks or even thought about them, he responded, "Not in a formulaic sense":

> I think it's less conscious, it's more issue specific. Some people may well have a calculated risk strategy, almost like a beta investing strategy. I suspect those who study university administration as an academic field may have that sense of it, but as a practitioner, I would not say I ever had anything like a philosophy or strategy or concept of risk taking or risk avoidance. It really depended on a particular issue. [In decision making] risk is only, I think, a relatively minor part of the calculus. There is only one way to go, and you just have to do your best and go forward. Actually, [in the removal of the black administrator during my first year at Virginia], once this person was gone, we were able to restructure the office of Afro-American affairs . . . achieving the highest retention rate of minority students of any AAU public institution. In order for that to happen, some-

body—and I happened to be the person who was there at the time—
had to pay a price.

Addressing the topic of risks he took at Michigan during the energy
crisis, Harold Shapiro, like James Freedman and Robert O'Neil, felt that
"for better or worse" there was "only one way to go." Shapiro's strategy
of growth in certain areas (primarily the professional schools where funds
were more readily available) and cutbacks in the arts and sciences until
the economy strengthened, placed him in an uncomfortable position, "I
was very conscious the whole time that I could be making a mistake. . . .
I knew that the strategy could be wrong, but I knew it was better than
just staying where we were." Asked to enumerate some of the risks he
saw at the time, Shapiro, again like Freedman and O'Neil, cited his relationship with the faculty:

> There were a lot of risks involved. We ran the big risk, in my view,
> of misunderstanding—of faculty in the core of the university think-
> ing that we didn't care about them, that they were being phased out,
> that the administration didn't care about anything except profes-
> sional education. . . . I think in this particular case we managed to
> avoid that, largely by not talking about the strategy too often. So I
> can't claim a whole lot of courage or credit because I tried not to
> force people to face up to this strategy more than was necessary to
> get the job done.

Shapiro went on to note some of the calculated financial and political
risks he also chose to take but set them in the context of an economic
situation that gave him an unusual margin of protection in the matter of
campus opinion:

> [In taking these risks I had the advantage of] an external circum-
> stance you could look at and everybody could read about in the paper
> every day, that had nothing to do with us. Normally, we [the ad-
> ministration] were held responsible for most things, but not for the
> energy crisis. That was the Shah of Iran's energy crisis . . . and it was
> before the U.S. automobile industry restructured itself. . . . I have the
> Ann Arbor paper at home which says in big headlines, "Shapiro Ap-
> pointed President," and on the right hand side it says, "General Mo-
> tors Lays off 36,000."

Perhaps Robert O'Neil's rule of crisis as experienced at Indiana University is applicable here: in a public emergency even academics will come
together behind the administration.

Our remaining four presidents form another interesting comparative group as each served only a single presidency and that one at a private university. Within this group Michael Sovern was least expansive, limiting his explicit discussion of risk to the circumstances of the Rockefeller Center land deal. The negotiations passed on to Sovern from President William McGill involved him in a risky business venture that "seemed to be moving for a while," until it became apparent that "the Rockefellers were not going to be sufficiently forthcoming." Acknowledging that holding out for a much higher offer (from $220 to $400 million) was a big risk, Sovern responded that selling at the lower price "just seemed to be a mistake." The risk was significant, however, in that "The terms of the lease were such that rental negotiations would reopen every 21 years. My nightmare was that [if we did not sell] the lease would reopen in the middle of a [real estate market] trough, and as it turned out, it would have." Of course, Sovern was not alone in his nightmare; the risk was shared with Columbia's trustees to whom he reported, as he says, "fully," and who had to approve the deal, but in the event of failure it was Sovern who would have taken the career beating, as every CEO knows.

Michael Sovern offered no particular risk-taking philosophy for university presidents, stating instead as a pragmatic rule of thumb that in the face of conflict, his job was "to do what was right for Columbia . . . in ways that would minimize people's anger or discontent," much as Harold Shapiro "tried not to force people to face up to" the unpleasant implications of necessary cutbacks at Michigan. Our focus on presidential risk taking did, however, prompt Vartan Gregorian, Donald Kennedy, and Benno Schmidt to formulate definitions of what presidential leadership should encompass, emphasizing, respectively, the moral, the political, and the managerial. To preface his comments on risk, Gregorian began with a provocative generalization:

> [Now, on the subject of risk taking.] First of all, there are two types of presidents: people who have served public universities and people who have served private universities. Public university leaders who go to private universities get paralyzed for the first year or two. Even though they are intoxicated with the freedom they're inheriting, they get paralyzed. After all, they have spent most of their time in the public university trying to legitimize their potential actions— touching base with a regent here, with a legislator, with the city there, with the tax assessor or whatever. At the private university, you don't have that constraint, but you're under the impression that you still do, so much so that you delay your actions because you think somebody may object to what you intend to do.

In the context of our study, James Freedman and Harold Shapiro appear to be exceptions to Gregorian's rule, having left the public for the private sector and acted, in their own opinion, somewhat incautiously during their first year or two. On the other hand, Paul Hardin provides a corollary: Moving from a private to a public university he acted perhaps too independently, began his term aggressively, and endangered his job through the resulting friction with the system president.

Vartan Gregorian's main theme when asked about risk taking was that university presidents must take the risk of speaking out on moral issues and acting on moral grounds. His determination not to use a spokesperson was part of that philosophy:

> On important issues, I did not keep myself [away] and then disown the university spokesman or decision makers. I spoke up. University presidents have to speak out on major academic, moral, and political issues, but many people don't. I don't know why—maybe because they are afraid to displease some trustees or some faculty. But in my case, I thought my role as an educator extended also to dealing with conflicts. I saw that conflicts gave opportunities to deal with crucial issues confronting the campus community.

Among the issues Gregorian notes educating the Brown community about were freedom of speech, especially in the context of political correctness (which he notably attacked in a *Rolling Stone* interview[7]), and tolerance, especially in the case of campus criticism when his successor, a Mormon, was named. In addition to seeing risk taking in the moral arena as part of his role as an educator, Gregorian cited three other reasons for his risky decisions: they were the right thing to do, they were the practical thing to do, and they were decisions within his purview as a leader, without reference to the faculty or trustees. In the case of inviting the Aga Khan to give a baccalaureate address, the first Muslim to do so at any American university, he says he "did not ask the faculty, do you think it's a nice idea? It was the right thing to do," just as it was the right thing to ask students' relatives who were teachers to march with the faculty at graduation:

> I thought it was the right thing to do, to honor all the teachers. Do you think this would have gotten done if I had taken it to the faculty and said, "What do you think?" "Define teacher," they would say. . . . But I did it in the name of the faculty and the faculty liked it. After it was done, I said, "This is what I am doing; I actually want to respect the teaching profession." They did not [react badly] be-

cause again, they know the overall thing, that you're trying to high-light nationally the importance of teaching. Brown could not be the site of educational reform if we didn't respect teachers whose children are graduating.

The pragmatism of Gregorian's sometimes risky idealism is also evident in his explanation about HELP (Health and Education Leadership for Providence), a consortium he was directly involved in creating: "You have to do it because you have to show . . . [what the university is doing] for the community in which you live. Not paying lip service, but trying to help, because if the community collapses they drag you with it." Citing another independent action, Gregorian clarified his relationship with Brown's trustees:

> The governor asked me to chair an investigation of the entire collapse of the Rhode Island Savings and Loan banking system. I was crazy to do that but I had to because it affected—among others—at least a thousand of our employees, many of them poor people whose savings were in danger. Members of our union, community, and others were affected. Some faculty members called me and said, "Don't do it, it's a very dangerous thing, the mob may be involved in this," whatever. But I had to do it because it was the right thing to do. [I did not discuss it with my trustees.] I told them I was invited by the governor and I intend to do it. . . . [Brown gave interest-free loans to employees, a somewhat financially risky decision I took alone. The trustees] could have gotten angry, but again, they knew why I was doing it, they knew the savings banks were very important. When the recession came, I had to find two million dollars to help parents who had lost their jobs, whose children were at Brown but they could not pay. We did not tell the children, "Leave school." We can't do that. . . . But again, I did not confront this issue [with the trustees] because in my opinion when they hired [me], they hired [me] as a leader rather than as a manager. Leaders can always hire managers. Managers never hire leaders. I did not just present the trustees with a fait accompli. I told them, we discussed it. But as president of Brown, I was also the chair of the executive committee of the board and therefore met with the chancellor regularly, every month. So there was opportunity to communicate all of these problems. The result was, we got tremendous positive reaction about the report of our commission, with gratitude that this was the best thing Brown had done for the community.

Vartan Gregorian's self-described leadership style is one of considerable risk taking in that these were decisions he says he arrived at independently, thus putting himself out in front of the faculty and the trustees, taking the chance that where he led, the institution may or may not have followed. By eschewing the use of a university spokesperson, he worked publicly without a safety net, and by making some internal decisions without building consensus first, he worked privately without a net as well. It is illustrative of the ingrained nature of his personal style that when he was asked, "As president, you were taking risks, but you didn't think of them in that way?" he responded, "All the time. All the time."

In contrast to Vartan Gregorian, Donald Kennedy viewed risk taking more from the political than the educational point of view, taking into account the president's place and responsibilities within the governance structure of the university, and the university's place and responsibilities within the civic structure of American society:

> Risk taking is a complicated matter for presidents because trustees and others regard the president as embodying the institution. One may talk about taking risks as though they are personal risks, but you cannot dissociate yourself from the institution. My attitude is that as the voice of the institution, the president ought to be willing to inject himself and it into important debates about what the institution's business is. But presidents should not inject themselves into issues in which they have neither personal standing by way of experience and knowledge, or in which there is no definable special university interest. . . . If there were a controversy about selective service as it applied to students or about student financial aid, I would certainly want to reflect my views and the university's on those issues. I would try to keep the trustees informed about what I was doing, but I wouldn't consider it their task to edit my remarks.

Kennedy's suggestion of tensions with trustees becomes a major thread as his comments on risk and the university president continue; at the same time he occupies common ground with Vartan Gregorian as he expresses the view that universities have obligations to be responsible participants in public life:

> Even if it does involve some personal and institutional risk, university presidents ought to seek ways of expressing themselves on such matters because universities ought to be centers of national dialogue. Many of today's trustees have a quite different view, that presidents, like nineteenth-century children, should be often seen and seldom heard. They don't want to see the name of their institution in the newspaper except for the sports page and an occasional op-ed policy pronouncement in an admirable context by some faculty mem-

ber. I just don't feel that trustees are into risk taking at all. Some presidents need to push [their] boards, to make it plain that it's important for their institution to be right in the middle of important policy issues. I made some decisions to be much more public about situations in which I thought there might be some risk, some public disapprobation that might cost me some of the confidence of the board. For example, I decided to debate the secretary of education on the McNeil-Lehrer program about the changes in the Stanford curriculum. It's not a light decision to exchange fairly harsh words with a member of the president's cabinet who is of the political party of perhaps half your trustees. But it never occurred to me not to do it. There's some risk of looking foolish, but I had done that sort of thing a fair amount and I wasn't worried about that. . . . I wanted my own community to know that I was not hesitant to go and argue our case on the merits with someone who had the advantage of position.

Where Kennedy's view differs most from Gregorian's is in the breadth of public leadership that should be expected of or taken on by a university president. Gregorian sees the president as an educator first whose business is anything that impacts the university community, while Kennedy sees the president's public role as more narrowly defined, more cautiously approached; he would draw lines as to what is and is not part of his and the university's business. He seems very much of the same mind as Gregorian, however, when he notes that while president at Stanford he made his own decisions in these matters without regard to questions of trustee approbation.

When Benno Schmidt considered our question of risk and presidential leadership, he construed the leadership role of the university president even more narrowly than did Donald Kennedy. While Schmidt saw Yale as the best of bully pulpits from which to expound the principles of liberal education and the importance of freedom of expression, he did not see it as an appropriate venue for political activism. In an interesting reversal, where Donald Kennedy referenced trustees who preferred a president *not* to be outspoken on controversial public issues, Schmidt described members of the Yale Corporation who held quite different views, especially Vince Scully whom Schmidt feels he "greatly disappointed" with his opposition to divestment: "[Vince] wanted the leader, the president of the university, to be a force for the cause of liberation and social progress, and I felt very strongly that that [shouldn't be] the case." More than either Gregorian or Kennedy, Schmidt focused on risk as it impacted management issues within the university. He began his response by second-guessing himself, as we have seen him do before:

[As to whether I thought about the risks I was taking when I made a decision,] I didn't think about it that way, but I think I should have thought about it that way. I didn't think of myself then so much as a risk taker as something a little different.

Using a baseball metaphor derived from childhood excursions to the ballpark, Schmidt encapsulated his management philosophy with a quote from his father who had taught him "that the people who really count have the big slugging percentage":

It's not the batting average, it's not how many hits. It's how many really big hits. It's how many home runs. It's what you *drive* in. I have always had the view in any job that focusing on the big issues, if they are given the right kind of attention and solved, will make a huge difference in the life of the institution. . . . It is far more important than trying to focus on everything, trying to solve little issues because solving all the little issues means you're not going to deal with the big questions. On the big questions there'll be drift. I've always held that view. That was my view as dean, that was my view as a professor, and it was *definitely* my view at Yale.

This philosophy of putting presidential energies where the "greatest consequences for the institution" lie, led Schmidt to "take what turned out to be some significant risks," such as pressing forward with plans for rebuilding Yale, proposing necessary if unpopular financial measures (including selective rather than across-the-board budget cuts in arts and sciences), and acting to resolve longstanding problems in Yale's school of management, its philosophy department and school of nursing:

Now, those are just a few of the issues that I felt it was important to tackle and focusing on them [made] a major and risky statement about the appropriate role of the president—[to take on these things] not because they are the big risks but because they are the big issues. But the reason they're the big issues is that people haven't tackled them before because they recognized the risk. Perhaps smarter. But my view was that if that's not what a president is for, what is a president for?

While Schmidt stands by this ultimate statement of the presidential bottom line, he has come to the view that such a philosophy does not preclude a president's choosing to minimize risk at times by treading more lightly on academic toes:

Each one of those [issues I named] is its own complicated question, and on a couple of those my view of the necessity of tackling those questions and forcing the issue from the president's office was wrong because it raised big governance questions.

I did think nothing was happening [on some of those issues,] but there are ways to address that without the president being front and center as the driving force.

NOTES

1. Allan R. Gold, "Dartmouth President Faults Right-Wing Student Journal; *The Dartmouth Review* Is Accused of Bullying," *New York Times*, March 29, 1988, Late Edition, p. A16.

2. Michele N-K Collison, "Dartmouth President Blasts Conservative Campus Paper for 'Poisoning' the College's Intellectual Atmosphere; Strongest Criticism of Controversial Publication in 8 Years Gets Warm Support from Faculty Members," *Chronicle of Higher Education*, April 6, 1988, pp. A27–A28.

3. "Review and Outlook [Editorial]: The Joys of Hypocrisy," *Wall Street Journal*, April 4, 1988, Eastern Edition, p. 1.

4. James Freedman, *Idealism and Liberal Education* (Ann Arbor: University of Michigan Press, 1996).

5. Maureen Dowd, "Columbia Is to Get $400 Million in Rockefeller Center Land Sale," *New York Times*, February 6, 1985, Late Edition, A1.

6. See, for example, William C. Rhoden, "At Chapel Hill, Athletes Suddenly Turn into Activists," *New York Times*, September 11, 1992, Late Edition, B9; "Dispute over Black Center Tears U. of North Carolina," *New York Times*, April 21, 1993, Late Edition, B11.

7. "Everybody is worried about not saying the 'politically correct' thing . . . people hate to be called racist or sexist. But I think it's myopic, it's historic retrogression. . . . I don't want people who come here to take their prejudices away with them. It will be far more strident prejudice if people are not allowed to discuss it." Asked about his friend James Freedman, the "politically correct" president trying to "banish" the *Dartmouth Review*, Gregorian continued, "I've followed that debate, and it's not as simple as the way you put it. The issue there is, Where [*sic*] does harassment begin, where does freedom of speech end? To discuss intellectual issues, to say that Freedman is a liberal and therefore wishy-washy is fine. But to put a Nazi emblem in the paper and run a cartoon portraying him as Hitler—to make fun of his Jewishness—why do we always have to go for the jugular, toward the ethnic and religious prejudice?" Norman Atkins, "The Making of the President: Brown's Vartan Gregorian on the Modern University," *Rolling Stone*, Issue 600, March 21, 1991, p. 91.

CHAPTER 3

Plateau

That period from the end of the honeymoon to the day a president starts to think of resigning.

The long haul from the end of the honeymoon to the beginning of the end of a presidency we characterized as the plateau, not because it lacks ups and downs (which it does not) but because most past presidents can identify a relatively stable period of accomplishment during their terms, when administration team members worked together effectively, the institution moved forward according to plan, and governance structures appeared to be meeting the needs of the university community. The plateau phase thus designates that long middle period of service gainfully occupied by the myriad tasks that Yale's Bart Giamatti once characterized as getting the university through the day.[1] The drama of beginnings is over, the drama of leave-taking has not yet begun, and the president has become a known quantity occupying familiar terrain.

Yet, conflict or the threat of conflict consistently marks this terrain as presidents pursue the everyday tasks of governance: implementing and altering agendas, making difficult choices, responding to the unexpected, conferring with and meeting the demands of governing bodies while maintaining the confidence and cooperation of their campus constituencies. Our interview questions on governance topics, designed to pinpoint areas of tension with the groups involved, encouraged our subjects to recall difficult situations and discuss their reactions and strate-

gies as they engaged in the overarching leadership task of conflict resolution. From their stories of getting the university through the day some
common themes and experiences emerged that suggest why the average
life span of research university presidencies today is relatively short.

CONFLICTS WITH FACULTY

While university agendas may be at least partially shaped by governing boards, impacted by legislative decisions, and interrupted or adjusted
by the demands of students, the actual implementation of an approved
plan falls to the president with, in most cases, the advice and consent of
the faculty. Thus, when presidents encounter faculty resistance, how do
they respond? Looking back over the course of their terms in office, our
presidents described not only the difficulties they faced in achieving successful institutional outcomes, but also some of the frustrations they experienced: satisfaction in an important job well done marred by a lack of
recognition or the lingering discomforts of dilemma, of having sailed between the Scylla and Charybdis of competing campus interests and left
disgruntled opponents in their wake. It is little wonder that several presidents seemed pleased to count coup with disasters that had *not* befallen
them—that during Michigan's financial troubles Harold Shapiro had *not*
been served with a faculty petition of no confidence, that except for the
Title IX case against Brown, Vartan Gregorian had *not* been sued, that
when Columbia went coed Michael Sovern had *not* been publicly de-
nounced as the "Butcher of Barnard."

It is ironic that the effectiveness of successful presidents is likely to be
undermined over time by their very willingness to deal aggressively with
problems; the good that they do lives after them in the form of adver-
saries as well as achievements. Michael Sovern recalls that his predecessor, Bill McGill, had advised him, "Don't serve more than ten years," but
Sovern says he "didn't listen." When he made some controversial budget
decisions during his second decade at Columbia, Sovern understood the
reason for McGill's advice: Catching "a lot of hell" from some of the faculty, he found that his opposition was led by "a man I had passed over
for provost and . . . a man I had fired as dean of the college. As you know,
friends may come and go, but enemies accumulate!" Benno Schmidt,
having served about six years to Sovern's thirteen, appears to have
learned the same lesson at Yale in less than half the time; he, too, believes that "while institutions and people differ," the "outside limit" for

the length of a presidency is probably ten to twelve years because "presidents who do things tend to use up a lot of their [political] capital."

Schmidt would probably agree that he had spent his political capital lavishly at Yale. One of the characteristics of the plateau stage of a presidency is the constant pressure to choose between change and no change, between maintaining the status quo and taking actions that will very likely face opposition unless, of course, the nature of the change is additive. But when something has to be cut or shut down, presidents face a painful and politically expensive process. Benno Schmidt's experience at Yale provides a textbook example of what can happen when the right agenda is chosen and implemented too rapidly for the faculty to keep up. Literally "shocked" by the condition of Yale's physical infrastructure, Schmidt believes his first mistake was thinking that "the university needed to share my sense of shock at the magnitude of the task":

> And so I went to the university . . . with an unvarnished view of the situation . . . a message of sacrifice and institutional fiscal discipline without the equal and comparable message of immeasurable opportunities. . . . The second thing that I think I did not convey adequately was that this was also a time [when] Yale's resources were in a period of unprecedented expansion. . . . The alumni were . . . respond[ing] . . . at levels of generosity approached [only] once in Yale's history. . . . Our endowment was outperforming that of any other university in the country. . . . Although I certainly tried to make the good news clear and shout it from the rooftops, the message . . . that we've got to rebuild the place and it falls to this generation to sacrifice perhaps more than others . . . tended somehow to drown out, among the faculty especially, what I thought was the compensating good news. . . . I blame myself for the fact that that rather dour and difficult message seemed to be a more basic theme in the minds of a lot of faculty and students than the fact of the expansion of the university's . . . academic resources. It was very odd . . . somehow the sense of difficulty and institutional choices that were hard and controversial, became ingrained.

Thus, Schmidt suffered the frustration of seeing his achievements go unrecognized by many, even as the evidence of his success at fund-raising and stewardship showed up on the university's balance sheet and on campus where the renovation of desperately deteriorated buildings was getting under way. Furthermore, his efforts in these areas were "interpreted by some [as] a greater concern for buildings than people," setting the stage for what Schmidt calls "the primacy of the symbolic over the real or empirically grounded views of a president." In other words, detractors were wrong if they thought Schmidt was concerned only about budgets and bricks and HVAC systems; his concern for Yale's excellence as an academic institution obviously was the very reason for his concern with facilities and just as aggressively pursued:

> It seemed to me clear that Yale couldn't be good at everything and it couldn't even be good at everything it was doing. The evidence for that was the great disparity in the quality and effectiveness of different departments and different schools. In most cases, these problems of quality and effectiveness were long-standing. On the other hand, there were areas of enormous excellence and energy . . . that had been starved for growth because of the very strong tendency of the institution, particularly in the faculty of arts and sciences, to pretty much take the status quo as given and view change in a very incremental, interstitial way. Now, I think that's the wrong view for a first-rate academic institution under any circumstances, but particularly under circumstances of financial stress and under circumstances where the *financial* status quo or the inertia of financial priorities, had gotten the institution deeply out of balance.

Schmidt's answer to the problem was hardly revolutionary: assess schools and departments in light of Yale's academic priorities and pursue a policy of enhancement, reduction, or elimination. But this part of his agenda met with vociferous resistance among the faculty of arts and sciences (though "[n]ot elsewhere," Schmidt says) for two reasons. First, it rested on the generally unpalatable (to faculty) need for academic prioritizing:

> Some of my friends warned me . . . and I can remember a couple of faculty members saying, look, you've laid out here a need to achieve a rather modest cutback in the faculty of arts and sciences budget. (I said it had to be 6 or 8 percent, and we could do that over several years.) They said, as long as you do that across the board, there will be grumbling about it, people won't be happy, but it will be doable. But if you say that you're going to do it selectively, with some departments having their budgets cut by 20 percent, 50 percent, other departments having their budgets increased—then that will be tremendously controversial. I disagreed, I still disagree, but it was tremendously controversial. The initial response of the faculty was to resist strongly although that's what has in fact happened. It's not uncommon that the first time or two something is tried there's immense resistance, and then eventually there is acceptance of the need to do something.

The second "very serious adverse reaction" to Schmidt's academic agenda occurred because sufficient confidence in his administration had not yet been developed within the faculty of arts and sciences:

> There's no question that the faculty was upset . . . and felt that the provost and the deans and the faculty committee members who had been appointed to lead that effort were not adequately reflecting all the views of the faculty. I expected trouble on that front—there was trouble through the spring of 1992 with faculty committees reporting their dismay at this whole process, and I expected that to continue into the next year. But on the other hand, I also had no thought of taking any actions until that process resolved itself one way or the other. I wanted to see how the reaction would play itself out because reality is constantly intruding on such reactions in the form of the university's financial situation, and in this particular reality, the fact is that Stanford, Columbia, and Harvard were all at the same time engaged in very similar efforts at budgetary restructuring, centering on the faculty of arts and sciences. . . . So I thought that that situation was going to continue to be a source of resentment and resistance . . . but I had no need and did not want to make the situation worse by forcing decisions. I was prepared to wait. My thought was that if I waited, the faculty and I would continue to learn about the financial realities we were dealing with. Every year is different.

But Schmidt did not wait to see the faculty confirm and adopt his strategy; he left in spring 1992 while they were still in "revolt against the notion that certain departments were to have their resources lessened on the basis of a qualitative judgment." His presidential experience at Yale had left him with a sense of the university as almost unmanageable due to its culture of inertia, a culture reinforced by an easily aroused attitude of suspicion on the part of faculty directed toward decision makers and by the unwieldiness of the faculty governance process:

> I think the modern university has become a deeply conservative institution. I think there's a kind of visceral reaction against and resentment of the possibility of change. I think there's a tendency to avoid difficult realities if facing up to them requires tough choices. There's a tolerance of or at least an acquiescence in, things that aren't working well because the process of coming to grips, of simply making a judgment that something is not working well, is [too difficult]. I mean, there had been a solid consensus at Yale, an absolute solid consensus, that the situation in the department of phi-

losophy for many years was out of kilter with a place like Yale. The last rankings of departments had the Yale philosophy department ranked something like fortieth . . . [while] *all* of the adjoining disciplines and departments in the humanities and social sciences are among the strongest in the world. There was no argument about the situation of the philosophy department on campus. But *nothing*, nothing decisive had ever been done about this situation, not for three decades. Now, I think I understand and appreciate the arguments for not doing something about that. Who wants to? Get on with your own work. It's an unpleasant kind of a thing to face. If you are going to deal with it decisively, it's going to take a lot of somebody's time. But I saw not only at Yale or even particularly at Yale, that the modern university is very adverse to facing up to tough choices. Maybe that's good, maybe that's bad, but I actually wasn't comfortable with that even when I was a faculty member. I used to find it wrong, but especially as a dean or a president I felt my role was to try to actually do something. . . . I'm not saying that the response [should be] some presidential edict. . . . There has to be a process in the university and an appropriate one that engages the university [community], but if you wait for consensus about everything, including processes—the time to do it, how we do it, who should do it—nothing will happen. And . . . I was very impatient with that.

Benno Schmidt's description of the difficulties encountered at Yale from 1986 to 1992 bears a striking resemblance to some of Harold Shapiro's experiences at Princeton and Michigan. We have already noted that Shapiro's situation in the early years of his presidency at Princeton (1988–2001) was analogous to Schmidt's at Yale in that both came in as outsiders and discovered bad budget news, which they announced immediately and began acting on before the faculty had become comfortable with their administrations. Shapiro, however, waited out the uproar until the realities of the early 1990s, "when a lot of universities started running into fiscal trouble," were "grudgingly" recognized and confidence in him had developed. His greater patience with the hostility and disbelief he encountered at first among Princeton's faculty probably owed much to his prior trials as president of the University of Michigan.

Earlier in the 1980s, Shapiro, like Schmidt, had faced the double whammy of a need for both budget and academic restructuring, though in Shapiro's case the cause was external to the university: The second energy crisis had precipitated a recession in Michigan that resulted in decreased state support. In order to sustain quality during lean times,

Shapiro adopted a strategy of selective growth, summed up in the slogan "Smaller but better":

> Now that slogan was not meant to say that smaller *is* better, but that in our circumstances, the only way to get better was to get smaller. That meant I had to start deciding where it was that we were going to get smaller since I had rejected the notion of just getting smaller everywhere by the same amount.

Having concluded, as Schmidt would a few years later at Yale, that resources would have to be redirected from some academic areas in order to support excellence in others, Shapiro incurred and suffered the consequences of faculty ire:

> We were faced immediately with the problem of identifying areas of the university that were going to have to be cut back or eliminated—always a hard thing to do. We closed some programs, we dramatically reduced the size of others, and each one of those decisions was the struggle you would expect it to be with the faculty in those areas that were negatively affected. . . . To give an example, we closed the geography department and the geographers of the world descended on us both in writing and in person to tell us how we were altering the course of Western civilization. . . . We closed a number of programs, but more commonly we reduced the size of other programs by 25 percent or 30 percent. . . .
> . . . That was difficult and I'm not sure we always did it in the best possible way, but we did do it. Although there was a tremendous amount of angst about it at the time—anxiety and accusations of various kinds—in the years since I have hardly met anybody from the University of Michigan who hasn't said how appropriate the strategy was under those particular circumstances. These latter-day allies were not there, I can assure you, during the hard times. No one was there telling me how wonderful it was then.

Although Harold Shapiro successfully weathered the storm over cutbacks at Michigan, his remarks suggest that he, like Schmidt, may have felt unappreciated at the time and certainly did feel uncomfortable with the faculty's reaction. His fear, that they would misunderstand his strategy as a lack of concern for "anything except professional education," was a realistic one, as demonstrated by Benno Schmidt's later struggles with the misperception at Yale that his strategy showed "greater concern for buildings than [for] people." Nevertheless, Michigan *was* Shapiro's home university, he was an insider, and he felt that he had credibility with the faculty despite tensions and outright anger among some groups. On the other hand, his fifteen years at Ann Arbor made the strategy that much more painful for him:

> I found it very upsetting. . . . No one likes to tell a group of colleagues who have worked loyally for the university for a long time, "You're not as big a part of our future as you were of our past." It's a very unpleasant prospect and I didn't like doing it. . . . There was a period when we were holding public hearings on all this, allowing faculty and students and others to protest, which they did. And they didn't bother using measured language as I would use measured language. And so, it was psychologically difficult to do it, but you know, you get the courage to do these things because you really believe in the institution and where you're going.

Although Shapiro was more patient than Schmidt with the consensus-building process that is chapter and verse at universities with strong faculty governance, he nonetheless came to the same conclusion, that it is a mistake to "wait for consensus about everything":

> We decided that in making our budget cutbacks, we would allow for extensive on-campus discussion, faculty review groups, students, etc., on the idea that if the community understood better, had a chance to participate in these difficult decisions, they would find them more acceptable. And we followed through on that plan. It is my judgment in retrospect that this process just prolonged the agony for everybody and was actually costly in the end. We had a longer period of uncertainty as people felt that they could in fact get in the way of change, and while I certainly did not learn from that experience that one shouldn't have such a process, I think we in fact erred on the side of having too much discussion, and it became costly. I think we could have served everybody better. We certainly learned something in this process, but we didn't learn much after a while—after a while it was just repeating with more and more vehemence, and more and more anger, and more and more this, and more and more that, and I think it wasn't serving anybody, either the individuals involved or the departments involved or the university or anybody, because it just got to be unproductive. I think some of that is very important, but in my view we overdid it.

Although taking away is always painful for somebody, adding to is not always viewed as desirable by faculty either, and the president who spins gold out of the straw of controversy and stalemate cannot necessarily count on getting credit for his efforts. In 1983, Donald Kennedy found himself placed between two hostile camps at Stanford: on one side, the director of the Hoover Institution, a conservative think tank on the Stanford campus, and its various supporters (conservative alumni, donors, board members, and scholars); on the other side, a large and vocal number of liberal Stanford faculty. The issue at hand was whether the university, via the Hoover Institution, would accept the Ronald Reagan Presidential Library:

> Hoover was a problem in two ways. The first is that W. Glenn Campbell, the [then] director, is a truly unpleasant person for whom conflict is entertainment. . . . He had been in constant battle with the two presidents before me, and with large numbers of the Stanford faculty, whom he regarded as leftists. Of course, some of those could not resist taking a poke at him and Hoover at every opportunity. He in turn couldn't resist annoying them with provocative statements.

When Campbell presented the Reagan Library proposal to Kennedy it came with a catch: The library would actually be a complex that included a museum likely to attract thousands of tourists and a public policy center "to be affiliated with the Hoover Institution." Kennedy did the prudent thing and appointed a "distinguished faculty committee to look at this proposal and make a recommendation":

> The committee reported that it would very much like to have access to the presidential papers, which would be a boon to Stanford scholarship and would bring other scholars here. But it concluded that the public policy center ought to be under normal academic governance. That produced a brouhaha in the course of which two trustees and I flew back to Washington to meet with Attorney General [Edwin] Meese in the White House to negotiate. Finally, it was decided that there wouldn't be a public policy center or a museum with memorabilia [on the Stanford site].
>   As things went along, I had to fight two battles, one against Campbell and his board and others who thought we were being picky about the public policy center, and a second against faculty and others who didn't like the idea of a Reagan *anything* on the campus. You can imagine how popular Ronald Reagan was on the average research university faculty. . . . [However,] a scholarly library containing presidential papers could hardly be turned down; if a higher education institution says "no" to that, it's open to charges of political correctness, especially when its own historians . . . are saying it's a good thing to have.

Risking "alienation from Stanford liberals," Kennedy resisted faculty pressures to withdraw support for the library while "at the same time hold[ing] Campbell at bay." Finally, in 1987, apparently tired of the wrangling with Stanford faculty over the siting and the size of the library and concluding that the planned (but banned) public affairs center should be located on the same site with the library after all, the Ronald Reagan Presidential Foundation withdrew its proposal. Kennedy and Stanford board chairman Warren Christopher issued a statement of disappointment at the decision, and Kennedy recalls the whole process (which lasted almost four years) as "a difficult time." Within a year, however, he had snatched one victory at least from the standoff: Glenn Campbell was forced into retirement[2] and under a new director the Hoover Institution began

> making all kinds of joint appointments with the Stanford faculty. They have a very valuable archive and twenty years from now nobody will remember that the institute was a terrible thorn in our side. That's one of the accomplishments of my time here which, because of all the acridity that accompanied it, won't be recognized. But we brought the Hoover Institution into the fold, and it is very valuable to the campus.

Kennedy's Hoover vignette, like Schmidt's and Shapiro's accounts, offers one more guide to some of the sources of fatigue and frustration that build toward presidential exits: the lack of appreciation or recognition while enduring slings and arrows over a sustained period; the wear and tear of lose-lose situations; and sometimes even a sense of futility in their efforts to secure informed faculty cooperation. Because university presidents must be tireless promoters of their institutions, ever accentuating the positive, such natural human reactions are seldom publicly acknowledged.

CONFLICTS WITH STUDENTS

Students have a special ability to place presidents in uncomfortable situations, even to affect university agendas through the power of disruption. None of our group of eight presidents lacked ample experience with student protests, petitions, and marches, but half, in retrospect, saw student activism as just another part of the university landscape with no significant impact on their presidencies. The other half, however, identified student unrest as a painful or difficult factor that *did* seriously affect them.

In the first group, Vartan Gregorian emphasized his preventive maintenance approach to Brown's student population, visiting dormitories, addressing students directly in speeches and letters on issues raised by the students themselves or by events, even marching with them in protests, "deal[ing] with student needs up-front." Gregorian admits, however, that his hands-on approach, intended to convey that he was "not relying on [the] dean of students to call . . . if there was trouble," is probably feasible only at relatively small universities like Brown. An additional note on student activism at smaller institutions was provided by Harold Shapiro who compared student manageability and student power as he experienced them at Princeton and Michigan:

> When you're president long enough, a protest is not a major deal, it's just all part of the environment. You get protests from time to time. I thought that there was never a student protest here at Princeton that was anything close to some of the situations that developed at the University of Michigan. I think there've been two or maybe three protests of one kind or another since I've been here, I can't quite remember, but for the most part they've been very mild, very appropriate, and you know, I don't consider any of them to have been inappropriately disruptive. Their *intent* was serious, the people were serious about what they were doing, but they weren't seriously disruptive, they didn't change what you did day to day. . . .
>
> . . . I have to say, in my own experience, the intensity, the level of organization of the protests here is a shadow of what could be mobilized at the University of Michigan. My view is that organizing protests is not a simple matter, and graduate students are much better organizers than undergraduates. They have experience, they've been through it before, they know what you have to do. Where you have a large group of graduate students, you have a large group of potential organizers. And where there are large graduate student bodies, you get better organized undergraduate political expression because you still need organizers, you can't just go out there and feel good. I mean, it doesn't last for more than a short time. So you need to get organized and know what to do, how to do it. I think at a university like Princeton where we have only 1,500–1,600 graduate students, it's a little bit harder.

In contrast to Gregorian's "teachable moment" philosophy, and much like Shapiro, Michael Sovern recalled the disruptive powers of Columbia students as just another factor to be considered in ordering the everyday business of the university. When students blocked the entrance to a classroom building, Sovern observes that they "had no knowledge of what had happened in 1968 and so didn't understand why I didn't call the police. But I didn't. We just sat 'em out." Over two years of anti-apartheid, pro-divestment protests by hundreds of students did lead eventually to the decision to divest Columbia's portfolio completely of stock from companies doing business in South Africa, but only because "Principle and pragmatism came together. We were all strong opponents of apartheid . . . [and] The contrary position would have left us with a mountain of residual ill will on campus." Donald Kennedy, too, is matter-of-fact in his references to the South Africa protests by Stanford students, "Occasionally, the trustees would appear with me at mass meetings, and we would explain our position to the students and get booed."

While in hindsight these four presidents describe student protests as never really breaching their comfort zones, even a small sampling of contemporary newspaper coverage suggests that activist students nonetheless produced headaches enough for them and numerous unpleasant confrontations. For example, in 1992, during Vartan Gregorian's tenure at Brown, 250 students were arrested after occupying the administration building. Harold Shapiro also suffered occupation of his administration buildings—at Michigan by more than 200 students in 1987 and an overnight sit-in by forty students at Princeton in 1989. In 1985, Michael Sovern had to deal with hundreds of student protesters at Columbia who had not only "chained shut" a building entrance but had apparently done so with the support of 200 faculty and fourteen students who were on a hunger strike. In the academic year 1985–1986, Donald Kennedy saw Stanford anti-apartheid protesters lying down in front of trustees' cars and a hundred more rallying at his home.[3] Whether because of outcome or interpretation or simply as a function of personality, these presidents struck a mellow note when recalling what had to have been stressful times with students, downplaying the impact of organized student dissent on themselves or their presidencies. Their attitudes are in sharp contrast to the retrospective views of Benno Schmidt, Robert O'Neil, James Freedman, and Paul Hardin, who recalled students as having produced some distinctively negative influences during their presidencies.

Benno Schmidt notes several times in his interviews that student reaction contributed to the creation of a campus, and then a public, view of him that he considered inaccurate but powerful. On the issues of maintaining two homes, his position on free speech as an absolute value, and his opposition to divestment, Schmidt speaks repeatedly of the responses of faculty *and* students. For example, on his wife's need to keep their home in New York City because of her career, he spoke at length about the campus response:

> The faculty and the students, at least in many quarters, felt that this [arrangement] reflected—I'm not sure what, and obviously one can't

speak of "the faculty" and "the students"—but I had a very clear sense that with some faculty and with many of the students, the perennial issue arose of the president of a major university not being around all the time, or not being as accessible to everyone all the time as they might like. This was put into the perspective that because Helen was not in New Haven full time as her base and we kept a home in New York as well as the President's House in New Haven, that that somehow represented a lack of commitment by me to New Haven and to Yale. . . . I was surprised when the most effective sign the pro-divestment student protesters were carrying around campus was, "Where's Benno?" . . . I said with great pride I thought her career was every bit as important and worthy of respect in terms of family arrangements as mine was. Yet there were significant elements of both the faculty and the student community that really didn't like that. . . .

    . . . The newspapers picked it up, it became one of the strong symbolic features of my presidency, and I never would have predicted it. . . . All presidents, many presidents, have to deal with the perception on campus that they're away all the time. Do you know the wonderful joke about Father Hesburgh that they used to tell at Notre Dame? What's the difference between God and Father Hesburgh? God is everywhere, including Notre Dame; Father Hesburgh is only everywhere. I love that. I think Ted told me that joke, actually. A university president, at least the Yale president when I was the Yale president, has to be on the road a lot. I had to raise a huge amount of money for the institution and a lot of what I had to do included taking a fairly strong role in Washington. Anyway, there was inevitably a fair amount of travel and because of that I actually took pains to have more lunches with students and more dinners and things like that with students, than any president had before. Notwithstanding, the perception was that I was away more, or as some people came to see it, a commuter president. And I think it was because most of the time people don't see the president, even when he's on campus. There are 25,000 people at Yale, students, faculty, staff—it's a pretty big place. Any president has a fairly hectic schedule so that these symbolic features of a presidency can assume much larger proportions than the reality would [warrant]. This was just one of those symbolic elements that took on a life of its own.

Life and prominence were certainly pumped into this symbol of campus skepticism by the national press in such articles as "Yale's Commuter President" (*Manhattan, inc.*), "New Haven Blues" (*Boston Globe*), and "'Where's Benno?' Refrain at Yale Belies Its President's Record" (*New York Times*),[4] but the spread of the myth of absentia appears to have been fueled as well by Schmidt's unpopular stands on free speech and divestment at Yale which he cites as further reasons for a continuing student disaffection toward him. His insistence that at Yale, "there was not going to be any requirement that speech be nice in order to be protected," branded him "a pretty uncompromising conservative" in the eyes of a generally politically correct student body, he believes, an impression strengthened by his opposition to divestment and to the larger issue of the university as a staging area for political action:

> This very, very deep, ingrained institutional habit of the university, of Yale especially in some ways, being the focal point for political agitation when something is wrong in the broader society—I was not sympathetic to that. And I'm afraid I made that clear. . . . The style in which I conveyed [my feelings on] that issue, the uncompromising language of principle, was a style better suited to the law school setting where students are more adult by definition. . . . In a college setting I'm afraid [I] . . . came across as very austere, unsympathetic, and, among my most extreme critics, even authoritarian.
>
> I don't think that last word is right at all because it never had anything to do with my having the answer or being unwilling to engage or participate in a full exchange of views and explain myself. It had nothing to do with an authoritarian streak, but it had a lot to do with my view of the university as a place that has to act in accordance with principle.

A friend at Yale, trying to give him some practical advice, urged divestment, but Schmidt, concerned about committing the university to an action that he perceived as not being "morally consistent," objected:

> Well, why South Africa, why start with that? I mean, there are so many evils in the world. "Because the kids are making a lot of noise and you've got to give the kids something. They're upset, they want the university to listen." So, well, I agreed, it's better to listen, I *have* listened. But the fact that they're upset doesn't mean anything to me. Well, I shouldn't say it doesn't mean anything. It means I listen, but the mere fact that they're upset as a guide to action? No way. His view was, "Oh, no, absolutely. If you're a university leader, you gauge when they're upset, and you comply with what they want, try to calm things down, and get on with life." I suppose that's a reasonable point of view, but it's certainly not mine, and I made it very clear that it wasn't. In the process I think I may have conveyed an unbending view which then was a negative when we got over into the totally different territory of, okay, granted we've got to rebuild the place and it's falling down, how quickly do we do it? I had people

who thought, gee, this is a character who comes to what he thinks
is right and then doesn't listen and doesn't bend much. I don't think
that was right, but I think that was definitely the feeling that some
people had.

Ironically, for all his pragmatism in the academic and physical realms at
Yale, it was Schmidt's idealism about the university—that it should remain on the high ground of neutrality where political controversies were
concerned—that served to alienate him from the idealists among the Yale
student body and that conveyed to the Yale faculty the impression, however false, of an autocratic president.

To the extent that conflicts between a president and any group of students gains press attention, personal discomfort, image problems, and disruptions of the university's daily business are likely to ensue, with
repercussions on the faculty's view of the president as well. For Benno
Schmidt, his lack of popularity with Yale undergraduates, while hardly a
deciding factor, did become eventually one more presidential frustration
and one more politically negative element to add to the growing list of
conflicts with faculty that made him vulnerable to outside offers.

For an example of a conflict with students that enhanced faculty support of a president, we can turn to James Freedman's experience with the
student staff of *The Dartmouth Review*. Still painful for him in the
retelling, the anti-Semitic attacks on Freedman in the *Review* are our
most extreme example of student power to disturb a president. Freedman's long and public battle with the *Review* on behalf of others attacked
in its pages as well as himself, was of course not typical of a clash between administration and student radicals; comparatively few students
were involved and they were not, strictly speaking, activists. But because
for a time they virtually terrorized the campus under the guise of free
speech/free press, Freedman feels that his early confrontations with these
students provided a bonding experience with the faculty that ratified his
presidency, "I have not had a fight with the faculty in ten years, and I
think it was in part because they saw I was willing to put myself on the
line for their values."

Robert O'Neil, on the other hand, provides a sort of inverted gloss on
Freedman's statement. O'Neil believes he raised doubts in the minds of
the Virginia faculty about where he might stand on the issue of student
power versus faculty rights when he removed an administrator in the face
of student protests about the man. Although he had done what he
thought was right and would inevitably have done anyway, looking back
on it O'Neil now believes that he weakened his presidency by not an-

ticipating student action and moving quickly to head off the demon-strations that alarmed faculty. "Somehow, there was an emotional reac-tion, one I think in some cases of fear, that if a group of angry black students—doesn't matter if they're right or wrong—can do this even to a *black* administrator, then we're in terrible trouble." Tellingly, O'Neil compared the impact of this incident on his own presidency to his UVA predecessor Frank Hereford's loss of credibility with the faculty when the *New York Times* publicized Hereford's membership in the all-white Farm-ington Country Club. "I think it was very difficult for Frank from that time on to move effectively in certain areas because of the intensity of feeling."

Although like James Freedman and Robert O'Neil, Paul Hardin had what he called a "top-of-the-chart crisis in racial conflict" with students, he did not place the struggle over a freestanding black cultural center (BCC) at UNC in the context of effects on his presidency or his rela-tionship with faculty. In fact, his ambivalence about how to evaluate the impact of the two-year BCC controversy was evident during our inter-view as he considered and then rejected it as a defining moment:

> I think that the defining moments probably ought to be . . . those that had thoroughly positive consequences. . . . But I think that the person on the street . . . would see the black cultural center contro-versy as the defining moment because through that long, arduous ex-perience I suffered more wear and tear than I ever have. I don't think I showed it, I've got a lot of stamina, but that hurt me a lot. . . . The BCC was a defining moment in the sense that I had to pick my way through my personal feelings and what I thought was best for the university, and I had to do it simply without regard to public opin-ion. . . . There was no way I could approach that problem in terms of what's going to make people happy. Absolutely no way.

Later, however, after reviewing what Hardin believes was agenda-driven press coverage by ABC, he firmly rejected the BCC controversy as a defining moment in his chancellorship:

> I would say that the competition for defining moments would be close in the public eye. When all the facts are on the table, I would choose that aggregation of confrontations with my president and with my two governors that had positive outcomes, protecting and strengthening the university.

What is clearly evident in Hardin's account is that he took personally—or perhaps more accurately, responded very personally to—the series of events that unfolded from fall 1991 to spring 1993:

Initially, as you'll recall, the advocates of an expanded black cultural center . . . wanted to take over Howell Hall where the school of journalism and mass communication was housed, but that was an inappropriate part of campus for a student activity. . . . I said something [then] that I still believe but that became an inflammatory comment: that we want for the black cultural center a forum, not a fortress. That if you have a freestanding building, it is likely to be seen as a fortress. Let's make sure that we're talking about a facility and a program that are not exclusive, that are open and affirming and educational. But it suited the proponents, the student activists, and the woman who then was in charge of the black cultural center, to treat that as a confrontation[al] [statement]. And so I became for a moment a reluctant hero with the conservatives who did not like the whole idea of a black cultural center and an enemy [among supporters of the BCC] which I think was an artificial construct and very hurtful. I had always championed diversity and had taken steps to establish diversity on this campus and had said that if you satisfy me that you're establishing an institution that would be open and that will be constructive, I will support it to the hilt. Later, when I had Provost Dick McCormick chair a committee to make recommendations to me, Dick tried to enlist those student activists on the committee, and they refused to cooperate just to show they were more interested in the issue than they were in a solution. Dick McCormick made the best of it without the students, and his committee recommended that the freestanding black cultural center go forward and be constructed on an appropriate site, that it be open programmatically to everyone regardless of race, and that it be an educational facility and not a segregated black student union. At which point I endorsed it and incurred the wrath of the conservatives. I think the true liberals were more or less people who think as I do about these things, who have an open mind and really want the races to work together, who believe in integration. I think we were all just kind of baffled about how these things got out of control. . . .

. . . Now, I did feel the weight of that black cultural center debate, and maybe one reason I didn't get beat down by it was, I was open about that. I said to the press, "This is the hardest thing I've ever confronted, and this is very wearing because I'm being caricatured by both sides of the argument. When I want to sit down and talk with the student leaders and I invite them to talk, they have a prearranged signal when they walk out. I'm not comfortable with that kind of conversation. That's a confrontation, that isn't a conversation. And you know, this is really tough."

Hardin's experience *was* tough and quite publicly so, with increasingly negative national press coverage throughout the nearly two years of student unrest and protest,[5] visits by Spike Lee and Jesse Jackson, and numerous marches, demonstrations, and sit-ins, including a takeover of his office that ended with the arrest of sixteen students (April 15, 1993). However, except for the length of time this conflict continued (extended by renewed disagreement over where to locate the approved BCC), Hardin's grueling experience seems no less severe than that of Harold Shapiro during the 1987 racial crisis at the University of Michigan. While in our interview Shapiro downplayed the impact on himself of two months of stressful interactions with students, the *Detroit Free Press* describes a series of tense, unpleasant, and at times threatening encounters between president, administrators, and regents on one side, and protesting students on the other.[6] The difference in perspective of these two presidents may be a function of temperament, or it may be simply the passage of time, some ten years having elapsed between Shapiro's student-orchestrated trial by fire and our interview, but only about four years between the resolution of the BCC issue and Hardin's recollections for our study.

As with many other aspects of the university presidency, lessons drawn from these presidential experiences with students are as complicated as the institutions and the people involved. Those who look back with equanimity and matter-of-factness on times of turmoil may have forgotten how difficult and uncertain the right path was at the time. Robert O'Neil reflects ruefully on what he *should* have done, suggesting that presidents need always to keep a close eye and ear to student concerns, yet Vartan Gregorian, who did just that at Brown, admits that it has its limitations at larger schools and besides, his practice did not prevent the occurrence of one of a president's many nightmares: having to call in the police to arrest hundreds of his institution's students. We might conclude from these interviews that idealism among university presidents is an expensive luxury: Benno Schmidt stood firm on his principles and suffered bad publicity throughout his term for his strained relations with students. Paul Hardin defended the principle of integration rather than segregation of the races and suffered for it. James Freedman stood up for a principle of civil behavior, suffered for it, but ultimately won. He still, however, recalls the pain.

CONFLICTS WITH GOVERNING BODIES

All things being roughly equal—mission, size, academic quality—the chief difference between heading a public and a private university lies in the nature of the governance structure above the level of president. Thus,

while all of our subjects had positive things to say about the supportive-
ness of their trustees, those who had headed public institutions said less
about difficulties with their campus boards and more about the conflicts
and complexities they encountered at the next higher levels of state governance. Among our presidents who spoke about their relationships with
trustees at private universities, two broad differences in descriptive emphasis emerged, a partnership model and a presidential responsibility
model.

Both Michael Sovern and James Freedman described strong boards
who appeared to be looking for an equal partnership with strong presidents. In Sovern's narrative, the Columbia trustees are a supportive but
powerful background presence as they join him in making tough financial decisions. Selling the land under Rockefeller Center, he reported
"fully to the executive committee of the trustees, and summarily to the
trustees as a whole, until . . . the deal was really struck . . . subject to
trustee approval." Deciding to exceed the endowment spending rule,
Sovern notes carefully that "the trustees and I agreed . . . one year we
spent as much as 8 percent instead of 5 percent . . . of course, with the
trustees' approval." With respect to divesting Columbia's portfolio of
stock in companies doing business in South Africa, Sovern notes again
that "the trustees and I agreed that we would in fact divest. . . . The leadership of the trustees was especially strong." He does not, however, suggest an equal partnership with his board in academic decision making; as
we have previously noted, when asked whether during the presidential
search Columbia trustees discussed an agenda of their own for the university, he replied succinctly:

> They did not. Of course, my views on many subjects were known.
> The education committee of the trustees is the provost's committee,
> so I was working closely with that group on a regular basis. . . . In
> the course of discussing [an important] report with the trustees' ed-
> ucation committee and the trustees, I did focus on things that
> needed to be done in the arts and sciences. . . . I had an agenda that
> was substantial, but it was . . . not one that I ever laid before the
> trustees as a master plan. It was my own judgment about what was
> needed.

James Freedman, too, describes a Dartmouth board looking for a president who would be a strong leader, but in partnership with trustees determined to reshape their university in the eyes of an academic world
that saw Dartmouth as "not a significant intellectual player" among its
Ivy League brethren. Like Michael Sovern, Freedman implies a sensible

division of leadership labor, one both parties understood: "The board clearly knew in appointing me that they were not hiring someone who was going to be a superb financial manager, who would understand the endowment spending formula to the umpteenth degree," but they did know Freedman's reputation as an academic leader, that he "spoke the values of the faculty," and the Dartmouth trustees "clearly wanted a president who had a national profile academically." Unlike Michael Sovern who was well known to his trustees both as dean and as provost at Columbia, Freedman was an outsider at Dartmouth who had served his presidential apprenticeship in the public sector, making him a surprising choice. In addition, the Dartmouth board had been perhaps overpersuaded, Freedman suggests, "whether reluctantly or enthusiastically," by a forceful chairman intent on change. The partnership had the potential to be an uneasy one, obviously a stretch and a risk for both president and board. In this light, the painful confrontations with the *Dartmouth Review* that left Freedman's trustees "so angry and so offended and so hurt," were in one respect at least efficacious, providing an early and powerful bonding experience for this academic odd couple, the unlikely pairing of an Ivy League board with the Jewish president of the University of Iowa. In the end, Freedman and his wife "always felt supported by the board at every stage," and the unlikely presidency continued successfully for eleven years.

James Freedman makes only glancing reference to a president's responsibility "constantly . . . to reeducate [his] board," as "a different story for a different moment," one overshadowed by the more important history of an unusually strong—one might even say pivotal—group of Dartmouth trustees. For our other private university presidents, however, the creation and re-creation of well educated, effective, and harmonious boards were the important trustee stories, a key responsibility and a hazardous one to lose sight of. Both Donald Kennedy and Benno Schmidt take note of trustee problems and tensions for which they blame themselves; Kennedy, however, is the more critical of the two. At one point, he underlines a general institutional loss:

> The group that was in place at the time I became president was a terrific board of trustees. I thought they understood the institution quite well, particularly the board's leadership. The board was somewhat weaker at the end of my presidency, and I can't blame anybody but myself for that. I thought we were making good appointments, but we didn't do as well as we might have. Part of what happened

was that over a period from the 1970s to the mid-1980s, we lost trustees who were deeply experienced senior figures from an era in which trusteeship was taken much more seriously by most people than it is now. . . . That kind of commitment, knowledge, and workmanship is pretty rare now.

At other times in response to our questions, Kennedy makes reference to conflicts with the Stanford board they were more specific or personal to him—his divorce, his support of a change in Stanford's housing policy that was perceived as a gay issue, and most important, his administration's open public relations posture at Stanford: "Frank pronouncements on behalf of the university" that made some trustees "wince." While Kennedy also acknowledges Stanford's trustees' support in many other touchy areas—divestment, the Nixon library, the Hoover Institution, and the indirect costs controversy—he suggests that conflict may be the norm in the present-day trustee/president relationship, a judgment summed up in his strong statement elicited during our discussion of risk taking, that "many of today's trustees" hold the view that "presidents, like nineteenth-century children, should be often seen and seldom heard."

Whether Benno Schmidt was seldom seen during his Yale presidency, he most certainly was often heard, taking strong public positions not all of his trustees agreed with. On the issue of divestment, for example,

> The Corporation was divided and deeply divided, but it did not cause me to lose any support. . . . Indeed, the people who most vigorously disagreed with me . . . turned out to be my biggest supporters—Paul Moore, Paul Tsongas. . . . Eleanor Holmes Norton bitterly disagreed with me but was a wonderful supporter of mine on the Corporation. So it didn't cause any problems with my relationships in the Corporation, not at all.

Despite this oft-voiced confidence in his trustees' support, however, Schmidt does believe that he made his board uncomfortable, first by insisting on an abbreviated search process that left some of them feeling "less engaged and a bit less a part of the process," and then by confronting them simultaneously with "a system of challenges that were beyond the memory of most trustees" and a "degree of turnover in the Corporation unprecedented in the history of the institution":

> Within two years a majority of those who were trustees when I was appointed had left, and new people came on in very large numbers.

I think some who left . . . partly because they had never had a chance to work with me . . . felt separated from Yale and from me, felt some slight sense of alienation. I probably could have reached out a bit more to them. The new members coming on felt a great deal of institutional responsibility and pressure because I was telling them and, if you will, leading them, teaching them, that Yale needed to undertake some fairly fundamental changes in its financial governance, and that these changes were going to be difficult at best. They felt great pressure at having to deal with institutional change of a fairly basic and controversial character at the same time that they were newly arrived and in some cases relatively new to being trustees of a university. They always gave me unstinting support, but . . . given that I was prescribing . . . a variety of actions that were difficult, it created more of a sense of institutional challenge, things not going along so much in a traditional way, and that, I think, was uncomfortable for all of us. You see, only a few years before [I became president], Yale had moved from a system of lifetime tenure for trustees to a system of trustee terms. . . . The upshot was that a Corporation that had been marked over the centuries by a very high degree of continuity (with some members serving for decades and decades), went to being one governed by [trustees with] limited terms in office. . . . At the same time I was saying to the Corporation and these new members, we really need to grapple with some realities about the university's financial and educational and institutional position, realities that really haven't been well understood or faced up to for many, many decades. I think I did not exaggerate the extent to which the institution had to change to put itself on a firm and promising foundation for the future . . . but it may be that my candid view was a little alarming to some of the new people.

Although he never actually characterizes himself as being in direct conflict with his trustees, Schmidt accepts responsibility for exacerbating tensions inherent to the Yale situation. To sum up the contrast with Donald Kennedy: while Kennedy points to a tendency for trustees to be too hard on presidents, Schmidt offers himself as an example of a president who was too hard on his trustees.

Vartan Gregorian and Harold Shapiro provided us with the most extensive commentaries about their philosophies for avoiding conflict with trustees while turning them into effective board members. Gregorian, in fact, offered a veritable tutorial in trustee management, explaining, "There are two ways you can work with trustees. One is to finesse them, flatter them, please them. The other is to involve them, to give them a sense of ownership not only of the general vision, but also an understanding of the intricacies [of the university]." To do this, to ensure that a board, "instead of becoming an overseer, an obstacle, becomes your ally," Gregorian offered some specifics from his Brown experience. To keep his board "abreast of things," he went as far as to meet individually with each of the university's twelve fellows and thirty-six trustees,

> so that there would be no misunderstanding as to my public statements and my actions. Every decision I took, even unpopular ones, had the full backing of the trustees and their understanding as to why I was doing what I was doing. So, my conflicts with trustees were practically nil, I hate to tell you! Practically nil.

To further ensure against conflict, he kept himself equally well informed on the "position of people [trustees] on various issues," so that he would not be surprised by disagreements and could avoid embarrassment to board members:

> The only time a vote was forced in the executive committee of the trustees [was when] a person disagreed [with me about] whether I should buy this [certain] building. . . . Naturally, I did not want that to happen again because I did not want this trustee to lose the vote; it [begins to appear] that you don't pay attention to his opinion.

"Conflict," Gregorian sums up, "comes with a surprise." A further way for both president and board to avoid surprises and stay informed was the Brown trustees' unusual practice (for a university) of reviewing annually the president's relations with the faculty, which Gregorian describes as a "safety valve so that issues don't get out of hand, so that you have indications where there are problems." The meetings, he carefully notes, were "not for adjudication," but rather "to say, this is what the faculty is worried or pleased about." These meetings also seem to have been another of the ways the Brown board could continue to learn about the complexities of the university and the very different culture of the faculty. In fact, Gregorian issued a caveat for presidents who may become confused in the course of acting as an intermediary between these two cultures:

> Since most trustees come from the corporate culture, presidents are forced to develop a schizoid language; they defend their [policies] to the trustees in corporate language and to the faculty and students in academic language. . . . It's hard to keep the two cultures talking without telling two different things to the inhabitants of those two

cultures. That's the most difficult task for a college president. In the 1960s, we saw many instances when university presidents fell as a result of the clash of these two languages and cultures by promising two contradictory policies, one to the trustees and one to the faculty. . . . So then the issue is, how do you explain efficiency and excellence without constantly resorting to bottom-line analysis? You can show academic excellence in Egyptology for example, but you cannot show a successful cost-benefit analysis of Egyptology when you have only a handful of students studying it. How are you going to explain that to the trustees? You have to explain the university culture to the trustees, its complexity, the fact that it's a 900-year-old academic culture that has evolved, and that you're heading this, gradually changing it, managing it, leading it, but it's not a uniform corporate culture. There's no clear vertical integration and horizontal integration in this business. All tenured professors are equal, not only in their departments but also in the university as a whole. Their salaries may not be equal, their stations may not be equal, the Wharton professor of finance and the classics professor may not drive the same cars or have the same lifestyle, but they all believe, "I have one vote and you have one vote and [we are both] members of this corporate academic body called the faculty." That's what gets leaders into trouble, how to talk one language with which you bring both parties to appreciate the academic culture despite its inane rules and its perceived inertia and seeming opposition to change.

Like Vartan Gregorian, Harold Shapiro, too, placed a strong emphasis on informing and instructing his boards because "if the president gets hit by the proverbial beer truck, somebody has got to be there who knows what's going on":

> It's surprising how many boards are quite ill informed. I am stunned by the number of boards that have only the most marginal idea of what the real situation is at the university. I mean, they love the university, they work for the university and all that, and they have all these commitments. But if you ask them any question about what really is the nature of your budgetary situation, it's very hard for them to say anything beyond, well, our budget is balanced or it's not balanced.

At Princeton, therefore, Shapiro "went to a lot of trouble to keep the board really fully informed." Acknowledging that this conscientious attention to teaching "takes a lot of effort," he nonetheless asserts its importance as a key presidential duty:

To understand how the whole university works, with professional schools, a medical center, and everything else put together, is a complicated issue, so it takes time. And you've got to be willing to invest the time in teaching your board. I think that many of my colleagues underestimate their obligation to be a teacher to the board regarding what's going on at the university in terms of the responsibilities the board has. They don't have to know what's going on in the latest biological research laboratory, that's not their direct responsibility, but there are some things for which they are directly responsible, such as the financial welfare of the university, and my view is you have to teach them a lot, and if you have a lot of turnover as we do on our board, you have to teach all the time. It's like having a new class. We don't get mad because we have to teach calculus every year. We don't think just because we taught it last year we don't have to teach it again. You have new students and you teach it once again. And it's the same thing with boards.

The philosophy that Harold Shapiro brought to the board at Princeton was first developed, of course, at Michigan where his tiny, eight-person board (compared with Princeton's forty or so board members) had been chosen in statewide elections. Because Shapiro was intensely aware of the potential for conflict with these elected regents, his "single highest priority" was "building and sustaining" the support of the board:

Nothing was more important because you don't need a majority to stop you. You can be stopped by much less than a majority because every member of that eight-person board has the capacity to hold up a lot of actions. They can be overridden eventually, but it's trouble. So I always put an enormous emphasis on keeping close to the board and sustaining their support. I don't want to give you the impression that was hard. It was not so hard in those years because they were very supportive. You know, you do start out with the support of the board. After all, they appoint you. Okay, so in the first year or two you're not about to lose their support. It really comes later if it's going to come. I was just very fortunate in that respect—I didn't have any real problem. I think part of the reason was that unlike some of my colleagues, I always—regardless of what I thought of the board members individually—gave them the utmost respect because I respected what they stood for. Even if I didn't always respect their opinions or didn't always respect them as people, that was in my view irrelevant. This was a group of people who in some sense owned the university, in the sense of having all the power, and for that reason they deserved respect. I suppose they could have done something outrageous that would have caused me to resign, but otherwise, I thought then that it paid enormous dividends for the president to respect the board, both individually and as a group. You take people seriously, they take you seriously; you take them lightly, they take you lightly. So I had very few and relatively minor problems with the board. They supported me steadily.

Although Shapiro speaks of his Michigan board as "having all the power" and indirectly acknowledges that the vagaries of the political process may not always have provided the best possible board members ("Even if I didn't always respect their opinions or didn't always respect them as people"), he also takes note of the ironic balance of power that was provided by the open meetings laws to which public universities are captive:

> To get around the hard problems you delegate to the president a lot. That's one of the unknown costs of the open meetings law. You may think you're going to see more, but you in fact actually see less because the board, in order to avoid dealing with a lot of these things in public, just delegates to the president. The president meets by himself, so what needs to be done gets done. Like many laws, open meetings laws have a lot of counterintuitive results, that is, unintended results. One of the results at Michigan when I was there is that the board gave even more leeway to the president because they felt some issues were inappropriate for public discussion.

For Harold Shapiro, then, the combination of careful attention to his board and the "unintended" increment of power and independence created by the open meetings law, gave him a strong element of control at the campus governing-board level. The real challenge he faced was the potential for governance conflicts above the trustee level, with the state legislature, where the purse strings, the political power, and the unpredictability lay. To move the University of Michigan forward in the 1980s in the midst of a recession, therefore, he had to take calculated political risks—generating funds for academic growth, for example, by increasing out-of-state enrollment (in order to collect the higher tuition), despite realizing that he might "offend the sensibilities of state legislators regarding what they thought was appropriate," especially in regard to undergraduates. Another gamble was proceeding with the desperately needed modernization of Michigan's medical center "without any final commitment from the state," which was dallying over the financial agreement:

> Inflation was proceeding at around ten percent a year, so that the state's fixed-dollar commitment was worth less and less all the time.

> I just felt we had to get ahead of inflation, we had to take that chance
> and demonstrate our confidence in what we were doing and our con-
> fidence that the state would in fact meet its agreement to support
> this project as we went along. And they did. But on the day we bor-
> rowed one hundred and some odd million dollars, we didn't know,
> no one knew.

Savvy enough to gauge just how far he could push the governance realities under which he and the university had to operate, Shapiro nevertheless seems to have been unprepared for the experience of being
personally attacked by legislators on his home ground. On February 4,
1987, racial tensions at the University of Michigan were inflamed when
a student disc jockey at the campus radio station permitted two callers
to make a series of scurrilous racist jokes.[7] On sabbatical at the time,
Shapiro returned to Michigan to contend with protests and disruptions
on campus and sharp public criticisms as the *Detroit Free Press* kept the
state informed. Especially difficult was the Michigan legislators' decision
to come to campus and hold a hearing to "investigate racism" at the university. On March 5, 1987, the higher education subcommittee of the
House Appropriations Committee, chaired by Representative Morris
Hood, D-Detroit, heard testimony from students, faculty, and staff, many
of whom apparently blamed the administration for the racial climate and
racist incidents on campus. While the following day's headline in the
Detroit Free Press must have been difficult for Shapiro to read: "U-M President Is Soft on Racism, Blacks Charge at Panel Hearing," (March 6,
1987), the newspaper kept the story short, ran few quotes, and did not
report at all what the legislators themselves had to say. Another administrator later described these hearings to a U-M doctoral candidate in so-
ciology as a "'media frenzy,' a 'witch hunt,' terribly unfair and causing
'serious damage to the University.'"[8] This, then, is the context for Harold
Shapiro's recollections of his emotional response at the time:

> I had a particular set of experiences with African American legisla-
> tors in Michigan and with certain kinds of talk radio in Michigan
> that led me to think two things: "Maybe I can't be a good repre-
> sentative of this university anymore. Maybe they need a different
> kind of person here." And in any case, even if that were wrong, even
> if my judgment were too harsh on myself then, I thought, "You know,
> I don't need to do this, I don't have to put up with this." I viewed
> myself as trying to provide a social product for the state, and then
> to have legislators who were trying to take advantage of a difficult
> ongoing situation to lay the burden of all the social pathology of this
> country on the university and on my shoulders—you know, I didn't

need that. In addition, my wife was particularly frightened by some anti-Semitic comments that occurred in and around that time on talk radio. I said to myself, "Gosh, what do I need this for? I've got a nice life, I don't have to put up with this."

Later, on March 23, Jesse Jackson calmed the waters at a massive rally described by Shapiro as a "stunning performance":

He had at that time these sayings, you know, "Up with life, down with drugs," I don't remember, but things that rhyme, and he had this audience repeat these statements, and they were screaming them by the time he was finished. And every time he said "Racism," and it was a topic he came to many times, he turned towards me and he said, "And anti-Semitism." . . . And he went on like this for about an hour and then came to a close, walked out of the back of the auditorium into a limousine, and he was gone.

I walked out the back with him, of course, and started walking across campus back to my office. Well, it was unbelievable, grown people would come over to me and say, "Bless you, Dr. Shapiro, it was such a wonderful time, isn't it wonderful we could all come together like this?" People from the state legislature whom I had had so much trouble with were all on the platform wanting to be there with him, of course, and saying how wonderful this was and everything that's been accomplished here, and how fantastic it is, and what a wonderful person I am. [Some of these were people who had been offensive to me, yet] they were saying what a wonderful person I was, and how great it was that I was at the University of Michigan. . . . And from that day, this issue that had generated so much tension was gone. It just went, like a wave, it just went. It's magical in a way, I mean, I can't even to this day explain it. The tension just went.

Tensions may have eased for students, faculty, regents, and legislators, but not for Michigan's president: "I didn't forget easily the reactions of some members of the state legislature or some of the reactions on talk radio that occurred in and around that issue—that part didn't leave me." It had been an experience over which Shapiro had been able to exert far less control than he wanted to or was used to, and one that exemplified the biggest drawback to heading a public institution. The legislative subcommittee did not need permission to meet on campus to remind the president of the 500-pound gorilla in Lansing. The president of the University of Michigan, in turn, accepted the presidency of Princeton one month later.

Around this same time period (April 1987), another Big Ten President was also opting for the Ivy League. Recalling his decision to leave Iowa for Dartmouth, James Freedman does not suggest that the governance realities at a large state university were a factor or even much of a problem, but he does acknowledge that the potential for conflict was there. The governance structure at Iowa is quite similar to Michigan's: Each university is governed by a small, politically chosen board with multiple campus responsibilities. At Michigan, eight regents are directly elected and are responsible for the university campuses at Ann Arbor, Dearborn, and Flint (Michigan State has a separately elected board). At Iowa, nine regents (one of whom is a student) are appointed by Iowa's governor, with no more than five from the same political party. The Iowa regents govern the University of Iowa, Iowa State, and the University of Northern Iowa.[9] Despite the strongly political basis for these board appointments, Freedman considered politics a benign factor during his recruitment process:

> The chairman [of the board of regents] . . . had been a state senator. One of the other members was a former lieutenant governor. . . . And so you had two people who had been involved in the politics of the state and that must have been helpful in negotiating the arrangements. . . . Another person on the board . . . was the Republican National Committeeman. So, you had people close to the Governor. I am surprised—I was going to say appalled, but surprised—these days to read that candidates for public presidencies now are interviewed by the governor. I did not meet the governor until many months later when he was asked at a press conference, "What do you think of the person who's coming up to be your new president?" and he replied, "I've never met him." [The chairman] called me and said, "We'd better get you out here to meet the governor." So I went out and I met the governor, which was a pleasure. But you know, it was entirely an apolitical process.

Although he found politics at Iowa to be a neutral or possibly helpful element during the presidential search, Freedman was nonetheless wary of the ever-present possibilities for political intrusion, as he indicated when recounting a run-in with the Iowa football coach over the construction of a new practice facility:

> [Athletics] had the money, but that was a year in which the legislature had voted no salary increases. So the entire faculty, the entire university, went without a salary increase for that year—zero. I felt

it was unmeet and inappropriate to announce we were going to build a two-and-a-half-million-dollar indoor practice facility when the faculty weren't getting increases. And I had said to the coach, and I thought I had his agreement, that . . . we could have everything ready to go, and the minute the legislature next year approved our appropriations with a salary increase, we'd put a shovel in the ground. . . . He accepted that, and the whole athletic establishment accepted that. But really, he didn't. And finally, at a press conference he said that he just didn't know how much longer he could be an effective coach without this kind of facility. Then I heard from the Governor, and the alumni and it was a big thing, all over the front page of the paper . . . and we announced we would build the facility, and I got virtually no flack from the faculty at all. . . .

. . . They understood. They knew the [political] realities. They saw it on the front page . . . all over the television. . . . They understood the realities and that I'd fought the good fight and that I'd lost. You just can't let an issue like that get into the legislature because once the legislature starts talking about it, you're going to lose. And if you're going to lose, you might as well lose in your own way and you might as well get it over with.

In his five years at Iowa, James Freedman was fortunate to escape with only glimpses of the sort of heavy-handed political interference Harold Shapiro had suffered at Michigan and the potential for battle within the bureaucratic structure of Iowa's university system: In 1985, the executive secretary of the board of regents attempted what one news report characterized as a "bold power grab," involving Freedman in a public and uncharacteristically rancorous exchange. Calling "offensive" the secretary's proposal to create "'a smooth running Regents machine'" by centralizing power in the Regents staff office, Freedman attributed the great strength of Iowa's universities to their presidents' direct lines to the board and legislature, communicating "without a mediator": "'What we have now is a gentleman who wants to diminish this power [of the presidents] and take it for himself. . . . If you want to ruin the state's fine history it's your prerogative but I will not let you do it without voicing my deepest opposition.'"[10] Looking back on the incident, Freedman is no longer fiery, noting that the board of regents secretary at the time "was a man who really is a fine person, who'd been the secretary of the board for fifteen years." But his understanding of the situation has not changed, and his concise analysis underscores the abiding necessity for presidents in multicampus systems to maintain a combative attitude:

There's a constant tension between the institutions that the board of regents governs . . . and the board itself. Furthermore, the board office had an enormous amount of power because every proposal we put to the regents, the board office passed upon. That is, they put in with the agenda their recommendations—you know, the board should be careful of this, or skeptical, or it's not clear that this much money is needed or we'd recommend further study. So every recommendation we made to the regents for a new building or for whatever, was also commented upon by the board office. We could live with that. But it does mean there's an adversary relationship built in. I think the board felt that this was healthy in that they got a skeptical, critical view of whatever we were always proposing. But the fight [the secretary] and I had, had to do with aggrandizing the powers of the board office vis-à-vis the institutions, moving things to a nonacademic central bureaucracy in Des Moines, away from the campuses, and diminishing the power of the presidents. . . . [But] he made a mistake in thinking we would be passive and quiet [in the face of his proposal]. . . . It just happened that of the three presidents—Iowa, Iowa State, and Northern Iowa—the president of the University of Iowa was always expected to be the one who took the lead. That was just the way the institutions were lined up, and I knew I would win on that, there was never any doubt. . . .

    . . . The board was not in a comfortable position because they dearly did not want to vote down the president of the University of Iowa, particularly as I was getting a little attention outside of Iowa, but they also didn't want to vote down the executive secretary who was absolutely indispensable to them, who was very competent and they absolutely needed him. Their real challenge was somehow to side with me but not to hurt him or insult him or injure him and his status and credibility. But in the end they had to make the choice, and they made it in our direction.

    Dealing in North Carolina with a larger and more complex university governance structure than those of Michigan and Iowa, Paul Hardin naturally spoke at greater length and in more detail than did either Harold Shapiro or James Freedman about the governance pressures under which he operated. The University of North Carolina System consists of sixteen competing institutions, each with a chancellor who reports to the institution's own board of trustees, as well as to the system president who in turn reports to a board of governors elected by the state's General Assembly. It is not surprising, therefore, that Hardin had no comment on tensions between himself and his trustees but had quite a lot to say about his battles with system president C. D. Spangler and two of North Carolina's governors. His choice of emphasis makes it clear that for Paul Hardin, who had moved from the private, church-related sector of higher education to the public sector, the chief difference between institutional cultures came not just at the governance level, but in relation to the various layers that constitute the governance level—presidential, board, and gubernatorial/legislative. In fact, Hardin's UNC experience, as he relates it, offers a lesson in the many permutations of tension that such complex systems can generate.

There was, as we have already noted, the tension between UNC's board of trustees and system president C. D. Spangler during the chancellor search because of an independent "management audit" contracted for by the trustees, a tension that Hardin now believes spilled over into his initial relations with Spangler. There was also the tension between Hardin and Spangler that spanned several years, perhaps exacerbated by the system president's residence on the UNC-Chapel Hill campus with the General Administration offices located nearby. As Hardin points out, "The system head feels so much at home in Chapel Hill that the relationship between the system head and [that] campus is quite different from the relationship between the system head and the other campuses." Hardin's insistence on lobbying the state legislature independently for fiscal autonomy created "ill feeling for a while" not only between him and his president (whose position was "Don't go to Raleigh, that's my job") but also with "many members of the board of governors" who did not favor budget flexibility for the individual campuses in the system. In addition, at a time when the tensions between Hardin and Spangler had reached a crescendo, with, Hardin says, Spangler threatening that some members of the board of governors "would like to hold my coat while I fire you," Hardin delivered a low blow by referring to dangerous tensions between Spangler and the board of governors, "Well, Mr. President, . . . I remember you went to Pinehurst once with the board of governors and the rumor was . . . they might be out to get you." Furthermore, there was always the pressure of tensions within the system, as individual chancellors competed for system resources:

> In a complex situation like ours . . . you'll find that the chancellors of the flagship institutions . . . [are] worried about the tendency to homogenize and to fund equally instead of equitably, and to fund to the lowest common denominator of success that a whole system can be brought to. Thus, I did find myself in subtle ways and in some di-

rect ways, making sure that I protected the majesty and the incredible quality and reputation of UNC-Chapel Hill. That will be the
driving life force in any chancellor of a major flagship public university, whereas chancellors of the newer up-and-coming institutions
will be fighting for a stronger share and a system head has to mediate all of that. Just as President Spangler didn't always approve of
my activity on behalf of the flagship, I didn't always agree with him
on the way that he was dealing with the system, but I never failed
to recognize, and I never failed to say when I was asked by the press,
"Well, remember, he has a different constituency. My constituency
is Chapel Hill, and his constituency is sixteen campuses of the University of North Carolina."

And, finally, there was the tension between the chancellors of the state's
universities and the state's political leadership, which Hardin illustrates
by aggressively describing his "confrontations" with two North Carolina
governors rather than his lobbying activities:

You know, in the public sector one of the things that we always get
caught up in is that we have to campaign, we have to get the attention of the legislature. . . . In the early days of the [bicentennial]
campaign . . . I found out that while I was [in Dallas] extracting a
one-million-dollar pledge from Ross Perot, [Governor] Jim Martin's
budget proposal had lifted $12 million out of our pockets at Chapel
Hill. The year before, the legislature, in a tight budget move, had
raised the legislative share of our overhead receipts on research contracts from 30 percent to 50 percent, but had promised that the next
year their share would go back down to 20 percent. . . . But instead
of bringing it down to 20 percent as promised, Jim Martin sent a
budget to the legislature that continued to send 50 percent of our
overhead research support to the state of North Carolina. . . . I called
the mansion and a courteous highway patrolman put me through.
Jim Martin came on and said, "I understand you're mad." . . . I said,
"Jim, I have never been as upset in my life." He said, "Well, calm
down . . . I did not know . . . what the legislature had promised the
year before, and I did not know that UNC-Chapel Hill accounts for
77 percent of that money . . . and I'm going to make a supplemental budget proposal, but if I'm going to do that I need you to stay on
my case." We talked about practical politics, and I called Larry Monteith [chancellor of North Carolina State University], and the next
day we had the first and only joint press conference ever held between the chancellors of the two flagships in North Carolina. We
excoriated Jim Martin and everybody must have thought we were

very bold, but we were doing it at Jim Martin's request, which I think is one of the great political stories of all time. I'm a Democrat, but I got along very well with Republican Jim Martin. I later had conflict with [Democratic governor] Jim Hunt when one of his budget proposals threatened the very life of our graduate program. I was in his office chewing him up and he changed that in our favor. So, I not only had to confront our president, but I had to confront Republican and Democratic governors alike without fear or favor, and both of those confrontations came out okay. But you just have to be alert because somebody is going to do you in if you're head of a public institution.

Robert O'Neil would probably agree with Paul Hardin's assessment of a public university president's special vulnerability. At Virginia, O'Neil found himself faced with a set of board and governance relationships so much more complex than those he had experienced at either Wisconsin or Indiana, that he considers the North Carolina system structure simple by comparison:

Now, the North Carolina campuses do have separate local boards which the Wisconsin campuses do not—there, one board of regents [is responsible] for all public post-secondary education. But the structure is so much simpler than that of states like Virginia where you have fifteen separate boards, you have a secretary of education, you have a state council for higher education which is itself a board and which has a director of the state council for higher education to whom, in a sense, the university presidents report. In another sense, they report to the secretary of education and of course, everybody ultimately reports to the governor. Much more complicated.

Despite the complexity of Virginia's governance structure, however, O'Neil is not sure "to what extent that makes governance more difficult ... how much structure as such really affects the dynamic." He prefers to emphasize how the political vulnerability of public universities can significantly reduce a president's control over his own and his institution's destiny, as, for example, was the case in 1989 when state legislators in Richmond mandated enrollment growth for Virginia's universities under pressure from their constituents. The resultant controversy had already heated up on campus and become an intense source of (apparently illogical) faculty criticism of the president by the time O'Neil announced his decision to step down.[11] Corollary to this lack of control is the swiftness of change in the public sector, which O'Neil il-

lustrates by citing the precipitate firing of Clark Kerr by the University
of California Regents:

> How soon was that after Ronald Reagan took office? Ten days. I
> think many people assumed that Reagan took office and gradually
> transformed the Board of Regents. Wrong. Within ten days of tak-
> ing office, he made a few appointments to positions that were gu-
> bernatorially appointed and had a majority to displace Clark Kerr.
> January 1967. So, in the public sector, you tend to live with dis-
> continuities of that kind. . . . Life is always somewhat chancy in the
> public sector, even for people who may have served many years. . . .
> Another example: Paul Verkeuil . . . [was] president of the College
> of William and Mary around the same time I was president [at UVA].
> About six weeks after I had left office, I saw Paul on a plane going
> to New York. . . . He said, "You won't believe how things have
> changed since you left office." I said, "Paul, it was only six weeks
> ago." He said, "I know, I know. We now have to file—" and he ticked
> off a list of reports that they had to file, all of which had been im-
> posed on them by state government in the six weeks since I had left
> [the UVA presidency].
>   The Wilder administration had begun while I was still in office
> but the fiscal situation had not become apparent until the summer
> of 1990. During the week I left office, two things happened. One,
> Saddam Hussein marched into Kuwait, which had very little effect
> on public higher education. Two, the degree to which the Virginia
> miracle had come to a halt became apparent, and it was a very differ-
> ent environment from that point on. Things like these massive
> record-keeping and reporting requirements had taken effect during
> that period. Now, those were things that do not have counterparts
> in the private sector. You will have, I'm well aware, outrageous
> alumni and major donors and so on who can almost come out of
> nowhere, but it's not the same. There may be a lot going on behind
> the scenes, but it's not out front in the way it is in the public sec-
> tor, and it's for that reason that I think a deterministic view, or even
> a cyclical view, an evolutionary view of the life cycle of a senior ad-
> ministrator, has a very different dimension [at public universities].

Rapidity of change, uncertainty created by political power shifts in
state government, and the extent to which political pressures can alter a
university's—and a president's—agenda would seem to sum up our presidents' perspective, that the basic difference between heading a public

and a private institution boils down to exacerbated unpredictability and diminished control.

NOTES

1. A. Bartlett Giamatti, "A Free and Ordered Space: The Real World of the University" (informal remarks at the Gannett Center for Media Studies' 5th Annual Leadership Institute, June 19, 1989), Special Report (New York: Gannett Center for Media Studies, December 1989), 3.

2. UPI, "No Reagan Library at Stanford," April 24, 1987; Jack McCurdy, "Reagan Library Drops Stanford U. Site, Looks South for a New Home," *Chronicle of Higher Education*, May 6, 1987, p. 2; "Stanford Plans to Replace Director of Hoover Unit," *Chronicle of Higher Education*, May 25, 1988, pp. A2–3.

3. For example, see UPI, "Brown University," April 23, 1992; Joel Thurtell, Karen Schneider, and Ruth Seymour, "Students Occupy U-M Building," *Detroit Free Press*, March 20, 1987, Metro Final Edition, sec. NWS, p. 1A; "Sit-In Protesters Take Appeal to the Alumni," *New York Times*, March 5, 1989, Late Edition, p. 51; Thomas J. Meyer, "Investment Policies Spark Blockade at Columbia U.," *Chronicle of Higher Education*, April 17, 1985, p. 3; "Protesters Lie in Front of Cars, Block Stanford Trustees," *Los Angeles Times*, May 15, 1985, Home Edition, p. 21; "Stanford University: Divestment Rally Draws 250 at Stanford; Trustees May Act on Three Firms Tuesday," *Business Wire* [electronic resource], May 12, 1986.

4. Lyle Crowley, "Yale's Commuter President," *Manhattan, inc.*, April 1989, n.p.; Charles A. Radin, "New Haven Blues: Yale President's Colors Not True to Tradition," *Boston Globe*, April 23, 1989, metro/region, p. 1; Nick Ravo, "'Where's Benno?' Refrain at Yale Belies Its President's Record," *New York Times*, May 29, 1989, National Edition, p. 17.

5. For example, stories appeared in the *New York Times*, *Los Angeles Times*, *Orlando Sentinel Tribune*, *Houston Chronicle*, *Newsweek*, *Newsday*, and *Jet*, and on NPR and ABC, among others.

6. See, for example, "U-M President to Meet with Students on Racism," *Detroit Free Press*, March 21, 1987, Metro Final Edition, pp. 1, 7A, where Shapiro is described as addressing "an emotional gathering" of 200 students, "nervous at times, with his voice cracking." One student told the president, "'Maybe it's time to turn the tables on you . . . for your children to be scared to walk to class, and for you to be scared to walk to your job.'" The meeting took place after students had "forced Shapiro to adjourn the regularly scheduled meeting of the board of regents . . . when they occupied the regents' chairs. . . . Then, as the regents left . . . a column of more than 100 chanting students followed Regent Sarah Goddard Power and Richard Kennedy, vice-president for government relations," demanding that they "get the administration" to meet with the students. Three days later on the morning after she had attended Jesse Jackson's successful rally, Regent Power, a revered figure in Michigan, in a presumably un-

related denouement to a period of dramatic turmoil for the university and its president whom she had supported and calmed, threw herself from the eighth floor of the University of Michigan bell tower ("U-M Rergent [sic] Dies in Plunge," *Detroit Free Press*, March 25, 1987, Metro Final Edition, sec. NWS, p. 1A; Karen Schneider, "The Private Sadness of Sarah Power," *Detroit Free Press*, June 7, 1987, Metro Final Edition, sec. MAG, p. 10).

7. See, for example, W. Kim Heron, "U-M Orders Probe into Racist Jokes on Radio," *Detroit Free Press*, February 21, 1987, Metro Final Edition, sec. NWS, p. 3A; Susan Watson, "Call to U-M Station Was a Lengthy One," *Detroit Free Press*, March 23, 1987, sec. A, p. 3; "Call to U-M Station Stirs Valid Outrage," *Detroit Free Press*, March 25, 1987.

8. Karen Schneider, "U-M President Is Soft on Racism, Blacks Charge at Panel Hearing," *Detroit Free Press*, March 6, 1987, State Edition, sec. NWS, p. 3A; Roderick Keith Linzie, "Analysis of the Anti-Racist Student Movement at the University of Michigan-Ann Arbor" (Ph.D. diss., University of Michigan, 1993), 150.

9. The Iowa regents are also responsible for the Iowa School for the Deaf, the Iowa Braille and Sightsaving School, the State Hospital School, and the Oakdale Campus of the University of Iowa, a research park.

10. UPI, "Presidents Oppose Regents Secretary," July 18, 1985.

11. See, for example, Thomas Boyer, "Unmaking of a U.Va. President," *Norfolk Virginian-Pilot*, October 8, 1989, sec. 1, pp. 1A, 3A; "Virtually every faction at UVa. has a different opinion on growth and the board may be fractured as well. . . . One of [O'Neil's] public statements, designed to reassure the campus by promising no more than 20 percent growth, has only angered many faculty members and students, who say O'Neil has prejudged the issue." Of course, as O'Neil told us in our interview, he himself "didn't have any particular viewpoint; [increased enrollment] was mandated by the State Council for Higher Education, so we didn't have any choice."

CHAPTER 4

Exit

That period from the day a president starts to think of resigning until
a successor has taken office and the ex-president's attention is engaged elsewhere.

In the normal course of events, a university presidency does not come
to an end on any one particular day; rather, it begins to end privately
at first, in the thoughts and emotions of the president for whom even
the inaugural festivities of a successor may not be the end of the story.
Whether the idea of closure matures swiftly or slowly, under duress or as
part of the natural flow of a career, announcing the decision to step down
triggers a series of more or less predictable consequences—press attention, the formation of a search committee, and the subtle shifting of campus interest away from the current administration toward speculation
about the future. As the search process gains momentum and candidates
appear on the horizon, an atmosphere of institutional uncertainty as well
as anticipation is likely to arise, and forward movement by the outgoing
president and administration may be slowed down or even stalled. After
a successor has been named, the period of transition and the first few
months of a new administration may prove awkward for the emeritus
president.

To explore this phase in the life cycle of a university presidency, we
asked our participants to describe what influenced their decisions to
leave, what happened between their public announcements of resigna-

tion and their departures, and how they think their own and their predecessors' denouements played out.

RESIGNATIONS

The reasons our small but significant sample of presidents gave for their
exits summed up why most presidents leave office—some combination of
age, ambition, opportunity, or duress. Age appears in these accounts both
as a personal benchmark and as a measure of time in office, one side of
an equation balanced by fatigue, disillusionment, the growing weight of
internal politics, and issues of control. Ambition is cited as a desire for
other presidencies at more prestigious institutions, a motivation differentiated from special or unique opportunities, invitations to follow cherished interests down alternative paths. Our one example of resignation
under duress is described as the result of an institutional misfortune that
could not be overcome without new leadership. Surprisingly, most of our
presidents placed less emphasis than we had anticipated on the achievement of specific goals as important in the timing of exit decisions.

For Paul Hardin, chronological age functioned as an artificial goad to
departure. Although he admitted to some fatigue—"I wasn't as fresh on
the day that I made my decision . . . as I was when I first came to the job
because I was six years older and I had not had a smooth, tranquil, totally positive experience"—more important to him than any weariness
he might have felt was his desire to exert control over his own destiny:

> Let me tell you how I came to step down. This almost goes back to
> my continuing albeit friendlier competition with the system. Presi-
> dent Spangler had made it clear that he wanted every chancellor to
> step down at age sixty-five, without any question. Now, that may not
> be legal, to demand that, but that was his decision. Incidentally,
> when he stepped down at sixty-five he didn't want to, but he had
> gotten himself into a corner by imposing that absolute edict on all
> the chancellors. I knew a couple of chancellors who wanted just one
> additional year to complete something, and he said, no, sixty-five is
> it. Well, I began to compute, and I was to turn sixty-five on June 11,
> 1996, about a month after commencement and just before the end
> of the fiscal year. I would have been required to step down then,
> willy-nilly. I've always wanted to step down when more people would
> say, why so soon? than would say, it's about time! I've always wanted
> to step down on my own timetable, and, too, I had a sneaky motive:
> I knew that on June 30, 1995, the month that I would turn sixty-
> four, we would conclude the Bicentennial Campaign for Carolina,

and I would be guaranteed to go out on a high note. Now, if tired was a factor, it was the fourth factor in there.

Paul Hardin served seven years as chancellor of UNC-Chapel Hill, putting him at the mid-range in our sample and respectably above the national average of 5.7 years of service for public Research I university presidents appointed between 1985 and 1989.[1] While a lengthier span than his service at either Wofford College (1968–1972), where he began his presidential career, or at Southern Methodist University (1972–1974), where he was forced out after disciplining the athletics director ("I had lost my job on the issue but had maintained my sense of dignity"), Hardin's long years of service at Drew University (1975–1988) and his subsequent willingness to serve as interim president of the University of Alabama at Birmingham (1997) suggest that, had he been given the choice, he may well have stayed longer at UNC to reap the rewards of a long but successful fundraising campaign.

In contrast to Paul Hardin, arbitrarily required because of his age to step down after a successful term of better-than-average length, Michael Sovern continued in office until he decided that he was tired of it all. Sovern served thirteen years at Columbia, the longest tenure among our presidents and certainly by modern measures a notably long presidency. It is also a duration more likely to occur at private research universities, where the average tenure of presidents in Sovern's cohort (those appointed from 1980 through 1984) was 11.2 years versus 7.1 years for presidents at public research universities.[2] For Sovern, sheer length of time in office and the resultant political weariness combined with unusual personal considerations to bring about his decision to step down at age sixty-one. In the early 1990s, Columbia was caught in a budget squeeze created by increasingly expensive medical benefits, a large cut in state support, and reductions by the federal government in the rate of indirect cost recovery. Sovern's solutions—and Sovern himself—"caught a lot of hell from some faculty":

> It was also a time in my life (and here I guess my circumstances were unusual, maybe unique among your group) when my wife was very ill.[3] Had I encountered faculty discontent during my first few years, I would have been out there morning, noon, and night, explaining, justifying, persuading, but I just didn't have the motivation. And that's ultimately what caused me to quit. I love Keith's [Brodie] idea that you quit when you've achieved your goals. I had achieved many of them, but I quit because I just felt I couldn't do it anymore, under

my circumstances. Didn't want to do it anymore, actually. . . . When these troubles started to develop, Jonathan Cole who was the provost, Jack Greenberg who was dean of the college, both friends, gave me advice. They said, "You really have to spend more time with faculty during this period." And I started to do it but found I no longer had the patience for it. It was then that I began to realize that I might be overstaying my time. We had a change in the chairman-ship of the trustees at that point; G. G. Michelson was stepping down and Henry King was to succeed her, and I felt I had an obligation to alert him to the fact that I was thinking about retiring. That would have been in the spring of '92 because Henry would have been taking over in the fall. I hadn't yet made up my mind, but I was re-flecting about it, and I made up my mind later that spring. So it was not a single moment; it was a period of reflection and a recognition that this is an all-consuming job, and if you're not prepared to give it everything, and I wasn't going to give it everything, then you should get out. And so that's what I did.

If Paul Hardin and Michael Sovern could be said to exemplify presi-dents who have aged out of office (albeit for different reasons), James Freedman and Harold Shapiro represent the opposite example of presi-dents too young in office not to heed the call of ambition. Courted early on in his Iowa term by other institutions, Freedman felt compelled to re-spond to these overtures despite his positive feelings about the Univer-sity of Iowa:

A couple of things were in the back of my mind. I clearly knew I would need a second presidency at some point because I was forty-six when I started at Iowa, and even if I had spent ten years there, I would still have been only fifty-six. I had to be alert to the possi-bility [of another presidency] because you couldn't stay more than ten years at one place, or so I thought. The second thing was, every-one in my group of presidents thought that people don't appoint presidents after fifty-two or -three or -four years of age. That's all changed now, of course. You know, Neil Rudenstine was older than that when he was appointed, Gerhard Casper was older than that. That's changed. But it was the folklore at that time, omnipresent in presidents' minds, and all the Big Ten presidents, when we talked, lived with the view that you really had to make your move before you were fifty-three or -four because no one would appoint some-one as old as fifty-five. So both thoughts were in my mind, and then . . . I started hearing from other schools much earlier than I'd ever anticipated. That's flattering, and so you do think you want to look. . . . What had really happened was that we had had such tough years economically in Iowa. Those were bad years for the Farm Belt, we had no resources. We had one year without any salary increases, and it's just discouraging trying to do things without the resources you need. . . . I don't know if [leaving Iowa after] five years was premature or not, but it was a mixture, I think, of ambition, of maybe too much ambition, of fear of getting too old to be appointed elsewhere, and a sense that Iowa was a tough place because of the economy.

Freedman's departure from Iowa might be considered premature if judged by the average tenure of his group of public university presidents—seven years to his five—but as he emphasized in his press statements at the time, the offer to lead Dartmouth was a "childhood dream-come-true."[4]

Harold Shapiro, Freedman's contemporary in the Big Ten and almost exactly the same age,[5] also resigned in April 1987 after suffering the stress of guiding his university through hard economic times. Recalling the timing of his decision, Shapiro identified three elements. First was the achievement of specific goals at the University of Michigan (i.e., the success of his strategy to strengthen Michigan's medical center and professional schools, and the completion of a capital campaign):

I had done a whole series of things I felt I had started out to do. . . . So I felt I'd come to a good point. And in fact, I had begun discussing with my wife whether I should return to the faculty. It wasn't being tired, and it wasn't that I thought I was underappreciated, quite the opposite. I felt good, I felt that people had been extremely appreciative of my efforts at Michigan, and the board had been supportive. But this assessment did coincide with a very interesting flare-up of racial tensions on campus.

Although in our section on governance conflicts, we quoted at length Harold Shapiro's reactions to the interference of Michigan legislators on the university's campus, it is important to note that he made those comments in the context of how he reached his decision to leave the Michigan presidency. The passage is therefore included here with the discussion of his exit from Michigan to show the extent to which state politics can contribute to making a university presidency personally intolerable:

I had a particular set of experiences with African American legislators in Michigan and with certain kinds of talk radio in Michigan that led me to think two things: "Maybe I can't be a good representative of this university anymore. Maybe they need a different kind of person here." And in any case, even if that were wrong, even if my judgment were too harsh on myself then, I thought, "You know, I don't need to do this, I don't have to put up with this." I viewed myself as trying to provide a social product for the state, and then to have legislators who were trying to take advantage of a difficult ongoing situation to lay the burden of all the social pathology of this country on the university and on my shoulders—you know, I didn't need that. In addition, my wife was particularly frightened by some anti-Semitic comments that occurred in and around that time on talk radio. I said to myself, "Gosh, what do I need this for? I've got a nice life, I don't have to put up with this." So those two things came together, both the completion of a phase at the university and a very unpleasant situation. And it wasn't the tension and issues on campus that were unpleasant, not at all. [It was the outside, public attacks.] And so I had those things in my mind, but I hadn't decided to do anything. This would have been in the winter/spring of 1987. . . . Then the third coincidence around this time was that Bill Bowen . . . resigned. All of a sudden Princeton was looking for a president. . . . I had no idea that I'd be interested, number one. Number two, I still was on a track of thinking either of continuing at the University of Michigan, or if I continued to feel badly about this [situation] then I would just go back to the faculty. That seemed like a very simple thing to do. But then in the middle of all this, even though the racial issue on campus had subsided . . . I didn't forget easily the reactions of some members of the state legislature or some of the reactions on talk radio that occurred in and around that issue—that part didn't leave me.

But I was completely undecided as to what if anything to do. And I certainly hadn't spoken to anybody at all except my wife about this. Then this opportunity at Princeton came along, and they asked me to think about it and I said no, I didn't want to leave Ann Arbor. I had turned down a number of other opportunities around the same time because for whatever set of reasons my experiences at the University of Michigan seemed to be getting some attention elsewhere. Almost every month I'd have a visit from a group who wanted me to become president somewhere. . . . But I said the same thing to all of them, "No, thank you very much, I'm not interested." Then Princeton came along and for me, Princeton had a number of differences: I had some emotional ties, I was a student here, which is important, and Princeton was a high quality place like Michigan but in other ways it was very different from a large state university like Michigan. Eventually, after thinking about it, I decided that as long as I only had one career, the chance to work in two places like these which were really so different, doesn't come along every day.

Harold Shapiro's situation differed from James Freedman's in that he had served as president three years longer (eight years to Freedman's five and a year longer than their cohort's average), suffering some disillusionment in the process, and had always intended to return to the faculty at Michigan when he left administration. Nevertheless, for Shapiro as for Freedman at the age of fifty-one, the chance to begin anew as a president at an Ivy League institution was irresistible.

Benno Schmidt, too, was relatively young as a president, just fifty, when he unexpectedly left Yale after only six years. Appointed in 1986, Schmidt took on his first presidency at a time when the average tenure of Research I university presidents had begun to drop dramatically at private institutions, from 11.2 years in the 1980–1984 cohort to 8.8 for those appointed between 1985 and 1989.[6] Schmidt's analysis of his decision-making process is the lengthiest offered by any in our group and a candid assessment not only of his Yale presidency but also of the type of leaders he believes that universities require today. Schmidt was first approached to lead The Edison Project (now Edison Schools) at a time when he felt he could not leave Yale because two of his goals were still to be accomplished. The first was a presidential commonplace, to raise the first half-billion dollars in Yale's new capital campaign, while the second was decidedly "odd," he acknowledges, in the context of a university. He "wanted to be the only Yale president in modern history who had never had a [labor] strike":

> Although there was an awful lot of agitation and static and noise, I *am* the only Yale president in modern times who never had a strike. I never would have thought this going up to Yale, there are strikes at Columbia all the time, but I actually concluded after I was at Yale and I saw how anxious and agitated the community was about labor relations, that if I could give Yale a period of labor peace and try to calm the thing down and make the process more professional and normal than this highly personalized, theatrical, hysterical process, that I would be doing the institution a great service. I think that. So I felt I could not leave when there was another round of collective bargaining coming up.

Because Schmidt had turned down Edison earlier in the year, he was surprised when they asked him to reconsider in late fall 1991. "I started thinking about it seriously in November. It took me about four months to conclude that this was something I wanted to do." Edison, he believed, offered him a "once-in-a-lifetime opportunity" to be an architect of genuine change in the public schools. Yet, Schmidt was more than a little ambivalent about leaving Yale:

> The question of going to Edison, despite the immense attraction that it held for me, was a very close question. I mean, that was not an easy decision, and as part of making that decision, I tried to think through very carefully what would happen if I did not go to Edison.

As we have already seen, Schmidt believed that his conflict with the Yale faculty over financial restructuring and the proposal to allocate resources selectively would "put itself into some perspective" as similar difficulties at peer institutions led to similar solutions. He also thought that "some of the fairly positive things that were going on had a momentum of their own":

> I'd just solved the labor problem again, no strikes. . . . I had proven myself to be Yale's most successful fundraiser . . . the results of that were beginning to be obvious in many ways programmatically and otherwise. I had just concluded an understanding with the mayor and the city of New Haven that gave Yale some benefits that it had been trying to get for half a century and more, first and foremost . . . [not to] challenge any of Yale's tax exemptions. . . . I'd gotten the state to commit to the biggest urban development project in the history of Connecticut in downtown New Haven next to campus. The mayor had agreed to turn over several streets that went through the Yale campus, something that Yale presidents had been trying to get for sixty years . . . [which] had a huge aesthetic and cohesive and, in fact, safety impact. The alumni . . . were really rallying around the university. The endowment had outperformed that of every university in the country, and . . . for all the controversies that I got into with respect to one thing and another, there had never been any issue of integrity or carelessness. This was when John Dingell was auditing every university president in the country and coming up with all kinds of mini-scandals and accusations . . . and some university presidents got embarrassed in that process. Although I had my detractors, I was pretty sure that I had seized the high ground . . . in my defense of free speech. That's a good place to be for the long run, if you're a university president.

With so many "very positive forces . . . at work," Schmidt calculated that he could "ride out this bit of a storm" over budgetary restructuring: "time was on my side."

While he could point to much that was being accomplished for Yale in his administration, Schmidt, like Harold Shapiro in one sense, was suffering feelings of personal disillusionment that were ultimately stronger than the reality of his presidential achievements. Weighing his decision, Schmidt concluded that there were "certain aspects of the modern university presidency that were not a particularly good fit in terms of who I was and what I thought was important." First among his frustrations was the difficulty of implementing change in the university, which he describes as a "deeply conservative institution," where a "visceral reaction against" change is the first response to even the "possibility of change." Second was his lack of sympathy with the university as a place that is "appropriate to use symbolically and in other ways as a lever for political change":

> The university of constant agitation and protests and chronic indignation about something or other is likely to be a university that is not spending enough energy defending its critical and unique mission, its academic mission, the predicate for which has got to be free inquiry. I also feel—and this sounds very old-fashioned, the students used to chuckle when I expressed this point of view—that in order to fulfill its mission, the university has to be at least to some extent a place of repose. A place of reflection. A place of—dare I use the word?—sobriety, or at least the sober second and third and fourth thought about things. . . . [Political] protest has a great role in American society and I go as far as anybody that I know to defend the right of protest and agitation, and in many respects, the value of it. But for the university to have become the center of that in our society seems to me to be deeply wrong. . . . I was out of sync with the modern university in that respect.

Third among the factors alienating Schmidt from the university, or more specifically, from the university presidency, was his sense of being out of step with the majority of his colleagues and therefore not the best leader for them:

> Many of my colleagues . . . wanted to make prudential political choices about controversies facing the university whether it was divestment or the right way to resolve the question of whether graduate students should form a union. My view was that for a university, the response to those questions had to be principled, had to be defended in terms of principle, that the implications of the response had to be viewed in a principled way for other issues. . . . That view of the university as needing to be more of a principled actor in those

areas as part of its commitment to academic freedom, was not the prevalent view. . . . Now, there were a lot of faculty members who agreed with me about this, but . . . it's viewed as kind of a minority and almost even a cranky position. . . . I felt that a large segment of the university community really didn't share those views and didn't particularly want to have a president who embodied those views. Which is fair enough. I think they are wrong, but they have a perfect right to prefer a president who more nearly embodies . . . the post-sixties institutional ethos of the place than I did.

For Schmidt, the attraction to Edison was the opportunity to foment revolution in the "most important sector of American society," elementary and secondary education, and, paradoxically, to take action in a venue that he considers as "incredibly resistant to change" as the university he was leaving:

[The public schools] haven't changed their calendar since this was an agrarian society; they make no serious use of modern information technology. They haven't changed their daily schedules since American mothers went to work. . . . I thought that Edison offered the opportunity to bring innovation into the most anachronistic sector of American society . . . and at the same time to focus all those changes on the poorest and most disadvantaged kids, which is what we're doing. And if that worked, it could be of historic importance. I still think that. I knew at the same time that it would be bitterly controversial. . . .

. . . So, no, [it cannot be said that I went from a tough job to an easy one,] but it *can* be said that I went from a tough job in which taking action and deciding on things that are necessary is very difficult to achieve, to a job where it's very easy to take action and it's very easy to [make decisions]. Edison is a cohesive, entrepreneurial organization that acts. We may not get it right, but [our organization] is highly responsive, it's highly creative, it's necessarily highly entrepreneurial and risk taking. . . . [Universities have] become so difficult internally to change and so adverse to decision making and priority setting, that Edison for all its difficulty is an enterprise I fit into much better than the administrative side of the modern university. . . . The kind of institutional habits that have developed have made university administration highly reactive and risk averse and anything *but* entrepreneurial.

Drawing on his experience as dean of the law school at Columbia to contrast it with the presidency, Schmidt compared the satisfactions of the one with the relative powerlessness of the other:

A dean can have a very clear sense of the collective consciousness of the faculty . . . [and] personal interaction with the faculty in shaping that collective consciousness is really possible. Indeed, it's inevitable. Deans have a degree of influence over all the things that really matter—budgets, appointments, promotions, standards of admission—whereas most university presidents have some limited degree of influence over budgets, have little or no influence over appointments even if they have a role in them (the president of Yale has no role in the process). Even where a president has a role in the appointment process it's only at the end. [Presidents have] very little role in the questions of individual promotion, sometimes a blocking role, but that's not a shaping role. [Presidents] can, through budgets, have some degree of influence over the general evolution of departments, but not on the most critical matters of appointment and promotion, and in the Yale context very little. Very little [influence over] the standards of admission for students. But deans are in the thick of it, and with that influence and working with the faculty whom they know well and have a real personal connection with, it really is possible for deans to have a very powerful and very constructive shaping role, and the measure of what counts as a good dean reflects that. But for university presidents in most situations, the measure of what counts is raising money, being a good ceremonial head of the place, and avoiding trouble. Those are hard things to do, now; I'm not trying to make light of it, not at all, I have tremendous respect for people who can do it and do it well and do it for twenty-five years. But in my own case, the things that have given me a lot of satisfaction as a professor and as a dean and indeed, as head of The Edison Project, aren't really the things university presidents are expected to do. That's one of those statements of the obvious that some people don't like to say, but I say it with a deep sense of affection. I really loved the university in many ways and a lot of the people [there], and some day, when I've satisfied my entrepreneurial and radical proclivities with respect to public education, I plan to go back.

Benno Schmidt is the only one among our group who rejected the university presidency as a good option for himself in midcareer. Harold Shapiro seems only briefly to have considered rejecting the university presidency at about the same point. Michael Sovern treated the presidency as part of his normal progression through the ranks of the Columbia faculty, as did Donald Kennedy at Stanford, while James Freedman, Paul Hardin, and Robert O'Neil seem to have viewed the office as a multi-institution career path from the beginning. Although like Schmidt, both Vartan Gregorian and Robert O'Neil eventually left the presidency for executive positions outside higher education, they conveyed no sense during their interviews that they were looking for escape from an uncongenial job choice; rather, they seem to have viewed their moves out of the academy as appropriate at the time and desirable for personal reasons.

It was in keeping with his own established pattern of seeking institutional and leadership variety that in 1997 Vartan Gregorian left the presidency of Brown University to head Carnegie Corporation of New York. After serving as provost at the University of Pennsylvania (1978–1980), he had been disappointed in the outcome of Penn's presidential search and reacted to the loss somewhat unconventionally by accepting the presidency of the New York Public Library (1981–1989). His departure from Brown, however, had nothing to do with disappointment but rather with a sense that things had begun to run too smoothly, that he might be in danger of "beginning to love the routine." It will be remembered that Gregorian had interpreted our question about the defining moment as the signal that it was time to leave:

> Right before we finished the campaign, in the midst of it actually, my defining moment was when Columbia University offered me the presidency. . . . I said, if you wait a year I may accept. . . . Subsequently, though, I asked myself, do I really want to continue as president of another university, or have I done the presidency? I concluded that I had done the presidency. I wanted to move on.

More than any other of our presidents, Gregorian explicitly linked his decision to move on to the achievement of his goals and the feeling that to stay longer would be to court the mischiefs attendant on complacency:

> My defining moment was actually one year before Brown's campaign ended. Once a campaign has ended, then something sets in with the president. You start competing against yourself, and you believe your own rhetoric and in people who say you can do more, you can do anything. You start acting; you become a caricature of yourself. And that's where you have to split, when you know you already have succeeded, you've accomplished the goals you've set for yourself, for the institution. The institution then needs new blood, needs to bring another wave of energy, vision, imagination, and challenge. Change does not come naturally.

Looking back not only on his accomplishments at Brown but also on the honors that accompanied the Brown community's affectionate farewell,

Gregorian judges that his tenure of a little more than nine years (slightly above the 8.8 average for his cohort) was just right, "I left Brown in great form. . . . People did not say, 'When is he retiring?'"

Gregorian's tranquil timing is in sharp contrast to Robert O'Neil's apparently abrupt decision to leave the Virginia presidency during a period when questions had arisen in the press about O'Neil's relationship with UVA's board. As controversy mounted over whether the president's style of consensus building was too time consuming, and the board's chairman was reported to be playing an "unusually and increasingly active role" in university leadership,[7] O'Neil shocked both supporters and detractors by announcing his resignation after only four years in office:

> I'd been doing this sort of thing for twenty years, and if I add the year and a half that I was executive assistant to the president at Buffalo to the four years at Cincinnati [as provost and executive vice president], five at Indiana, five at Wisconsin, five here,[8] that's actually a little over twenty years. I also figured that [it was time to leave] if I were going to do anything else of substance. I'd seen lots of other people who remained in administrative office until they were sixty or older and found it very hard to get back into scholarship. Though I had always taught at least one course, and I had usually had a student research assistant, and I'd tried to keep up with the field, even so, there comes a stage in life where it gets awfully hard to go back into whatever your field is.

More important to O'Neil's timing than the potential loss of relevance as a scholar, was the inducement of an opportunity as uniquely suitable for him as The Edison Project had been for Benno Schmidt, to become the founding director of The Thomas Jefferson Center for the Protection of Free Expression. As a young professor of law at Berkeley, O'Neil had worked pro bono for the ACLU—"The very first case I ever got involved in was trying to keep the California Alcoholic Beverage Control Department from closing down a gay bar in San Francisco . . . where Melvin Belli and others went for lunch"—and the prospect of some special association with a new center for similarly radical undertakings was included in the recruitment package:

> The very first thing that the first member of the board of visitors who came to visit with me in Madison in November 1984 had said was, "You should know that a fellow member of the board of visitors just announced a very substantial gift to create a First Amendment center at the university. Does that sound like something that would be attractive to you?"

The idea was "very appealing" to O'Neil, and even more appealing when the donor's intentions were clarified:

> The person within the donor's organization who was working on the structuring of the Thomas Jefferson Center came to spend a day or so with me in Madison in the spring of 1985 before I'd left there and said to me, "There seems to be some thought," (this is back in Charlottesville), "that it should be a think tank or just a research center and," he added, "my boss," (the donor), "doesn't see it that way. He thinks this ought to be an activist organization." I said, "Absolutely, that's exactly the way I would see it."

Thus, "when it came time actually to get the center up and running," O'Neil realized that he would either have to "recruit somebody else to take it over" or resign the presidency. Although he says he did not feel "worn down or burnt out or anything like that," he does emphasize that "twenty years [of administration] in four institutions is quite long enough," and a few more years of the same was not worth losing a second chance at his first love.[9]

Robert O'Neil's pattern of serving no more than five years at any one institution is quite different from the career path of presidents like Michael Sovern and Donald Kennedy, who are more committed to an institution than to a particular role in that institution, a factor that also contributes to lengthening presidential tenures.[10] This mind-set— summed up by Kennedy in his statement that "the presidency, after all, is an episode in an academic career"—must have made all the more painful for him the external circumstances that forced him to leave office before he was ready, the only one among our group who resigned because of scandal. So powerful were the political and press-fueled distortions of Stanford's disagreements with the federal government over billing for the indirect costs of research[11] that the smearing of Kennedy's (and Stanford's) reputation by U.S. Representative John Dingell left unresolved and almost irrelevant any actual questions of integrity, ineptitude, overly aggressive accounting practices, or failure of oversight. When the Dingell investigation began at Stanford in summer 1990, Kennedy had just recently celebrated with the trustees his tenth anniversary in office and was guiding the university through the financial consequences of a slowing economy and the Loma Prieta earthquake.[12] He harbored no thoughts of stepping down:

> How long would I have stayed had the indirect cost controversy not happened? I tend to be a person with considerable inertia. All it takes to keep me on the same path for an extra year or an extra

month normally is one more interesting challenge, or a problem that
I don't feel good about leaving unresolved. What I had in my head
was a couple of years, but it might easily have turned into five. Some
people whom I regard as the most successful presidents actually went
seventeen or eighteen. That's true of Bill Bowen at Princeton and
Frank Rhodes at Cornell, and Derek Bok went almost twenty at
Harvard.

Throughout the academic year 1990/1991, Kennedy recalls, he and his
provost attempted to get on with university business, "executing some
considerable budget cuts" while simultaneously "preparing for the onslaught from Dingell." Early reports in the local press of an investigation
that fall gave way by December to a sustained national furor. Even a limited sampling of headlines illustrates how excoriating and seemingly uncontrollable the story became: "Stanford Charged Taxpayers for Yacht,"
"Stanford Billed Taxpayers for Flowers," "Stanford's Image: It's One of a
Greedy School that Sees the Government as a Reservoir to Be Tapped,"
"Turning Labs into Cedar Closets," "U.S. Funds Used for Wedding,"
"Stanford to Return U.S. Funds Used for Upkeep of Tomb," "School for
Scandal," "Sleaze Knows No Class," and so forth. An additional fillip of
scorn was added in the British press with "Top Scientist Pays for Uni-
versity High Life." Months after Kennedy's resignation was announced,
Reader's Digest kept the story alive by glorifying the navy accountant who
went after Stanford in what is surely a *Digest* classic, "He Caught the
Campus Chiselers" (January 1992).[13] These and numerous other all too-
frequently distorted stories hammered Kennedy and Stanford relentlessly
despite the efforts of Stanford's trustees and administration to set the
record straight.[14]
  At the Congressional hearing on March 13, 1991, Stanford "looked
terrible . . . although not as terrible as the local press made us look in reporting it":[15]

> Time passed. Commencement happened, and we started putting to-
> gether the committees to do this next round of budget cuts. As I
> talked to faculty about these things, it became evident that you
> couldn't get them settled down to talk about budget cuts because
> they were busy asking themselves, what's going to happen? what's the
> subcommittee going to do? what's OMB going to do about circular
> A-21? Is Kennedy a lightning rod for this problem? There was so
> much uncertainty that it was hard to focus on normal, necessary busi-
> ness. The board had a scheduled midsummer meeting, and having
> talked to the chairman, several board members, and some faculty, I
> decided that unless we could precipitate the uncertainty out of the

situation, we weren't going to get anything done. So I announced my resignation a year hence, and that clarified the situation.

Kennedy had taken the heat for about nine months (measured by the rising crescendo in the press) before announcing on July 28, 1991, that he would leave the presidency the following summer. Throughout the ordeal, amid increasing calls for his resignation both from within and without the Stanford community, Kennedy says Stanford's trustees were "terrifically supportive" though he is realistic about their private opinions:

> There was probably a variety of views among [the thirty-two] different board members; I had calls from some saying, "Don't even think about resigning," and I know there were two or three who were very anxious to have me gone. But I think they behaved like responsible trustees and let the board leadership speak for the board to the press.

The leadership included chairman Jim Gaither and former chairman Warren Christopher, "who actually wrote a letter to Chairman Dingell explaining the president's house accounts," but to little avail: "Once a process like that gets going, it's pretty hard to stop. One knew that it wasn't going to stop":

> What the board would have done about leadership in the institution had I not decided to resign, I don't know. I suspect that they would have pushed me pretty hard to step down; once an issue of that kind gets personalized, it's pretty hard to separate institution and person successfully. The way I put it to the board was that if you are perceived as part of the problem, it's very hard to be part of the solution. To repeat: the chairman of the board was unfailing in his support, and the board never took any unsupportive public action. But I believe their feeling would have been, had you asked them to express it, "We've got to have a change."

Just as state politics had at least temporarily made the Michigan presidency personally intolerable for Harold Shapiro, so national politics had made the Stanford presidency impossible for Donald Kennedy. He was sixty-one-years-old and had served as Stanford's president for twelve years when he stepped down, almost a year longer than the average for his cohort.[16] He did not leave Stanford and he had not been ready to leave the presidency.

LAME DUCKS?

Once having announced their resignations, did any of our presidents feel that their effectiveness was seriously hampered as they completed their terms? Had theirs become functionally lame-duck administrations? Two of our participants avoided the situation by exiting promptly: James Freedman left Iowa July 1, 1987, just two and a half months after announcing his departure for Dartmouth, and Benno Schmidt was gone from Yale even more swiftly, in little more than a month, on the advice of his board chairman, Vern Loucks, Schmidt's "closest confidant, supporter, and mentor on the Corporation":

> When I concluded that [leading The Edison Project] was something that I wanted to do, which was in April, I went to see Vern in Chicago and told him. I explained what Edison was and a little about why I wanted to do it, and Vern's view was, if you want to do it, you *should* do it. . . . We then talked about what was the best way for Yale and for me to make the transition. Vern and I agreed in April (or it may have been March, I'm not sure, it was in the spring), that the best way to do it would be to say nothing until graduation so as not to disrupt the school year. But I should announce it right after graduation as soon as possible in order to give the Corporation the maximum amount of time to respond before the next school year started. Vern's advice was that I should not have a lame-duck period, that is, that once I decided there was a specific other job that I wanted to do, I should do it. . . . That was my preference, too.

Schmidt's announcement on May 25, 1992, came on graduation weekend, when both he and Loucks could "talk to the whole Corporation face-to-face" and insure that the news did not become public until after Yale's commencement "so that it wouldn't interfere with the seniors." If Yale's trustees were not prepared for Schmidt's announcement (the *New York Times* described them as "stunned"[17]), Schmidt himself was not prepared for the nature of the publicity:

> I did not really appreciate how big a national story that was going to be. I knew it would be controversial for me to leave Yale for Edison because I knew Edison was controversial . . . but I didn't know—and here I think I just failed to understand how the publicity was going to appear—I didn't [realize] the way the timing of the announcement would make it look as if I had perhaps [tried to] maximize the [impact of] "Yale President Goes to The Edison Project" rather than Benno Schmidt goes to The Edison Project as his next thing.

Despite an initial impression that Schmidt might remain through the fall semester (the *New York Times* reported that Schmidt would "leave Yale by Jan. 1, 1993, at the latest"[18]), he was rapidly succeeded on July 1, 1992, by acting president Howard Lamar, a Yale history professor whose appointment was announced only three weeks after Schmidt's resignation.[19]

Although more than eight months passed between Vartan Gregorian's announcement that he was stepping down as president of Brown (January 7, 1997) and his departure (October 1, 1997), he, too, feels that he avoided any lame-duck problems through careful timing:

> You become a lame duck—it doesn't matter when you step down— if your stepping down coincides with a budget cycle. As long as you are in control of the budget, you are not a lame duck. . . . That was learned from Martin Myerson's experience at Penn and from others as well. When you announce your resignation or retirement, they always like [for it] to coincide with the academic year and, therefore, nobody feels compelled to call on you. But if you are controlling the next year's budget, it doesn't matter what you call yourself, lame duck or not lame duck, you are still in charge. I made lots of decisions in the last three months when I was quote unquote the lame duck. Important decisions. Up to the very last day. I learned it the hard way. So "lame duck" is "budget duck"!

Similarly, Harold Shapiro considers that the eight months he remained at Michigan after announcing his resignation were quite productive, though he cites a different reason:

> People didn't say, "Well, we have to wait until the next person." Quite the opposite. People wanted me to do things because they knew me and knew what I would do, and so there was a lot of pressure to keep on doing things. And what I had to do was resist the temptation to start committing my successor to things he might not want. So those were very easy months. I didn't have any feeling of losing authority or anything like that because that's the way other people treated us, so I had no serious problem with that transition.

Shapiro's goal for his last months at Michigan was to prepare the way for the next president, to "accumulate some resources, make no long-term commitments, try to make sure that my successor would have lots of options before him." Paul Hardin and Donald Kennedy also had goals in mind for the remainder of their lame-duck presidencies, but goals they felt could best be met by the very fact of announcing that they were entering the waning days of their administrations. Hardin saw the timing of his announcement as a response to, or a solution for, the built-in lame-duck effect of UNC System president C. D. Spangler's mandate that all of his chancellors had to step down at age sixty-five:

> My board of trustees, whether they approved of President Spangler's policy or disapproved of it, were very aware of it. Now, why did I announce it a year and a half in advance? I felt, although I didn't feel worn out or defeated, that I didn't have the same automatic, full-hearted, positive response of my board when I made various proposals as I had enjoyed in the early phase. That's just a natural human process, [but] I felt like it might be time to let them know that I wanted to renew our mutual commitment and get going. So I wrote out by hand, longhand, a careful retirement statement that I had rehearsed only with the board chairman and made it at a board meeting with the press present. They had no idea it was coming. This was almost exactly a year and a half prior to the end of the campaign, at the January board meeting in 1993. I told them that I would step down in June of 1995 at the end of the campaign, that there would be a success there, and I would not be able to stay in office long enough under the age sixty-five expectation to preside over the new surge of energy that the campaign would be bound to give to the university. I wanted to bequeath that to a successor. So in order for the trustees to absorb that and to make plans for a smooth succession, I was announcing right then that I would retire at the end of June 1995, and I asked the trustees to launch the search process in a timely fashion so that there could be a smooth transition. Then I said, "I'm not tired, I'm exhilarated about working with you to complete this campaign and to do all the other things a chancellor does. So, let's not make much over this announcement, let's go back to work." One board member, I later learned, was sort of a General Bullmoose character who thought that once a CEO announces his intentions to step down sometime later, he might just as well get out of the way right now. That's true if he's being forced out. If a man is being forced out, or a woman, he or she ought to get on out of the way; if it's a violation of the contract, the board ought to pay off the person because it's not a good working relationship. But I did this at a time when we did have a good working relationship, and the full board, if they discussed this in executive session, obviously decided to accept my timetable. I took a calculated risk that instead of having a negative lame-duck period, I might have a reenergizing, and that's what happened. . . .
>
> . . . I have a hunch that people who might have challenged me if I had not announced my intention to retire, decided to wait and challenge somebody else. . . . I had some tough times; I lost a lot of

sleep at Carolina, but I think that by some accident or some intuition and by a lot of luck, my resignation was appropriately motivated and somehow rather fortuitously smooth.

The length of time between Paul Hardin's resignation and his departure
(January 28, 1994–June 30, 1995) is by far the longest among our small
group and probably unusual for most departing academic leaders. Our
next longest gap was Donald Kennedy's thirteen months (July 28,
1991–August 31, 1992), which allowed time for the completion of necessary university business once the certainty of Kennedy's departure had
"precipitated out" the governance uncertainty created by the Dingell investigation:

> If I can characterize the modal faculty reaction during the indirect
> cost recovery investigation, it was, "Kennedy's been a pretty good
> president. I think he missed seeing something on indirect costs and
> we're paying a price for that. I don't know whether Dingell has some-
> thing personal here, but I wonder if, as long as Kennedy continues
> to be president, we won't continue to be attacked in this way? So
> I'm pretty nervous about it." When I said in July, "I'm done after this
> year," all that was clarified; the attitude was, "Now, let's get down to
> business and search for a successor. We'll do the work we need to do
> with respect to budget cuts and so forth." . . . On balance, I didn't
> feel like a lame duck at all. Now, you will hear faculty say Building
> 10 (the president's and provost's offices) lost a lot of its authority in
> that period of time, but I don't think we needed a lot of nominal
> authority. We had a strong provost who was running a good budget
> reduction process along with a faculty-trustee committee. [My resig-
> nation in fact facilitated] an ambiguity reduction that was enor-
> mously helpful. Although it was not a very happy year in terms of
> public relations, it worked fine.

While six of our presidents chiefly recalled the lame-duck period in
terms of administrative strategy (including the quick exit), both Robert
O'Neil and Michael Sovern emphasized a different dimension, a psychological bonus that afforded them the freedom to do and say what they
thought best, whether it was professionally prudent or not. Robert O'Neil
says that during his final months at the University of Virginia (October
4, 1989–August 1, 1990), he "never felt any lack of authority or of either persuasive or dissuasive power." In fact, "it went very smoothly . . .
and we got quite a bit done that spring":

> I resolved some issues—I had some just terribly messy sexual ha-
> rassment cases on which I had to rule, and I think I felt freer to do

the right thing there than I might have if I had been continuing. I went to meet with a gay and lesbian student group which I thought was important to do—I would never have dared do that if I were still in office, I don't think. And several other things—I went and dealt with legislative committees and I told it like it was. I think people appreciated that candor. [I felt unfettered] and that may have been partly because it's the only time when I was not going on to another office somewhere else, so that if I really spoke my mind, let's say in Bloomington, somebody in Madison would hear about it, or if I said something in Madison that was outrageous, somebody in Charlottesville would hear about it. If I did that as I felt freer to do in the spring and summer of 1990, it wasn't going to have down-stream impact on anything else.

And O'Neil was, after all, leaving the University of Virginia to head a center for free expression.

Michael Sovern, too, felt a certain rare freedom to take on controversy after announcing on June 6, 1992, that he would step down from the Columbia presidency, effective June 30, 1993. During that time, he says, "The knowledge that I was leaving was liberating." As he dealt with the need for a "gentle" financial retrenchment at Columbia that was being met with some very public resistance on campus and faculty criticism that was amply reported in the national press,[20] Sovern believes that one of the most important measures taken to ensure Columbia's long-term solvency might have been impossible without his resignation, that is, to "actually cut the pension program":

> I'm not sure if I hadn't announced my retirement whether we would have been able to do it. . . . [Our pension plan] was grossly excessive. Before I became an administrator, it was clear to me that under the Columbia plan, I would retire at considerably more than I was earning. . . . Our plan was far, far too generous; it made absolutely no sense. But faculty, of course, regarded it as an entitlement. Anyway, we took out two and a half percent. Let me be clear about that. For example, when I reached age fifty-five with twenty-five years of service, Columbia would have increased its pension contribution for me to 20 percent of my salary above a certain level each year. We knocked that down to 17.5 percent. Another step would have gotten 15, we knocked that down to 12.5. So everybody still has a very generous pension program, but we saved a lot of money. . . .

> . . . I think the pension change was easier to achieve [because I was leaving]. It was very unpopular, and we had countless meetings. I didn't go to all of them; in fact, I didn't go to most of them . . .

but I was part of it. If I had intended to stay longer, I'd have had to think about the effect of that change on my ability to lead, it was so unpopular. . . .

. . . I haven't seen any other university that's done it. Others have very rich pension plans, and they still have them. I'm not saying we wouldn't have done it, but I do have to ask myself the question, did my freedom from fear affect that judgment?

AFTERMATH

What actually happens when a university presidency ends? That is, as the transition occurs, how do old and new presidents interact? How do they approach the private, personal aspects of beginning and ending a highly visible job? We asked our participants to describe their experiences both during and after the changing of the guard. Not surprisingly, for some the process of presidential transition had its awkward moments. Michael Sovern recalls that after resigning (but before stepping down), he hit a "bump" in the transition that heralded changes to come:

> We had a vacancy for the vice president for arts and sciences post, and it was clear that the search committee, once I had announced, was not going to give me a recommendation. I was unhappy about that because it was an important vacancy. . . . When George Rupp was announced, then, of course, you began to get a shift. In fact, he actually indicated his intention to fire a couple of deans while I was still in office. I was not thrilled.

Robert O'Neil remembers as "almost comical" that during the transition at UVA he had to defend to the press his successor John Casteen's installation of a Jacuzzi in the presidential residence. "I said, 'Well, he has a bad back, for heaven's sake!'" More on the painful side of awkward, however, was Donald Kennedy's experience:

> I'll be frank to say that the transition was a difficult one for me, partly because I had to cope with both a drop in my own interaction rate and the sense that there was a deliberate effort to make a sharp break with my part of the institution's history. That was a little difficult to take for a while; it took me about two years to adjust and move on. Several people that had been important parts of my life in the institution, including the general counsel and the vice president

for public affairs, were terminated. The new general counsel had the idea to outsource virtually all of Stanford's legal work and to shrink the staff abruptly; my wife was the first to go, in a rather public way. That was a little hard to take.

There was also something alienating about the style of the presidential transition itself. The search committee had been working away for a few months, and in casual conversation a faculty member told me that they were about three weeks away from a decision. The chairman of the board called me up one morning just a couple of days later and said, "I assume the search committee's been keeping you up to date on progress?" And I said, "Well, no." And he said, "Oops," and then he announced the selection of Gerhard Casper who, he said, was getting on a plane in Chicago that morning. So I said, well, of course he must stay with us, etc., and that came to pass. The transition was perfectly cordial, but it started in an awkward way, [then] was followed by a fairly low interaction, and I don't know the extent to which that differs from the standard experience. It does seem to me that it could have been handled differently, but there's a strong view among many managers, including my old boss in government, Joe Califano, that if you come in from the outside, you want to make the sharpest break you can—get rid of anybody you think may be loyal to others and create a new inner circle of management. Increasingly, some trustees are echoing calls from industry that universities should work toward a more corporate model. There's a lively debate about that.

The question of interactions between predecessors and successors— their quantity and manner—drew several instructive responses from our presidents. Donald Kennedy implicitly contrasted his own transition style with that of his successor when he referred to his relations with his predecessor as president of Stanford, Richard Lyman:

> Dick Lyman went to head the Rockefeller Foundation; he met his last commitments to Stanford, flew to New York, and took right over. Dick and I are good friends. We've had a close relationship, and during the first year I tried to make sure that every achievement of the Lyman presidency was given lots of attention.

Benno Schmidt (who did not remain long enough at Yale for issues of transition in his own presidency to arise) also described his relations with his predecessor, A. Bartlett Giamatti,[21] and offered his observations about

Giamatti's exit philosophy and some of the emotional impetus that lay
behind it:

> Bart was tremendously helpful to me in every way that he could be
> in the six months before I started. I developed in that time a tremen-
> dous regard for his intellect and his courage, both in his institutional
> character and personally. But at the same time, Bart had a very
> highly developed and precise view of what his proper relation to me
> was, and it was pretty much that the minute he stepped down and
> I became president, he was off to other responsibilities and what he
> owed me and the institution, he felt, was essentially withdrawal. I
> think Bart had felt to some extent in his own presidency that the
> shadow of Kingman Brewster had been a little more pronounced
> than it should have been, and so he took pains to withdraw. Not
> personally at all—we would see each other in a very friendly way,
> but he got away from the place, and many of his friends on the fac-
> ulty would remark to me how much they missed him and how much
> they felt that he had really withdrawn as he went into baseball. Now,
> it has to be said because it's true, that Bart was a wonderful presi-
> dent, in many ways beloved, but he also had in many ways a very
> difficult time. The strike in 1984 was extremely difficult for him per-
> sonally. He felt very badly about the way the faculty responded, very
> badly, and I think some of the faculty's response during the strike
> was irresponsible and was a betrayal. This was puzzling to me because
> Columbia had strikes . . . But somehow at Columbia resentments
> didn't last, [whereas] the pain of that 1984 strike hung over Yale like
> a pall. . . . I think Bart was hurt by a sense of mistrust and a gulf that
> he felt existed between the faculty and the president and the ad-
> ministration. I mean, I was shocked when I arrived at Yale . . . and
> a number of faculty members told me . . . that no administration was
> to be trusted, that the administration and faculty historically had a
> healthy sense of mutual skepticism if not downright antagonism, as
> a part of the institutional character of the place. I was just shocked
> at that. . . . Bart had been a faculty member, and he found many of
> his old friends and colleagues approaching him, the administration,
> with distrust and an absence of institutional cohesion and harmony,
> particularly when things got difficult around the strike or around a
> few other tough issues. That troubled Bart, troubled him deeply. We
> talked about it; it's among the reasons that he thought the proper
> role for a president was to withdraw. And, by the way, I think there
> is a great deal of wisdom in that.
>   [I did have occasion to call on him for advice.] We would make
> sure that we had lunch or dinner at least three or four times during
> the course of the academic year. I did the same thing with Kingman,
> as a matter of fact, and that was also quite helpful and very, very

pleasant and cordial. But I think they both had a sense from their own presidencies that once you're not in there, you're not in there. I mean, you can be a great source of advice and Bart was tremendously helpful about a lot of things, and there is obviously a continuity that they can speak to. But at the same time, they both had a sophisticated and circumspect view about the proper limits of their advisory function or capacity, and so, as time went on, the separation would increase. I don't have any sense of a growing separation or alienation or anything; I [just] mean on the day Bart left, he left. He [remained] friendly and helpful, but there was a clear sense of the crossing of a divide. I begged him to stay and teach, but fortunately or not for him—and indeed, this turned out to be the case for me—being president of Yale is something one does and then moves on, not back.

Robert O'Neil offered similar examples of a philosophy of cordial distancing between an institution's presidents (and in passing, a lively snapshot of Bart Giamatti):

If I take the three [executive] offices I have held, in each case I would say I knew my predecessor a bit, but got to know him (and they were all male) somewhat better afterwards. The one structured relationship [I had was with] Byrum Carter,[22] who was chancellor at IU-Bloomington [before me] and was really the first person to hold that office. I was essentially the second; a man named [John W.] Snyder had held it for only a few months before Byrum, but practically speaking, Byrum was the first chancellor. He was a political scientist from Oklahoma and had spent most of his life at Bloomington. When I was appointed, he said, "I will be happy to talk with you for one hour about administration and then that's it." Now, we often went to the Carters' house, we had them to our house, we saw one another around the community (Bloomington's a fairly small place). Scrupulously did he observe [his dictum], and I felt that I had to as well, so that even if I had a pressing issue on which I figured Byrum had some experience, he had raised that wall and I respected it. In other situations, at Wisconsin, for example, my relationship with Ed Young,[23] my predecessor as system head, was de facto almost the same as the de jure relationship that Byrum Carter's injunction had created, and here [at UVA] I'd have to say that my relationship with Frank Hereford[24] has been in all cases cordial but distant. . . . Ken Gros Louis,[25] who is now finishing twenty years as my successor at Bloomington, has called me only once about an issue, and I think that was almost more to just let me know that he was still there. I don't think that in any of these roles I contacted my predecessor more than once or twice. It's an interesting question why that happens; I think it's probably a healthy sign. There is perhaps a feeling that your two situations aren't really comparable, and therefore you're not going to find out that much. Also, [there is] a feeling that you probably have to make your own judgments. But even so, I think it's surprising that there is so little reliance [on experienced hands] even when the relationship is entirely cordial. My successor at Wisconsin, Buzz Shaw,[26] who's chancellor at Syracuse—we hadn't really known one another before he succeeded me, and I was gone from Madison by the time he got there. We did meet at AAU meetings—they seated people alphabetically. That's how I got to know Bart Giamatti; Wisconsin and Yale were seated next to one another, so my perspective on Bart is very much of someone sitting in the next chair waving his arms wildly.

Anyway, I don't know about other people's experiences—this is something on which I'm not sure I have ever compared notes. . . . It's comforting to know that the person is there if you ever really needed to call on him, but in fact, you seldom do.

Leaving one university presidency to go on to another does not of course raise the same personal issues as leaving the presidency for retirement from the administrative life. Interestingly, three of our presidents who specifically addressed the psychology of uncoupling were all returning to the faculties of the private universities where they had served:

Michael Sovern:

Letting go is hard. I still remember the moment when I knew I had fully let go. I'm a trustee emeritus as well as president emeritus, and so I am invited to all the trustee meetings. I figured I'd go, keep an eye on things, and it was about a year after I'd left office that I was sitting in a trustees meeting and was delighted to observe myself bored stiff.

Donald Kennedy:

Many people manage the problem [of letting go] by going away and doing something quite different. I have essentially given my entire career to this institution. I care a lot about it and I wanted to stay in it. I also think that it's useful to demonstrate occasionally that the presidency, after all, is an episode in an academic career. Going back to the faculty has been a wonderfully positive experience for me. I've done a lot of teaching in different areas, especially with undergraduates. I think I'm good at that, and it's been very engaging. I've made a fair number of outside commitments to keep myself busy and to take me away from time to time.

Harold Shapiro:

[In response to your question about how presidents prepare for what really will be a personal loss when they step down,] . . . most of our colleagues don't really prepare for it and don't really think about it that way. . . . It will be a big loss—I mean, I won't have all these people wanting to see me, and calling me up and making appointments and telling me how important I am and so forth, and I'm sure that's going to be an adjustment. Until you do it, you don't know how you're going to experience it. I'm preparing for it by trying to develop a new agenda of activities. As you may know, I'm chairman of the National Bioethics Advisory Commission. Well, I accepted that with some of this in mind, that I wanted a new aspect to my life. It certainly will be different, and I don't have any magic bullet here, but I do consciously think about it and consciously do things. I don't think I would be teaching now if it wasn't that I think of myself as preparing for another stage in my career. So while I enjoy the teaching, what I really have in mind is that I'm building up my capacity, or rebuilding my capacity, in this area, which would be very hard to do if I just had to start cold turkey. We did something else: my wife and I moved out of the president's house at Princeton because I didn't want us to have two losses at the same time—our house and my job the same day. . . . I told the trustees the only thing I want when I leave here is an "O" parking pass. That means you can park anywhere on campus. I think they have given only three of them out, to me and to the two former presidents. That's the only thing I want.

NOTES

1. Art Padilla and Sujit Ghosh, "Turnover at the Top: The Revolving Door of the Academic Presidency," *The Presidency*, Journal of the American Council on Education (winter 2000): vol. 3, no. 1, p. 34. Unlike ACE's profile series *The American College President* (and other college and university leadership studies), Padilla and Ghosh do not define presidential tenure as length of service as of the date the president fills out the questionnaire ("Years in present job"), nor do they combine statistics from different categories of colleges and universities (e.g., ACE surveys Research I and II and Doctorate I and II universities under the single category, "Doctorate-granting Institutions"). Instead, they analyzed presidential tenures at Research I universities only and defined tenure as "total or start-to-end," that is, from "initial appointment to separation," with averages figured in five-year intervals from 1950 through 1989.

2. Padilla and Ghosh, p. 34.

3. Joan Sovern died in September 1993 after a battle with cancer.

4. Cohort 1980 through 1984, Padilla and Ghosh, p. 34; UPI, "Freedman Denies Departure Linked to Funding Problems," April 15, 1987.

5. Shapiro was born June 8, 1935, Freedman September 21, 1935.

6. Padilla and Ghosh, p. 34.

7. See Ruth S. Intress, "O'Neil's Resignation Came Down to Style," *Richmond Times-Dispatch*, October 8, 1989, sec. Area/State, p. A1, and Debra E. Blum, "U. of Virginia Board Redefines President's Job, Gives Provost Oversight of Daily Operations," *Chronicle of Higher Education*, July 19, 1989, pp. A9, A12.

8. O'Neil announced his decision on October 4, 1989, having begun the Virginia presidency on September 1, 1985. He ultimately stepped down after serving 4 years, 11 months (John Casteen took over on August 1, 1990). The average tenure for public university Research I presidents appointed between 1985 and 1989 is 5.7 years (Padilla and Ghosh, p. 34).

9. Robert O'Neil's intention to lead the Jefferson Center as an activist organization has borne fruit. See http://www.tjcenter.org/ for reports on the litigation, testimony, and other activities of the center's director and staff.

10. Padilla and Ghosh, p. 34, note that they "detected differences in average tenures between 'internal' and 'external' presidents. Individuals promoted to the presidency from within the institution tend to have longer tenures than do those who are hired from outside the university. Public universities recently have been more likely to hire people whose immediate previous employment was at other institutions—which may be a function of an increased use of search firms—and this has contributed to the decline in presidential tenures."

11. Informative accounts of the indirect cost controversy and the attack on Stanford and Donald Kennedy by Chairman Dingell and his Subcommittee on Oversight and Investigations (House Energy and Commerce Committee) can be found in Donald Kennedy, "To Discover," in *Academic Duty* (Cambridge, MA: Harvard University Press, 1997); Jerrold K. Footlick, "How High the Cost: Indirect Costs at Stanford University," in *Truth and Consequences: How Colleges and Universities Meet Public Crises* (Phoenix, AZ: American Council on Education and Oryx Press, Series on Higher Education, 1997); and Robert M. Rosenzweig, "The Rules Change I: Matters of Policy and Politics," in *The Political University: Policy, Politics, and Presidential Leadership in the American Research University* (Baltimore: The Johns Hopkins University Press, 1998). To summarize, the investigation dealt with two issues: (1) the results of pool accounting, an accepted method of figuring indirect costs to an institution of federally sponsored research whereby the government was billed an agreed-upon percentage of expenses in particular categories or indirect cost pools, thus lumping together everything classified in that category, and (2) charges that a series of overly generous memorandums of understanding between Stanford and representatives of the Office of Naval Research had been developed without official approval. These charges were eventually proved false.

12. The October 17, 1989, Loma Prieta earthquake registered 7.1 on the Richter scale and did $160 million in damage to the Stanford campus.

13. Jeff Gottlieb, "Stanford Charged Taxpayers for Yacht," *San Jose Mercury News*, December 5, 1990, p. 1A; Jeff Gottlieb, "Stanford Billed Taxpayers for Flowers," *San Jose Mercury News*, December 14, 1990, p. 1A; "Stanford's Image: It's One of a Greedy School that Sees the Government as a Reservoir to Be Tapped," *San Jose Mercury News*, March 17, 1991, p. 6C; "Turning Labs into Cedar Closets," *Newsweek*, February 4, 1991, p. 70; David Dietz, "U.S. Funds Used for Wedding," *San Francisco Chronicle*, February 15, 1991, Final Edition, p. A2; "Stanford to Return U.S. Funds Used for Upkeep of Tomb," *Los Angeles Times*, September 6, 1991, Home Edition, p. A3; Valerie Richardson, "School for Scandal," *Washington Times*, March 20, 1991, Final Edition, p. E1; Robert J. Samuelson, "Sleaze Knows No Class," *Washington Post*, March 27, 1991, Final Edition, p. A23; "Top Scientist Pays for University High Life," *New Scientist*, vol. 131, no. 1781, August 10, 1991, p. 14; Eugene H. Methvin, "He Caught the Campus Chiselers," *Reader's Digest*, vol. 140, no. 837, January 1992, pp. 81–86.

14. See, for example, Larry Gordon, "Stanford Goes on Offensive to Rebut Government's Charges," *Los Angeles Times*, February 5, 1991, Home Edition, p. A3; "Stanford Bills Justified, Trustees Say," *San Francisco Chronicle*, March 9, 1991, Final Edition, p. A5; "Stanford Trustees Back Kennedy," *San Francisco Chronicle*, April 10, 1991, Final Edition, p. B6; Bill Workman, "Stanford President Denies Whistle-Blower's Charges," *San Francisco Chronicle*, January 31, 1992, Final Edition, p. A15. Kennedy cited media reports of Stanford's government billing that were "egregiously inaccurate," such as $1,200 urns said to cost $12,000, and a nonexistent purchase of $7,000 worth of sheets brought up at the hearing as "supposedly for my bed," see Thomas G. Keane, "Stanford Getting a Top Accountant," *San Francisco Chronicle*, March 25, 1991, Final Edition, p. A2. Kennedy's wife Robin expressed her view of the press and the politicians as "attackers . . . irrational, uninformed," who "don't give a damn about the truth," see Karen Grassmuck, "How Donald and Robin Kennedy Handle Negative Publicity," *Chronicle of Higher Education*, May 15, 1991, p. A27.

15. According to one article, Dingell accused Kennedy of "incompetence" and "rascality," see Bill Workman, "David Packard Says Hearing Was 'a Sad Day for Stanford,'" *San Francisco Chronicle*, March 15, 1991, Final Edition, p. A2; in another, the hearing is described as a "marathon" at which Kennedy "appeared pained and kept his eyes down," see Colleen Cordes, "Angry Lawmakers Grill Stanford's Kennedy on Research Costs," *Chronicle of Higher Education*, March 20, 1991, p. A1.

16. 1980–1984: 11.2 years, see Padilla and Ghosh, p. 34.

17. Deborah Sontag, "Yale President Quitting to Lead National Private-School Venture," *New York Times*, May 26, 1992, Late Edition, pp. A1, B8.

18. Sontag, p. B8.

19. Lamar was reportedly named acting president on June 17, see Jennifer Kaylin, "Probing the Presidency," *Yale*, October 1992, p. 52, but the appointment was not official until voted on by the Yale Corporation on June 26; the "acting" was dropped in April 1993, according to William R. Massa, Jr., Public Services

Archivist, Yale University Library, in his letter of April 30, 2002 to Leslie Banner. Lamar was succeeded that same year by Richard C. Levin.

20. For example, see Anthony DePalma, "Columbia President Warns of Need for More Cutbacks," *New York Times*, December 10, 1991, Late Edition, p. B3; Anthony DePalma, "Short of Money, Columbia U. Weighs How Best to Change," May 25, 1992, Late Edition, pp. A1, 25; Liz McMillen, "Columbia U. Arts and Sciences Chiefs Won't Cooperate in Further Cuts," *Chronicle of Higher Education*, December 4, 1991, p. A47; "Columbia U. May Face $87-Million Deficit," *Chronicle of Higher Education*, December 18, 1991, p. A4; Robert L. Jacobson, "Clash Over Money Management at Columbia U. Averted," *Chronicle of Higher Education*, May 6, 1992, p. A37.

21. Giamatti was president of Yale, 1978–1986; president of the National League, 1986–1989; and commissioner of baseball, April 1989 until his death, September 1, 1989.

22. Byrum Carter served as Indiana University-Bloomington chancellor from 1969 to 1975; John W. Snyder had served as Acting Chancellor during 1969.

23. H. Edwin Young served as University of Wisconsin System president from 1977 to 1980.

24. Frank Hereford served as president of the University of Virginia from 1974 to 1985.

25. Kenneth Gros Louis stepped down as chancellor of Indiana University-Bloomington in 2001, having served since Robert O'Neil's departure in 1980. He was succeeded by IU-B's first woman chancellor, Sharon Brehm.

26. Kenneth A. Shaw served as president of the University of Wisconsin System from 1986 to 1991.

CHAPTER 5

Summary of Findings

We based our study of research university presidencies on three premises: (1) that examining the university presidency in terms of a developmental model would yield useful insights; (2) that representative illustrations of conflicts and attitudes common to their positions could be drawn from interviews with past presidents of comparable institutions; and (3) that our life cycle hypothesis would have predictive value.

For what we called the prelude phase of a presidency, we asked our subjects to describe the conditions surrounding their candidacies, their preparations for office, the assembling of their administrative teams, and the origins of their institutional agendas. In these discussions we wanted to discover if they were aware of any ambivalence on their own parts during the search process and what, if anything, during the performance of their earliest presidential tasks might be identified as having led to conflicts later in their terms. The three internal candidates (Kennedy, Shapiro at Michigan, and Sovern) were serving as provosts when they were tapped for the presidency and not surprisingly, characterized their promotions as easily accepted, logical progressions, as the appropriate extension of what they were already doing. Consequently, they felt no ambivalence about accepting the job. Among external candidates, only Benno Schmidt indicated any early ambivalence and concluded that his own insistence on secrecy and speed during the search process created some initial strain among Yale's board members, most of whom met him for the first time the day he was offered the job. The external searches were described as providing largely positive experiences at the time, but in retrospect only James Freedman's recruitment to Iowa emerged as having no hidden or delayed negative elements. In fact, Freedman felt that the careful organization and the tenor of the Iowa search actually served to strengthen his presidency from the very beginning by creating strong faculty and board alliances and providing sources of political advice. In sharp contrast to Freedman's experience, Vartan Gregorian, Paul Hardin, Benno Schmidt, Harold Shapiro (at Princeton), and Robert O'Neil (at UVA) saw their early presidential terms impacted by what might be seen as the search anomalies of board members who either did not volunteer crucial information (Brown, UNC), did not grasp the implications of crucial information (Yale, Princeton), or apparently did not understand basic information about their own institution (UVA). For our external candidates and for internal candidate Donald Kennedy, however, personal desires and the prestige of the institutions where they were being asked to serve essentially overrode conscious recognition of any factors that might otherwise have given them pause. Their attitude toward researching the jobs they were considering was not rigorous; in fact, Robert O'Neil felt there was no way he could have prepared himself for the culture shock of UVA, while James Freedman simply overlooked (and his board evidently underestimated) the resistance to change among Dartmouth alumni. In the case of Donald Kennedy, misgivings about an inadequate period of presidential apprenticeship while provost (later borne out in personnel decisions) seemed less important at the time than his commitment to Stanford.

The question of change versus no change among university officers as a new president contemplates taking office elicited a lengthy disquisition from Vartan Gregorian on the negative consequences of moving quickly and of *not* moving quickly to appoint a new team. Robert O'Neil, Harold Shapiro, and Benno Schmidt agreed that in general, continuity among high-level personnel should be maintained—except when it should not, as Donald Kennedy's problems at Stanford illustrated. Overall, the presidents who spoke to this subject admitted to difficulties and mistakes that came back to haunt them, confirming the importance that conventional wisdom places on a leader's ability to appoint capable lieutenants, appropriate in skills and character to the tasks assigned, matched equally with a president's openness to recognizing and correcting personnel misjudgments in a timely fashion. More central to intrainstitutional conflict than the selection and performance of university officers, however, is the implementation of a new president's agenda for action. As our respondents indicated, the source and control of major portions of that agenda will not necessarily lie with the president himself, even at a private institution. Vartan Gregorian, Benno Schmidt, Harold Shapiro, and Michael Sovern all found that financial realities in the private sector—just as in the public sector—shaped major goals and actions early in their terms. In addition, as James Freedman and Paul Hardin learned, university trustees sometimes come to a presidential search with specific agenda items of their own that can put a new president into an uncomfortable, even controversial position.

Conflicts that are unanticipated or unavoidable at the beginning of a term in office will eventually require presidential action that ends the putative honeymoon period of general goodwill and support on campus. Thus, we were interested in looking beneath the theoretical calm of this honeymoon phase for presidents' attitudes and approaches to making unpopular decisions. Specifically, we asked whether our presidents felt they had had a honeymoon period, whether they could identify the moment when they had incurred serious political consequences on campus, and whether considerations of the risks to their fledgling presidencies had influenced the timing of any decisions. The response to our relatively simple inquiry about an initial honeymoon period proved to be quite complicated, with only Robert O'Neil describing our posited period of institutional and personal calm, his having lasted at UVA approximately nine months and having been ended by a racial protest that he believes left a residue of skepticism about his administration among some faculty. Other honeymoon reports ranged from ten years (Sovern), to variable in time according to constituency (Kennedy), to immediate institutional angst coupled with a neutral personal reception (Gregorian, Schmidt), to immediate institutional angst coupled with presidential excoriation (Freedman at Dartmouth, Shapiro at Princeton). The theme of first impressions was taken up spontaneously by both Vartan Gregorian and Benno Schmidt, who noted the persistence for good or ill of early perceptions of a new president. Gregorian believes he managed these effectively during his first months at Brown, while Schmidt thinks his "uncompromising" style of expression and decision making, carried over from the law school at Columbia, alienated many at Yale.

Equally complex were the responses to our concept of the defining moment as the first presidential decision that results in a significant and lasting negative reaction on campus—the moment when enemies begin to accumulate. With the exception of Benno Schmidt, who ruefully noted early decisions at Yale rendered in such a way as to give a lasting impression of him as authoritarian and inflexible, our presidents who addressed this issue did not want to describe as negative anything in their

presidencies that was to be labeled "defining." Robert O'Neil, for example, chose as defining moments two early public crises at Indiana that
united the academic community behind his administration, rather than
the racial crisis at UVA that ended his honeymoon there. James Freedman and Harold Shapiro, while talking candidly and at length about
their negative experiences, selected as their defining moments tough battles that after the passage of time resulted in stronger presidencies as well
as widely acknowledged positive outcomes for their institutions. Paul
Hardin and Michael Sovern chose risky decisions outside the academic
arena that they could count as presidential triumphs, and Vartan Gregorian selected as his defining moment the point at which he began to think
he had "done the presidency" and was ready to move on.

Our third question about the honeymoon period—whether considerations of risk led to the delay of any presidential decisions during the first
year—evoked a decided "no," accompanied by numerous comments
about and discussions of the risks inherent in the job. Benno Schmidt
and Harold Shapiro thought that they should have been more cautious
with some of their decisions at the beginning of their terms, while James
Freedman, Robert O'Neil, and Michael Sovern recounted administrative
and governance risks that had to be faced and dealt with immediately,
regardless of any damage to their own positions, a philosophy that had
plunged Harold Shapiro into hot water soon after arriving at Princeton.
For Paul Hardin, the special risks in heading a public institution brought
to mind the levels of command that had to be negotiated above that of
board of trustees; and Vartan Gregorian, Donald Kennedy, and Benno
Schmidt took the question of risk taking further, to expand on what presidential leadership should involve, answering the question (as Schmidt
posed it): if taking on the "big issues" (and therefore the "big risks") is
"not what a president is for, [then] what is a president for?" Gregorian
considered that a president is first of all an educator and therefore has a
responsibility to speak out on campus about issues of right and wrong regardless of trustee or faculty displeasure; Kennedy felt that the role of university president included an obligation to American society to represent
the views and best interests of higher education in public policy debates,
no matter the political fallout; and Schmidt reflected on questions of risk
in terms of the stewardship responsibilities of a president to address a university's toughest problems, whatever the peril to his tenure.

Another way to look at the strains that accompany effective governance is to examine some of the specific conflicts that arise between presidents and their major constituencies. Under the rubric of the plateau,
the workaday years of presidential administration, we asked for accounts

of difficulties and battles with faculty, students, and higher authorities. In relation to faculty, a picture of real frustration emerged among some of our presidents, ranging from Michael Sovern's references to grudge-holders who caught up with him during the final years of his presidency, to detailed accounts by Donald Kennedy, Benno Schmidt, and Harold Shapiro of painful and contentious interactions with faculty over long periods of time. Donald Kennedy recalled his failed four-year struggle to bring the Reagan presidential papers to Stanford, illustrating how thank-less a task is a president's responsibility to look beyond current contro-versy to make balanced, long-term decisions for the institution. In Benno Schmidt's case, the legitimate feeling that he should "actually do some-thing" about longstanding problems at Yale collided sharply with what Schmidt called a "deeply conservative . . . visceral reaction against . . . change" among the faculty. Both he and Harold Shapiro described hos-tility in the face of efforts to deal responsibly with bad budget news and saw the time-honored process of consensus building among the faculty as an appropriate governance tool that could be carried to the point of detriment to the institution. For Harold Shapiro the problem was exac-erbated at Michigan, where his close ties to longtime faculty colleagues made it "psychologically difficult" for him to endure their openly ex-pressed anger.

If faculty frustrate and wear presidents down with inertia, indecisive-ness, and politicized opposition, students have the power to create im-mediate havoc. Less rational and predictable than faculty, they can deplete a president's physical and psychological reserves and take a toll on both image and effectiveness. Judging from the press coverage, all of our presidents had negative, even alarming experiences with student protests, but interestingly, half downplayed such disruptions as business-as-usual while the other half described strongly negative impacts on their presidencies. Gregorian, Kennedy, Shapiro, and Sovern portrayed their confrontations with large numbers of students matter-of-factly, noting that student protests are the order of the day at universities and there-fore should be anticipated. All true, yet newspaper reports during their presidencies also indicate that they suffered occasions of actual physical threat when hundreds of students rallied en masse, invaded presidential and trustee precincts, halted classes and traffic, and were hauled off to jail. In retrospect, these presidents clearly felt that their tenures in office had not been seriously impacted by conflict with their student bodies and they did not refer to memories of being personally disturbed, though they very likely were at the time. A contrasting picture was presented by Freedman, Hardin, O'Neil, and Schmidt, who described serious effects stemming from difficulties with students. While James Freedman and Paul Hardin did not feel that students had inflicted any lasting damage on their presidencies, they did recount at length the painful, exhausting nature of long-running battles that garnered bad, even vituperative national press and numerous hurtful interactions over the course of several years. On the other hand, Robert O'Neil and Benno Schmidt did not report taking their troubles with students personally, but in their analyses they saw student protests and disaffection as having had political repercussions that spread to other constituencies.

The difference between leading a private and a public university emerged most distinctively in our discussions of conflict at the governance board level. The trustees at Brown, Columbia, Dartmouth, Princeton, Stanford, and Yale were described as generally strong, supportive partners to their presidents, but nevertheless, partners whom the presidents were responsible for educating. James Freedman and Michael Sovern emphasized that the division of labor, or more accurately perhaps, realms of expertise between themselves and their boards were clearly understood—academics on the presidential side, finances on the trustee side. Benno Schmidt and Donald Kennedy felt responsible for occasional tensions with their boards, Schmidt because he created additional discomfort for them during a time of change by the degree of urgency he communicated—"my candid view was a little alarming"—and Kennedy because trustees appointed during his tenure, he believes, were less experienced and knowledgeable, resulting in trustee attitudes that led to more conflict with the president, a concern he generalized to other universities today. In Kennedy's view, university trusteeship is not taken as seriously as it once was. Harold Shapiro, too, deplored the extent to which many of today's boards appear to be relatively uninformed, and both he and Vartan Gregorian discussed their strategies for avoiding conflict with trustees by continuously educating them and keeping them fully informed. In addition, Gregorian warned of the dangers for presidents when translating the two cultures, academic/faculty and corporate/trustee, to each other: "That's what gets leaders into trouble, how to talk one language with which you bring both parties to appreciate the academic culture despite its inane rules and its perceived inertia and seeming opposition to change."

Educating and developing strong partnerships with their boards are tasks common to presidents whether at private or public universities; it is the political element in state systems that creates an additional, unavoidable layer of governance conflict, as the experiences of James Freedman, Harold Shapiro, Paul Hardin, and Robert O'Neil clearly showed.

Freedman felt that he was quite fortunate in regard to his Iowa board of regents who, despite being political appointees, understood the importance of the university to the state, were respectful of the views of its leader, and apparently remained free of the politicized decision making that currently afflicts so many state universities. He was mindful of state politics, however, wary of the legislature, and took a publicly aggressive stance when the state system bureaucracy attempted to institute greater central control over Iowa's universities. Harold Shapiro's experience at Michigan, where the small governing board is elected, was far rockier, not because of his board, whom he made a point of educating and treating with respect—"You take people seriously, they take you seriously; you take them lightly, they take you lightly"—nor because he was politically unaware—he took care to move within legislative realities where funding for the university was concerned; but because when racial conflict exploded at the University of Michigan, state legislators took advantage of the situation to make political points for themselves, actually holding hearings on campus to "investigate racism" at the university. Shapiro found such heavy-handed interference intolerable and accepted an offer to lead Princeton shortly afterward. At the University of North Carolina at Chapel Hill, Paul Hardin worked within a structure more complicated than that of Iowa and Michigan. Conveying a sense of always having to watch his back, he recalled the proliferation of tensions throughout the university system—between himself and the system president, two of the state's governors, and the university system's board of governors; between the UNC-CH trustees and the system president; between the system president and the board of governors; and finally, among the chancellors of the individual campuses as they competed for funding. Any tensions between himself and his own board at Chapel Hill appear to have been the least of Paul Hardin's governance worries. Robert O'Neil pointed out that as complicated as the North Carolina system may seem, to his mind Virginia's governance relationships are even more complex, with the addition of a secretary of education and a state council for higher education "to whom, in a sense, the university presidents report." He felt, however, that structure per se affects a president's ability to exercise control less than sudden shifts in the political winds. Citing the imposition of legislative mandates during his own presidency at the University of Virginia and later, he concluded that such political pressures on leaders of public institutions are "without counterparts in the private sector" and constitute a "very different [administrative] dimension."

The final stage we examined in the life cycle of a university presidency, the exit, we viewed as encompassing the entire period during which a president reaches the decision to step down, announces that decision, lives with it administratively, and then departs. Given the complexity and irreconcilable tensions of these positions, we hoped to explore both the psychology and the reality of the end phase. Thus, we asked how the decision to leave office was reached, whether effectiveness diminished during the months prior to departure, and what the postpresidential experience was like. The representative value of our small sample was further confirmed when we found that their leave-takings provided illustrations of the most common reasons for a change in leadership at a research university: aging out of the job, whether because of reaching the age of retirement or simply reaching a critical point of fatigue between institution and leader; moving on to a more prestigious institution; leaving the academy for an attractive outside opportunity; or being forced out because of an unmanageable or untenable situation. In this last category we had only one president who resigned under pressure, Donald Kennedy, who gave up leadership of Stanford when it became clear that he was too closely identified with the indirect costs controversy to continue effectively.

The resignations of Paul Hardin and Michael Sovern fell into one of the more usual categories of leave-taking, aging out of office. Facing an arbitrary retirement age of sixty-five, Paul Hardin decided to choose his own moment by resigning early but giving his trustees a long lead time before actually stepping down, a strategy meant, as he said, to reenergize his board. Michael Sovern, who was by no means required to retire, nonetheless felt that by year twelve in the job, he "no longer had the patience for it." With his wife Joan seriously ill at home as well, he concluded that although only age sixty-one, he no longer wanted to tackle the "all-consuming" tasks of a president. Despite somewhat mixed circumstances, James Freedman and Harold Shapiro fell primarily into our second category, that of ambition, when they left large midwestern universities to head Ivy League institutions while both were still in their forties. For Freedman, who had planned to pursue another presidency rather than return to teaching law, his own relative youth was the major factor in his being open to outside offers, although the timing of his departure from Iowa was determined by the coincidence of economic difficulties in the state and recruitment by prestigious Dartmouth College in his home state of New Hampshire. Shapiro's situation was somewhat more complicated in that he had planned to return to the faculty at Michigan rather than continuing a presidential career, but the lure of Princeton was a powerful one, reinforced by the coincidental interference of legislators when racial tensions roiled the Ann Arbor campus. While both men cited their particular vulnerabilities at the time, both also indicated that the idea of heading these particular institutions (Dartmouth and Princeton) was profoundly persuasive.

Three of our presidents left university leadership—and the university—entirely, citing attractive opportunities elsewhere and a sense that they were ready to move on. Their situations differed in intensity, however. Vartan Gregorian left Brown to become president of Carnegie Corporation of New York because, in his words, he had "done the [university] presidency." That is, he was reasonably satisfied with his accomplishments at Brown and rather than become stale in the job he preferred to seek new challenges and allow Brown to bring in "new blood . . . another wave of energy." Gregorian made it clear in our interview that his exit decision was not given any impetus by frustration or fatigue; the operative emotion seemed to be a dislike of complacency (which we might be forgiven for reading as boredom or restlessness in the face of the too well known). Although Robert O'Neil also eschewed any description of himself as "burnt out," he nonetheless indicated that his departure from the University of Virginia presidency was a case of career weariness meets golden opportunity. He had spent a total of twenty years in senior administration at universities and felt that if he was ever "to do anything else of substance" it was time to leave that path and accept the offer to head the newly established Thomas Jefferson Center for the Protection of Free Expression (also in Charlottesville). Although press accounts of his surprise announcement reported the usual faculty disgruntlement and, more concerning, suggested possible administrative interference by the UVA board, O'Neil did not mention these factors as influencing his decision. Certainly, the active and highly visible role he has played since 1990 as director of the Thomas Jefferson Center gives ample evidence of his genuine enthusiasm for the change. A similarly appealing opportunity drew Benno Schmidt away from the presidency at Yale, but with the difference that in his account he laid far more stress on the negative aspects of his decision than did O'Neil. Schmidt was courted by The Edison Project at a time when his presidential difficulties and his frustration with the process of dealing with those difficulties had been mounting. After careful thought, he left Yale because the Edison venture sparked in him an idealistic zeal to effect real change in the public schools and because he had become disillusioned with the culture of the university, especially its resistance to change. Schmidt concluded that his entrepreneurial and aggressive leadership style did not fit very well into the mold of the modern-day university president, for whom, he contends, "in most situations, the measure of what counts is raising money, being a good cer-

emonial head of the place, and avoiding trouble." (To be absolutely accurate, both Schmidt and his critics agreed that he was good at raising
money.)

To sum up the exit decisions we surveyed: Most of our presidents left
office on a personal timetable compounded of psychology and circumstance rather than any checklist of accomplishments. Our one exception,
Donald Kennedy, speculated that had he not had to leave office when
he did, a sort of inertial administrative carpe diem would have carried
him forward indefinitely, so long as there was "one more interesting challenge, or a problem . . . unresolved," suggesting that there may be no logical end point for most university presidencies, just an emotional one.
Certainly most of the emotions we heard about with regard to exits (ranging from the negative to the neutral) implied closure: anger (Shapiro),
frustration and disillusionment (Schmidt), defeat (Kennedy), weariness
(Sovern, O'Neil), pride (Hardin), and boredom (Gregorian). Only James
Freedman seems to have gone happily and unambivalently from Iowa to
Dartmouth, with some later regrets.

Having decided to leave office, how did our presidents fare in the waning days of their administrations? By leaving Iowa and Yale soon after
they announced their resignations, James Freedman (at two and a half
months) and Benno Schmidt (at five weeks) avoided any questions of
lame-duck presidencies. Freedman's abbreviated leave-taking seems to
have been just a matter of circumstances, but the swiftness of Schmidt's
departure was advised by Yale's chairman of the board specifically to avoid
a lame-duck period and to allow both Schmidt and the university to get
on with their own agendas. Vartan Gregorian and Harold Shapiro remained in office at Brown and the University of Michigan, respectively,
somewhat longer—approximately eight months each—but discerned no
lame-duck difficulties during that time. Gregorian's strategy was *not* to
step down coincident with the academic year and therefore the budget
cycle, for "if you are controlling the next year's budget . . . you are still
in charge." Shapiro may not have developed a strategy for exercising
power during his final months, but others at Michigan had. Rather than
waiting for the new president to make decisions, "People wanted me to
do things because they knew me and knew what I would do." His task
became one of resisting the pressure to act rather than enduring the in-
dignities of being ignored. Paul Hardin and Donald Kennedy, on the
other hand, planned lengthy periods between announcement and departure (seventeen months and thirteen months, respectively), specifically
to preserve the ability to act—Hardin to neutralize the potential effects
of the UNC system head's mandatory retirement rule and Kennedy to fa-

cilitate a difficult budget process by resolving the question of his presidency during the indirect costs investigation. Shifting the focus from the realm of the political to the psychological, Robert O'Neil and Michael Sovern described a sense of empowerment during their final months in office (ten months for O'Neil, almost thirteen months for Sovern), a license to speak and act without regard to career consequences. O'Neil recalled dealing candidly with members of the Virginia state legislature—"I told it like it was"—and feeling "freer to do the right thing" with regard to some sexual issues on campus, and Sovern cited his work on important but unpopular changes in the Columbia pension plan that he might not have supported had he been apprehensive about the subsequent effect on his ability to lead the university: "I do have to ask myself the question, did my freedom from fear affect that judgment?"

Finally, as power actually changed hands, what was the experience like emotionally as well as practically? Presidents who stay on at their universities after the advent of a successor should probably expect some jolts: Both Michael Sovern and Donald Kennedy cited as a source of unhappiness the firing of personnel from their administrations, especially awkward for Kennedy whose wife was one of those who were terminated "abruptly." Kennedy and Harold Shapiro (who was anticipating his retirement at Princeton) also noted the psychological impact of a drop in the past president's on-campus "interaction rate" (or, as Shapiro put it, the dearth of people "calling me up and making appointments and telling me how important I am"), and the prudence of accepting invitations and appointments that would periodically take them away from campus. On the topic of predecessor/successor relations, the consensus was that these tended to be cordial but distant, a somewhat regrettable but realistic circumstance. Donald Kennedy clearly would have been comfortable with a higher level of interaction between himself and both Richard Lyman and Gerhard Casper. Robert O'Neil, looking back at his own arrivals and departures at Indiana, Wisconsin, and Virginia, expressed surprise at the infrequency with which contact is made from the incumbent side of the presidential gulf: "It's an interesting question why that happens . . . so little reliance [on experienced hands] . . . It's comforting to know that the person is there if you ever really needed to call on him, but in fact, you seldom do." Benno Schmidt's reflections on his relationship with predecessor A. Bartlett Giamatti led to an affectionate and unexpected portrait of Yale's famous president, including Giamatti's "precise view" that what he owed Yale and Schmidt was "essentially withdrawal," and some of the reasons for that attitude: The "shadow of Kingman Brewster" on Giamatti's own new presidency, and his painful sense that once he became president, "old friends and colleagues" approached him "with distrust."

The predictive value of the life cycle hypothesis, that is, whether one must accomplish the tasks and resolve the conflicts associated with one stage of the presidency before moving on to achieve success in the next, was most pronounced at the prelude and honeymoon stages of our subjects' presidencies, when a lack of institutional knowledge or pertinent experience had led most of them into difficulties, some of lingering duration. These negative examples were balanced, however, by less dramatic, positive illustrations of tasks undertaken or conflicts anticipated or resolved successfully at each stage—judgments and decisions that buoyed a presidency as opposed to missteps. James Freedman's accurate estimate, during the prelude phase, of the boards that recruited him to Iowa and Dartmouth, proved to be one of the keys to his later success at these universities. Vartan Gregorian began his honeymoon period at Brown by inserting himself personally into campus conflicts, but with the intention of controlling early perceptions of his presidency among students and faculty, establishing credibility and a style of communication that saw him through subsequent trials. Harold Shapiro secured a long and successful plateau period at Princeton by staying the course of his controversial early decisions there, while Robert O'Neil cited crises during the plateau phase of his chancellorship at Indiana that, negotiated well, had created a bond with the faculty and made a noticeable difference in later cooperation with his administration. Paul Hardin, Donald Kennedy, and Michael Sovern prevented presidential stalemate and negated conflict during the exit phase of their terms by using their resignations as tools for further end-stage presidential accomplishments.

For the most part though, our subjects' narratives suggest that beyond the earliest stages of a presidency, predictions based on the intersection of time, task, and conflict must take into account the diffuse and cumulative nature of conflict within the research university community, the various constituencies that wield power within that community, and the intervention of unpredictable, and uncontrollable, forces from without. Michael Sovern, for example, had a long and generally successful run as Columbia's president, yet with the passage of time he felt the weight of administrative history, of the accumulated enemies and repetitive battles that can weary and eventually stymie a president. Benno Schmidt's much shorter tenure at Yale illustrates that there is no *one* bottom line for such a complex enterprise: His success at the essential presidential tasks of fund-raising, institutional stewardship, labor relations, and garnering the support of important constituencies, in his case Yale's alumni and trustees, was not enough to offset the failure to resolve his image problems among faculty and students. Similarly, Donald Kennedy was able to chart the rise and fall of his fortunes with various university interests across a long career as Stanford's president, underscoring the reality that presidential success and failure at the research university tends to be multilevel and simultaneous. Finally, outside forces may intervene at any time during a presidency and logic, expertise, goodwill, and careful planning count for little. James Freedman, Harold Shapiro, and Donald Kennedy, despite being administrators of proven ability and integrity through years of solid accomplishment, found themselves attacked unfairly and ferociously in the press and in political arenas. When the legislature mandated increased enrollment at the University of Virginia to the vociferous dismay of faculty and students there, Robert O'Neil's hands were tied. As he pointed out in our interview, state politics and bureaucracies can and will disrupt public universities almost overnight, altering agendas and budgets, and straining presidential relations on campus and off. Beyond these and other irrational, political, and bureaucratic human factors of normal dimensions, presidents of both private and public universities may face the task of leading their institutions through unforeseen external realities of near apocalyptic dimensions, including from our sample alone such events as the largest outbreak of Legionnaires' disease at any college or university (Robert O'Neil), the collapse of Rhode Island's Savings and Loans (Vartan Gregorian), the Loma Prieta earthquake (Donald Kennedy), and the Iranian revolution, also known as the second energy crisis (Harold Shapiro).

Overall, we concluded that approaching the university presidency in terms of a life cycle provided a useful paradigm for helping others to understand the conditions under which presidents must operate and for presidents themselves to detect patterns and direct their attention to the long-term consequences of actions and decisions. We found that the developmental model generated a productive interview format that engaged our subjects and garnered quite a lot of frankly and concisely expressed administrative wisdom. This response probably owed much to two factors: the psychological aspects of our questions about their experiences and the admittedly negative cast of our focus, an unusual approach for a higher education leadership study. Because our outline and questions were oriented toward finding specific points of conflict, the resulting texts and analysis yielded a sort of presidential troubleshooting handbook, couched more in the language of problem solving than theory, with specific examples of hard-earned experience, emotional wear and tear, and the mature attitudes and perspectives of old hands at the research university helm. Taken together, their accounts offer evidence for a number of administrative caveats that ring true. It should be noted, however, that these negatives are less pronounced in the context of the individual narratives, where the presidents relate their positive experiences alongside their problems, as readers can discover for themselves in the following pages.

PART II

The Narratives

Donald Kennedy

Stanford University 1980–1992

After earning degrees in biology from Harvard University and holding a tenured position at Syracuse University, in 1960, Donald Kennedy accepted an assistant professorship at Stanford. By 1965 he was a full professor and chairman of the department of biological sciences. Kennedy's national reputation grew swiftly, leading to his appointment as President Jimmy Carter's FDA commissioner in 1977. In 1980, Kennedy came to the presidency of Stanford with broad campus support after serving one year as its vice president and provost. At that time, the university had approximately 1,900 faculty and almost 13,000 students divided about equally between its undergraduate and graduate/professional schools that included business, earth sciences, education, engineering, humanities and science, law, medicine, and a number of research laboratories, centers, institutes, and programs. Stanford's budget of $487 million and endowment of $643 million (the fourth largest in the nation among universities) were not adequate to meet the institution's pressing needs, necessitating budget cuts and an unprecedented $1.1 billion fund drive.[1]

Despite financial concerns, Stanford prospered during the 1980s under Kennedy's leadership, an era summed up in a *Time* magazine accolade of May 16, 1988: "Excellence under the Palm Trees: Brash and Exuberant, Stanford Jostles the Ivies at the Top Ranks of U.S. Universities." But in October 1989, the Loma Prieta earthquake, measuring 7.1 on the Richter scale, caused $160 million in damages to the Stanford campus, increasing the urgency to renew the university's aging science and technology infrastructure. Then, less than a year later, Stanford became the first of a number of research universities attacked by U.S. Representative John Dingell's Subcommittee on Oversight and Investigations (House Energy and Commerce Committee) for their accounting practices used to recover indirect costs of research from the federal government. After nearly a year of negative and frequently inaccurate press attention, Kennedy announced his resignation, effective August 1992. A consensus gradually emerged that Stanford had been a scapegoat, and many supporters echoed Stanford's trustee chairman James Gaither, who judged that Stanford was losing the "best president any university has had in modern times." Donald Kennedy left to his successor an institution whose budget had grown to almost $1.2 billion and whose endowment had more than tripled, to $2.428 billion.[2]

> Donald Kennedy's account of some aspects of his presidency is an edited transcript of his interview with Leslie Banner at Stanford University, July 14, 1998. The questions that prompted his comments have either been omitted or indicated with bracketed material to create a more readable narrative.

I had joined the Stanford faculty in 1960 in a fairly standard role, starting as an assistant professor. I was department chairman in biology for seven years and then got engaged with the founding of the program in human biology. I had also started to do a lot more with science policy and spent six months or so loaned part-time to the new Office of Science and Technology Policy in the Ford White House. Then I did a two-and-a-half-year stint as Commissioner of the Food and Drug Administration during the Carter presidency. I left that position when Stanford invited me to come back as provost in 1979, and about eight months after I started, Dick Lyman announced that he was going to step down from the Stanford presidency and take over the Rockefeller Foundation in New York.

So a search was started, and the provost is a pretty obvious candidate. [Stanford] has had a very good experience with internal candidates for senior academic jobs; at the time, the university had made only internal appointments to the provostship. It had made only one external appointment of a president and that was not successful. Stanford's a place that has always considered that it has a rather special culture, and understanding that culture is important. So I think my faculty experience helped. There was a fair amount of speculation, but the search committee insisted that they were going to look broadly and I suppose they did, although no one has ever told me anything about the operations of the search committee. My appointment was announced right at the time of commencement in 1980. It was a little difficult being that obvious a candidate while continuing to do the provost's work, [having to] avoid commenting on the search, and stay[ing] away from the whole issue. You get a fair number of press inquiries, but I think I contrived to duck those reasonably well.

I don't think anybody who takes a provostship ought to have [the presidency] completely out of mind. Suppose the president dies? If you have a serious commitment to doing academic administration in an institution that you care about—and this has really been my only institution—then you have to consider that as a possibility. However, my expectation was that Dick would go for at least a few more years, and that if I ultimately became a candidate for the presidency, I would be reasonably well prepared. In point of fact, compared with what would have been my preference, it all happened too fast. [I would have preferred] more time to make some judgments about my fellow vice presidents in a collegial setting. When I came back to Stanford from Washington, I knew every single person who was on the senior management team. I joined it, and we became a very collegial unit. We had agreed to meet together for lunch on a weekly basis. We had decided that after ten years, Dick's focus on the job was very good, but his enjoyment of it—the intensity of his engagement with it—had attenuated a little. So we felt that he needed extra support from us. I think it's fair to say that we were very loyal to him, very fond of him. And so we formed a little entente: "Let's give Dick more support, let's figure out for ourselves some things that we should suggest to him." That's a very good circumstance for unity and loyalty to develop in a group of people, and although it is plain that the provost is *primus inter pares* in that group, there was no sense in which I was the boss. I might have been the quarterback, but I wasn't the coach.

Then I became president and the question became, would I keep the players from the Lyman administration? We had a team relationship already. I wasn't coming in on a parachute and looking around saying, "Okay, who are the troops?" I'd worked with them, I'd developed some trust in them, they'd developed some trust in me, and that's a very strong incentive to keep a team together. Which is, in fact, what I did, although I now believe that I made a few mistakes in that department. I was serious about giving people annual performance evaluations and discussing with the board the performance of all of the vice presidents. One of the vice presidents had a difficult problem with clinical depression. He [had] reached a point at which it made him much less effective in his job. I

kept him on too long, trying out modifications in his position that I
thought might allow him to continue. It was a serious mistake. We lost
a lot of effectiveness in that job, and I let his staff get a little too uncomfortable with the lack of leadership. In the end, when I finally did
act, the delay had created an unreasonable climate of expectations on his
part so that the blow came much harder because it was later. The ending was very uncomfortable. The vice president for business and finance,
although he was very smart and still enjoys a good reputation as a consultant on higher education productivity and policy, turned out not to
have terrific judgment about people he was appointing in certain spots—
internal audit, for example—and I relied a little more on his judgments
about appointments than I should have. In the end, when we had our
difficulties with the Dingell subcommittee on indirect costs, he was disappointing in his unwillingness to take personal responsibility and to support the people on his own staff. Now I think I was too tolerant because
we had formed a rather strong bond among us when we were all working for Dick, and that made it more difficult for me to make hard evaluations *de novo*. That was a disadvantage of being an internal candidate
in a particular role, under a particular set of circumstances. What I should
have done is to say to each of those people independently, "Look, I've
got to make sure that we've got the best set here. I've got every reason
to have confidence in you and the way you do your job, but I've got to
go around and get some views about how best to deploy the players we
have in the positions that we have to fill, so I'm going to be asking some
hard questions, and then you and I are going to have another conversation." That way you deflate expectations a little bit, so that people say,
"Okay, now he's the boss, and he's going to take a fresh look at things,
and it's going to be different from the way it was when he was provost."
There is a way to do that.

I don't think the trustees had a particularly strong, positive relationship to some [of these officers] as opposed to others. Two of the vice presidents concerned them, and it was largely a matter of style. There were
reservations about my general counsel because he had a rather close-to-
the-vest air about him, and that put some of them on edge. The lawyers
on the board (there were several successful partners in good private law
firms) believed that nobody who is in-house counsel can be any good.
Thus, because of his personal style, because of this attitude, and because
he would occasionally take a tough line with the board on some conflict
of interest problem, some trustees were not positive about him. The vice
president for public affairs unhesitatingly spoke uncomfortable truths
about certain matters and had a very strong philosophy about the public

affairs posture at this place; it was, "Let it all hang out." The director of the news office covered Stanford like a reporter. He made stuff available to outside journalists and would report Stanford events very objectively—no spin. Both men were enormously respected by the outside media because they knew Stanford would tell it straight, sometimes self-critically. Frank pronouncements on behalf of the university would sometimes give offense on the outside. Some trustees would wince when an acquaintance at the California Club in downtown Los Angeles would say, "What's this I read about Stanford?" Trustees get very edgy about that sort of thing; they ask, "Is he trying to get us in the papers all the time? For God's sake, can't we *not* talk about 'X'?"—not realizing, of course, that *not* talking about "X" just absolutely makes reporters insistent on finding out where under the rug "X" has been concealed.

Actually, I believe that Stanford's general openness and its willingness to let institutional controversies hang out—and I'm thinking here about the "Western Culture" debates, among others—was healthy. After all, one of the university's roles is to sponsor wider discourse about important matters. But I think our policy made our trustees uncomfortable, [though] I didn't really [hear about it from them] until the transition to my successor when it became evident that the trustees were now saying, in effect, "We've had enough of 'letting it all hang out.' " [It's true that] the press treated Stanford badly in the indirect cost business, but I don't think most trustees blamed Stanford's public affairs policies for that. Almost everybody saw that as a breaking political wave that nobody could do much about. It happened to hit us first; it could have hit anybody. There were other issues on which we could have voluntarily maintained a silence and on which the trustees did more blame fixing.

The group that was in place at the time I became president was a terrific board of trustees. I thought they understood the institution quite well, particularly the board's leadership. The board was somewhat weaker at the end of my presidency, and I can't blame anybody but myself for that. I thought we were making good appointments, but we didn't do as well as we might have. Part of what happened was that over a period from the 1970s to the mid-1980s, we lost trustees who were deeply experienced senior figures from an era in which trusteeship was taken much more seriously by most people than it is now. We had people like Bob Brown, a San Francisco lawyer of great distinction and wisdom, who had been a trustee for two long terms and was deeply knowledgeable about the institution. Bob chaired our committee that worked on a lot of the changes in the medical school. That kind of commitment, knowledge, and workmanship is pretty rare now. My relationship with that board was excellent and I think it continued to be excellent for most of my twelve-year term. But beginning in 1987, several events made it a bit bumpier. One was my divorce and remarriage. That's an unusual thing for a president to do in office, and I think some board members said, "What's the matter? Presidents just don't do that. They're not supposed to be like other people and have disruptions in their personal lives." I don't blame the trustees for their reaction.

The second event occurred when, after much internal fussing, we reported to the board a change in housing policy that would have permitted domestic partners to share university housing. Of course, this was widely seen publicly as a "gay" issue. In fact, at the end of the dramatic year in which this decision was made, there were ten domestic partner couples, nine of them, as one waggish correspondent from the San Francisco newspaper put it, "ordinary Jacks and Jills." Although the ratio of symbolism to reality here was pretty high, it was important to report it to the board. I did, and although I asked for comments, there were none. The trustees, after they had a chance to see some press reaction, came back in the next meeting and said, in effect, "What did you pull off on us?" That was a second issue on which I lost some board support.

But had it not been for the indirect cost controversy, those would have been vanishing ripples, I think. During the indirect cost controversy, the board was terrifically supportive, particularly its chair, Jim Gaither, as well as all of the past chairs including Warren Christopher who actually wrote a letter to Chairman Dingell explaining the president's house accounts. But once a process like that gets going, it's pretty hard to stop. One knew that it wasn't going to stop. What the board would have done about leadership in the institution had I not decided to resign, I don't know. I suspect that they would have pushed me pretty hard to step down; once an issue of that kind gets personalized, it's pretty hard to separate institution and person successfully. The way I put it to the board was that if you are perceived as part of the problem, it's very hard to be part of the solution. To repeat: The chairman of the board was unfailing in his support, and the board never took any unsupportive public action. But I believe their feeling would have been, had you asked them to express it, "We've got to have a change." There was probably a variety of views among [the thirty-two] different board members; I had calls from some saying, "Don't even think about resigning," and I know there were two or three who were very anxious to have me gone. But I think they behaved like responsible trustees and let the board leadership speak for the board to the press.

[In regard to the timing of stepping down,] I learned a lesson from Dick

Lyman. At his inauguration Dick was asked by a reporter how long he thought he was going to be president. He said, "Well, I don't know, about ten years," which is what most presidents will say if you just ask them, stone cold, "How long do you think you're going to serve?" That's a number that pops into one's mind; a decade sounds respectably long and doesn't tie you up for the rest of your life. Well, Dick said it. What he discovered is that reporters have tickler files. So in the ninth year, he starts hearing, "When are you going to step down?" Having learned that you should never do that, I didn't say anything.

What was in my mind? It's hard to say. In 1990, the trustees had an event to celebrate my tenth anniversary; it was a wonderful evening and they gave me some nice mementos. I believed that the board had adjusted to my new marital state; they knew Robin because she had worked for the university and they had started to think, "Well, this is really okay. This new wife must be very committed to the university because she's got a demanding full-time job as a Stanford lawyer, and she's being a heavily engaged presidential partner for another thirty-five hours a week." In June we had the Gorbachev visit, which was a huge event here, and a wonderful commencement; then, in July of 1990, the Dingell committee arrives. For the next academic year, I was totally absorbed in trying to deal with that problem and executing some considerable budget cuts. The economic glass had turned dark in 1990, and everybody was looking around. We had gotten a jump on the problem with a significant budget cut early on; it produced a story the trustees actually liked on the front page of the *New York Times*, headlined, "How Stanford, Wealthy and Wise, Is Cutting Costs to Stay That Way" [July 8, 1990]. So, we had another cut coming, and the provost, an economist, and I were working hard at that and preparing for the onslaught from Dingell. There soon followed a volley of leaked stories to the newspapers, particularly the *San Jose Mercury-News*, a paper that is much read around here. The hearing was in March; we looked terrible in the hearing, although not as terrible as the local press made us look in reporting it. Time passed. Commencement happened, and we started putting together the committees to do this next round of budget cuts. As I talked to faculty about these things, it became evident that you couldn't get them settled down to talk about budget cuts because they were busy asking themselves, what's going to happen? what's the subcommittee going to do? what's OMB going to do about circular A-21? Is Kennedy a lightning rod for this problem? There was so much uncertainty that it was hard to focus on normal, necessary business. The board had a scheduled midsummer meeting, and having talked to the chairman, several board members, and some faculty, I ation, we weren't going to get anything done. So I announced my resignation a year hence, and that clarified the situation.

How long would I have stayed had the indirect cost controversy not happened? I tend to be a person with considerable inertia. All it takes to keep me on the same path for an extra year or an extra month normally is one more interesting challenge, or a problem that I don't feel good about leaving unresolved. What I had in my head was a couple of years, but it might easily have turned into five. Some people whom I regard as the most successful presidents actually went seventeen or eighteen. That's true of Bill Bowen at Princeton and Frank Rhodes at Cornell, and Derek Bok went almost twenty at Harvard.

[My presidency began with a honeymoon,] no question about it. I think you can't define "honeymoon" until you specify, honeymoon with whom? The president has a number of constituencies; we've talked about changes in my relationship with the trustees and the events that might have, at various points, attenuated the solidity of that relationship. There's an equally important relationship with the faculty, and I would say that went on very well until the late 1980s when various kinds of faculty concerns arose, some about political issues, some about the rate of increase in indirect costs, which involved publicly aired dissatisfactions about the rate. Among the science faculty there was a feeling that I did not respond early enough to their complaints. So in 1988 or 1989 there was a fairly significant drop in my relationship with some faculty. As to the student body, I had a reputation as a teacher long before, and I think students appreciated the fact that someone had been appointed to the presidency from the faculty who really cared about teaching. I liked to participate in student life, to invest in it through initiatives like public service and our new campus in Washington, D.C. I would say that I had good relationships with the student body all along although the controversy over South African divestment hurt that relationship for a period in the mid-1980s. Some of the faculty—a small, far-left fraction—and significant numbers of students wanted blanket divestment of all stock in all companies doing business in South Africa. I never was convinced that was the thing to do. We did actually adopt, and the trustees actively supported, a policy in which companies doing business in South Africa were contacted and asked about their compliance with the Sullivan principles and their future plans. If we were troubled, we would request a change in policy and/or further information, and if the company stiffed us, we divested. We didn't do that with a great many companies, but we did it with some. Occasionally, the trustees would appear with me at mass meetings, and we would explain our position to the students and get booed. Some of our trustees were really good about standing up for Stanford's policies.

My relations with alumni were pretty good. Alumni are distant from the president of the university. I think their picture is apt to be derived from what they read about the president and what he is doing, and they see that through the lens of their own political convictions. Some conservative alumni were unhappy with the degree to which I was committed to increasing minority enrollment, promoting public service, and supporting changes in the Western Culture curriculum—they saw those things as rather left-liberal. But they found that very hard to square with other positions, that I was quite supportive of the athletic program, for example. So they confronted various versions of me which they got through the press or through occasional talks I gave. It's very difficult to generalize about alumni, but the institution was doing well, the fundraising went very well, and generally Stanford was seen favorably by the world, except during the indirect cost controversy.

[In regard to my attitude toward risk taking, I think that] risk taking is a complicated matter for presidents because trustees and others regard the president as embodying the institution. One may talk about taking risks as though they are personal risks, but you cannot dissociate yourself from the institution. My attitude is that as the voice of the institution, the president ought to be willing to inject himself and it into important debates about what the institution's business is. But presidents should not inject themselves into issues in which they have neither personal standing by way of experience and knowledge, or in which there is no definable special university interest. If, in some national debate about the new drug approval process, I were invited by the *New York Times* to express a view as the ex-commissioner of the FDA, I would feel perfectly comfortable doing so because my personal experience with the issue is considerable and because it's so plainly unrelated to my present role at the university. Nobody would mistake it as somehow involving Stanford. If there were a controversy about selective service as it applied to students or about student financial aid, I would certainly want to reflect my views and the university's on those issues. I would try to keep the trustees informed about what I was doing, but I wouldn't consider it their task to edit my remarks.

Even if it does involve some personal and institutional risk, university presidents ought to seek ways of expressing themselves on such matters because universities ought to be centers of national dialogue. Many of today's trustees have a quite different view, that presidents, like nineteenth-century children, should be often seen and seldom heard. They don't want to see the name of their institution in the newspaper except for the sports page and an occasional op-ed policy pronouncement in an admirable context by some faculty member. I just don't feel that trustees are into risk taking at all. Some presidents need to push boards, to make it plain that it's important for their institution to be right in the middle of important policy issues. I made some decisions to be much more public about situations in which I thought there might be some risk, some public disapprobation that might cost me some of the confidence of the board. For example, I decided to debate the secretary of education on the McNeil-Lehrer program about the changes in the Stanford curriculum. It's not a light decision to exchange fairly harsh words with a member of the president's cabinet who is of the political party of perhaps half your trustees. But it never occurred to me not to do it. There's some risk of looking foolish, but I had done that sort of thing a fair amount and I wasn't worried about that. I expected that the people who favored Secretary Bennett's point of view were going to think that he won the argument and that those who favored mine were going to think that I won. But I wanted my own community to know that I was not hesitant to go and argue our case on the merits with someone who had the advantage of position. Bennett did say unpleasant things about Stanford, but fortunately the people at Stanford knew they weren't true.

[You asked about the Hoover Institution:] Hoover was a problem in two ways. The first is that W. Glenn Campbell, the ex-director, is a truly unpleasant person for whom conflict is entertainment. That's not just my opinion; eventually it came to be shared by his own board of overseers and his colleagues. He had been in constant battle with the two presidents before me, and with large numbers of the Stanford faculty, whom he regarded as leftists. Of course, some of those could not resist taking a poke at him and Hoover at every opportunity. He in turn couldn't resist annoying them with provocative statements. At one point Campbell and others persuaded Ronald Reagan that he should locate his presidential papers and the presidential library on the Stanford campus. When he presented this to me, I said that an allocation of Stanford land to this purpose would have to rest on whether the Stanford faculty saw an advantage to scholarship in having the presidential papers. Campbell then added that there would be a museum and a Ronald Reagan Center for Public Policy to be affiliated with the Hoover Institution. So we appointed a distinguished faculty committee to look at this proposal and make a recommendation. The committee reported that it would very much like to have access to the presidential papers, which would be a boon to Stanford scholarship and would bring other scholars here. But it concluded that the public policy center ought to be under normal academic governance. That produced a brouhaha in the course of which two trustees and I flew back to Washington to meet with Attorney General Meese in the White House to negotiate. Finally, it was decided that there wouldn't be a public policy center or a museum with memorabilia.

As things went along, I had to fight two battles, one against Campbell and his board and others who thought we were being picky about the public policy center, and a second against faculty and others who didn't like the idea of a Reagan *anything* on the campus. You can imagine how popular Ronald Reagan was with the average research university faculty.

A lease negotiation followed over a piece of Stanford land in the foothills, and soon faculty and neighborhood residents were raising issues about visual impairment of space, architectural design, land use and land planning, traffic—most of them stalking horses for unrelated political objections. I had to resist that, and at the same time hold Campbell at bay. It was a difficult time and certainly did involve some risk. The Stanford trustees were sympathetic and helpful. A scholarly library containing presidential papers could hardly be turned down; if a higher education institution says "no" to that, it's open to charges of political correctness, especially when its own historians, including some who have written long critical articles about the Reagan administration in the *Atlantic Monthly*, are saying it's a good thing to have. Eventually, with help from trustee negotiators, we got the Hoover Institution Board of Overseers to usher W. Glenn Campbell out. He's been replaced by a thoughtful, conservative, thoroughly decent man, and the Hoover is now making all kinds of joint appointments with the Stanford faculty. They have a very valuable archive and twenty years from now nobody will remember that the institute was a terrible thorn in our side. That's one of the accomplishments of my time here which, because of all the acridity that accompanied it, won't be recognized. But we brought the Hoover Institution into the fold, and it is very valuable to the campus.

[The governance structure of the Hoover is confusing to many.] The ultimate terms negotiated between Herbert Hoover and Stanford describe it as an "independent institution within the frame of Stanford University." The director of the Hoover Institution reports to the president of Stanford University, and the board of trustees of Stanford University owns the Hoover Institution, lock, stock, and barrel, although the past director tried to pretend that wasn't so. The Hoover Institution has a board of overseers that appoints new members and meets regularly; it is an oversight committee but has no fiduciary responsibility whatsoever.

[Stanford can get rid of a director of the Hoover,] but it would be very unwise to do that without the support of the board of overseers. We had to bring that board along; they didn't want to recognize reality for a long time, but finally they did. I pushed hard to take Hoover on where it needed to be taken on, but I supported the Reagan Library. Both of those were somewhat high-risk decisions. In doing the first, I risked some opposition from trustees and conservatives; in doing the second, I really risked some alienation from Stanford liberals.

[Did I become a lame duck during the end phase of my presidency?] No, it was an unusual circumstance. Lame-duckness only matters in terms of the relationship between the president and the faculty and the senior administrative officers of the institution. The latter were pretty much aligned with me in trying to get through the business and resolve it. If I can characterize the modal faculty reaction during the indirect cost recovery investigation, it was, "Kennedy's been a pretty good president. I think he missed seeing something on indirect costs and we're paying a price for that. I don't know whether Dingell has something personal here, but I wonder if, as long as Kennedy continues to be president, we won't continue to be attacked in this way? So I'm pretty nervous about it." When I said in July, "I'm done after this year," all that was clarified; the attitude was, "Now, let's get down to business and search for a successor. We'll do the work we need to do with respect to budget cuts and so forth." I brought in a terrific guy to work with me as a deputy, Ted Mitchell, a young former trustee who had been on the faculty at Dartmouth and now is dean of education at UCLA. On balance, I didn't feel like a lame duck at all. Now, you will hear faculty say Building 10 (the president's and provost's offices) lost a lot of its authority in that period of time, but I don't think we needed a lot of nominal authority. We had a strong provost who was running a good budget reduction process along with a faculty-trustee committee. [My resignation in fact facilitated] an ambiguity reduction that was enormously helpful. Although it was not a very happy year in terms of public relations, it worked fine.

[You asked whether I had discussed an agenda for my presidency with the trustees.] I had had some discussions at the time [of my appointment], and then I tried to lay out some institutional needs in my inauguration talk in October of 1980; that is as close to an agenda as I had. A writer here decided to do a piece for the Stanford Historical Society on what had happened during my presidency and its relationship to the agenda I'd set out in my inaugural. I think she concluded that we did do most of the things that I felt were important. We needed a reemphasis on the humanities, and we made a lot more appointments in that area and established a Humanities Center that I think is one of the best in the country. We needed to restore some serious attention to undergraduate education, and I think we made some progress on that. There was a set of facilities needs and we met some of those. I think there was some resistance [to the emphasis on undergraduate education]; some faculty thought that I had been too negative about how well we were doing in that area. There were three views: One, "We're doing fine; what right does he have to come and tell us what we ought to do differently?" Two, "Well, there certainly is some room for improvement, but it may be unwise for him to make his views public because it implies that we're not already doing good things." And then the third group, probably smaller than the second, said, "Boy, that's what we need!" There was a diversity of reactions, some of it negative, [but] once we got it into the conversation, more and more people started talking about it. My successor appointed a commission to evaluate undergraduate education at Stanford, and some excellent innovations have come out of that, so I think we started a good process.

[In regard to budget cutting and faculty attitudes:] There is always some skepticism. We tried to spare academic programs as much as we could, and we managed to take the first $40 million out of the operating budget without seriously damaging academic programs. After that, it became harder. If somebody tells you he wants a budget cut, the first thing to ask is, "Have you done this before?" because each time an increment is taken it gets harder to do it again. [Fortunately,] we had a very strong provost who was an economist respected for his businesslike approach, and his knowledge of numbers helped a lot. [We maintained credibility] through two rounds of hard budget cutting. Now, there was one problem with the trustees. When the joint trustee-faculty committee discussed further budget cuts, the trustees looked for a dramatic sign that we were evaluating large units, not just cutting across the board. I think they wanted to see a school or a department or two go. I felt that by selectively pruning a little farther out from the big branches, we could achieve the same result. It would be unfair to characterize our strategy as across the board, but it certainly was not at the level of whole schools or even whole departments. I can't judge what has happened since. The Food Research Institute was eliminated; it was always an odd department in the school of humanities and sciences. I suspect that they cut one large unit just to satisfy everybody that they were serious and eliminated the weakest one they could find. Unfortunately, it was the only large unit at Stanford seriously engaged with the developing world. Trustees do have a right to say, "As you prepare your budget for us to approve, we would like to have a clear view of your strategic thinking, and we reserve the right to ask whether you are comparing effectiveness at the level of whole programs." That's a legitimate concern for the board. I just happen to think that in this instance they pushed too hard for cuts at the major branch level.

[To respond to your question about the psychology of uncoupling from the presidency:] Many people manage the problem [of letting go] by going away and doing something quite different. I have essentially given my entire career to this institution. I care a lot about it and I wanted to stay in it. I also think that it's useful to demonstrate occasionally that the presidency, after all, is an episode in an academic career. Going back to the faculty has been a wonderfully positive experience for me. I've done a lot of teaching in different areas, especially with undergraduates. I think I'm good at that, and it's been very engaging. I've made a fair number of outside commitments to keep myself busy and to take me away from time to time. I'll be frank to say that the transition was a difficult one for me, partly because I had to cope with both a drop in my own interaction rate and the sense that there was a deliberate effort to make a sharp break with my part of the institution's history. That was a little difficult to take for a while; it took me about two years to adjust and move on. Several people that had been important parts of my life in the institution, including the general counsel and the vice president for public affairs, were terminated. The new general counsel had the idea to outsource virtually all of Stanford's legal work and to shrink the staff abruptly; my wife was the first to go, in a rather public way. That was a little hard to take.

There was also something alienating about the style of the presidential transition itself. The search committee had been working away for a few months, and in casual conversation a faculty member told me that they were about three weeks away from a decision. The chairman of the board called me up one morning just a couple of days later and said, "I assume the search committee's been keeping you up to date on progress?" And I said, "Well, no." And he said, "Oops," and then he announced the selection of Gerhard Casper who, he said, was getting on a plane in Chicago that morning. So I said, well, of course he must stay with us, etc., and that came to pass. The transition was perfectly cordial, but it started in an awkward way, [then] was followed by a fairly low interaction, and I don't know the extent to which that differs from the standard experience. It does seem to me that it could have been handled differently, but there's a strong view among many managers, including my old boss in government, Joe Califano, that if you come in from the outside, you want to make the sharpest break you can—get rid of anybody you think may be loyal to others and create a new inner circle of management. Increasingly, some trustees are echoing calls from industry that universities should work toward a more corporate model. There's a lively debate about that now, people like Dick Mahoney, the ex-CEO of Monsanto, saying to universities, "What's the matter with you guys? Why can't you be more like us?" Dick Lyman went to head the Rockefeller Foundation; he met his last commitments to Stanford, flew to New York, and took right over. Dick and I are good friends. We've had a close relationship, and during the first year I tried to make sure that every achievement of the Lyman presidency was given lots of attention.

NOTES

1. Stanford University, *Stanford Facts 1980/81*, pp. 5, 9, 12, and Stanford University, *Courses and Degrees 1980–81, 1990–91*, provided by Department of Special Collections and University Archives, Stanford University Libraries; Don F. Speich, "Donald Kennedy, Stanford Provost, Named President," *Los Angeles Times*, June 14, 1980, Morning Final Edition, sec. 2, p. 1.

2. Nadine Brozan, "Stanford President's Decision Is Praised," *New York Times*, July 31, 1991, Late Edition, p. A16; Stanford University, *Annual Financial Report 1992*, Department of Special Collections and University Archives, Stanford University Libraries; "The Nation: Resources—College and University Endowments Over $35-Million, 1992," *Chronicle of Higher Education*, August 25, 1993, p. A40, survey by National Association of College and University Business Officers.

Harold Shapiro

University of Michigan 1980–1987
Princeton University 1988–2001

Only forty-four years old when he was named president of the University of Michigan on July 27, 1979 (to take office in January 1980), Harold Shapiro had spent his entire academic career at Michigan. Arriving in 1964 with a Ph.D. from Princeton, the increasingly distinguished economist climbed the ranks from assistant to full professor in only six years. From 1974 to 1977 he served as chairman of the department of economics and from 1977 to 1979 as vice president for academic affairs (provost). The scope of the job Shapiro accepted in 1979 after only five years of experience in academic administration can be illustrated by a thumbnail institutional profile of the time: The university's endowment had a reported market value of $100.5 million and its budget was $584.4 million; the 2,465 faculty members taught 47,081 students, of whom 32,971 were undergraduates. When Shapiro stepped down in 1987, the number of students had increased only slightly, to 49,244 (with 35,216 undergraduates), but the faculty had increased to 3,619, the budget to $1.327 billion, and the endowment to $287.5 million. By one estimate of his presidency, Harold Shapiro had "lifted Michigan in seven years from financial crisis to a prosperous institution loaded with new research facilities."[1]

The contrast with Princeton, where Shapiro was installed as president in January 1988, was striking. On the Ann Arbor campus, the University of Michigan consisted of some eighteen schools, both professional and academic,[2] while Princeton was composed of five much smaller schools: Undergraduate and graduate study in the arts and sciences; architecture, engineering, and public affairs. The faculty of 931, student body of 6,190 (4,564 undergraduates), and budget of $372 million were comparatively small, but Princeton's endowment of $2.308 billion dwarfed Michigan's.[3]

Harold Shapiro's account of selected aspects of his presidencies combines edited transcripts of his two interviews with Leslie Banner, the first, on March 26, 1997, in the Office of the President at Princeton University, and the second, on March 31, 1998, by telephone from Duke University. The questions that prompted his comments have either been omitted or indicated with bracketed material to create a more readable narrative.

My appointment as president coincided with the second energy crisis which occurred in 1979, and if you lived in the state of Michigan at that time, you knew what the implications were: Energy prices skyrocketed again and the American automobile industry entered a very troubled period of its history, bringing a recession to the state of Michigan. This meant that state support for the university would undoubtedly fall, which became quite clear almost right away.

Therefore, if there was a honeymoon period in my presidency, it was short. I saw immediately that the only way to sustain the quality of the university in these circumstances was to make it smaller, and so I adopted a slogan, "Smaller but better." Now that slogan was not meant to say that smaller *is* better, but that in our circumstances, the only way to get better was to get smaller. That meant I had to start deciding where it was that we were going to get smaller since I had rejected the notion of just getting smaller everywhere by the same amount.

There were parts of the university for which I thought growth was very important, and we had to finance that growth from somewhere. At the same time, we not only needed to find resources for selected growth but also to make up the shortfall in state funding which lay ahead. And so we were faced immediately with the problem of identifying areas of the university that were going to have to be cut back or eliminated—always a hard thing to do. We closed some programs, we dramatically reduced the size of others, and each one of those decisions was the struggle you would expect it to be with the faculty in those areas that were negatively affected which, as you know, is not at all uncommon. To give an example, we closed the geography department and the geographers of the world descended on us both in writing and in person to tell us how we were altering the course of Western civilization and so on. We closed a number of programs, but more commonly we reduced the size of other programs by 25 percent or 30 percent. I was determined, one, to do what I could to sustain the quality of the university, and two, to enable the university to grow in areas where we could not afford simply to maintain the status quo. Whether it was the library or the law school or the business school or whatever it was, I really did want to work out strategies that would permit the university to grow and contract at the same time—that is, to grow in selected areas.

That was difficult and I'm not sure we always did it in the best possible way, but we did do it. Although there was a tremendous amount of angst about it at the time—anxiety and accusations of various kinds—in the years since I have hardly met anybody from the University of Michigan who hasn't said how appropriate the strategy was under those particular circumstances. These latter-day allies were not there, I can assure you, during the hard times. No one was there telling me how wonderful it was then. But now, looking back, they all say it. I was just speaking recently to the new president of the University of Michigan, Lee Bollinger (who had been dean of the Michigan Law School and then provost at Dartmouth before going back to Michigan as president), and he said, "You know, I remember the seventies and early eighties and we were in all that trouble, and I got the highest raise I ever received in all my time as a professor. It really made the point to me that what you were trying to do was see that the people who were really carrying the load would be treated well no matter what the circumstances were."

All that happened very, very early in my presidency, [but because] I had spent three years as provost, I felt I knew what the university needed to do. And even though I didn't anticipate the energy crisis, which made the situation more dramatic, I had worked out in my head a strategy for where to take the University of Michigan, with or without an energy crisis. For example, I had decided that at a place like Michigan, given its situation at that time, in the late 1970s, the way to strengthen the overall university was to begin on the periphery by strengthening the professional schools—not at all an obvious strategy, I don't think. Most people would say, that's not the core of the university, you've got to start with the arts and sciences. In Michigan's circumstances at the time, I came to exactly the opposite conclusion, to strengthen the periphery and then move that strength into the core. It wasn't a matter of philosophy so much as just what was possible at the time, given the way you could generate resources in these professional schools—you weren't quite so dependent on the state. And therefore, rather than just wait until the state's economy improved, what I thought we would do is strengthen the periphery while we had a chance, try to focus on the smaller-but-better strategy in the core until the situation improved. The periphery would be strengthened, we'd also get better in the arts and sciences core though a little smaller, and then that would give us something to work on in future years. We had a double-pronged strategy. I don't mean to be repetitive, so you'll excuse me, but what you've got, if you think of it three, four years ahead of time, you have your periphery strengthened, you have your core a little smaller but stronger, and then when times get better you can move to expand. That was the overall strategy.

I knew that there were selected professional schools I wanted to strengthen (the law school and the business school were both dramatically improved during that period) and I knew that no matter what happened, we had to find some way to revolutionize our medical center, which meant spending hundreds of millions of dollars. And I knew that I had a budget problem on my hands. I had a pretty good idea of what the issues were, and indeed, when I was provost, I had adopted a strategy of taxing every department's budget throughout the whole university one percent a year. Everybody thought, "One percent, that sounds reasonable, fine." It doesn't sound like a lot, but I assure you this adds up. Michigan's a big university—even in those years we're talking about millions of dollars. I accumulated this tax in a pot, so to speak, and I would then allocate it to our highest priority needs. So some departments might end up way ahead out of this little reallocation. It meant that I had some resources, even when I was provost, to begin doing things, to begin showing the faculty and others that I meant what I said. In the first year I put it all in the library's acquisition budget, something which everybody could support. The next year most of it went to graduate student support. People began to see that yes, we were in a difficult situation, but somebody here has a notion of what should be happening. When, as I became president, the energy crisis hit, the situation changed quantitatively but not qualitatively. The campus had been prepared, if anybody was listening, because during the time I was provost we were moving in these directions. The energy crisis just made it mandatory that we move more quickly.

Many faculty may not have agreed with my strategy, but they knew I'd spent fifteen years at the university and had some basic understanding of the situation. It's like anything else—when you announce a strategy like this, you want to focus on the need—above all—to sustain quality. You don't want to just go on as you were, you want to change for the better. So everybody says, "Yes, yes, yes, yes." Obviously, the logic of such a policy is at least somewhat compelling. Until, of course, you start to implement it, and some people have to say, "Hey, that was *me* he was talking about when he said some departments will have to be cut back or eliminated." Then, of course, those who are unaffected go about their business as usual and it's not their problem, while those who are affected are understandably very upset. I found it very upsetting myself. No one likes to tell a group of colleagues who have worked loyally for the university for a long time, "You're not as big a part of our future as you were of our past." It's a very unpleasant prospect and I didn't like doing it.

There was a period when we were holding public hearings on all this, allowing faculty and students and others to protest, which they did. And they didn't bother using measured language as I would use measured language. And so, it was psychologically difficult to do it, but you know, you get the courage to do these things because you really believe in the institution and where you're going. I was very conscious the whole time that I could be making a mistake. After all, nobody is sure. I knew that the strategy could be wrong, but I knew it was better than just staying where we were. At least, I sensed that we really had to demonstrate movement. So if you look at the University of Michigan in all those years—1979, 1980, 1981—you'll see very rapid growth in some of the professional schools, rapid growth in the library budget, pretty good salary increases, but we had to pay for all those things. We had to pay by becoming less of a presence in certain areas in order that we could move forward. Now, we also did other things. We increased our federal research budget, we increased our tuition—it wasn't all accomplished simply by this reallocation. But that was a major component of it. And I still believe, in retrospect, not that I would have done everything the same way, not at all—maybe I chose the wrong departments, maybe I should have done more, I'm sure there were better ways to do it—but that the basic strategy was right because we came out of the energy crisis in 1984, 1985, 1986, in much better shape than we went into it. And that was very satisfying.

There were a lot of risks involved. We ran the big risk, in my view, of faculty in the core of the university thinking that we didn't care about them, that they were being phased out, that the administration didn't care about anything except professional education. The big risk there, in that sense, was misunderstanding, and I think in this particular case we managed to avoid that, largely by not talking about the strategy too often. So I can't claim a whole lot of courage or credit because I tried not to force people to face up to this strategy more than was necessary to get the job done.

But to go to the issue of what risks were taken: In the medical center, where the hospital was built in the 1920s and was hopelessly antiquated and the medical school had missed some steps as we went from specialization to subspecialization to subsubspecialization, I felt that we weren't as good as we thought we were. During the early 1980s I predicted it would take a billion dollars to reconstitute the medical center, and we managed to do that despite the recession in Michigan. We borrowed lots of money and we weren't sure what it would mean to pay it back, so in some sense we went into debt in a major way in order both to get matching funds and to do all kinds of things before we had any final resolution as to whether we would have the ability to pay it back. Let me give you an example. The state said if we would make a substantial investment in the construction for the medical center, they would also make a very large commitment. Well, at that time if you recall, inflation in the early eighties was rising very quickly, and the state couldn't quite decide just how to finalize this agreement with the university. So I decided that I would put our investment in anyway and begin constructing our new medical center without any final commitment from the state that they would come across with their share because inflation was proceeding at around ten percent a year, so that the state's fixed-dollar commitment was worth less and less all the time. I just felt we had to get ahead of inflation, we had to take that chance and demonstrate our confidence in what we were doing and our confidence that the state would in fact meet its agreement to support this project as we went along. And they did. But on the day we borrowed one hundred and some odd million dollars, we didn't know, no one knew.

So that's an example of what you might think of as a financial risk, as opposed to other kinds of risks. To go to another risky area, one of the ways we built up some of the professional schools at that time was by following two strategies: increasing the proportion of out-of-state enrollments where fees are a lot higher and increasing the fees themselves very quickly. That was a combination of financial and political risk, i.e., would the increase in out-of-state enrollments offend the sensibilities of state legislators regarding what they thought was appropriate? and second, would we in fact run ourselves ahead of the market? That is, would we continue to be able to attract the quality of student body we wanted? It was a risk because at that time University of Michigan out-of-state tuition was very close to private university tuition, and so we had both a political and what you might call a market risk at stake. Both of those happened to work out very well. We did reach a political ceiling on out-of-state enrollments eventually. When we started doing this, we were at something like 18 percent out-of-state enrollment on the undergraduate level. I think we ended up over 30 percent. Then subsequent to my leaving for Princeton, the university did run into some political issues in this area, but by then, I believe the risk had paid off—we had been able to gain some strength during a difficult period economically although the strategy did cause some problems later on, there's no question about it. We had used the argument that this was actually doing a "favor" for the rest of the universities in the state, who would then have better quality in-state students for themselves. That played for a while! You know, some of these arguments are a little humorous. Ours was actually true, but nevertheless also very self-serving.

To give you an idea of a risk that I think didn't work out—and again, it's of a different kind—we decided that in making our budget cutbacks, we would allow for extensive on-campus discussion, faculty review groups, students, etc., on the idea that if the community understood better, had a chance to participate in these difficult decisions, they would find them more acceptable. And we followed through on that plan. It is my judgment in retrospect that this process just prolonged the agony for everybody and was actually costly in the end. We had a longer period of uncertainty as people felt that they could in fact get in the way of change, and while I certainly did not learn from that experience that one shouldn't have such a process, I think we in fact erred on the side of having too much discussion, and it became costly. I think we could have served everybody better. We certainly learned something in this process, but we didn't learn much after a while—after a while it was just repeating with more and more vehemence, and more and more anger, and more and more this, and more and more that, and I think it wasn't serving anybody, either the individuals involved or the departments involved or the university or anybody, because it just got to be unproductive. I think some of that is very important, but in my view we overdid it.

[How long it went on] I don't really remember, but I would say, once a preliminary set of propositions was announced—this is what we might do, this is what we suggest—maybe a year. Now, I know if someone called me back and said I've checked the date and it's eight months, I'd believe that, too. I just don't remember. You see, what happens is, nine-tenths of the campus are completely unaffected because they escape, they go about their business and disappear into the woodwork. And everyone else mobilizes themselves as if the world is coming to an end. I often say to students, "Try the best you can to maintain a sense of perspective: not every disappointment is a holocaust." There are some things that are really tough and big and awful and dangerous and so on, and some things are just unpleasant. Quite understandably, many people have a very hard time with these types of issues when they touch on something that matters deeply to them, as opposed to abstract budget principles.

[In taking these risks I had the advantage of] an external circumstance you could look at and everybody could read about in the paper every day, that had nothing to do with us. Normally, we were held responsible for most things, but not for the energy crisis. That was the Shah of Iran's energy crisis, that was when the Shah was deposed and oil prices skyrocketed again, and it was before the U.S. automobile industry restructured itself. So they had both the oil shock and these tremendous inroads made by the Japanese auto companies to deal with. I have the Ann Arbor paper at home which says in big headlines, "Shapiro Appointed President," and on the right hand side it says, "General Motors Lays off 36,000." These things were coincident with each other. So I knew going into the presidency I was going to have to do something. This wasn't going to be business as usual.

[By 1984, 1985, we had entered] a somewhat more normal phase. It wasn't an expansive phase, but the sharp decreases in state support had more or less stopped, we were starting to see small increases, and the state was beginning to get itself together again after a very difficult adjustment. Throughout this whole period I had the support of the board. I had a very, very good board, an excellent board. And I certainly couldn't have done the kind of things we needed to do in the very late seventies and early eighties without the full support of the board. The board at Michigan is very small, only eight people, elected in a statewide election. You always know whether or not you have the support of your board. I placed my single highest priority on building and sustaining their support. Nothing was more important because you don't need a majority to stop you. You can be stopped by much less than a majority because every member of that eight-person board has the capacity to hold up a lot of actions. They can be overridden eventually, but it's trouble. So I always put an enormous emphasis on keeping close to the board and sustaining their support. I don't want to give you the impression that was hard. It was not so hard in those years because they were very supportive. You know, you do start out with the support of the board. After all, they appoint you. Okay, so in the first year or two you're not about to lose their support. It really comes later if it's going to come. I was just very fortunate in that respect—I didn't have any real problem. I think part of the reason was that unlike some of my colleagues, I always—regardless of what I thought of the board members individually—gave them the utmost respect because I respected what they stood for. Even if I didn't always respect their opinions or didn't always respect them as people, that was in my view irrelevant. This was a group of people who in some sense owned the university, in the sense of having all the power, and for that reason they deserved respect. I suppose they could have done something outrageous that would have caused me to resign, but otherwise, I thought then that it paid enormous dividends for the president to respect the board, both individually and as a group. You take people seriously, they take you seriously; you take them lightly, they take you lightly. So I had very few and relatively minor problems with the board. They supported me steadily throughout all this. I never had any serious problems.

I may be fooling myself, but in terms of the overall faculty I believe I had their support throughout this period. There was never any problem in the faculty senate of any major proportions. Now, people came in and complained but I never had any serious problems. There were some tensions, but they were really very modest in terms of this issue because intellectually I had taken a defensible position. There were some faculty who were extremely angry—some individuals, some groups of faculty. But—to use one measure as an example—you sometimes read in the paper that faculty somewhere have signed a petition of no confidence in their president—nothing like that ever happened. I don't know the reason. It was early in the game. In those years, the early eighties, the rest of the country was more or less booming and there weren't that many universities in trouble. It was only later that the states started feeling some pressures and a lot of state universities got into trouble. But in the early eighties there were not many universities in our position.

[My decision to leave Michigan came about when several] things happened to coincide. First, I had completed a set of big projects that I had set in motion. The medical center was completed in an almost revolutionary way. The professional schools we had started to strengthen were in excellent shape—if you look at rankings they were all much higher than they had been in the past. I had done a whole series of things I felt I had started out to do. I completed the first capital campaign Michigan had had in fifteen or twenty years, which by today's standards was modest, but anyway, it was done and completed. So I felt I'd come to a good point. And in fact, I had begun discussing with my wife whether I should return to the faculty. It wasn't being tired, and it wasn't that I thought I was underappreciated, quite the opposite. I felt good, I felt that people had been extremely appreciative of my efforts at Michigan, and the board had been supportive. But this assessment did coincide with a very interesting flare-up of racial tensions on campus.

I had a particular set of experiences with African American legislators in Michigan and with certain kinds of talk radio in Michigan that led me to think two things: "Maybe I can't be a good representative of this university anymore. Maybe they need a different kind of person here." And in any case, even if that were wrong, even if my judgment were too harsh on myself then, I thought, "You know, I don't need to do this, I don't have to put up with this." I viewed myself as trying to provide a social product for the state, and then to have legislators who were trying to take advantage of a difficult ongoing situation to lay the burden of all the social pathology of this country on the university and on my shoulders—you know, I didn't need that. In addition, my wife was particularly frightened by some anti-Semitic comments that occurred in and around that time on talk radio. I said to myself, "Gosh, what do I need this for? I've got a nice life, I don't have to put up with this." So those two things came together, both the completion of a phase at the university and a very unpleasant situation. And it wasn't the tension and issues on campus that were unpleasant, not at all. [It was the outside, public attacks.] And so I had those things in my mind, but I hadn't decided to do anything. This would have been in the winter/spring of 1987. [In February, the school radio station was closed because of racist comments.] I was on sabbatical when this incident happened—in London to do some research in January, then at the Ford Foundation in February, and I was getting ready to go back to campus in March. Then the third coincidence around this time was that Bill Bowen, my predecessor at Princeton, resigned. All of a sudden Princeton was looking for a president. I didn't have any idea of coming here, I had no idea that I'd be interested, number one. Number two, I still was on a track of thinking either of continuing at the University of Michigan, or if I continued to feel badly about this [situation] then I would just go back to the faculty. That seemed like a very simple thing to do. But then in the middle of all this, even though the racial issue on campus had subsided (it came and went very quickly, I can describe that to you in a minute if you'd like, it's a side issue), still, I didn't forget easily the reactions of some members of the state legislature or some of the reactions on talk radio that occurred in and around that issue—that part didn't leave me.

But I was completely undecided as to what if anything to do. And I certainly hadn't spoken to anybody at all except my wife about this. Then this opportunity at Princeton came along, and they asked me to think about it and I said no, I didn't want to leave Ann Arbor. I had turned down a number of other opportunities around the same time because for whatever set of reasons my experiences at the University of Michigan seemed to be getting some attention elsewhere. Almost every month I'd have a visit from a group who wanted me to become president somewhere. So there were a lot of opportunities around, but I said the same thing to all of them, "No, thank you very much, I'm not interested." Then Princeton came along and for me, Princeton had a number of differences: I had some emotional ties, I was a student here, which is important, and Princeton was a high quality place like Michigan but in other ways it was very different from a large state university like Michigan. Eventually, after thinking about it, I decided that as long as I only had one career, the chance to work in two places like these which were really so different, doesn't come along every day.

[I had never thought of myself as making a career as a university president.] I can say that when I got a call from the president of the University of Michigan that he was interested in my becoming provost, I'm not sure that I knew what a provost was. I know that I didn't know what a president did. I always remind myself that when I first went to the University of Michigan as a faculty member, not only did I not know who the president was, I didn't care who the president was. I thought whoever it was he was doing his job and I was doing my job and the two of us would probably never meet, and we didn't, of course, for many years. That was just fine, I'm sure, with him; it was certainly fine with me. So I had absolutely no concept. I had become chairman of the economics department at Michigan, but this was a rotating chairmanship, so it wasn't any big step or decision. While I was relatively young for the job, I knew I'd only have it for three years, and then I'd go back to the faculty.

Then the summer of 1977, when I was preparing to go back to the faculty, preparing my courses for the fall, I got a call from the president who informed me that the current provost, the vice president for academic affairs, was going to Cornell to be president and would I come see him? I went to see him and he essentially offered me the job. I knew so little about it that if I'd had to leave town to do it, if someone else had offered me the same job somewhere else, I never would have done it. It just did not occur to me then that I might be president. However, I had enjoyed being chair of the department for those three years, and I didn't have to leave town, and I thought it would be an interesting and exciting experience, so why not? And that's how I became provost. Then it was only two and a half years or so before I was appointed president, and of course, I had begun to understand what the issues were. It was only in that position that I finally began to understand what a president was. Before this, I had never known a university president, didn't know anyone who knew a university president, so I was at least two degrees of separation away from *any* university president.

You know, I never found, in general, that there were tremendous psychological pressures. I found it mostly to be a big high, that is, interesting problems, exciting, risky, making decisions in areas you aren't a deep expert in but somebody has to make the decisions—I have found that all very exciting. There are unpleasant moments, but let's face it, most jobs have unpleasant moments. What happened in Michigan with the state legislature, that incident in 1987, was very atypical. Maybe that's why it hit me as so unusual, because I had never experienced anything like that, I'd never experienced any kind of psychological pressure. Now, I didn't like it in those early years when a faculty member would get up at one of these public hearings and say, "Well, if anybody had any intelligence they wouldn't do this, and it's only people who don't know—" But that lasted a half an hour and it went away and I didn't think about it anymore.

So while I don't want to minimize those things, I never felt any particular pressure more than I did when I was a faculty member, for example. The job [of president] is a lot more demanding, not because it is psychologically so difficult, but because your whole life transforms itself, from working on problems that you choose and mold to really working to enable other people to work on problems that they choose. My work moved from focusing on econometrics, on problems of interest that I chose in that area, to having a different agenda, to make it possible for students and faculty at the University of Michigan to do what they wanted to do, not what I wanted. And that's a psychological transformation. It involves a different perception of your own work. The presidency is a much more service-oriented job. That was the biggest change to me, that I was doing things much more for others than for myself. Now, obviously I got satisfaction out of that, so I don't mean to say that this was some kind of calling and I sacrificed myself—that would be the opposite of the truth. But it was a change. That was more important and more striking to me than any kind of external pressure.

Obviously, [I had my wife's support in coming to Princeton]. That was central. I wouldn't have even considered it without her support. But I have to say, the move was harder than we expected. Our children were grown and had all left home, and we said to ourselves, "Gosh, we're still relatively young, at least in our view, not in everybody's view, but in our view, and we don't have children here anymore, they've all moved away, none living in Ann Arbor, so this ought to be pretty straightforward." In fact, it was a lot more difficult than we had fully thought out. And this had nothing to do with Princeton or Michigan. It was just not knowing where the drugstore is or what doctor to have or who to call. It's a whole set of things after living for almost twenty-five years in Ann Arbor, the whole set of things that are attachments to a community. It's where our children grew up, where we went to all the PTA meetings, where we went to little league games, and we did all those things that you do when you have a family growing up in a town and are able to set up relationships which, of course, can never be rebuilt somewhere else. We had not, I think, been fully appreciative of how difficult that would be to give up. And who knows what we would have done if we had realized? So in that sense the move was harder than I expected, but again, it wasn't related to either Michigan or this university, it was just related to personal experience.

[The last months of the Michigan presidency] went really very smoothly in my case, partly because the big projects I had in the way had been completed early in 1987, as completed as projects ever get. But I felt pretty good about where we were. So in the last months what I was trying to do was make it as easy as I could for the next president—accumulate some resources, make no long-term commitments, try to make sure that my successor would have lots of options before him. I felt like a lame duck in a way, but I didn't have any problem. I mean, people didn't say, "Well, we have to wait until the next person." Quite the opposite. People wanted me to do things because they knew me and knew what I would do, and so there was a lot of pressure to keep on doing things. And what I had to do was resist the temptation to start committing my successor to things he might not want. So those were very easy months. I didn't have any feeling of losing authority or anything like that because that's the way other people treated us, so I had no serious problem with that transition.

[In accepting the Princeton presidency, I didn't do any homework.] I just said to myself, "Well, here's a great university. It's got to have its own problems, but I don't need to know those. Those aren't going to determine whether I do this or not. Here's a university that's so good it must know what it's doing." I had a lot of respect for Bill Bowen and Neil Rudenstine who were running it at the time, and I knew that it had to be on a pretty good path. I told myself that I would go to Princeton and learn and then think about what to do. That was my attitude.

[The honeymoon did not last very long] because one of the things that I learned within months was that, much to my surprise, although the university had just finished a big and successful capital campaign, the operating budget of the university had what I would call a structural deficit. That is, it was actually in deficit and the kind of deficit that would grow over time. So my experience at Michigan had taught me, I thought, that when a problem like this arises nothing is gained by delay. You've just got to address it. It's tough, but you get it over with and you go on to the next stage. Well, when I informed the community here that we had a budget problem, I was met with absolute incredulity. That is, it couldn't be possible, it must be made up, it must be social engineering of some kind. I think people here had begun to believe their own rhetoric, that is, that everything had been so successful, the money was coming in over the transom, and there really couldn't be a problem. Besides which, Princeton was sitting there with a two-and-a-half-billion-dollar endowment. How could anybody be in trouble?

Of course, we weren't in trouble like survival trouble, but we still had a serious deficit in our operating budget and I proceeded to announce that we were going to do what was necessary to get the budget under control, and that faculty salaries were at something like 98 percent of our peer group, and I wanted to move over a number of years to 103 percent of our peer-group average and this would involve adjustments. Well, people just thought this was some kind of ridiculous idea that I had. There was a lot of concern. Now, this is a place that is unlikely to mobilize itself in the way that a lot of other places will, that is, here the president is chairman of the faculty, there's no faculty senate, it's just an open meeting of the faculty, and I serve as chair. It's quite different than at most places where the faculty have a representative system of governance. Nevertheless, there was a lot of disbelief, a lot of grumpiness, a lot of whining about it. And so that was hard to get over. On reflection, thinking about this now in retrospect, had I thought just a little bit more about it, I may have found some way to hide the problem for a year or two, in order to gain some better sense of the institution—after all, I hadn't been on the faculty here—and then come at the issue afterwards. But I didn't have that perspective then, and so I just went ahead. A lot of unhappiness came out in various ways, but then, this was 1988/1989, and by the early 1990s when a lot of universities started running into fiscal trouble, we were in good shape. We had taken our lumps, and while everyone else has been faced with cuts and so on, we've had none of that in the last four or five years.

And so I think people grudgingly realized that there really may have been something to being ahead of the curve in the financial area. But getting back to your question, how long did the honeymoon last? It didn't last long because I decided to take that issue on right away. You know, I don't remember if it was in the first semester or the second semester—I think it was in the fall of 1988. [I don't recall a moment with the faculty that I would call a defining moment.] I think these things build slowly and change slowly, [become perhaps a defining situation]. I think that once we got over what was a bumpy period those first two or three years, my sense is that there has been a growing level of confidence and enthusiasm. At least, that's my view. But there wasn't a moment—it's just that slowly you do things that begin to have some kind of impact. We did restore our faculty salaries to 104 percent of our peer group—we're not only 104 percent of the average, we're higher than anybody in that group. So we've done things. Now we're in another capital campaign which is going very well, so I think these things happen slowly.

As I've probably told you, I had a very good experience with the Michigan board and felt the whole time I was there that despite issues that came up from time to time, we had a very good working relationship. I'd have to say that at Princeton, first of all, the structure is different. They're a much larger board of close to forty and therefore a lot of their work is done through committees and through an executive committee. But I just have to say that I can't imagine having a better board than I have here at Princeton. I've been very fortunate in my career as a university president; I've always had good boards to work with.

[On the Princeton board] turnover is built-in. We have probably an average of four or five people changing every year because while the majority are only appointed for four years, some are appointed for ten, and you cannot be reappointed without leaving the board for a year. And so, yes, there is steady turnover, but the majority of the board is self-appointed, that is, the board forms a nominating committee and appoints successors. A minority, maybe a third or so, is elected by our alumni, and both processes are very careful and very thoughtful.

[In terms of their philosophy or attitudes,] I think the board has shown a willingness to change over time. Indeed, I think our board is startlingly progressive. Somehow, I've even managed to convince them that you stay good by changing. I could compare the boards. For example, one board meets in public and one doesn't. That is in itself a big difference because that means that things can be in general much franker; the board doesn't need to delegate so much. One of the ironies of a public board with public meetings is that to get around the hard problems you delegate to the president a lot. That's one of the unknown costs of the open meetings law. You may think you're going to see more, but you in fact actually see less because the board, in order to avoid dealing with a lot of these things in public, just delegates to the president. The president meets by himself, so what needs to be done gets done. Like many laws, open meetings laws have a lot of counterintuitive results, that is, unintended results. One of the results at Michigan when I was there is that the board gave even more leeway to the president because they felt some issues were inappropriate for public discussion. It's inevitable that when you meet in public, no matter what kind of person you are, you're talking not only to your colleagues but to everyone else who is present—to the press, to the students, to the faculty, to members of the public. Whereas when you meet in closed session, those audiences are in your mind but you're not speaking to them. My general experience is that the closed sessions do not deprive the university of any crucial information. You know, we pub-lish our agenda, we publish our board books, we publish our minutes so that everybody knows what's going on. But they allow for much more productive discussions.

There are some [trustees still here who were on the board when I was named president] because some have left and come back on the board. Trustees do have to leave for a year after their term is up, but then they can be reappointed. The current chairman of our board was not chair-man at the time I was appointed, but he's still on the board. To tell you the truth, I've never counted, but somehow I feel that I know these people so well they must've been around a long time. There's probably at least 25 percent of the board who have been here the bulk of the time I've been president.

[During the time when I was delivering the bad economic news, the Princeton board and I] were discussing it in pretty much detail, and they were very supportive. I don't know what exactly their motivations were, but I think probably a combination of things—that they had invested in me and wanted to support me. My philosophy on boards is that the bet-ter informed they are, the better the university is served. Therefore, I went to a lot of trouble to keep the board really fully informed. I formed a special budget committee and had them work month after month. I had them report to the board every time we met. They issued a report, they laid it out. I really believe in informing the board because if the president gets hit by the proverbial beer truck, somebody has got to be there who knows what's going on. It's surprising how many boards are quite ill informed. I am stunned by the number of boards that have only the most marginal idea of what the real situation is at the university. I mean, they love the university, they work for the university and all that, and they have all these commitments. But if you ask them any question about what really is the nature of your budgetary situation, it's very hard for them to say anything beyond, well, our budget is balanced or it's not balanced.

[I have found this to be the case equally with private and public boards.] It takes a lot of effort, you know. These are complicated institu-tions. To understand how the whole university works, with professional schools, a medical center, and everything else put together, is a complicated issue, so it takes time. And you've got to be willing to invest the time in teaching your board. I think that many of my colleagues underestimate their obligation to be a teacher to the board regarding what's going on at the university in terms of the responsibilities the board has. They don't have to know what's going on in the latest biological research laboratory, that's not their direct responsibility, but there are some things for which they are directly responsible, such as the financial welfare of the university, and my view is you have to teach them a lot, and if you have a lot of turnover as we do on our board, you have to teach all the time. It's like having a new class. We don't get mad because we have to teach calculus every year. We don't think just because we taught it last year we don't have to teach it again. You have new students and you teach it once again. And it's the same thing with boards.

[On the subject of team building at Princeton,] I had the same attitude as when I came in at Michigan. My presumption was that I could work with the existing team, I didn't have to bring my own people. The existing team would be good enough, enthusiastic enough, eager enough so that we would get to know each other and work well, and go that way. I've always had the view that it's a mistake to come in and sweep clean unless there's some kind of crisis. Many of the senior people on the team that we have here were hired by Bill Bowen and I'm still working extremely effectively with them. Inevitably, of course, there's some turnover. Neil Rudenstine left not long after Bill left, and so I had to replace the provost and then the dean of the faculty. But I didn't come in to replace them; turnovers happen as a matter of course and then you slowly build a new set of arrangements among the existing people, some new people, and yourself. So that's the way I look at it, that you're always in the process of team building because people are always moving on. Ruth Simmons went to become president of Smith, Hugo Sonnenschein went on to become president of the University of Chicago, Henry Bienen to become president of Northwestern. Janet Holmgren went on to become head of Mills College. There's always turnover at a place like this because a lot of these senior people are very attractive for other positions. That's very satisfying and it's nice to see your colleagues go on to bigger and better things, if that's what they want to do, but the result is that you're always in the process of team building, it never ends. So I view it as a process that goes on year after year. You make some mistakes. Not every appointment works out. I have made my share of mistakes, but on the whole I like to think of people as long-term colleagues. I don't like to change. I think that people work more effectively the longer they work together.

[To answer your question about the racial protests at Princeton:] When you're president long enough, a protest is not a major deal, it's just all part of the environment. You get protests from time to time. I thought that there was never a student protest here at Princeton that was anything close to some of the situations that developed at the University of Michigan. I think there've been two or maybe three protests of one kind or another since I've been here, I can't quite remember, but for the most part they've been very mild, very appropriate, and you know, I don't consider any of them to have been inappropriately disruptive. Their *intent* was serious, the people were serious about what they were doing, but they weren't seriously disruptive, they didn't change what you did day to day. For the most part they didn't have the standard racial overtones, so I'm a little surprised to hear it phrased that way. But let's go back to the one at Michigan. The Michigan one, which as I said was much more serious, occurred toward the end of my time as president. It wasn't the first protest by any means but probably what most people consider the most serious one that occurred there.

Somewhere in the middle of this tension-filled environment at that time, I get a call from the Reverend Jesse Jackson from wherever he was, saying that he thought he could come to campus and help out. Would I mind if he came? I did not know the Reverend Jackson then, I'd never met him. The students had come up with twenty demands, and the Reverend Jackson called me on a Saturday, and I said if he wanted to come that would be fine. I knew who he was but only as someone who read about him in the newspaper. So he agreed to come to my office at ten o'clock on Monday morning, and at eight o'clock on Monday morning I was to see in my office two students who were part of this group that was very agitated and upset. Well, first of all, these students came in dressed as if they were about to go to Wall Street. Now, I had never seen these kids other than in dungarees, jeans, and baseball caps, and here they were in dark suits and white shirts and ties informing me that yes, we were going to have a meeting, but they knew I was meeting with Reverend Jackson later and so they would meet with me some other time, they didn't want to preempt Reverend Jackson. I found out later, of course, that he had met with them and others the night before and had instructed them that they weren't to show up in my office in jeans. He also had met the previous evening with some of the faculty and students who had concerns and with some of the local ministers.

Anyway, Reverend Jackson eventually came to my office and we talked about the twenty demands or maybe there were nineteen or maybe there were twenty-six, I don't remember. So he said to me, "Well, what do you think?" And I said, "Well, look, there are some of these that we can discuss, but there are some of these that are just nonnegotiable issues that we can't make any progress on at all." And he said, "Which are those?" And again I'll make up the numbers—"It's these eighteen," or these fifteen or whatever. "Really, there's no movement allowable there at all, the best we can do is just talk past each other." So he says to me, "Well, I understand, I'm on the board of. . . " he named the university, but I don't remember—"and we have a very hard time getting African-American professors," and so forth, "and so I understand." "All right," he says, "I've told everyone else to meet us here at ten-thirty," some of the students and faculty whom he had met with the previous night. "Could we meet with them?" I said, "Fine."

After our discussion we went to the conference room next door, and there were maybe thirty people in there, and Reverend Jackson and I walked in and after some general pleasantries the Reverend Jackson said, "Well, President Shapiro and I have talked over all these demands and we've decided that these fifteen we have to put aside." And so there's a lot of grumbling around the table, and he stands up and says, "Okay, everybody who's with me, stand up." Well, they shot out of their chairs like they had a cannon underneath them and everybody stood up. He says, "That's fine, that takes care of those fifteen." And then we went on for a few hours to discuss what we might do. In the meantime, the students had scheduled a rally for him to speak at, and there was a sack lunch and of course, by this time there were newspapers and TV reporters around. So we finished that meeting and came up with some agreement on these items, and we went back to my office and he says, "Well, we have to speak to the TV people, what should we tell them?" So I said, "Well, you can tell them anything you like but I really don't want you to speak for the university. I'll speak for the university. I don't want to put any restrictions on what you say, but I want to speak for the university." Finally he says, "Let's go out and talk."

So we went outside and the TV cameras were all there and he immediately started saying what a wonderful meeting it was, how wonderful I am, what a progressive educator, etc. He then announces that we've come to a wonderful agreement and he's very happy and everybody's happy and so on and so forth. And then they asked him, "Well, what is the university going to do?" and he goes along completely with our agreement— he turned to me and said, "Well, President Shapiro will tell you that." By then it was time to walk over to the rally, and there was a considerable amount of tension out there. By the time we got over to the rally which was in an auditorium that seats 4,000 people, it's full, packed, another three, four thousand people standing outside waiting to get in. And we go into this, which is a kind of concert hall, and onto the stage, which is where we'll speak from, where he will speak from principally—you know, it was really for him—and it looks like a revival meeting. He's invited all the local ministers, they were there with their families, children running along on the stage and so on. The students are there who organized the rally, and he says to them right away, "Before I speak I want you to introduce President Shapiro and I want him to speak regarding things that impact the university, and then I'll speak."

Well, I don't think the students were entirely happy with that, but they certainly weren't going to confront him. So anyway, I got up and I thanked him for coming, and then went on to say what I would do on the five items we agreed were actionable items. Every time I completed one section of this, he started clapping, and of course, the whole audience starts clapping. This audience was mainly a white audience, there were a lot of African Americans, but it was a mainly white audience of different ages, but obviously, they were all completely in his hands. This went on, and every time I completed something, he would clap his hands, and everybody else would cheer, and everything was wonderful and fantastic.

Then he got up to speak, which of course is exactly what they were all there for, and he started to give those students an argument, saying that they really hadn't figured out what the problem is, that there's starvation around the world, there's nuclear war, there's all these things, and they're worried about someone telling a joke on the radio station. He says, "Does anybody remember the name of the person who sent Joseph out of the inn into the stable? Nobody remembers that terrible person. Is anybody going to remember who said this ridiculous thing on the radio?" So he immediately began by trying to move them to a different plane and taking away this issue that he characterized as trivial, unimportant, not worth thinking about, the issue that had caused all this. Then he goes on to give a rousing speech on much bigger issues. He had at that time these sayings, you know, "Up with life, down with drugs," I don't remember, but things that rhyme, and he had this audience repeat these statements, and they were screaming them by the time he was finished. And every time he said "Racism," and it was a topic he came to many times, he turned toward me and he said, "And anti-Semitism." And he went on like this in a stunning performance. It could take your breath away, it was scary in its own terms, but it was stunning in other ways. And he went on like this for about an hour and then came to a close, walked out of the back of the auditorium into a limousine, and he was gone.

I walked out the back with him, of course, and started walking across campus back to my office. Well, it was unbelievable, grown people would come over to me and say, "Bless you, Dr. Shapiro, it was such a wonderful time, isn't it wonderful we could all come together like this?" People from the state legislature whom I had had so much trouble with were all on the platform wanting to be there with him, of course, and saying how wonderful this was and everything that's been accomplished here, and how fantastic it is, and what a wonderful person I am. [Some of these were people who had been offensive to me, yet] they were saying what a wonderful person I was, and how great it was that I was at the University of Michigan. I met some regents on the way back and they said, "Well, this is fantastic." And from that day, this issue that had generated so much tension was gone. It just went, like a wave, it just went. It's magical in a way, I mean, I can't even to this day explain it. The tension just went.

Now, I wouldn't say that [the students then trusted me and the administration,] but they behaved as if that were true, let me put it that way. [Our efforts for affirmative action were accepted,] and the immediate tension around that issue just went away. And so Reverend Jackson was, in my view, enormously helpful and very, very responsible. At that time, in that year, he was also being considered as a possible presidential candidate, running in a few primaries. So, he had a lot of opportunities to talk. People asked him about the situation at Michigan, and to his great credit he never forgot our agreement—he never talked about the university's decisions, he always talked about the reaction to his experiences there. He never forgot or appeared never to have forgotten what he told me. And I had, of course, very limited experience with Reverend Jackson, but that experience I had was very positive, and so, you know, even though I disagree with him on things, I had a very positive view of him as a person because he simply didn't forget. The whole truth is he never took advantage of the situation to serve his own needs as opposed to those of the university. Now, I don't doubt that he had his own reasons for doing all these things, but it was an extremely positive experience and the immediate tension went away as quickly as it came. It was just absolutely stunning.

I could have [said I didn't want Jesse Jackson coming on campus and meddling with this issue,] but if anybody had asked me, "Would you object to my coming onto campus?" I would never say I object. The campus is an open community, you can't start deciding who is going to come and who is not going to come, it's a bad position to be in. While it was very nice of him to ask, I'm sure he knew that I would never say, "No, I don't want you here." I wouldn't have said that to anybody.

You know, here at Princeton, the protests mostly had to do with whether we should add another person to be an advisor in issues of sexual harassment. That was the one which seemed to mobilize more attention than the others. But I have to say, in my own experience, the intensity, the level of organization of the protests here is a shadow of what could be mobilized at the University of Michigan. My view is that organizing protests is not a simple matter, and graduate students are much better organizers than undergraduates. They have experience, they've been through it before, they know what you have to do. Where you have a large group of graduate students, you have a large group of potential organizers. And where there are large graduate student bodies, you get better organized undergraduate political expression because you still need organizers, you can't just go out there and feel good. I mean, it doesn't last for more than a short time. So you need to get organized and know what to do, how to do it. I think at a university like Princeton where we have only 1,500–1,600 graduate students, it's a little bit harder. That's my explanation, I don't know if it's correct but that's my explanation.

It's very, very hard to say [how being president of two research universities has affected me personally]. You know, I've been in university administration now at a senior level for twenty years, and during that twenty years I have changed a lot, but perhaps I was going to change a lot anyway in twenty years. That's a long period of one's life. When I became president at Michigan in 1979, I was forty-four-years-old, and now it's eighteen years later and there are lots of ways I've changed.

The way I look at it is, being president enables you to enlarge and refine your understanding of the university. I think it was James Madison who said that the responsibility of a legislator is not simply to respond to the latest expression of interest in the population or to hold a poll. The idea was to take public opinion and respect it but enlarge it and refine it and focus it on a legislative program—that was Madison's idea. And I think a university presidency is the same way. You now have a responsibility for a much larger vision than you ever were required to have before as a faculty member. And you get lots of input about what to do—this department wants this, that department wants that—and your responsibility is to both enlarge that, make it more than it is, a separate stimulus, and to refine it, that is, focus it in a way that you think can carry the institution forward. That's an experience that's very hard to have as a faculty member, and I've had a lot of that now as president both at Michigan and Princeton. My impression is that it has caused me to grow in a way that may have eluded me had I stayed in the faculty. I don't know that, I'm just imagining that to be the case. You become very aware that what people value in different parts of the university is very different. What someone values in engineering, what someone values in philosophy, and what someone values in music or law or medicine, it's just all different. And that's what enlarges your scope of understanding of the whole endeavor, at least in my thinking.

[In response to your question about how presidents prepare for what really will be a personal loss when they step down,] I always have thought a lot about this because, as Keith [Brodie] has suggested, most of our colleagues don't really prepare for it and don't really think about it that way. I have a natural advantage in this area because my wife, who used to teach at the school of social work at Michigan, has all her life worked on the issue of loss—how people cope with it, what it is you have to prepare for, and how it is you experience it. So this has been a kind of long-running conversation over many, many years for us. And so, yes, that is a big issue. I'm preparing for it myself by visualizing a transition period, that is, I expect to go back to the faculty here. As a result, I've kept up my teaching. I teach one course a year, and I keep preparing new courses so that I will have a teaching program. It will be a big loss—I mean, I won't have all these people wanting to see me, and calling me up and making appointments and telling me how important I am and so forth, and I'm sure that's going to be an adjustment. Until you do it, you don't know how you're going to experience it. I'm preparing for it by trying to develop a new agenda of activities. As you may know, I'm chairman of the National Bioethics Advisory Commission. Well, I accepted that with some of this in mind, that I wanted a new aspect to my life. It certainly will be different, and I don't have any magic bullet here, but I do consciously think about it and consciously do things. I don't think I would be teaching now if it wasn't that I think of myself as preparing for another stage in my career. So while I enjoy the teaching, what I really have in mind is that I'm building up my capacity, or rebuilding my capacity, in this area, which would be very hard to do if I just had to start cold turkey. We did something else: My wife and I moved out of the president's house at Princeton because I didn't want us to have two losses at the same time—our house and my job the same day. Moving is always difficult, as you probably know from your own experience, so we went ahead and moved and made all the decisions you make when you move— what you're going to give to the children, what you're going to keep, what you're going to throw out, all those things that you do.

That was very conscious on our part. It wasn't that we didn't like where we were living, or didn't enjoy having all the services of the university facility, but we said, you know, we've got another stage in our life coming, and we have to think about it. I told the trustees the only thing I want when I leave here is an "O" parking pass. That means you can park anywhere on campus. I think they have given only three of them out, to me and to the two former presidents. That's the only thing I want.

None of us are totally ready, but my wife and I thought about it so that she can manage her own career, and both of us hope to do some projects together when I retire, and so we're working on that agenda, what kinds of things match her skills and my skills. I don't want to claim too much here. All I want to claim is that we are thinking consciously about it, and we think that will help. What it will be like, I'll tell you when it happens.

NOTES

1. "Fact-File: Market Value of Investments at 147 Colleges and Universities," *Chronicle of Higher Education*, March 24, 1980, p. A5, survey by the National Association of College and University Business Officers; "U-M Budgets Better, Not Smaller," *Detroit News*, April 29, 1987; faculty and student numbers provided by reference department, Bentley Historical Library, University of Michigan, September 9, 1998; "Growth of College Endowments Found to Have Slowed Last Year; Value of 296 Funds Placed at $4.7-Billion," *Chronicle of Higher Education*, June 1, 1988, p. A35, survey by the National Association of College and University Business Officers; "A New Kind of Tiger," *Time*, May 11, 1987, p. 77.

2. The schools were architecture and urban planning, art, business administration, dentistry, education, engineering, graduate studies, information and library studies, law, "LS&A" (literature, science, and the arts), medicine, music, natural resources, nursing, pharmacy, physical education, public health, and social work. Information provided by reference department, Bentley Historical Library, University of Michigan, September 9, 1998.

3. Office of the President, Princeton University, August 24, 1999; "The Nation: Resources; College and University Endowments Over $100-Million, 1988," *Chronicle of Higher Education Almanac*, September 6, 1989, p. 22, survey by the National Association of College and University Business Officers.

Michael Sovern

Columbia University 1980–1993

A graduate of both Columbia College and Columbia Law School, Michael Sovern joined the university's faculty as a visiting assistant professor in 1957, commencing an extraordinary career there as legal scholar, civil rights activist, labor relations specialist, and academic leader. After successfully mediating the spring 1968 student strikes that threatened to shut down Columbia, Sovern was appointed dean of the law school, serving from 1970 to 1979, when he became provost and executive vice president of the university. He succeeded to the presidency in 1980. At that time Columbia had a student body of 18,069, more than two-thirds of whom were graduate and professional school students (undergraduates 5,719), a faculty of 1,772, a budget of $317.2 million, and an endowment of $553 million.[1] When Michael Sovern stepped down in 1993, the student mix was approximately the same (undergraduate 5,690/graduate and professional 11,564), the faculty had increased to 3,063, the budget was $1.008 billion, and the endowment had grown to $1.847 billion. Retrospectives of his presidency noted that he had been the most successful fund-raiser in Columbia's history, increasing faculty salaries, establishing 120 endowed chairs, building minority enrollment to 35 percent (more than any other Ivy League institution), and "rebuilding Columbia's confidence and reputation."[2]

Michael Sovern's account of some aspects of his presidency is an edited transcript of his interview with Leslie Banner at the Columbia University

*School of Law, December 4, 1997. The questions that prompted his com-
ments have either been omitted or indicated with bracketed material to create a more readable narrative.*

It was highly significant [that] not only had I been dean [of the law
school] and provost, but I had gone to both Columbia College and Columbia Law School, and probably most important, in 1968, when Columbia exploded in student unrest, I was elected chairman of an
executive committee of the university faculty. You put all those things
together, and by the time I was tapped to be president, I had a broad acquaintance across the university. I was well positioned to stay in touch
with many of my colleagues on an informal, social, and friendly basis,
and I found that enormously helpful.

[I did not anticipate the presidency.] My first epiphany on the subject
took place in 1968–1969, when I discovered that I enjoyed the work I
was doing in my capacity as chairman of the executive committee of the
faculty. But I had no burning hunger for academic administration. I
looked forward to getting back to teaching and writing, and I did. In fact,
I remember a lot of people were surprised. One of the things we had done
in that committee was to open up Columbia's governance by creating a
university senate, and many people were surprised when I declined my
colleagues' invitation to accept a senate seat. But I enjoyed my teaching
and I enjoyed writing. Then the dean of the law school indicated that
he was about to retire, and it was obvious to me and to others that if I
wanted the job it was mine. The chance to help shape the law school's
future proved irresistible. I decided to do that; it was my first serious commitment to academic administration.

Shortly before, the law faculty, with my strong support, had agreed that
the dean should serve no more than ten years—a six-year term renew-
able once for four years. I had just begun my ninth year as dean when
one of my colleagues called on me and said he wanted me to know that
the faculty would be very happy to waive the ten-year limit. I thanked
him and said, "No, I want to go back to teaching and writing."

Then the provostship became vacant, and the president of the university, Bill McGill, asked me if I had an interest in the job because if I
didn't, he wanted me on the search committee. I said, "Put me on the
search committee." And so I was serving on that committee when Bob
Merton, an old friend, called and said he was the "rump committee" of
the search committee, talking to those members of the committee who
had been nominated by others. Would I come have a drink? My first impulse was to say, "Bob, I don't want to waste your time." But he was an

old friend and a senior colleague of enormous distinction, and that impulse struck me as rude, so I went to have a drink. After the pleasantries I said, "Bob, this is not a job I would want except under the most unusual circumstances." Being a good scholar he said, "What circumstances?" And I said, "Either of two. One, if you can't find anybody good, I would do it for a couple of years as a kind of draftee because this is an important job and we want it done right. The other is, if Bill McGill is going to step down as president, then I might be interested in the provostship with a view to succeeding him." And that was the first time I had ever acknowledged any interest in the presidency even to myself. The next day Bill McGill called and told me on a confidential basis that he intended to announce his retirement the following year. I then accepted the provostship in the middle of my ninth year as dean, in February. Bill McGill announced his retirement in June of that year, to take effect the following year. In January of 1980 the trustees picked me to serve as president beginning on July 1.

So it really was a series of accidents that led me to the presidency. My youthful ambition was to be a justice of the Supreme Court, not president of a university! I won't take you through all the things that led to my being chairman of the executive committee of the faculty in 1968; that was another series of accidents. That inscribed resolution on the wall is signed by all the members of that committee who served during 1968/69: Lionel Trilling, Richard Hofstadter, Ernest Nagel, who was then America's foremost philosopher; Polykarp Kusch, a Nobel Laureate in physics; Eli Ginzberg, Daniel Bell, Fred Friendly—it was a wonderful, wonderful group. We spent an extraordinary year working together. I thought of myself as a faculty person, but now that I've served as president, I would hate like hell to have missed it. It was a stretching, satisfying experience, but at that point in my life I really wasn't looking for it. It's very funny: For a post that I had not sought until that moment that I described to you, it's almost as though I had spent my life in training for it. And as I say, just a series of accidents took me on that path. If it hadn't happened, I would have gone along enjoying myself and who knows? maybe become a justice of the Supreme Court!

[Did the trustees discuss with me an agenda they had for the university?] They did not. Of course, my views on many subjects were known. The education committee of the trustees is the provost's committee, so I was working closely with that group on a regular basis, and I attended all the trustees' meetings. I was an outspoken supporter of the college's core curriculum as well as its need-blind financial aid system, both of which we preserved and enhanced. As provost I had arranged for the first faculty to live in student residence halls, a program I would expand as president. I had also taken the first steps toward making Columbia College fully residential, an objective we reached several years later.

More comprehensively, I shared my views on a number of key issues with both trustees and a number of faculty in response to an important committee report. Professor Steven Marcus had led a major study of Columbia's arts and sciences departments; the Marcus Commission had been appointed by McGill before I became provost, but they reported during my time as provost. They had done some work on teaching, but mostly the report was about Columbia's arts and sciences graduate and research enterprise. In the course of discussing that report with the trustees' education committee and the trustees, I did focus on things that needed to be done in the arts and sciences. But I did not ever lay out a master plan for them, for the university as a whole, and I didn't have one. In anticipation of your visit, I looked this morning at my inaugural address to see what I said about these things, and I had an agenda that was substantial, but it was the product of lots of conversations and almost osmotic relationships over the years. It was not one that I ever laid before the trustees as a master plan. It was my own judgment about what was needed, much of it at a level of generalization, it has to be said, that would not have provoked opposition. To say we needed to strengthen our schools and departments, to have better community relations, to keep the university's door open to needy students—these are not controversial ideas, and I really thought we could do them all, so it wasn't a case of having to choose at that point. Later in my tenure we'd make some tough choices, but this was still the beginning.

I did [have a honeymoon]. For a while, it seemed as though it might never end. In my sixth year the committee conducting Columbia's periodic reaccreditation reported that "Hope and confidence have been restored. Urgent problems have been effectively addressed and in some areas already resolved. Prolonged depression has been succeeded by optimism. President Sovern's leadership has earned a consensus of full confidence and deserves enormous credit for this transformation. He is rightfully perceived both as its principal agent and personal symbol." Life went on like that for a few years longer. In fact, I didn't have serious difficulty with a substantial group of faculty until I was in my second decade as president. There were individual things—I stumbled into an Ebenezer Scrooge situation my first semester with one of our very substantial enterprises, now called the Lamont Doherty Earth Observatory. Its director was a distinguished scientist who was doing a pretty good job, but there was a lot of discontent with him and I came to the conclusion that he had to go. I then had a three-provost system and the relevant provost was Peter Likins, who later became president of Lehigh and of the University of Arizona. We agreed that Pete would go talk to this man and work out an amicable arrangement for his retirement from the leadership post. However, it blew up in our faces. He didn't want to have an amicable arrangement and I found myself firing him shortly before Christmas. It was messy. But it was a very discrete problem in one sector of the university; we met with the relevant faculty and calmed the storm, and so that was not the sort of thing that ends a honeymoon.

Bill McGill had told me, "Don't serve more than ten years," but I didn't listen to him. I ran into significant difficulty around my twelfth year. But I don't think of it as a defining moment because at the time it came, I was getting close to the end anyway. So I think of it as a tailing off. It was not a defining moment for me; it was an unpleasant time, and it didn't have much to do with anything I accomplished at Columbia. It was a distraction, and it came so late that much of what I had wanted to do I had already done anyway.

There were decisions to be made early on. At the very beginning I was of the view that I did not have a candidate within the arts and sciences who was strong enough to be provost. Here I was, coming from a professional school, and I thought that having another professional school person as provost would cause concerns in the arts and sciences faculty. So that's when I went to what I referred to a few moments ago, the three-provost system. That was the motivation. I appointed Fritz Stern from arts and sciences, a distinguished scholar and teacher and friend, and Pete Likins from the engineering school, and then I appointed a man whom I had recently appointed vice president of health sciences, Bob Goldberger, as the provost of health sciences. That was my answer to the problem and it had the unexpected advantage of causing me to be more hands-on in the first few years than I otherwise would have been because I had to work with all three of them. Then Pete left to be president of Lehigh and I went to two provosts. Fritz Stern never intended to serve for a long time—he didn't really have a taste for administration. So Bob Goldberger soon became the sole provost. We had evolved into a state of affairs in which we had a president from the law school and a provost from the medical school, and at that point I don't think it caused great concern.

Back in those early years the two most important decisions I made were, one, to take the college coed, and it wasn't that the decision was difficult—it was clearly the right thing to do. It was to handle it in such a way that we didn't savage Barnard because the risk was that if we ad-

mitted women into Columbia, Barnard would be in terrible shape. On
the one hand, I had the college faculty who had passed resolutions for
years going back to my predecessor's administration about wanting to go
coed, and they were right. On the other hand, since Barnard began because the Columbia trustees refused to admit women, for Columbia to
cause them great distress seemed to me unacceptable.

I saw my job as Columbia's leader to insure that we behaved ethically,
decently. That theme would recur—vis-à-vis South Africa, for example.
Our strong stances on affirmative action, freedom of expression, and ci-
vility also exemplified my view that a university's own actions are powerful lessons and that it is the president's responsibility to see that the
university lives up to its ideals. Students have a keen eye for hypocrisy.

It took us a while to work the coeducation issue through with Barnard,
but we finally made the change as part of a package that was acceptable
to them, and we announced the new era together. We were immeasur-
ably strengthened—Columbia College received over 12,000 applications
this year [1997], up from over 3,000 back then—and Barnard has continued to flourish.

The other transforming action in my early years was the sale of the
land under Rockefeller Center. [It was never controversial], but it too was
difficult to execute. The land was subject to a very long-term lease to the
Rockefellers. Under the terms of that lease we were getting about $10
million a year in rent. Columbia was in very bad financial shape at this
point, and in fact, Rockefeller Center represented roughly half of our
total endowment and almost all of our unrestricted endowment. And that
was *not* a desirable state of affairs. So my predecessor had opened negotiations for a sale to the Rockefellers, but those negotiations had stalled.
The Rockefellers offered, finally, $220 million to buy the land. At that
point, U.S. Treasuries were paying about 15 percent, so had we accepted
the offer, instead of getting the $10 million a year in rent, we would have
gotten over $30 million a year in interest. Hard to turn the offer down.
But we did, and it took more than a year before we got $400 million.
And then we sold. But it was very difficult—it took that long for the
Rockefellers to believe that I meant it when I said we would not sell for
less than $400 million, and their circumstances made a purchase desir-
able. With the $400 million, of course, the $10 million became $60 mil-
lion a year.

[The faculty were not following the negotiations]; we kept these conversations confidential, and I would report fully to the executive committee of the trustees, and summarily to the trustees as a whole, until the
point at which the deal was really struck. It was, of course, subject to

trustee approval. In those days the trustees used to meet on the first Monday of the month. We closed the deal on a Sunday, and it was approved the following afternoon. This was in February of 1985—it was a front page story in the *New York Times*.[3] That was a transforming event. We first took the $400 million and put it in Treasuries; I didn't want to go into the stock market yet because if the stock market went down, I didn't want this great inheritance to diminish in value. So we put it in Treasuries for a year or two, got a cushion, then moved into equities, and I think it's fair to say that that $400 million is probably worth well over a billion dollars today—it's the core of our endowment—and we may well have spent another half billion as a consequence. It was the single most important financial event of my term, perhaps of any Columbia president's term.

There is no tradition at Columbia—and it is not unique in this—of faculty participation in management of the university's investment portfolio. The only issue was sell or not sell, and at $400 million, nobody in his right mind was going to object. You know, we caught the peak of the real estate market. I don't think you'd get $400 million even today. The terms of the lease were such that rental negotiations would reopen every twenty-one years. My nightmare was that the lease would reopen in the middle of a trough, and as it turned out, it would have. The real estate market was in the pits in 1993–1994, which was when we would have reopened for negotiations. And you remember, there was a series of deals the Rockefellers did involving the Japanese, and the reason that enterprise went bankrupt was that the rents they had assumed they would get were not available because of the decline in the real estate market.

[We were taking a risk in holding out. The risk taking started,] actually, from day one, because I picked up the negotiations when my predecessor retired, and they seemed to be moving for a while, and then it was clear the Rockefellers were not going to be sufficiently forthcoming. I've forgotten exactly when we broke off, probably a year into my tenure. It was still going on the summer after I took office because I remember an investment banker flew up to Cape Cod where we were vacationing to raise the offer from $200 to $220 million.

[I realized what a big risk we were involved in, but] we couldn't sell at that price. It just seemed to be a mistake. And we knew that the Rockefellers were hamstrung to some degree by not owning the land. They could not have done the deal they did with the Japanese unless they could put the buildings and the land together. Now, I didn't know they were contemplating that particular deal. It was also the case that they had difficulties with their tenants. As I told you, the lease would reopen in 1993 or 1994, and most of the people renting space in Rockefeller Center had leases that also ended then because the Rockefellers couldn't easily enter into leases going beyond that period without knowing what they were going to have to pay us. So, as we got closer to that point, they were under increasing pressure to make a deal. And we decided to wait for all that pressure to build.

[The sale] certainly enabled us to address some critical needs—faculty quality, for example. When I was provost, I refused to accept as justification for a second-rate appointment the claim that the candidate was the best we could do, but I would hear it more often than I liked. With the income from the Rockefeller Center sale, we were able to increase faculty salaries and improve the facilities that support teaching and research. And in the years that followed we were able to attract outstanding faculty from all of our peers. In my last year we even recruited Simon Schama from invincible Harvard.

Yes, the Rockefeller transaction was clearly the most significant financial event of my presidential tenure, but I take greater pride in what we accomplished in the intellectual realm. Columbia's trustees put it generously:

> Perhaps his most difficult and enduring accomplishment has been the successful preservation of the university's central and traditional strengths through farsighted policies of change. He has actually fostered new cross-disciplinary programs and academic centers while steadfastly maintaining Columbia's renowned role in quality general education. He has encouraged the growth of pioneering research while nurturing our university's primary mission—to teach.

Our finances were beginning to turn around then anyway. We had started a capital campaign somewhere in there, and giving was going up substantially. We also started—and here faculty were involved after the fact, and were intense negotiators—to take advantage of our intellectual property rights. Around 1980 or 1981, Congress passed a statute, the details of which I no longer remember, that in essence gave universities the right to exploit intellectual property, scientific patents, that had been developed with federal support. So even though research had been governmentally funded, we could patent it as our own. Until then, if faculty members developed something in a lab with Columbia resources, and the faculty members wanted to patent it for themselves, it was theirs. And so during the summer of 1981, we put in a whole new policy providing that from then on Columbia would own the patents, and faculty would get a share of the resulting revenues, and the department would get a share, the school would get a share, and the university would get the lion's share. The trustees adopted that policy, I believe, at the June meeting that year. And so the faculty came back in the fall to find that the university had a new policy on the ownership of intellectual property and not everybody was thrilled by it. Modifications, none of them major, took another year or two during which a [faculty] senate committee reviewed the trustee resolution, made some suggestions, and in essence renegotiated the policy. From zero revenue in 1980, Columbia is now earning almost $50 million a year. As you can see, significant income came out of that particular development, and as I said, faculty were very much involved in that. But not in the first instance.

I consulted [the faculty senate] quite a lot. The structure of the senate is such that the president of the university presides and is a member of the executive committee. So I would discuss lots of issues with the executive committee. I would also discuss issues with the senate. [In regard to the patents change], I just think it happened to be June when we focused on it, and we wanted to get it done as quickly as possible. Once faculty expressed concern, we did in fact work very closely with them. And, of course, I consulted broadly with faculty and others outside the formal organs of governance. Though the president must lead, he had better be sure that someone is following, and that will not happen unless he shares his ideas, his hopes, his vision, and allows others ample opportunity to affect them and to participate in the choice of the institution's goals and the means to achieve them.

[In 1987 I took a sabbatical.] The way I used to describe that was, I had the place running so smoothly that it could run without me for four months and not a moment longer! [I did not leave New York.] I had done this as dean, and I knew what I was doing. I knew that I would not in fact get a full sabbatical, but that I could probably get at least half-time off. The biggest benefit of that sabbatical was the summer time; instead of cranking up in August to get to work in September, we spent the whole summer at Cape Cod. Then we came back to the city. No, I didn't go away and that was deliberate. I knew there would be things I could not avoid doing. For example, I had to recruit Herb Pardes to be our dean of the medical school and vice president. He was then chairman of the psychiatry department and had an offer to run one of the hospitals in New York at some obscene salary, and I had to manage our recruitment of Herb to be dean and vice president at a point when the search committee hadn't yet finished its work. I spent a fair amount of time on that during my sabbatical. I do remember I passed on receiving the crown prince and princess of Japan who are now the emperor and empress, but we would meet on other occasions. So I got rid of all the ceremonial stuff and a lot of the meetings. I obviously didn't go to the senate meetings, didn't preside at any faculty meetings, and so I was able to get some time free of the job. It was very good. Came back with fresh blood.

We were still going gangbusters. At one point we charted the rate of rise in university expenditures, and I think we were growing at something over 13 percent a year for my entire first ten years. And that doesn't count hundreds of millions we were pouring into renewal of our physical plant. At the same time our endowment was soaring. In fact, the year after I returned from my sabbatical, we persuaded Moody's to raise our bond rating to triple A. It had been only a single A in 1980, fine in the classroom, not as good in the market.

The perturbations in my life during that period were a couple of episodes of student unrest, one on South Africa, which we dealt with sensibly, and one involving a fight between a black student and a white student. I think it happened late on a Friday night, and Saturday morning I got the call about the episode, and I said, there goes the spring! And what happened was—I don't know if you've been following the defamation action coming out of the Tawana Brawley case in upstate New York? Maybe it's just a local thing, but the *Times* has had it well covered. The same characters who were involved in that case, Vernon Mason and Alton Maddox, were involved in our affair, and it was a nasty time. But again, didn't leave any scars, and we managed it just fine. In the South African episode, there was great sympathy on campus for the students who chained themselves to the front door of Hamilton Hall. Most of the students had no knowledge of what had happened in 1968 and so didn't understand why I didn't call the police. But I didn't. We just sat 'em out. They spent, I think, three weeks out there, and we went on about our business. Before coming back in the fall, however, the trustees and I agreed that we would in fact divest.

[In coming to that decision] Rockefeller Center is relevant again. Columbia's total stock portfolio before we sold the land under Rockefeller Center was only about $150 million. Of that, less than $40 million was invested in companies doing business in South Africa. As a compromise, I agreed with a [faculty] senate committee that Columbia would freeze the magnitude of its investment in such companies and would not go above $40 million. Then the Rockefeller Center sale produced $400 million. My promise precluded us from putting any of that money into the stock of companies doing business in South Africa. It made no sense to me or to the trustees to have continual disruptions for the right to invest only $40 million in the stock of companies doing business in South

Africa. Also, none of us, and I most particularly, felt fully comfortable with our policy. It was based on a complex, difficult, and not altogether persuasive argument. I still remember the trustees' vote was very collegial, though not everybody agreed with what we were doing. Columbia has twenty-four trustees including the president; the vote was twenty-one to divest, and three abstentions. Nobody voted no. That was wonderfully supportive. The leadership of the trustees was especially strong: Chuck Luce was vice chairman, head of Consolidated Edison here, and he thought we should get out; Sam Higginbottom, chairman of the board, was head of Rolls Royce America, and his parent company had facilities in South Africa. The parent company didn't like our action, but Sam told them that if they didn't like it, they could fire him. They didn't. In sum, we had a consensus that divestiture was the right thing to do, and so we did it.

We were the first university with real money to divest. I mean, a number of colleges had voted to divest, but their votes were symbolic because they didn't have much of an endowment. I had to do some damage control; I remember meeting with the head of Mobil Oil who came to lunch with a classmate of mine who was his vice president, Herb Schmertz, and it was not easy. I still remember, at the end he said, "Well, would you still accept gifts from us?" I said, "You bet we will!" And I had a very rough session with the head of Citibank. He really didn't like what we were doing. But I'm happy to say there didn't seem to be much disposition in corporate America to punish us.

Principle and pragmatism came together. We were all strong opponents of apartheid. The issue was whether divestiture would in fact weaken that regime or whether companies that remained in South Africa could be more helpful in opposition. We finally came down on the side of divestiture. And that was also helpful at home. The contrary position would have left us with a mountain of residual ill will on campus. For example, we deal with about a dozen unions, and they were all supportive of the students in this. Our community relations policies were producing a major turnaround for the university, and the South African issue was relevant here, too.

A number of my colleagues leading other universities were upset by our decision; it increased the pressure on them. But my job was to do what was right for Columbia. I was criticized on another front as well. We went to Washington and lobbied for facility support directly in the federal budget. As a result, we have a chemistry building that was substantially paid for by the federal government. We did that successfully—at the city, state, and federal levels—several times. A number of my colleagues around the country were upset by our federal effort because they believed it would subvert the system of peer-reviewed federal research grants. My position was that we fully supported the system of peer review for research grants and that we would support such a system for facilities construction as well, but no construction program existed. When it came to construction, the choice was not between peer review and politics but between doing without and politics. But it was the subject of discussion at virtually every AAU meeting for the next few years, and I still remember—and I didn't fight hard there, I saw no point in it— one university president saying, "Well, if others are going to do this, we will have no choice but to do it, too," and I had to hold back because I wanted to rise and say, "I did what I thought was right. You are proposing to do what you think is wrong." But I didn't!

I tried to do [what was right for Columbia] in ways that would minimize people's anger or discontent. The coed decision was the best example of that. I really am proud of having brought that about in a joint announcement with Barnard rather than my going down in history as the Butcher of Barnard.

Before you asked [whether I saw the budget crisis at Columbia coming], I was about to say it really wasn't a crisis. That's part of why I don't think I did see it coming. There was a confluence of events—federal pressure on the indirect costs of research. You remember the Stanford yacht stuff. So we were under pressure on costs on the federal side, and at the same time New York State cut its general support to us from about $13 million a year to about three. And then there were the runaway medical costs of our fringe benefits package. Those three things were happening all at the same time. So we were getting upward pressure from the fringe costs and downward pressure from the cuts, and we were spending more than our stated spending rule called for.

Are you familiar with those rules and the motivations for them? When I became president, because we had just finished our first budget without a deficit, it was time to begin to focus on assuring the future as well. Most of our peer schools were only spending about 5 percent of endowment corpus. The basic theory is that you want to plow back enough to maintain the constant value of the endowment. Now, when the capital markets are doing very well, if you spend only 5 percent you are in fact plowing back much more than enough to keep the endowment at constant value, and I had no principled objection to that. But it seemed to me to be a foolish thing to do if you had immediate needs to attend to. It was in my administration that we first imposed the spending rule, but the trustees and I agreed that since the endowment was growing at a very

healthy pace and we had important current needs, the prudent course
was to exceed the rule's limits. After several years, that led to a lack of
discipline about the rule; in fact, one year we spent as much as 8 percent
instead of 5 percent.

[We were making that decision annually] of course, with the trustees'
approval, but you'll recognize that when the percentage you're spending
floats up like that, it's very hard to bring it back down. Now, we were not
so profligate as it sounds because the base is a three-year rolling average,
so that it may be 8 percent of that three-year rolling average, but if your
endowment value is going up, it's much less than that of the actual value.
You follow? So I was not terribly concerned about it. But it was in danger of getting out of control. And so we decided we had to bring it down
over time. And that's the point at which we had a set-to with some of
the faculty.

There is one other factor that's pertinent here, and that is that Columbia had never had a vice president for arts and sciences. Peculiar history: We originally had four schools in the arts and sciences—the college,
the graduate school, international affairs, and general studies, which was
devoted principally to adult education. The faculties of those four schools
overlapped 90 to 95 percent. There was not an arts and sciences faculty
as such and therefore no vice president for arts and sciences. In the mid-
1980s I created the post of arts and sciences vice president with responsibility for the faculty in those four schools. (We later added the school
of the arts.) But there was considerable opposition to creating a single
faculty of the arts and sciences for fear that it would subordinate the college. [They didn't see it as an added strength] and I did. So it took several more years, but I finally persuaded the trustees to create the faculty
of arts and sciences. A substantial majority of the faculty was all for it,
but those with the strongest commitment to the undergraduate school,
the dean of the college and a cadre, opposed it. But they were a minority of the faculty. In fact, the faculty polled themselves, and they were
overwhelmingly in favor. The trustees were skeptical. I thought it was a
good thing. I believed it would lead to responsible governance. I was mis-
taken.

The new organization took hold just as our budget difficulties were
coming to a head. The arts and sciences faculty elected an executive committee chaired by a man I had passed over for provost and had as another
of its members a man I had fired as dean of the college. As you know,
friends may come and go, but enemies accumulate! All that came together, and the funny thing is—I told you about this period in which we
were growing about 13 percent a year—we only came down to about 8

or 9 percent a year. In other words, the budget continued to go up during this period. We never cut the budget. We never had a deficit. That's why I say it wasn't a crisis: We managed our finances very well, but we caught a lot of hell from some faculty.

It was also a time in my life (and here I guess my circumstances were unusual, maybe unique among your group) when my wife was very ill. Had I encountered faculty discontent during my first few years, I would have been out there morning, noon, and night, explaining, justifying, persuading, but I just didn't have the motivation. And that's ultimately what caused me to quit. I love Keith's idea that you quit when you've achieved your goals. I had achieved many of them, but I quit because I just felt I couldn't do it anymore, under my circumstances. Didn't want to do it anymore, actually.

So all this was going on at the same time, but we put together a very good plan and we executed it. As I said, once the percentage of your endowment that you spend goes up, it's very hard to get it back down, and so we set up a three-year plan in which we would squeeze out about $80 million worth of growth from a billion-dollar budget. In other words, we did what the Department of Defense does. When they say they're taking a 5 percent cut, that's after they've increased the budget for inflation. It was that kind of very gentle retrenchment. No actual cuts, no hiring freezes, nothing of that sort. We would increase revenue and slow expenditure growth until we finally squeezed out what we would have spent had we continued to overshoot the spending rule.

[So we were slowing the rate of growth at the school, and although it was reported that Columbia was going to have a smaller faculty], we weren't reducing the size of the faculty. You have to know that some of the reporting—the guy I passed over for provost and his cadre generated reports and sent them to the press before they sent them to me, and, to put it very generously, they were less than accurate. Let me give you my favorite illustration. The leader of the group had served a relatively brief tenure as vice president for arts and sciences. During that time he persuaded us that about five years into the future we would have a crisis of recruitment because so many faculty were scheduled to retire that we wouldn't be able to find enough high-quality replacements to keep our faculty from either shrinking or deteriorating. Consequently, we decided to recruit in advance of those retirements, thereby temporarily increasing the size of the faculty, with the explicit understanding we'd bring it back down as the retirements occurred. And the man who urged that course was the very same man who cited that reduction from the excess to the goal as evidence that we were shrinking the faculty! Isn't that nice?

I was [infuriated], and so were the trustees, who had been persuaded to accept the extra costs of a temporary bubble in the size of the faculty. And so that's what was going on during that period. No, we didn't cut. The one thing we did do, but we hadn't done it yet, and I'm not sure if I hadn't announced my retirement whether we would have been able to do it, we actually cut the pension program.

We did two things on the expense side that were terrific. I don't know what the Duke pension plan is like; ours was grossly excessive. Before I became an administrator, it was clear to me that under the Columbia plan, I would retire at considerably more than I was earning. That's when the retirement age at Columbia was sixty-five or sixty-eight. Then, of course, it went to seventy, and then it came off altogether. Our plan was far, far too generous; it made absolutely no sense. But faculty, of course, regarded it as an entitlement. Anyway, we took out 2.5 percent. Let me be clear about that. For example, when I reached age fifty-five with twenty-five years of service, Columbia would have increased its pension contribution for me to 20 percent of my salary above a certain level each year. We knocked that down to 17.5 percent. Another step would have gotten 15, we knocked that down to 12.5. So everybody still has a very generous pension program, but we saved a lot of money.

The other thing we did—on the health side—was to make very good use of our medical school. We entered into an agreement with one of the point-of-service health care organizations to let all of our medical faculty who wanted to come in join that program for the sole purpose of serving Columbia faculty who opted for that program. Then we made the program more financially attractive than the old indemnity plan, and more than half the faculty who had an indemnity plan elected to move into managed care, and that saved a lot of money.

[In regard to a statement by a faculty member to the New York Times that Columbia had not had much of a direct faculty role in governance], that's not a specious statement. Historically, the statement was true for arts and sciences faculty, and that was one of the reasons I wanted them to have their own faculty, so they could take a responsible role in governance. I think the university senate was an important governance instrument, but it didn't deal with many issues at the faculty or school level. [Participation of the arts and sciences faculty in governance issues was still in the process of maturing at the time I stepped down.] It was ironic, however, that but for me they would not have had an arts and sciences faculty [or much of a faculty senate either]. I really was and am a believer in faculty governance. But I have since developed some skepticism about it!

When these troubles started to develop, Jonathan Cole, who was the provost, [and] Jack Greenberg, who was dean of the college, both friends, gave me advice. They said, "You really have to spend more time with faculty during this period." And I started to do it but found I no longer had the patience for it. It was then that I began to realize that I might be overstaying my time. We had a change in the chairmanship of the trustees at that point; G. G. Michelson was stepping down and Henry King was to succeed her, and I felt I had an obligation to alert him to the fact that I was thinking about retiring. That would have been in the spring of 1992 because Henry would have been taking over in the fall. I hadn't yet made up my mind, but I was reflecting about it, and I made up my mind later that spring. So it was not a single moment; it was a period of reflection and a recognition that this is an all-consuming job, and if you're not prepared to give it everything, and I wasn't going to give it everything, then you should get out. And so that's what I did.

Coming back to Keith's letter, I don't really believe that in an organic institution you ever achieve all of your goals. The way I used to put it is, you can't get bored on this job because you can only do part of it at any one time anyway, so if you get bored with one piece, you just move on and tackle another of the challenges. I see my successor building on things I did; you just never finish. As far as the decision to leave is concerned—Derek Bok put it very well one summer, some years before either of us was thinking of retiring. Derek had been doing the job for more than a decade when we had this conversation. I said, "Derek, do you ever think about leaving the presidency?" And he said, "Yes. When I come back in September and I'm not all charged up for the year, that's when I'll go." And that captures my mood about it, too.

The tension between my original goals in joining the university and the demands of the presidency was growing stronger. It is thrilling to be leading an enterprise that aspires to transmit the heritage of civilization, to prepare tomorrow's leaders in virtually every field of human activity. It is exciting to go to work each day knowing that you are contributing, in however modest a way, to the work of scientists and scholars who are exploring the cosmos, unlocking the treasures of the past, seeking answers to the mysteries of life itself.

And yet—I became a professor in the first place because I believe in the value of helping others to grow and contributing something to knowledge and understanding. While making it possible for others to do that at the highest possible level can be very satisfying, it remains the case that one's original purposes now lie at one remove. Though the presidency is indeed "a bully pulpit," it is a pulpit without intimacy, without the sustained dialogue of the nourishing teacher-pupil relationship.

[In regard to the year between my resignation and my departure], I think the pension change was easier to achieve. It was very unpopular, and we had countless meetings. I didn't go to all of them; in fact, I didn't go to most of them. We had a vice president for administration named Joe Mullinix, and [he and] Jonathan Cole carried the heaviest load, but I was part of it. If I had intended to stay longer, I'd have had to think about the effect of that change on my ability to lead, it was so unpopular.

The knowledge that I was leaving was liberating. And I haven't seen any other university that's done it. Others have very rich pension plans, and they still have them. I'm not saying we wouldn't have done it, but I do have to ask myself the question, did my freedom from fear affect that judgment?

I didn't hit a lame-duck period until my successor was announced. But there was a bump; we had a vacancy for the vice president for arts and sciences post, and it was clear that the search committee, once I had announced, was not going to give me a recommendation. I was unhappy about that because it was an important vacancy. That's the only one I remember. When George Rupp was announced, then, of course, you began to get a shift. In fact, he actually indicated his intention to fire a couple of deans while I was still in office. I was not thrilled. On the other hand, he wanted to hit the ground running, so he wanted to be able to make his own plans. But I worked until the very end. I think I was in the office on June 30. There were things I wanted to finish.

[As to whether there is a place for an elder statesman role for the past president], it has to be the incumbent's choice.

Letting go is hard. I still remember the moment when I knew I had fully let go. I'm a trustee emeritus as well as president emeritus, and so I am invited to all the trustee meetings. I figured I'd go, keep an eye on things, and it was about a year after I'd left office that I was sitting in a trustees meeting and was delighted to observe myself bored stiff.

NOTES

1. *Columbia University 1980 Annual Report*, p. 11; faculty count found in "1980 Annual Update of Affirmative Action Plan" (total includes both full- and part-time instructional personnel), tables II-1 through II-18, pp. 7–24, Columbia University Archives and Columbiana Library; "Fact-File: Endowments of

192 Colleges Ranked by 1981 Value," *Chronicle of Higher Education*, March 17, 1982, p. 8, survey by the National Association of College and University Business Officers.

In addition to Columbia College and the graduate school of arts and sciences, the schools included architecture and planning, the arts, business, dental and oral surgery, engineering and applied science, general studies, international affairs, journalism, law, library service, social work, and the College of Physicians and Surgeons (*1980 Annual Report*, p. 26).

2. "1994 Financial Report," *Columbia* [1994 annual report] (Fall 1994): 54; faculty count found in "1994 Update to Columbia's Affirmative Action Plan" (schools of nursing and public health had been added, and the school of library service had been closed), pp. 29–30, 33–34, tables P-1, P-2; budget figure from *Columbia University 1993 Annual Report*, p. 12, Columbia University Archives and Columbiana Library; "The Nation: Resources; College and University Endowments Over $44-Million, 1993," *Chronicle of Higher Education*, September 1, 1994, p. A38, survey by the National Association of College and University Business Officers; William H. Honan, "Sovern Era Ends at Columbia: A 'Most Extraordinary Chapter,'" *New York Times*, June 30, 1993, Late Edition, B8; Anthony DePalma, "In Troubled Time, Columbia's Chief Is Stepping Down," *New York Times*, June 7, 1992, Late Edition, A1.

3. Maureen Dowd, "Columbia Is to Get $400 Million in Rockefeller Center Land Sale," *New York Times*, Late Edition, February 6, 1985, A1.

James Freedman

University of Iowa 1982–1987
Dartmouth College 1987–1998

A graduate of Harvard and of Yale, where he received his LL.B. in 1962, James Freedman began his teaching career at the University of Pennsylvania Law School in 1964. He was serving as dean there (1979–1982) when, in 1981, he was named president of the University of Iowa. At a time of economic recession and state budget cuts, Freedman enthusiastically took over leadership of a massive institution then educating more than 18,000 undergraduate and nearly 8,000 graduate and professional school students, with a faculty of approximately 2,600, a budget of $138.4 million, an endowment of only $13.6 million, and the largest university-owned teaching hospital in the country.[1] When he departed in 1987 to become president of Dartmouth College, Freedman left an institution that had continued to grow in reputation and size despite battles over money with the state legislature. The student body approached 30,000 and the faculty nearly 3,100, the budget had increased to $193 million, and with the impetus of a new fund-raising campaign, the endowment had reached $22.6 million, enabling the creation of the university's first endowed chairs.[2]

Leaving a major research university for Dartmouth College brought Freedman to a much different academic landscape: a student body of less than 5,000, a relatively small faculty (947), only four professional schools, and a budget of $106.6 million. During his eleven-year presidency, Dartmouth's budget increased to $335.8 million and its endowment from $537.3 million to $1.52 billion.[3]

*James Freedman's account of selected aspects of his presidencies is an ed-
ited transcript of his interview with Leslie Banner in the Office of the President at Dartmouth College on May 8, 1997. (President Freedman
announced his resignation only a few months later, on September 25, effective the following June.) The questions that prompted his comments
have either been omitted or indicated with bracketed material to create a
more readable narrative.*

I thought my recruitment to the Iowa presidency was extremely well
done. I knew the University of Iowa because I had taught there one summer in the law school for eight or ten weeks. So we'd lived in Iowa City
for two months, I had taught at the law school, I had a lot of friends on
the law faculty, including a law school classmate who's a very close friend
and two or three others who are close friends. I knew a lot about the institution. I also admired my predecessor, Sandy Boyd, whom I did not
know but had heard of, and I just knew that any place that Sandy had
been came with a momentum for respect and for being a good place. So
I really was able to know a bit about the university before I even started
the process. That was one very fortunate thing which you don't have in
every recruitment—some inside friends and some prior experience with
the institution.

The second thing is, there were two key people. Iowa has an odd faculty arrangement by which every year when they appoint dozens of faculty committees, they appoint what is essentially a search committee for
a president, a provost, or a university-wide vice president, should one be
needed. So every year there's always a chuckle and the chairman of the
faculty senate says, "You know, we're not really going to need you, of
course, but we'd rather have a committee in place." And lo and behold,
occasionally a president retires and indeed, you do need the committee.
So a committee was in place and the chair of that committee has become one of my dearest friends, which happened almost immediately. He
was someone I could trust, he was someone who was fair, I could really
talk with him. The other person was the chairman of the board of regents, a man named S. J. Brownlee, who was one of the finest men I've
ever known and one of the people I professionally became very close to.
I knew from the first minute I met him that we were made for each other.
He was honest, he was a straight shooter, he had the right values, he was
just a remarkable man. And that reassured me greatly.

So I was greatly impressed both with the chair of the search committee whom I had a lot of conversations with, obviously, and with Mr.
Brownlee, and that helped a lot. They also were absolutely honest with

me. The salary that they could offer had already been in the press—the board of regents had had a public meeting and voted—"We're going to search for a new president and this will be the salary." I knew nothing about public schools, I didn't have any idea, and I said to him, "You know, that's lower than the salary I'm making as the dean of Penn Law School," to which he said, "I knew that would be the case and there is just nothing I can do about it, and we will try in every way we know how to make it up to you when we can. It's not something that we're going to forget, but the way the system works is, we just can't do anything on that, it's not negotiable, our hands are tied." And he was right about that, but I just knew he was honest, I just knew that he would try to make it up to me, and the board would, and they did in dozens of ways thereafter.

So I felt the recruitment was very well handled. The other thing I liked is that although the university was required by the public records law to reveal the names of the candidates, the board negotiated with the newspapers and got agreement that only the last seven names would be published. The board had asked for I don't know how many names, but the search committee gave them seven, and those names were in the press. Ironically, they either were never in the Philadelphia press, or it may have been there was perhaps only half an inch—I've forgotten. But no one in Philadelphia knew, even though this was on the front page of the Iowa papers, and the Iowa papers were calling around everywhere to find out about these seven people. I don't know that they ever called anyone, though, about me. So I really suffered none of the consequences that people suffer today. I was not exposed at all. Obviously, I told the president of the University [of Pennsylvania] when I went out there [to Iowa] (I went out twice for interviews). And then the board won me over. There were nine members, a very high-quality board, and they told all of us what they were doing: they were going to a hotel in Des Moines, the Marriott, and they were interviewing all seven people over the course of three days—three in the morning, and then an afternoon to consider those three, and then three more and an afternoon to consider those, and then one more, and then they were going to pick.

I happened to be the seventh, the very last. They must have been well along in evaluating those first six because at the end of my interview the chairman of the board said, "Could you come on upstairs to my room and we'll talk a little bit," and essentially he offered me the job. So I didn't have to go home and wait and think. He told me all the terms and the like, and I wanted it so much that I said, "Can I call my wife?" And he said, "Sure. I'll step out of the room." And I said, "You don't have to step out of the room!" From his hotel room I called my wife and I said, "Here's where we are. They are prepared to offer me the job and the salary will be a little lower"—we're not talking hundreds of thousands here, only a few dollars lower—and she said, "If that's what you want to do, that's what of course we'll do." We had decided we would do that if I wanted it. I liked the board, I thought they were just very good people. And so that was that. Then he said to me, "The meeting when we'll vote will be on a certain day, and we have to vote in public, and I have to call you on the telephone, and we'll set a time of 11 AM. I will leave the committee room, I will call you, you'll say yes, I'll go back in and say you've said yes, and then we'll announce it." There was also no public discussion at that meeting. It had all been arranged that one member would say, "I would like to nominate Freedman for president of the university," someone else would say "second," no other nominations, and it was done. So I didn't suffer my name in the local paper in Philadelphia, I didn't suffer a long, prolonged business, I had an opportunity to meet the entire board, which is not always common.

I was also impressed with the way they did business. They essentially had a list of about twenty questions which they'd asked every single candidate, so none of us were subject to the whim of the moment and none of us got derailed on some hobbyhorse or other or on our own hobbyhorse. We were each asked to respond to the same twenty questions in the same order, to discuss our views about education and public education and the like, and it was very, very well done. I went there without an apprehension in the world except about my own capacity to do the job. But not about the university. I was lucky it was a university I knew. The only thing that I would say was not covered [before I accepted the job] was the publicness of public universities. I had not the slightest notion about that—how every repair to the house was going to be in the newspaper and all of those things that happen in public universities. But the search process forged a bond between the chairman of the board and me. I don't know if that was by design, but that was what happened. It also gave me someone on the faculty—the chairman of the search committee—whom I had as a friend, someone I could ask during those first few months, "Is this wise? is this sensible? what's the culture here? I'm doing this kind of thing, what do you think?"

I don't recall any of what they now have in these searches—open meetings on television where you give your speech and the whole community is there. I did meet with groups of faculty. After I was appointed, before I took office, I went out to Iowa every few weeks, and I would meet with women's groups and students' groups and faculty groups, and so on, so that I could get a feel for the place. But I thought the recruitment was virtually a model. In retrospect, I didn't know at the time how good it was, how exceptional it was. It was especially interesting because of the nine people on the board, the chairman, Mr. Brownlee, whom I'm so fond of, had been a state senator. One of the other members was a former lieutenant governor under then Governor Ray. And so you had two people who had been involved in the politics of the state and that must have been helpful in negotiating the arrangements—that the search committee would not reveal the list of 300 names and wouldn't tell when the candidates were on campus and wouldn't hold public interviews, but would give out the seven finalists' names. The fact of having some politically astute, experienced people had to be a big help.

There was another person on the board who later became chairman (I think they call it president) who was the Republican National Committeeman. So, you had people close to the governor. I am surprised—I was going to say appalled, but surprised—these days to read that candidates for public presidencies now are interviewed by the governor. I did not meet the governor until many months later when he was asked at a press conference, "What do you think of the person who's coming up to be your new president?" and he replied, "I've never met him." Mr. Brownlee called me and said, "We'd better get you out here to meet the governor." So I went out and I met the governor, which was a pleasure. But you know, it was entirely an apolitical process.

I was going to say in response to your question, "Was there something that was a defining moment?" that [the conflict with the anatomy department in 1982] was surely one of them. They had a system out there in which if you were denied tenure, as a man named Professor Black was denied tenure in that department, you could appeal to a faculty committee which was of the whole university. He appealed to a three-person grievance committee made up of faculty (there was an art historian and I've forgotten who the others were) who were from other departments in the university. They found that the process by which he was denied tenure was flawed. I had no problem with that recommendation and would have been perfectly glad to say to the department, "Do it again. Start over and cure the flaws." But the committee then said, "And therefore he's entitled to tenure because we have read the record and we've read the file and there's no reasonable way on this record you couldn't give him tenure. We order that he be granted tenure." And I just took the view that that couldn't be, that you couldn't have a committee of three people from other disciplines, indeed other schools, award someone tenure, although I was perfectly glad to have the department do it over. That was hard for a number of reasons, the first being that in accepting the part that we would do it over, we were obviously going in the face of the dean of the medical school, and all the people who had gone through the process of denying tenure. But the more important thing was, I had gone in the face of the faculty. I was called before a meeting of the faculty senate, which was eighty people elected from throughout the university, and had to defend this. Like a lawyer, I parsed the language, "Look what it says," and all that was well and good and it sounded reasonable—lawyers talk in ways that make things sound reasonable—while in fact I had rejected the Faculty Grievance Committee's recommendation. That was really a defining moment because it didn't hurt me with most of the faculty, I believe, and it established me in the state as someone who had a set of convictions and was prepared to stand up for them. I never felt threatened through any of it. I always thought I was right, for better or worse. And I just thought, in the end this will be persuasive evidence of who I am.

[That was fairly early in my presidency to be taking a risky stand, in terms of whether the faculty might become alienated,] but if I hadn't, then I would have been prey to every other grievance committee down the road. Furthermore, I would have had very powerful faculty forces saying, "This is outrageous, that an art historian, a sociologist and a chemist"—or whoever—"should be granting tenure in the anatomy department." You know, I would have had real problems down the road. The fact is, as I think back on it, there were two stages. I first wrote the grievance committee a letter and said, "I'm having a lot of trouble with your recommendations for the following reasons—and could you answer these questions—" (this was fifteen years ago). That letter irritated a lot of people because it sounded too legalistic, and I began to learn that I just could not behave like a law school dean in these settings; that was not the lingua franca of the larger academic community. But that was all minor. I didn't really feel that I was running a big risk there. I do think that these early problems are useful because when they're shaped on the right kind of issue and they're focused on principle, you're in your best circumstance. It's much better than a problem with students or a sit-in or something else because it's on your turf. It's academic values and quality. And that, I think, was fortunate, that the first challenge that gave me a chance to respond was one on academic issues and tenure, the most important value in the institution.

[Getting back to the board:] You have to appreciate how modest Iowans are, and how people on the board felt very comfortable and appropriate in dealing with cultural and financial issues, questions such as, "How high can tuition really be in a farm state like Iowa?" But they were very modest people on issues of education. They respected me and I could tell that the first day. They may have respected all seven candidates—I do know they treated me with great respect. They obviously approved of what I told them, of why I wanted to be a president, what I wanted to do. And I think that this issue was seen by them and by others as, "We have a president now who will not be pushed around by the faculty." That is always a great fear. That was not a fear at Iowa—my predecessor Sandy Boyd was never pushed around, he led that place—but I think it was a way of saying, "I won't allow myself to be pushed around by other groups." And you can do that and be a damn fool about it where in fact you've misperceived the situation entirely, and what you're doing is being rigid or stubborn or foolish. But fortunately, this worked out okay.

You know, [my agenda for Iowa] got changed a lot when I was there because I came to learn much more about public institutions. My agenda was obviously to make it the strongest place I knew how, and it's very clear for me, in all fifteen years I've been a president, that my principal constituency is the faculty, that's the group I get my support most from. I'm never going to be a terrific person on the alumni circuit. In Iowa, people were very respectful—I think they respected me as I think now people here do—but I'm never going to be an old boy, and I'm never going to be a glad-hander, and I'm just not cut out to do that—I do it, I have to—but I'm not natural at it, and I'm not exceptional at it. The faculty has always been my natural constituency. I truly wanted to make the faculty better, and almost every talk I gave there was about the dignity of being a faculty member, the responsibility, the opportunity, the significance of the academic life, the loneliness of it, the aspiration of it. I really wanted to make Iowa a place [where the faculty were] self-consciously proud about being academics.

What I came to see during my five years there, though, was so many other rich things the place did that I came to think of as important and which I never knew about in my naïveté and insularity before I went to Iowa. The most important of those is what that university adds—the value added [that] the university provides for students. I saw students there who were just splendid. We had more Rhodes Scholars there in my five years than we've had in any five years I've been at Dartmouth, slice them any way you want. We had wonderful students at the very top. I taught all the time I was there and I saw these kids who came to the university from nice homes but often not homes with a lot of books. You ask a group of eighteen-year-olds the first day, "How many of you have ever been out of the state of Iowa?" and you often get half of them who've never been outside the state. If you ask, "Where have you been?" it's Chi-

cago, but they've never been further than Chicago. These are not kids
who come from wealthy families that are well traveled, who've been to
Europe, who've been to New York, who've seen operas and symphonies
and read Plato and had authors around the house and book talk. They
went to Iowa high schools, which cover, of course, a very wide spectrum
of quality from some very good ones to some very ordinary ones. And
they come to that university and they're suddenly lit up when they read
Plato and they read Aristotle, they read Locke, they read Dostoevsky.
And the value added in those four years, in my view, is far greater than
the value added at the great, private eastern universities of this country.
It may be that in the eastern places you push further because you started
up at a higher level, and kids come from much stronger secondary schools
and from homes that are much more enriched. But, boy, what Iowa does
to enrich those people's lives carries them much further. They start at a
lower point, perhaps, but they travel further because there's further to
travel.

The second thing I saw was that that state couldn't exist without that
university and others. You couldn't imagine that state without the university because the university trained the predominant doctors, lawyers,
nurses, pharmacists, businesspeople, engineers. Go through all of our professional schools: Most of the graduates are in the state of Iowa. Two-
thirds of all the people in the state doing any one of those professions is
a graduate of the University of Iowa or [one of the state's] other universities. But, you know, that state, it's losing people, it's not bringing them
in. I don't know where it would have the quality that it has in all of those
professions if these universities weren't there. And obviously the other
thing is that we had at that time the largest university-owned teaching
hospital in the country. This was a gem in the middle of the prairie there,
to have a teaching hospital of that quality and the medical school that
we had. So that I really came to respect the public mission immensely.

[As for other notable conflicts at Iowa:] It had been the desire of the
football coach to have an indoor practice facility, and after Iowa lost
twice at the Rose Bowl, we had a go-round. It was my view that we could
build the facility—athletics was a tub on its own bottom and most of its
money was football money. They were on television, they went to bowl
games, they were fine in terms of raising money. And we had the money,
but that was a year in which the legislature had voted no salary increases.
So the entire faculty, the entire university, went without a salary increase
for that year—zero. I felt it was unmeet and inappropriate to announce
we were going to build a two-and-a-half-million-dollar indoor practice
facility when the faculty weren't getting increases. And I had said to the

coach, and I thought I had his agreement, that we could start hiring the architect, we could make the plans, we could have everything ready to go, and the minute the legislature next year approved our appropriations with a salary increase, we'd put a shovel in the ground and be ready to go, there wouldn't be a minute's lost time. He accepted that, and the whole athletic establishment accepted that. But really, he didn't. And finally, at a press conference he said that he just didn't know how much longer he could be an effective coach without this kind of facility. Then I heard from the governor, and the alumni, and it was a big thing, all over the front page of the paper for a few days, and we announced we would build the facility, and I got virtually no flack from the faculty at all. I think everyone understood I had tried. This was not standing up for a great principle, it was just a sense that it wasn't appropriate, it didn't look right, and I had wanted the faculty to know that we were all suffering together for a year.

They understood. They knew the realities. They saw it on the front page of the papers, it was all over the television for a few days. They understood the realities and that I'd fought the good fight and that I'd lost. You just can't let an issue like that get into the legislature because once the legislature starts talking about it, you're going to lose. And if you're going to lose, you might as well lose in your own way and you might as well get it over with.

Another interesting thing that I would tell you about Iowa relates to the inaugural address. At Dartmouth, a president does not take office and report to work until the day of his inauguration. Until the day I was inaugurated, I was not the president. That's always been the tradition here. At Iowa, I showed up April 1. My inauguration wasn't until October, and by that time I was kind of familiar goods, and the possibility of using an inaugural speech to focus the attention of the university on my agenda had been dissipated because I had had six months to do that. I'd been talking all over the place, obviously, as the new president.

It was very different at Dartmouth, where the inauguration was the first time anyone here (except a few people) had ever seen me. I had met the search committee which had seven faculty members, and between the day I was appointed (April 13) and the day I took office (July 19) I had come here once a month and met with fifteen faculty at a time for three days, so I had met a lot of faculty, but it was more social and more getting to know them, showing appropriate interest and curiosity about the place. But the inauguration at Dartmouth was my first occasion to speak out as president. I'm only saying Iowa did not offer that opportunity.

[The Dartmouth trustees] certainly knew my views. I had dinner two nights ago with the person who was the chairman of the board then. This was a remarkable search process here, in its own different way, because he just said to this board, "Before we do a search we've got to find out what the rest of the world thinks about Dartmouth." And he and members of the search committee interviewed Bart Giamatti at Yale, David Riesman, Henry Rosovsky, Hanna Gray, many eminent people. Essentially the message they got back was that the rest of the world doesn't know Dartmouth academically. You're an undergraduate college, you're a nice place, nobody associates educational innovation with you, many people think you barely belong in the Ivy League, you certainly make sense in a football league because there are eight of you clustered up there geographically, but nobody puts Dartmouth in the same breath as Harvard, Yale, Princeton. You're just not a significant intellectual player by comparison with those.

This really affected him. He came back and reported to the board, and he tells me the board shrugged and basically said, "That's not credible, that's not the Dartmouth we know. That may be what these people think, but you know, this is Dartmouth and this is a wonderful place." But Sandy McCollouch had a bee in his bonnet which was that every president of this place since 1822 had been a Dartmouth graduate or a member of the faculty when he was made president. John Kemeny, my predecessor but one, was not a graduate, but he had been on the faculty twenty-five years. Every president [save one] since 1822 had been a graduate and everyone assumed the next president would be a graduate, whomever they chose. And Sandy McCollouch just decided, "We are going to break with that. We're going to have a national search for the best person, but it's not going to be a Dartmouth graduate." That was never announced, but Sandy will tell you he was very determined that they were going to say, "Dartmouth is part of a larger world of higher education," and that's one way to show it. So they had this national search based upon the sense that, "We really need to do some things academically and intellectually, that's what we need." And clearly, that's why they hired me. I mean, we had very good discussions about it. I will tell you why I wanted to leave Iowa, or was prepared to leave Iowa at that point, but I didn't need to leave, I was doing fine there, and I could have stayed longer with perfect ease. So it was easy to be candid in saying to the Dartmouth search committee, "If I come here, what I really want to do is—," what I [later] said in my inaugural address. [I told the board,] "Everything I know about Dartmouth is, it's too male-dominated, it's too much of a jock school, it's too concerned with well-rounded people," and that speech says well-rounded people may have no point at all. It talks about creative loners. You know, the words "creative loner" and "translating Catullus" and "playing the cello" are in the student newspaper day in and day out— op-ed pieces once a week. There's a defensiveness and there's a humor and there's teasing and there's ridicule, all these things. But those phrases stuck.

Sandy McCollouch had this view that Dartmouth had to become a much more serious place. These [eminent] people said, "No one gives it a second thought if they get admitted to another Ivy school and Dartmouth, no one's going to go to Dartmouth instead of Harvard or Yale or Princeton." We're now at a point where we still lose three-quarters of the people who were accepted by both, but our freshmen this year, by all national indices, are the fifth best in the country. So we have brought ourselves up into the very highest echelons in terms of student quality, and that was what I was brought here to do.

Interestingly, today as I'm finishing ten years, there's not a member on the board who was here—we have a ten-year term—there's no one left of the board that chose me. So we've got a very different [group] today that does not remember any of that history, none of the fourteen people who chose me, who were all under Sandy McCollouch's spell and whether reluctantly or enthusiastically, became persuaded Dartmouth needed to make a very significant change of emphasis. And, you know, you constantly have to reeducate your board. But that's a different story for a different moment.

[In regard to thinking about leaving Iowa:] A couple of things were in the back of my mind. I clearly knew I would need a second presidency at some point because I was forty-six when I started at Iowa, and even if I had spent ten years there, I would still have been only fifty-six. I had to be alert to the possibility [of another presidency] because you couldn't stay more than ten years at one place, or so I thought. The second thing was, everyone in my group of presidents thought that people don't appoint presidents after fifty-two or -three or -four years of age. That's all changed now, of course. You know, Neil Rudenstine was older than that when he was appointed, Gerhard Casper was older than that. That's changed. But it was the folklore at that time, omnipresent in presidents' minds, and all the Big Ten presidents, when we talked, lived with the view that you really had to make your move before you were fifty-three or -four because no one would appoint someone as old as fifty-five. So both thoughts were in my mind, and then what happened was that I started hearing from other schools much earlier than I'd ever anticipated. That's flattering, and so you do think you want to look. I really only

looked at one, which was Texas, with very much seriousness, and as I got
to be one of the finalists, it was in the paper.

What had really happened was that we had had such tough years economically in Iowa. Those were bad years for the farm belt, we had no resources. We had one year without any salary increases, and it's just
discouraging trying to do things without the resources you need. So I did
look at Texas and talk to those people, and that was on the front page
of the *Des Moines Register*. We'd been down there twice and Texas was
not the place for us. I don't know if five years was premature or not, but
it was a mixture, I think, of ambition, of maybe too much ambition, of
fear of getting too old to be appointed elsewhere, and a sense that Iowa
was a tough place because of the economy.

[I became involved in a public argument with the board of regents secretary in 1985.] This was a man who really is a fine person, who'd been
the secretary of the board for fifteen years. There's a constant tension between the institutions that the board of regents governs (there were five
of them, three universities, an institution for the blind and one for the
deaf) and the board itself. Furthermore, the board office had an enormous amount of power because every proposal we put to the regents, the
board office passed upon. That is, they put in with the agenda their recommendations—you know, the board should be careful of this, or skeptical, or it's not clear that this much money is needed or we'd recommend
further study. So every recommendation we made to the regents for a new
building or for whatever, was also commented upon by the board office.
We could live with that. But it does mean there's an adversary relationship built in. I think the board felt that this was healthy in that they got
a skeptical, critical view of whatever we were always proposing. But the
fight he and I had, had to do with aggrandizing the powers of the board
office vis-à-vis the institutions, moving things to a nonacademic central
bureaucracy in Des Moines, away from the campuses, and diminishing
the power of the presidents. It just happened that of the three presidents
—Iowa, Iowa State, and Northern Iowa—the president of the University of Iowa was always expected to be the one who took the lead. That
was just the way the institutions were lined up, and I knew I would win
on that, there was never any doubt, I was not taking a huge risk.

The board was not in a comfortable position because they dearly did
not want to vote down the president of the University of Iowa, particularly as I was getting a little attention outside of Iowa, but they also didn't
want to vote down the executive secretary who was absolutely indispen-
sable to them, who was very competent and they absolutely needed him.
Their real challenge was somehow to side with me but not to hurt him

or insult him or injure him and his status and credibility. But in the end they had to make the choice, and they made it in our direction.

[To clarify:] The Board of Regents is nine people appointed by the governor, and the executive secretary is the full-time staff person whose job essentially was supposed to be focusing on the financial things. For example, when we projected enrollments and on the basis of that projected tuition income, he might say, "This is a very rosy enrollment projection, I think it's too high, and maybe there won't be all that income, and if there's not all that income, maybe you can't give salary increases at this level." I think he made a mistake in thinking we would be passive and quiet [in the face of his proposal].

[Coming back to Dartmouth:] What I had done at Iowa was once a year to publish a booklet with my talks. So what the [Dartmouth] board had when they appointed me was five years of these booklets from Iowa. They already knew what my values were and that I'd spoken on these things, and that I was a faculty's president—I spoke the values of the faculty. The board clearly knew in appointing me that they were not hiring someone who was going to be a superb financial manager, who would understand the endowment spending formula to the umpteenth degree. And they clearly knew they were not getting someone who was going to be exceptionally good at palling around with students and being in the fraternity living rooms and all that kind of stuff. All that's part of the job, but they were getting someone whose basic interest was outlined in all of these speeches that I'd always published. I thought the Dartmouth inaugural address was my opportunity to speak to the faculty and to the larger community who didn't know [me]. That was really my occasion to say, "Let me tell you what I hope we're going to be able to do here." I don't know if you've read my book, but there is a chapter that says, "This is the best moment you'll ever have, everyone's listening, everyone's looking, everyone's watching, you'll never have a better moment than that moment." And that was really very important, and it obviously hit a bell because we heard for years and years after that, from all of the alumni and from others.

You know, I've never had any problem with students anywhere. I am not a Mr. Chips kind of president. I know a few who are like that, and some are very good at it, but none of them are at really good institutions. I never had problems with students when I was dean at Penn or president at Iowa—I think students see you for who you are and they respect you for who you are. And if you're shy or if you're quiet or if that's not where you want to spend all your time, they understand that. They're not angry at you; they may not be entirely happy, but I never expected problems with students and I never had any. But I didn't expect there the same kind of enthusiasm that I did hope to have from faculty.

I wasn't [concerned about the Dartmouth alumni] when I came, but boy, I learned soon after. I had no idea of the way in which alumni then felt entitled to run this place and entitled to be heard. They were here constantly; every weekend the place was overrun with class officers and club officers and the alumni council and all these boards of overseers. I just had no idea of the prominence of alumni. It's not that they make a lot of policy and it's not even that they influence academic policy—I don't think they do. But their omnipresence here, and their sense of engagement in the place and entitlement to be engaged in the place was just far greater than anything I'd ever known. I should have taken my cue from the beginning because the difference in the inaugurations at Iowa and Dartmouth said worlds about the differences between the two schools. The Iowa inauguration, first of all, had dozens of university presidents there. All the Big Ten presidents came. Harold Shapiro spoke on behalf of the Big Ten presidents; Stan Ikenberry, who happened to be at Illinois, spoke on behalf of the AAU. Academics spoke on behalf of the academic community. There was a sense of, "Iowa is part of a national academic community and we want that represented here." Dartmouth set up the inauguration for July 19, in the middle of the summer. Not a single academic was here. Not a single academic was asked to speak. I was allowed to have a speaker, and my speaker was Vartan Gregorian. At Iowa it had been Lou Pollak, who'd been a teacher of mine at Yale and then dean of Penn Law School, my predecessor as dean, a dear, dear friend. And here it was Vartan, who's also a dear friend. But the Dartmouth inauguration was set up for the alumni. It wasn't set up for the national academic community, it was set up for the alumni. And no one gave a thought [to this]. It wasn't [that] they made a decision against it, it just never occurred to them that this ought to be an event in the academic life of the college and you ought to have other presidents here, certainly the Ivy presidents, and there ought to be people bringing greetings from the Ivy League, or greetings from some other outfit. It never occurred to anybody. This was an in-house event, this was a bar mitzvah, this was a wedding. And that's when I first should have begun to be quite aware that alumni play a big, big role here.

There's no question that in my early years we had alumni more upset over the *Dartmouth Review* and over the old line that "In New England, all people want is to see their names in the paper when they're born, when they're married, and when they die." That's what they wanted from Dartmouth. They just were very distressed that Dartmouth's name was in the paper a lot, and that there was all this trouble with the *Review*. That had started before my time. There was an incident on the Green that was talked about as the "shanty incident," for divestment [from stock in companies doing business in South Africa]. That's what really upset them, and then of course my ideas upset them. At every alumni dinner I went to those first few years you could always count on people saying, "Are you going to—" the word "Harvardize" became a word here, that I was trying to "Harvardize" because I was the first president who wasn't Dartmouth. "We're not Harvard and who would want to be, and Harvard's all nerds." The students had this attitude as much as the alumni. Harvard was the symbol of everything that was wrong, and it bespoke such an inferiority complex. What I'd really learned in my years at Penn, where there was of course an inferiority complex in regard to Princeton and Yale and Harvard, I learned from Vartan who, when he was dean and when he was provost, constantly said, "We are a wonderful place. We are Penn. And what Penn is, is seriousness of purpose and outstanding this and wonderful that and unique the other. We are Penn, and we don't compare ourselves to other people." And that's what I wanted Dartmouth to do. We are a wonderful place. We're not Harvard, we're different. We're not inferior, we're not superior. There are some things where we may do a better job than Harvard if those are what you value. There are other things where Harvard does a better job than we, if those are the things you value. We'll never be Harvard in a research sense, but we may be better than Harvard in a nurturing sense, in a small class sense, in a sense of school collegiality and spirit and belonging, and even—the lists are endless. But the sense of inferiority here was all focused on my having come from Harvard and sounding as if I had a Harvard agenda, which was intellectual seriousness, great dignity, aspirations for the faculty, wanting students who were not every single one well-rounded, but students who were themselves achievers, who in high school had shown they were debaters or musicians or athletes or school editors or poets or cellists or translators of Catullus or something. Students with an edge to them. All of those values should be Dartmouth's values, but people saw that as saying, "You're unhappy with Dartmouth because it isn't like Harvard, and that's what you're trying to do to us."

Easterners are different from Iowans. Iowans welcomed us. I mean, we were strange creatures out there, a little different. But they welcomed us. You've got to remember, I should go back and say, Iowa had a wonderful tradition of presidents—Howard R. Bowen was president there, who as you may know was a great man. Howard was an intellectual and a very severe man in a way, but an intellectual. My predecessor, Sandy Boyd, came next, and Sandy was an intellectual and wonderfully active, an absolute model. So I came into Iowa where people expected the president to be the kind of president I was there. I was no different than President Boyd and President Bowen, even though I was an outsider. People welcomed us. The Jewish issue never arose in Iowa. No one said a word to me about it. The board would have if they had thought it would be an issue because they were that kind of board. But no one ever did. The only place it arose was in the Jewish community that wanted to invite us but wasn't sure if we were Jewish. They didn't know how to ascertain it. They started doing profiles on us; my wife's maiden name was Bathsheba Finkelstein, and they got a hint from that! But it never was an issue there. Here [at Dartmouth], it was, of course, something of an issue, and all the issues of anti-Semitism were connected with the *Review*—as you know, anti-Semitism was a leitmotif through the history of the *Review*—we can talk as to whether that's fully justified or not—but that had to have something to do with the reaction in alumni land, too. It wasn't against Jews, but "Jewish" was itself a surrogate word for intellectual, for Harvard, for a set of values that they did not see as Dartmouth. Now, you put together Jewish, Harvard, intellectual, and you know you're talking about a creature they thought was not really of the history of Dartmouth, although that's not true, I think, and they began to see the board was really trying an experiment here in social engineering. The board had gone out to get someone whose reputation was as an academic builder and that's what they really wanted. And the alumni weren't so sure why the place had to be changed. What was wrong with it? You know, it was perfectly good. And I try to tell people it *was* perfectly good and it *is* perfectly good, and you couldn't change a 220-year-old institution if you wanted. But you do have to keep up with the times and you do have to keep up with the competition. And if we had not made the moves we've made these last ten years, we'd have slipped because all the other places were moving. The whole cohort is moving, and if you're not moving, too, you're losing.

My inaugural speech was hardly a turning [point because] it was the first day I was president. I think the faculty listened and said nice things, but faculty are skeptical and I think [the] faculty thought, "These are high-sounding words, but let's wait and see, we don't know this person." The *Dartmouth Review* speech was in March, I think March 28, 1988, so it was just a few months later. That really was a turning point because this place had taken the strategy until then of ignoring the *Review*, of not responding, of not protecting faculty, and I might well have done the same thing those years, but when we had another incident, it was a different point in time and my only point—I hadn't been here the earlier times. So I thought it was necessary to [speak out about the *Review*]. And standing in front of that faculty, I'll tell you, my knees—I was nervous. I mean, this was a big moment. I could have lost everything. That was a far bigger moment than anything at Iowa. I was doing something that had never been done here. It was taking on the *Review*. We had told the newspapers I was going to do this. The *New York Times* was here, and of course there was a story in the *Times* the next day. I knew that I was stepping onto a larger stage and it was a big risk; I was throwing down the gauntlet. So that really was a defining moment. One of the most senior faculty women here, Marysa Navarro, got up at the meeting and cried, and said, "I have been waiting all these years for a president to do this," and came to the front of the room and gave me a great big hug. And I'll tell you, that was quite a moment, really an emotional moment.

What followed that was, the *New York Times* called and asked me to do an op-ed piece, which I did, which they labeled, "Bigoted Students, Doting Adults" [*New York Times*, October 11, 1990, p. A25]. That piece, too, was a [defining] moment because that was really taking on the right wing and the *Review* and William Simon, who was their biggest person, and Bill Buckley, in the *New York Times*. Simon did reply. I was so naïve as well, I had no idea that once the *Times* asked me, they would then go ask someone to reply. I was sitting in a hotel ballroom and lo and behold, Bill Simon's piece was in [the paper] attacking me. Suddenly I had stepped out from Dartmouth, and this was an issue with some national visibility and attention, and then it got written about everywhere. I think another wonderful thing that happened was that when I took office, Ted Fiske, who was then a very prominent person with the *New York Times*, did one of those long interviews with me on the back page of section 4, "The Week In Review," and it was maybe half a page. That gave me a chance to state my views on education and what I hoped to do at Dartmouth. It was wonderful that Ted Fiske knew higher education well enough to know what the board of trustees was trying to do and that I was to be the instrument of that. That was a week or two into my presidency, probably. It was a question and answer format which gave me a huge platform, and once you're in the *New York Times*, you gain a legitimacy with the community, whoever that may be, alumni certainly.

[Returning to the March 1988 speech:] Once I got here I appreciated the agonies that my predecessor had to live through for six years with the *Review*, and I just knew I had to do something, and the speech was the something I had to do. As I say in my book, it is not my nature to confront and to denounce and to invite controversy. But I felt I had absolutely no choice. Sometimes these things just fall into your lap, they are fortuitous, and you have an opportunity to show who you are and what your values are. As it happened, in retrospect, as painful as all of that was and those years were, it was fortuitous that it came early and it did give me an opportunity to say, "I am going to defend this faculty, and I'm not going to allow the *Review* to drag our faculty and the name of this college in the mud and to make us a constant subject of controversy on the national scene." I have not had a fight with the faculty in ten years, and I think it was in part because they saw I was willing to put myself on the line for their values. Being a lawyer and a law professor gave me credibility in speaking about issues of the First Amendment and a commitment to it. You know, so many people who talk about the First Amendment don't have much more than a sloganized, clichéd idea of what it's about. I think being a lawyer and a law professor made people think I probably understand it a bit more than I would if I hadn't been a lawyer and a law professor.

[When the *Review* targeted me for anti-Semitic attacks,] I can't tell you I ever thought about leaving, but I did think a lot about, "How is this ever going to end? When and how are we going to bring this to an end?" The board was scared to death I was going to leave. No one ever said that to me, but they had made a huge investment in me because I was so different and because the mission was so significant, and were I to have left after a couple of years, it would have hurt Dartmouth because it would have confirmed in the national press that this is an ungovernable place, run by the right wing and a bunch of people like Buckley and Simon and a man named George Champion, who was the retired chairman of Chase Manhattan Bank, a Dartmouth graduate. I never really thought of leaving, but the anti-Semitism was the absolute—you know, when they did that business of me in a Hitler uniform [October 26, 1988] and the article titled, "Ein Reich, Ein Volk, Ein Freedmann" [October 19, 1988], that was the bottom. The board was so concerned, their question was, "How do you respond to that? How does the board respond?"— since I couldn't respond because it was about me, but it was so ugly. The response was a letter from the board to me saying how offended they were by all this and how inappropriate and terribly out of place this was at Dartmouth. [Then the letter was released to the press] and that was a very clever way to do it because it didn't attack the *Review*. I mean, our great concern was that every time we attacked the *Review* we got more publicity. Nothing is greater than "President Attacks a Bunch of Kids," and "President Attacks His Own Students," and "President Attacks

Newspaper." The awkwardness of all this was that it was a bunch of kids, but in fact, they were the cat's-paws for these adults.

[My wife and I] always felt supported by the board at every stage, and indeed, a constant issue in those days was the issue of—I can't tell you how omnipresent this became and how intense, it was day after day for several years—whether to sue the *Review* to take off the name "Dartmouth." That had been an issue for all three presidents, starting in 1981 or 1980 when the *Review* was founded. In the early years the board decided not to do it because it looked like anti-freedom of the press and it looked like taking on your students and "Maybe they won't always be like this." They also had legal advice at the time that an awful lot of things have been called "Dartmouth" around here over the generations: there's a Dartmouth co-op which is not ours, there's a Dartmouth bookstore that's not ours, Dartmouth taxicab which is not ours, Dartmouth dry cleaning—I mean, everyone uses the name, it's part of the community, everyone around here calls themselves "Dartmouth," and the main street's full of these places. How are you going to persuade a judge that there's a problem when a newspaper does it, when there isn't a problem when a dry cleaner does it or a bookstore does it or other things?

So when I became president and all this started, there was again another serious push, "Why don't we sue them and get them to stop using the name 'Dartmouth'?" The faculty clearly wanted to do that and the board did not, but there were real divisions on the board. There were people on the board who were so angry and so offended and so hurt that they wanted to do anything, as I did, really, obviously, to try to stop all this. But the board decided not to sue, and we never have. [The *Dartmouth Review*'s influence has waned, and it now has a much lower profile.] You know, I don't know when it comes out—it does not come out regularly. It does come out a few times, though, each term, maybe more than a few. It's much less belligerent and antagonistic, it doesn't get any attention. No one talks about it, it's nothing, it says many outrageous things still, but people today just take it as journalism, bad journalism. The cover this week has a photograph of our dean of students who's black. To me it looks no different than the cover that *Newsweek* did of O.J. Simpson where they darkened it. They took a photograph of O.J. when he was first arrested and made it very, very dark. And *Newsweek* finally apologized. Well, they have a photograph in the *Review* in which they've done that to Dean Pelton, and in my view, it may be innocent kids, but I don't know. They have a story in there about me. I was invited by a student group over at the Rockefeller Center, which is our social science center. We've got about twenty students who are in the group, and they have speakers and they have lunches and they do projects. I went to Vietnam, and they invited me to come talk about it. I did. I thought, I'm talking to a group of students about what I saw in Vietnam and the government. There's a story in the *Review* this week with a lot of things in there I never would have said publicly. I'm perfectly glad to say them to a group of students. But some student in that room was a *Review* reporter who took notes. Everything he said was accurate, I did indeed say those things, but they don't tell you like any other newspaper will.

There were really two great *Review* controversies: the first was with Professor Cole and when I gave my speech, and the second was the one on *Mein Kampf* and everything. The Jewish one was just in between there somewhere. But all of that is so far behind us now. What has happened is that all of the alumni are proud of the fact that Dartmouth [has changed]. The *U.S. News* rankings have been a blessing for us because they have put us up with the big players when we are not a research university. We're the only nonresearch university up with those big players like Harvard, Yale, Princeton, Duke, MIT, Cal Tech. The alumni, I think, have grudgingly come to the view that, "We may not agree about everything with Freedman, but we also want to see Dartmouth ranked way up there." And they're thrilled with the quality of the students we're getting.

[To compare the Iowa presidency:] I would regard Iowa as kind of a routine series of concerns, the concerns every president has of fiscal resources. But that was not a place where you had to fear the right-wing crazies or where you had to fear—I mean, the alumni just worshipped the place, and for anyone who was president, it was like being chief justice of the United States. That was a very honorific position.

The places I've been most successful are the places where I've in a sense encroached a bit on faculty things because I've encouraged them or wanted them. One of the things I do here is insist—and people are glad—that we have poetry readings. I introduce every poet or novelist who comes to read because I love that, I enjoy it, and we always have a dinner party at our house afterward. Well, that's something which at some places people would say, "What's the president horning in on this for? This is an English Department thing." But here they welcome it. Which is wonderful, which is really wonderful. So I've been most successful in all those areas that are the academic sides because I think people have seen that that's what I'm genuinely interested in. But this has been a much rockier, uneven, un-plateau kind of experience. The last few years have been fine, and of course, we've just finished this huge fund-raising campaign that was successful beyond all dreams, and that makes the alumni peaceful. I'm not on the defensive all the time anymore, and the alumni speech that I give—I've given all ten years—now is accepted. I was in Hartford last night for an alumni dinner, and when I tell them, "Our students have median SATs of 1440"—you know, in the olden days they would say, "Who wants those people?" but now they're very proud of those people.

I have lunches at this table with students, I had one yesterday, and they still want to know, "What do you mean by 'creative loner,' and do you really think that's what we ought to be?" And they talk. All I mean is, I've been able to set the agenda, and that first speech was the most significant part of setting the agenda.

I should say another thing that the Dartmouth search committee and board of trustees told me in the interview phase, "Whoever's the next president, we want that person to be a player, visible on the national scene. We want that person to speak on educational issues, to find a way to get some attention, and to be one of those people who are taken seriously as a president because of his views on education." Whether I've done that or not I don't know, but I've published all these things, I'm in the op-ed page whenever I can be. The *Times* runs something maybe every other year, the *Boston Globe* probably three times a year. They don't want more than that. They've just taken another piece. I wrote this book which people are proud of in the sense that very few presidents write books while they're president. All I mean is that my own ambitions and their employment expectations conjoined to give me great satisfaction. There's obviously great satisfaction. I'm reaching now the senior statesman stage where I get many more invitations than I used to, to speak at events and meetings, and that's all very, very satisfying. But the Dartmouth board clearly wanted a president who had a national profile academically, and that's what I wanted to do, and that's what I've tried to do, and you know, you're at the mercy then of the press and of how good your stuff is, and whether it's worthy of respect.

NOTES

1. "The University of Iowa Comparative Enrollment Report 1981–82," pp. 1–2, "UI Faculty 1982–83," no page, "The University of Iowa General Educational Fund Summary 1981–82," p. 2, "Balance Sheet, June 30, 1982," p. 4, Special Collections, University of Iowa Libraries; Tamara Henry, "Regents Name Freedman as UI President," UPI, July 31, 1981, no page.

The *University of Iowa General Catalog 1980–82*, "General Information," p. 2, lists colleges of business administration, dentistry, education, engineering, law, medicine, nursing, and pharmacy; and schools of journalism, library science, music, and social work. It omits specific mention of the college of arts and sciences and the graduate school. Special Collections, University of Iowa Libraries.

2. "The University of Iowa Comparative Enrollment Report 1986–87," pp. III–8, III–9, "UI Faculty 1987–88," no page, "The University of Iowa General Educational Fund Summary 1986–87," p. 2, "Balance Sheet, June 30, 1987," p. 4, Special Collections, University of Iowa Libraries; Regional News, UPI, May 9, 1987, no page.

3. "Dartmouth College Enrollment, Registered Students, Fall Term 1987," p. 319, "Dartmouth Faculty, Fall 1987" (Dartmouth is composed of the college of arts and sciences and the graduate school, and four professional schools: computer and information systems, and the medical, engineering, and business schools), no page, *Dartmouth: A Financial Report of the College 1987–1988*, p. 3, Dartmouth College Library Special Collections: Archives, Manuscripts, Rare Books; "Growth of College Endowments Found to Have Slowed Last Year; Value of 296 Funds Placed at $4.7-Billion," *Chronicle of Higher Education*, June 1, 1988, p. A35, survey by the National Association of College and University Business Officers; Office of Public Affairs, "Some Statistics and Facts about Dartmouth," http://www.dartmouth.edu, posted 12 February 1998 (computer and information systems is no longer listed as a separate professional school); "Facts and Figures: 506 College and University Endowments," *Chronicle of Higher Education*, from issue of February 19, 1999, http://chronicle.com, survey by the National Association of College and University Business Officers.

Robert O'Neil

University of Virginia 1985–1990
University of Wisconsin System 1980–1985
Indiana University-Bloomington 1975–1980

A first-rate legal scholar with a remarkable breadth of experience in public university administration, Robert O'Neil earned bachelor's, master's, and law degrees from Harvard University. He began his academic career at the University of California-Berkeley in 1963 as a professor of law and left in 1967 to serve as executive assistant to the president and professor of law at SUNY-Buffalo. O'Neil returned to Berkeley in 1969, but in 1972 left again when he accepted the position of provost at the University of Cincinnati, where he became executive vice president in 1973. In 1975, he took over leadership of Indiana University's Research I campus at Bloomington, a university of almost 29,000 students and some 1,500 faculty. During the tough economic times of 1975–1980, the university's modest endowment grew little (from $14,371,149 to $15,591,544), but the budget was increased from $88,533,450 to $113,095,584.[1] In what may be a unique departure from academic custom, from February to June 1980, O'Neil actively held both the de facto chancellorship at Indiana-Bloomington and the presidency of the huge University of Wisconsin System. At that time the fourth-largest higher education system in the nation, Wisconsin consisted of thirteen, four-year campuses and fourteen, two-year campuses or "centers" with a total enrollment of 155,499 students, 6,858 FTE (Full Time Equivalent) faculty, a $1.1 billion budget, and an endowment of $37,453,000. Once again accepting leadership at a time of economic uncertainty, Robert O'Neil departed five years later having built Wisconsin's endowment to $70,937,000 and increased the system's budget to

$1.375 billion. Most notably, perhaps, to those anticipating his presidency at the University of Virginia, were his successful lobbying efforts at Wisconsin for faculty "catch-up" pay raises as the state's finances improved, with a controversial provision that heavily favored faculty at Madison, the University of Wisconsin's Research I campus.[2]

At the University of Virginia, O'Neil found the contact with students, opportunity to teach, and identification with a single educational institution that he had missed at Wisconsin, in comparison with which Virginia presented a tiny academic domain: 16,531 students (10,962 undergraduates) and 1,669 full- and part-time faculty in the schools of arts and sciences, architecture, business, education, engineering, law, medical technology, nursing, and medicine (a significant difference from IU-B). Virginia's budget of $244 million (increasing to $392.5 million by 1990 when he left the presidency) was comparatively quite small, of course, but its endowment, at $256.5 million ($487 million in 1990) was more comparable with that of a private institution. When Robert O'Neil announced his resignation in October 1989 (effective August 1, 1990), the *Washington Post*, noting especially the soaring endowment and significant increases in faculty salaries and outside funding for research, declared that "all of the traditional barometers of a university's health indicate prosperity during O'Neil's tenure."[3]

> Robert O'Neil's account of some aspects of his presidencies combines edited transcripts of his two interviews with Leslie Banner at the Thomas Jefferson Center for the Protection of Free Expression in Charlottesville, Virginia, on June 25, 1997, and May 26, 1999. The questions that prompted his comments have either been omitted or indicated with bracketed material to create a more readable narrative.

Since your first question has to do with recruitment to Virginia, I would say it differed from any previous experience because the initial contact came to me from the incumbent president. He had been deputized by the search committee of the board of visitors to contact, as I later learned, several candidates whom he had known. Thus, I came to a relatively unfamiliar institution through a quite familiar channel. Actually, I had never been to Charlottesville before. I had visited extensively in other parts of Virginia, in Roanoke and the Shenandoah Valley, Richmond, Williamsburg, and so on, but for whatever reason had simply never been to Charlottesville.

My first visit therefore was in January 1985 to meet with the board of visitors as one of three candidates. Curiously, I learned much later, of the three candidates for this supposedly traditional southern institution, I, in Madison, Wisconsin, was the southernmost. The fact that the other two came from places north of Madison may give you a sense of how anxious the board of visitors and its search committee were to make this a truly national search. In terms of the more or less concurrent search at Duke, for example, I think they already felt that they had achieved national status so that they were free to choose a president from within. But there was some feeling here, a conviction, that even though there were some very good people within, somehow they had to go not only outside but far afield. Now, if you go to the next three or four of a group of twelve people who showed up both on the faculty list and the student list, and that the search firm had checked out and found were potentially available and acceptable, one of those people was considerably further to the south, Bill Frye, but he really was not interested. He wanted to stay at Emory. His presence on the list was, however, also a national phenomenon. I think of the last six or so candidates, probably no one was within two hundred miles of here. But that's just a hunch, I can speak only for the finalists.

For the crucial interviews, [there were] three of us. I found the interviews with the board of visitors as probing and as candid as any of the several comparable experiences I've had. I particularly recall one person (whom I've since come to know extensively in other contacts) asking about my politics. One is, of course, perplexed by that sort of question, particularly if one interviews with a state university board. So I said, "Well, in fact, I have been registered and have voted in both parties, and I'll simply tell you what one of our favorite legislators in Wisconsin said" (she actually represents the university district in the Wisconsin legislature), "One of your predecessors would never invite a Democrat to the President's House, the other would never invite a Republican. What we particularly enjoy about what you and your wife have done here is that you treat us all pretty much alike even though you recognize there are times when Democrats would like to be with Democrats and Republicans with Republicans," which we did. So I felt that sort of comment was fairly comforting.

The chairman of the board [at Virginia], whose title is "rector," had been in touch on almost a daily basis leading up to this crucial session. He wanted me to ask questions of him. He also wanted me to understand that, following the interview, they might immediately put to me the question, "Would you accept our offer?" so that one could not come and say, "Gee, that's interesting—I'm deeply honored, let me go home and talk to my family and friends and think it over and I'll come back and I'll let you know in a couple of weeks or even a couple of days." They made clear, and I think this was a perfectly reasonable expectation, that they might want an answer on the spot, which indeed they did, because I was the third of three candidates. Now, if the offer had gone to the first or the second person, it would then have been different. It just happened (I think it had to do with my schedule and theirs) that I was the third of the three candidates to be interviewed, so roughly an hour after the interview ended, the rector came and said, "Remember that question I asked you on the phone a few days ago? It was hypothetical then, it's now real. Would you join us?" I said yes.

I did so not out of any lack of enthusiasm for Wisconsin—we had five wonderful years there and it's an extraordinary institution—but more, I think, because having spent those five years as the head of a multicampus system, I did feel somewhat distanced from the life of a functioning academic institution. Our offices actually were on the top floor of the largest building on the Madison campus. You rode up and down in the elevators with faculty and students from the language departments. So we were not [as] isolated as the system offices are in places like California (Oakland), Texas (downtown Austin), and Maryland (Adelphi). Increasingly, the multicampus system offices really are remote. That's not true at Wisconsin—it's still very much a part of the Madison campus. But the administrative role was one that was more closely tied to the state government and less closely tied to faculty and student issues. So I welcomed the opportunity to return, as I had been at Indiana, to a central, single campus role.

I suppose there may have been questions I could have asked [in the interview], but in order to appreciate the differences between Virginia and any place I'd been in the past, one could not find that out by asking questions. The ideal way of knowing what those differences were, I suppose, would have been to be able to come here, say, as a visitor for a year, and then all of a sudden to be engaged in the presidential search. By that time you would know the institution. My experience has been unusual. Four times I have come in as an outsider. And each of those four times I had very little prior knowledge of the institution. I had in each case visited once before, except on coming here when I had not been near until that meeting with the board of visitors. But at Cincinnati, at Indiana, at Wisconsin, and at Virginia, I was totally an outsider and really knew next to nothing about the institution. Being an outsider has some advantages, but it also has disadvantages in that there are lots of things you just simply don't know and can't know if you come upon one institution from the perspective of another. So I think my answer to the question, were there questions that I should have asked? is that I don't think such differences as later proved to be significant could have been gleaned from simply asking questions.

I would say the [board of visitors'] expectation, more than agenda, was to make this a more national institution than it had been, although there is a curious underappreciation [here]. Berkeley may be a classic example of an institution which, extraordinary as it is, could never be quite as good as it thinks it is. I would describe Wisconsin and Indiana as places that are pretty objective about where they are. Virginia is a place that has had historically a kind of underappreciation of itself. There was always here, and I think to some extent still is, a sense that this university was until quite recently a small, semiprivate southern men's college. For example, many people would say [the University of Virginia] became a research university only since World War II. That is demonstrably untrue. Virginia became an AAU member in 1904 and would have been a charter member in 1900 almost certainly had there been a president. For the first eighty years there was no president; Thomas Jefferson's theory ("That government is best which governs least") was that the chairman of the faculty, on the European model, should be the senior administrator. So it was not until 1904 that a president was appointed. Almost immediately after [Edwin] Alderman came here from Tulane [where he had been president, to be UVA's first president], the charter group of about a dozen institutions that constituted the AAU in 1900 invited Virginia to join, by many years the first additional member in the southeast. I contrast that statement, that fact, with the perception that Virginia has become a research institution only in the last few years. It's a curious kind of underevaluation. Now that's something that it would take months to understand; you can't ask the question, "How do you see yourselves?" although I did have a bit of an inkling when among these expectations were things that seemed to me had already been achieved.

This is one of the great mysteries to me; there has always been here a certain discontinuity or disparity between the external reality and an internal perception that one could paraphrase as, "We've only just arrived," when that's clearly not true. [While president] I was never clear (nor am I to this day) why it's advantageous to speak in those terms. Most of my experience has been at places like Berkeley, for example, where people tend to project the institution's history further back. When the University of California (as it then was) celebrated the centennial in 1968 and the 120th anniversary [of the state charter in 1969], you would have thought that in 1849 there had been this great research institution in the East Bay. Stanford and Chicago people do this all the time—they seem to think that in the 1890s the Stanfords and the Rockefellers created these institutions full blown, roughly comparable to what is there today. Virginia is the only place I've been where the perception shortens, rather than lengthens, the actual time frame. I'm not sure what explains it or what impact it has on people. They seem to overlook that the University of Virginia could not have attracted the president of Tulane in 1904 unless it had been a more prestigious institution than this backward projection suggests. Around 1925, the American Historical Association did a survey of doctoral programs in history and Virginia's came up as one of the ten or twelve best programs in the country. There are very few surveys of the quality of academic institutions that go that far back. But history was one field that seemed to do it fairly often, and it's not surprising to me. But there is a strange sense in which people here have a false modesty about their predecessors, instead of, as I say, the typical pattern in American academia, which is just the opposite.

To return to the question of expectations, as I said, I think they are very difficult to define, and they weren't ever explicit. If one had asked, and I certainly made efforts to ascertain from the board of visitors what their expectations were, I don't think they had anything very clearly in mind except this "national presence" notion, which to a greater degree than I think they realized, was already achieved and would have continued to be, regardless of whether they had chosen a president from inside or outside. It was not in my interest, I guess, to tell them before the appointment was made that that factor would probably make a whole lot less difference than they may have assumed. In fact, I believed at the time and have continued to believe since then, that more emphasis was placed on origin, experience, background, and so on, of the next president than was really warranted.

So that's kind of an overview of the process of how I came here and a sense that asking questions, even if you knew exactly what questions to ask, which one never does, would not have significantly altered the process of orientation or transition.

[As far as an agenda of my own,] I sensed that there were some critical needs. External support for research was a classic example. Among public AAU institutions with medical centers, Virginia at that time ranked next to the bottom in sponsored research. The University of Missouri-Columbia was the only one below us, of AAU public institutions with medical centers. That struck me as surprising. Partly it's a function of size, although size isn't everything as places like Princeton and Vanderbilt illustrate—institutions that are objectively much smaller yet have achieved eminence even in some science fields where you tend to equate quality with quantity, physics probably being the outstanding example. So it wasn't only a function of size, though for the record this was the smallest save one in terms of enrollment, of AAU public institutions, UCSD [University of California-San Diego] being then slightly smaller. Now, I think, Virginia must be the smallest of public AAU institutions. I soon discovered that the constraints were not the ones I had supposed but rather were constraints of space. There simply was not anywhere near adequate laboratory space at that time, and it took many years with rather complex funding formulas to increase the available laboratory space to the point where you really could go out and aggressively seek the kind of sponsored research that parts of this institution did not have.

A second area in which I was very interested to work was the international. The first foreign student was personally admitted by Thomas Jefferson to the second entering class, the class that entered in the fall of 1826, the year in which he died on July 4. Much of the original faculty was recruited from European universities simply because Thomas Jefferson (who could on occasion be an elitist) did not believe that there were people worthy of teaching at his institution to be found anywhere on this continent. So a substantial number of the charter faculty was recruited from abroad. [When I arrived] I was startled at how small was the international enrollment compared not only to places like Berkeley and Madison but also to a place like Bloomington, [which had] a substantially larger foreign enrollment, and how relatively limited was student participation in overseas study compared to Duke and other places with which I was familiar. So we restructured international studies. For whatever reason, it turned out that was not universally a high priority, and I would have to say that that part of my personal mission which had come quite naturally from experience at Indiana and Wisconsin did not transplant very easily here.

Another hard-to-digest issue had to do with research policy. My experience, going back to Harvard and through Berkeley and Bloomington and Madison, was one which assumed that classified research was not acceptable. That's partly a principled view, but it also proceeds in part from the practical notion that federal funding agencies sometimes have flexibility in whether they will authorize a project to be funded as classified or not, and if the institution has a prohibition they will find a way to declassify or non-classify it. I discovered there was already a classified research project here which was phasing out. As soon as it had terminated, I asked the faculty senate to consider the issue of classified research. They appointed a committee, went to work and, to my amazement, came back six months later with a recommendation that classified research should not be forbidden but rather that it should be subject to certain disclosure requirements, and there should be a faculty committee with the authority to approve specific classified projects.

In that respect the culture here proved to be much more different than I would have expected and for reasons that now, twelve years later, I still could not readily explain. It's simply a difference. Another experience that didn't translate, which I think is interesting, is gender issues. We had had a very successful task force on the status of women in Wisconsin, and we had learned some things about how to do it. Soon after arriving here, I discovered that fifteen, sixteen years after coeducation had nominally occurred there were still a lot of unresolved gender-related issues. So I thought, what could we do better than appoint a task force on the status of women? It didn't quite translate. That group did some very useful things, but I think it sent a different signal, and that may be the difference between a historically coeducational institution like the University of Wisconsin and a relatively recently coeducational institution like Virginia. Even though there were three male members, and one was the chairman of the English Department—these were well-respected people—even so, I think there may have been an implication of trying to unsettle things more than was the intention. [Some people had negative reactions,] in some part even to the creation of such a task force, but more specifically to some of their early recommendations which were misunderstood. Now, that could happen anywhere. [I was given credit for improving the status of women at Virginia,] although I'm sorry to say that in terms of appointments we were able to do less here than I was able to do in Wisconsin. It's interesting. There, I appointed the first woman chancellor, the first woman vice-chancellor, first woman vice president who, as I said, is now president. We just did a lot of things there. Here, the openings didn't happen in the right places at the right times. There may have been credit for trying, but I felt that in terms of accomplishments, we did a great deal in terms of minority affairs here, but in terms of status of women in senior administrative roles, I was not nearly as happy as I would like to have been, although as I say, I think we get some credit for trying at least.

So those are examples of things that look as though they ought to translate from one institution to another, turn out not to translate very easily or comfortably, but for reasons that would be virtually impossible to isolate or identify. [Another example of this also speaks to your question about the honeymoon period at Virginia.] The closest thing to a crisis, I guess, in my first year here was a protest initially by the undergraduate and then the graduate African American students in early April of 1986. Up to that point, everything had gone very well.

That was a very messy situation. If you can imagine the president of the Virginia NAACP coming from Richmond to demand the removal of the person who was then the highest ranking black administrator here, that indicates how difficult a situation it was. I had looked at the structure of the office of Afro-American affairs, and the structure seemed to me fairly familiar. I then discovered that my predecessor had brought in as a consultant Herman Hudson, who had been the dean of Afro-American affairs at Indiana University-Bloomington. He had designed a structure which, as I well knew because I had been close to it, worked perfectly at Indiana. But for some reason, which may be partly structural, partly personal, that structure not only did not work here but was in fact the target of a protest which led to the complete revamping of the office. [The students were concerned about] the particular person who was in that job. [They found him] distant, unresponsive. Whether that was fair, I don't know because this began so soon after I got here that I really never had an adequate opportunity to judge either the structure or the person. He was willing to resign and it seemed to me essential that he leave the office. Probably earlier in the year, either the vice president for student affairs, to whom he reported, or I should simply have taken the matter in hand and removed him. But we didn't have anybody else ready to take over. This was somebody who had been chancellor at UMass-Amherst and had had a very bad experience there. He came here as dean of Afro-American affairs and didn't do any better. I think some feeling was expressed [by faculty who were critical] that when an administrator holding faculty rank is attacked by students, then the administration should stick up for him. I had actually been through a strikingly similar experience much earlier and will just recount it.

In the mid-1960s, the dean of the law school at Berkeley had appointed a Hispanic graduate as assistant dean, the first Hispanic administrator there. The Hispanic, mainly Chicano, students learned about his appointment and were indignant to a person because they felt this was a person [whom we might liken today to a] Clarence Thomas or Ward Connerly, who would be likely to say, "Well, I got here on my own efforts," and pull the drawbridge up behind him. What the dean agreed to do was to allow the students to interview him, which probably was a mistake, and then appointed a faculty committee that I chaired. Mike Heyman was one of the members, and I forget who the third person was. We ended up listening to the interviews that the students had had with this putative assistant dean (the interviews had been taped, as was understood would be the case). Actually, somehow Mike (and this was long before he became chancellor) had listened to the interviews first and said, knowing what my disposition was, "You're really going to like this. He really folds, he's inconsistent. But I still think we ought to back Ed," who was the dean that appointed him. I said, "Mike, we can't. The students—I hate to say it—the students are right." So, although none of us were very happy about it, and even though [the candidate] had been a very good student of mine my first year there and I liked him, I convinced them that this was the right thing to do. Some of our senior colleagues probably to this day are bitter about the fact that we, and myself in particular, capitulated to minority student pressure, and the dean had to withdraw the offer. [Yet] bringing him in under those circumstances would have been as bad for him as for anyone else.

You see how remarkably similar that case was [to the Virginia situation]. [Despite faculty criticism,] you really can't say anything, but the last thing you want to do in a situation like that is to persuade the person to stay because it's totally untenable. Probably the most honest thing is, just before the students get there, to go yourself, or I should have insisted that the vice president for student affairs go and get him to resign. In effect you say (and I've done this on other occasions), "Okay, either do it for me or wait until the students get here because they're on their way." The irony is that some of those who rallied around this person also had no particular use for him. Somehow, there was an emotional reaction, one I think in some cases of fear, that if a group of angry black students—doesn't matter if they're right or wrong—can do this even to a *black* administrator, then we're in terrible trouble. So I think that was the point at which [the honeymoon ended]. [For me, in terms of angering one or more constituencies,] it was definitely a no-win situation. We didn't realize how bad it was until a few days before [the protest] happened, but with better foresight, the thing to do clearly would have been to head it off earlier.

[The honeymoon] had lasted a fairly long time, three-quarters of the first year, and that's not bad. There really wasn't too much going on during that period, up to that point. But from then on, I suspect, there was some skepticism created by that incident. Frank Hereford, my predecessor, had a somewhat similar experience over the use of Farmington, an all-white country club, which got into the *New York Times*, played big day after day around here. And I think it was very difficult for Frank from that time on to move effectively in certain areas because of the intensity of feeling about Farmington. Now, at a place like Madison or Berkeley, there are enough controversies that something like [the Farmington issue] might last a week or two, but eventually would go away.

[This brings me to your question about building administrative teams.] In every situation I think I probably tended to rely perhaps more than one should on the people who were already there. I had a wonderful experience in Cincinnati as provost where we had six vice provosts, if you can imagine. The director of intercollegiate athletics actually reported to the vice provost for student affairs. There was one vice provost whose title was vice provost for educational innovation. She was independently wealthy, one of the first women Ph.D.'s at the University of Chicago, never married, lived with her sister in a very comfortable house in Cincinnati, a really quite majestic person—very thoughtful—and I enjoyed having her around. I thought I ought to take some time to evaluate the positions but then one of the other vice provosts said to me, "Lillian doesn't understand why you haven't replaced her." So I decided I should talk with her. She said, "You know, I haven't the vaguest idea of what I'm supposed to do in this job. I wish you would let me retire. I expected when you came in that that's what you would do—you'd look at this position and say, 'I don't know what she does, it must have been something my predecessor created to keep her here,' and you would let me go." "Well," she said, "I have hung around for a year, but this is ridiculous. I can spend a couple more years teaching educational philosophy and then retire outright." Now, that's an interesting commentary, somebody who was just waiting to be pushed out. But I have heard accounts of people who come in and just fire everybody. Make a complete change. And I think that's not good either. There is a happy medium somewhere. Actually, at Indiana I did more of that, but it was for a different reason. The titles were changing, and therefore in a sense each office had to be refilled. That enabled me quite painlessly to get rid of one person who didn't quite fit at Bloomington but later went on to become a very senior administrator at another institution. I rehearsed and rehearsed how to deal with him, and finally decided that we were going to have to review each of these offices as the titles changed. So I was prepared to go through all this and got together with him and said, "I'm thinking that we do have to conduct a review as the title changes," and he said, "I was planning to resign anyway, I've got to get back to my lab." I will never know whether he would have done so had I not indicated that there would have to be a review by a committee as the office was restructured. You just never know.

[The title change] was the result of a change in the IU system offices. Both my predecessor and my successor had the title chancellor as well as vice president. Shortly before I got there the title chancellor was taken away at Bloomington and Indianapolis and then reinstated later on. [It follows then that] you can't have vice chancellors if the vice president is not also a chancellor. My responsibilities were no different than those of Byrum Carter, who preceded me, or Ken Gros Louis, who succeeded me. But John Ryan [the system head] decided during that period he wanted to try just calling Glen Irwin, who was my counterpart at Indianapolis, and me, vice presidents. So the only title we could use for these erstwhile vice-chancellorships was dean, and two of them were "acting" anyway. We restructured two and then had some kind of search for the others. So it was a convenient opportunity to do what's probably the right thing. But I have always felt that coming in as an outsider is a situation in which, other things being equal, you are probably well advised to keep as many of the people who are already in place as you can. And on the whole, I think that's been a wise policy everywhere.

[You asked whether I thought about risk taking.] Not in a formulaic sense. I think it's less conscious, it's more issue specific. Some people may well have a calculated risk strategy, almost like a beta investing strategy. I suspect those who study university administration as an academic field may have that sense of it, but as a practitioner, I would not say I ever had anything like a philosophy or strategy or concept of risk taking or risk avoidance. It really depended on a particular issue. [In decision making] risk is only, I think, a relatively minor part of the calculus. There is only one way to go, and you just have to do your best and go forward. Actually [in the removal of the black administrator during my first year], once this person was gone, we were able to restructure the office of Afro-American affairs and bring in a new person who is still here in his twelfth year as dean and is responsible for such things as achieving the highest retention rate of minority students of any AAU public institution. In order for that to happen, somebody—and I happened to be the person who was there at the time—had to pay a price to get that office restructured.

[In reply to whether, during my first months on the job at Virginia, I felt the board of visitors was supportive], the answer is yes, although the board relationship here was not the same as it had been in Wisconsin, which is not to say that one is better or less good than the other, just somewhat different, again for reasons that would be very difficult to identify. Part of it is the structure of the state. Wisconsin, like North Carolina, has a very simple public higher education structure. There was essentially no one between the president of the university and the governor. The governor may have an advisor on higher education, but that's it. There is one board. Now, the North Carolina campuses do have separate local boards which the Wisconsin campuses do not—there, one board of regents [is responsible] for all public post-secondary education. But the structure is so much simpler than that of states like Virginia, where you have fifteen separate boards, you have a secretary of education, you have a state council for higher education, which is itself a board, and which has a director of the state council for higher education to whom, in a sense, the university presidents report. In another sense, they report to the secretary of education, and of course everybody ultimately reports to the governor. Much more complicated. The simplicity of the structures in Wisconsin and North Carolina has, I think, many advantages, and that tends to mean that the board of regents or the board of governors, respectively, in Wisconsin and North Carolina, have a kind of responsibility which I think creates a bond that is less likely to exist when you have fifteen boards with interests that are to some extent parallel but in other respects divergent and competitive.

Periodically, the Virginia state council would convene meetings of representatives of the various boards of visitors, which got awkward. I remember once in Wisconsin I asked the president of the board of regents whether he would like to have a meeting of the heads of campus advisory boards or [the] chancellors' advisory councils—maybe half the campuses had created informal groups of this kind. The response from the president of the Board of Regents was, "No way; that would legitimize them. There is only one governing board. If the chancellor wishes to meet with his or her advisory council (or whatever it's called), it's up to the chancellor, but I don't think we ought to recognize them even in this way." And that, of course, is the one structural difference between Wisconsin and North Carolina. But in other respects they share, I think, an admirable simplicity in structure. Now, if things are going badly, I suspect that may be difficult because there is no buffer between the university and the governor or between the university and the legislature, but if things are going well as they certainly were when I was in Wisconsin, I think it's a much more efficient structure and is generally advantageous.

Here in Virginia even the composition of the boards of visitors is somewhat complex. At least five of the members—and it's typically more than that—must be graduates of the university appointed by the governor following the submission of a list of candidates by the alumni association. It doesn't say they must be appointed from that list, although that tends to be the practice. The statute also provides that no more than three of the sixteen members of the board of visitors may be [from] out of state, and that creates another complexity. So this is in contrast to the Wisconsin statute, which simply says the board of regents shall have sixteen members who are appointed by the governor and confirmed by the senate, period. Now, it's understood that you don't appoint people [from] outside Wisconsin, although we did have one union official who, during the time he was on the board, was appointed the UAW secretary/treasurer and had to move to Detroit. I recall when I was at Berkeley I actually worked for one University of California regent who became the secretary to the Kennedy cabinet, Fred Dutton. So every month at his own expense he would fly from Washington to San Francisco where the regents were meeting, and no question was raised that Fred Dutton was out of state or Ray Majerus was out of state, although the understanding was that if they left [during their] term, that did not create somehow an out-of-state seat. Maybe in that sense the Virginia statute is better because it does have this three-seat limit. But for a university which draws nearly forty percent of its student body from out of state, it is somewhat constraining to limit the number of out-of-state members of the board to three out of sixteen, but that's the way it's set up in the statute.

So, yes, it is complex, and to what extent that makes governance more difficult, I don't know. I think there are a lot of things that one can do in a single statewide system. I've compared notes with Bill Friday [founding president of the UNC system] and more recently with Dick Spangler, and some of the things that you can do in North Carolina you can't do here, and Wisconsin is similar. But I'm not sure how much structure as such really affects the dynamic.

[I have told you that it would be very difficult to identify a defining moment in the presidency at Virginia.] I'd contrast it in part with my experience at Indiana where there were two clearly identifiable crises. One was the largest outbreak of Legionnaires' disease at any college or university, second in numbers only to the Bellevue-Stratford American Legion convention in Philadelphia [1976] and roughly two years later, in the summer of 1978. The other was a coal strike earlier that same year [1978]. Indiana was at that time 97 percent coal dependent for its electric power, so when there was a coal strike in Kentucky and Tennessee it had a drastic impact on Indiana's operation of electricity-dependent facilities. One of the things I learned: What percentage of the electric power on a campus like that goes for lighting? Less than 10 percent. Ninety percent goes for machinery, air conditioning, all kinds of other uses. Lighting was a tiny fraction of the total. Anyway, it was hard even to keep the lights on, and finally we did decide, with a little lead time but not much, that we had to close a week before the scheduled spring vacation. I think we may actually have extended the spring vacation, so that instead of one week it was a three-week period, and in the remaining weeks of the spring semester we then tried to make up those lost class days, which by the end of the session we had.

A crisis of that sort really does serve to bring people together under most circumstances, in a way that in my experience then makes easier addressing other issues as they may arise. When I felt we ought to start a freshman seminar program at Indiana—a large public institution with an entering class that is close to six thousand—it seemed to me that if we could get 100 faculty willing to teach a freshman seminar, we could at least provide half the freshmen with some kind of meaningful contact with a senior faculty member. When an appeal of that kind went out to the senior faculty—this may be a year after the coal strike and the Legionnaires' disease, which came very close on the heels of one another—I think some of the contacts that had been developed in the course of working through those two very painful experiences served us well in mobilizing support [for the freshman seminars and] on other issues.

[The crisis occurred about midway in my chancellorship and I did notice a difference], one reason being that faculty governance was unusually strong in Bloomington, and I think still is to this day. It wasn't quite like what I had been accustomed to at Berkeley, where the academic senate really is an extraordinarily powerful body, but the Bloomington faculty council was a very strong faculty arm that transcended discipline, department, school, building, anything else; they really saw themselves as a whole that transcended the sum of the parts. That's probably been less true elsewhere, although Wisconsin faculty governance, like Berkeley's, has a long and distinguished tradition and does certain things, promotion and tenure for example (which are done at Wisconsin on a divisional basis), but also rises to specific needs. The Bloomington faculty council I found extraordinarily flexible and adaptive and willing to address interesting and challenging issues. I put to them one day this question: Who has the responsibility for the makeup, the composition, of our baccalaureate degree? Whose responsibility, whose authority is it to define what a baccalaureate degree from this institution means? And they went back and forth, and finally I said, "Well, it seems to me that what you have done is what I had hoped you would do and that is to conclude that you, the faculty council, probably have that authority. So the next question is, what if the school of"—and I used the school of agriculture, which of course doesn't exist there, as a hypothetical— "What if the school of agriculture decided to eliminate any requirement of written or spoken communication as a part of the baccalaureate degree, would you be prepared to override that judgment?" Well, we were about out of time, so I left that as a partly rhetorical question, but I think they were willing to take that issue on. I posed the same question to the faculty senate here [at UVA] with a much less conclusive response, and we never really did get resolution of it, which suggested to me that there was a kind of cohesiveness in the Bloomington faculty council, which I had seen at Berkeley in a rather different form. At Berkeley, they would sometimes overdo it and become preemptive. I was part of that; I chaired the senate committee on academic freedom for several years, and there were times when I felt that the balance was somehow out of kilter. But that question, to my knowledge, has never really been addressed here [at UVA], and I'm not sure why. It isn't one of the questions that Thomas Jefferson posed at the Rockfish Gap conference at which the design for the university was created. And indeed, the structure of the Rockfish Gap report is somewhat compartmentalized, on a European model—people study a discipline, they prepare to practice a profession. In some curious way the locus of responsibility for general education wasn't diffused at Rockfish Gap, and now almost 180 years later, it still hasn't been diffused in a way that would be meaningful to faculty at Berkeley and at Bloomington, and less so to people at Madison where there's a higher degree of divisionality.

[So at UVA there never was a defining moment for me in that] there wasn't a crisis. Conditions here in the 1980s were so good in objective terms that far from having a crisis, the real question was, could you continue upward in this same way? And the answer, of course, is no. Between 1982 (which is three years before I got here [UVA] but this is the relevant period) and 1990, the average full professor's salary went from the top of the bottom third of the AAU, to the bottom of the top third. That is, jumping over one-third of AAU members, all of whom are of course trying frantically to keep up in competitive salaries. It meant that among public institutions, our full professor average was behind only the three University of California campuses, ahead of Michigan, ahead of Illinois. Now this is slightly skewed by the fact that it's a full professor's salary, and if you did all ranks it would be a little less favorable, but still pretty close. Virginia in the 1980s had a truly golden era. This was the great expansion of beltway business and all kinds of things happened. The port of Hampton Roads stole, at one point, something like a third of the tonnage away from the port of Baltimore, a good bit of which I think has now gone back. The state could do no wrong and as a result, when Gerry Baliles took over as governor in 1986, one of the first things he said to a standing ovation on a cold day in January was, "Virginia higher education is on a roll, and we mean to keep it that way."

[When I was recruited to the Virginia presidency, I knew that the state was in good shape economically,] although I didn't know the details. And, in fact, some of the details did not come out until the gubernatorial campaign, which took place that fall, but it soon became apparent that the state was in even better shape than people had supposed. I went with the rector, the head of the board of visitors, to call on the chairman of the senate finance committee, now long deceased, and he outlined how it was with difficulty they were going to be able to spend in the next fiscal year an $800 million surplus. I turned to the rector after we came out of Senator Willey's office, and I said, "Here you call him a conservative, in Wisconsin we'd describe him as a radical." An $800 million surplus in the 1986–1988 biennium—the sky was the limit. I think, in part, the expectations at that time were very high, probably higher than anyone could have fulfilled, whereas in my other experiences the expectations were not low, but modest. But by the time I got here, partly because of the flush times, the expectations were very high.

[You asked about the turmoil among faculty and students over the possibility of expanding the size of the University of Virginia.] The whole question of size, which now has been resolved in favor of a modest expansion, always puzzled me because size as such has seldom seemed to me sacrosanct. When Harvard, for example, addressed the question of admitting women as undergraduates by, I think, roughly doubling from the size of the typical Radcliffe class the number of women who would be admitted as freshmen at Harvard, I don't recall any concern, even though that meant a significant increase in the size of the Harvard/Radcliffe undergraduate population. At other places I'd been—not at Berkeley because Berkeley was about the same size when I left as it was when I got there, 27,500—but at other places, particularly public institutions, growth has been seen as sometimes even beneficial. It means that you will have a larger physics department and you will be closer to critical mass in certain areas. It is true, however, as I said earlier, that this is the smallest save one—or was even at that time the smallest save one—of the AAU public institutions, but conversely, substantially larger than most of the AAU private institutions. Is there any magic in a particular size? Probably not, but I think what may have influenced a lot of undergraduate students is a feeling that even with the present undergraduate enrollment there are many things that they felt were beyond reach, such as close contact with senior faculty. Now, I could say that even as a Harvard student who had grown up in Cambridge, I had close contact with senior faculty only (a) in my senior year and (b) through people who were friends of my parents, or parents of my friends who had grown up there. The average person coming to Harvard in the 1950s did not have meaningful contact with many senior faculty. But there's a lot of nostalgia—every institution has it; even at Berkeley there are people who describe themselves as "Old Blues" and really are, but the nostalgia level at Berkeley on the whole is fairly low, even among Old Blues. The nostalgia level *here* is relatively high, which is not bad, I think it's a neutral factor, but it's just a distinguishing characteristic.

I think there is another sensation and again, it's a dissonance between the perception and the reality: As close by as College Park, only two hours up the line, is the only really big state U in this part of the world. College Park is virtually indistinguishable from East Lansing or Champaign-Urbana or Madison, not necessarily in quality or mix, but just in sheer size. So it's not as though you're talking about some exotic place that's a thousand miles away, and most people here, if you asked them, "Were we to expand by 10 percent, would we be larger than the University of Maryland-College Park?" I suppose would have said, "No, that's a much larger institution." Yet there was somehow this feeling that Virginia was already a huge institution where traditions and personal relationships had been strained, and if there were further expansion, they would be strained beyond the breaking point. [During that time when growth was an issue], I didn't have any particular viewpoint; [increased enrollment] was mandated by the State Council for Higher Education, so we didn't have any choice. But I did have a fair number of discussions [with faculty and others], and I don't think anyone could ever pinpoint rationally what it was, what would be lost. I think some of the nostalgia here may relate to the honor system, but of course, what's strained the honor system isn't so much numbers as the same sort of things that strain the simple life in the Amish community. It's just so many more pressures from outside, a much more complex world in which giving one's word or the expectation of character isn't quite as dependable as it once was. From time to time mention would be made of the honor system as a concern, and it is true (I think this is correct) that this is the largest institution that has ever maintained a functioning honor system. That, I think, is one factor. But in other respects, I think there was a sense that certain values would be lost if there were significant growth. No one really enjoys the sheer size of a large state university, but at most other places it's [regarded as] simply a fact of life.

[With reference to the difference between experiences at public and private institutions,] my sense is that the degree of control or destiny, which Keith's hypothesis envisions or presupposes, would be more familiar to people in private than in public institutions. Things can change so quickly in the public sector. I'll give one small example. Many years ago I was working with the American Association of University Professors on loyalty oaths, and we finally got a group of people together who would challenge the Colorado loyalty oath. Just before we filed the suit, John Holloway, the general counsel of the University of Colorado, came to me and said, "Look, you don't have to put your people at risk. I will file suit on behalf of the board of regents." "Wonderful," I said, "That's perfect." He did so. The Colorado trial court threw the case out on a state law doctrine that an administrative agency can't sue to declare unconstitutional a statute by which it's governed. He thought, and I agreed, that this wouldn't apply to the Board of Regents, so if we could get to an appellate court it would be overturned and the suit would go forward. At that point the 1966 election occurred. Mr. Coors and a couple of his like-minded colleagues created a new majority on the University of Colorado Board of Regents. One of the first things that they did was to tell John Holloway that under no circumstances was he to proceed with the loyalty oath litigation. It was gone. By this time I couldn't reactivate my individual plaintiffs. Another case from another state reached the desired result within a year or so. That's an example of how fast things can change.

Also speaking of loyalty oaths [in January 1967], on the very day on which the Supreme Court decided the case striking down the New York loyalty oath, two things happened. One, the Supreme Court struck down the law that imposed the oath, which had come from SUNY-Buffalo, so we were having a party celebrating it. While we were celebrating in Buffalo, many of us being Californians or sometime Californians, we got word that that afternoon the University of California Regents had fired Clark Kerr. How soon was that after Ronald Reagan took office? Ten days. I think many people assumed that Reagan took office and gradually transformed the Board of Regents. Wrong. Within ten days of taking office, he made a few appointments to positions that were gubernatorially appointed and had a majority to displace Clark Kerr. January 1967. So, in the public sector, you tend to live with discontinuities of that kind. I just mention these two from California and Colorado, a year apart in what are admittedly more volatile times than those in which we now live, but life is always somewhat chancy in the public sector, even for people who may have served many years, like Bill Friday, who probably served more years in heading a public AAU university than anybody else I can think of. Even so, I'm sure Bill Friday would be the first to agree that life is always a bit chancy in the public sector. Another example: Paul Verkeuil, who is now dean of the law school at Cardozo, had been president of the College of William and Mary around the same time I was president here [at UVA]. About six weeks after I had left office, I saw Paul on a plane going to New York. I said, "Hi, Paul, how are things?" He said, "You won't believe how things have changed since you left office." I said, "Paul, it was only six weeks ago." He said, "I know, I know. We now have to file—" and he ticked off a list of reports that they had to file, all of which had been imposed on them by state government in the six weeks since I had left.

The Wilder administration had begun while I was still in office [at UVA] but the fiscal situation had not become apparent until the summer of 1990. During the week I left office, two things happened. One, Saddam Hussein marched into Kuwait, which had very little effect on public higher education. Two, the degree to which the Virginia miracle had come to a halt became apparent, and it was a very different environment from that point on. Things like these massive record-keeping and reporting requirements had taken effect during that period. Now, those were things that do not have counterparts in the private sector. You will have, I'm well aware, outrageous alumni and major donors and so on who can almost come out of nowhere, but it's not the same. There may be a lot going on behind the scenes, but it's not out front in the way it is in the public sector, and it's for that reason that I think a deterministic view, or even a cyclical view, an evolutionary view of the life cycle of a senior administrator, has a very different dimension [at public universities].

The differences between public and private institutions cut both ways [in terms of advantages and disadvantages]. A public institution is vulnerable to political pressures in ways that private institutions clearly are not, [as] private institutions tend to have a degree of financial independence. In public institutions anything that has direct consequences has to be discussed in public, whereas a private college or university board can essentially have a meeting by phone and do anything they want, and they certainly can do anything behind closed doors. I recall once when I was with Martin Meyerson [the acting chancellor of the University of California-Berkeley] and Ed Campbell, who was probably politically the most influential [member of the Board of Regents] in the early years of the Reagan administration in California. Ed called one day and demanded that something-or-other be done, and Martin, who as acting chancellor sensed he wasn't going to be there too much longer, said, "Well, Ed, I understand what you're saying and if you bring that up at the next regents' meeting, we'll have a chance to discuss it," knowing perfectly well that [Ed's concern] was not something which would be brought up in public. So that's a sense in which a public institution has protection in its public character that private institutions obviously do not; [the public institution] can insist that anything that really affects its status be done at some point in public. That's something that a private institution is never required to do. Some in fact do so, but often you suspect there are things that go on entirely behind closed doors, and in fact you never invite the media to a meeting of a private university board. It just never happens, I'd guess. Of course, I have absolutely no administrative experience in private institutions, so I don't know, but I would assume so. I well remember an incident during the accreditation visit to Duke in 1988. [Our group] had made some quick critical comments about the state of Duke's computer equipment at that time. I think there had been some expectation that things would work out as part of a triangle universities consortium. That didn't happen, however, so Duke was left somewhat behind, and Judy Woodruff [at that time a Duke trustee] pressed me fairly hard on some of those issues in a way that I doubt she would have done in a public meeting. Nor, do I suspect, would anyone else. Well, I had to look around and then very quickly remind myself, "No, this is a private university, they don't have any reporters here," even though this was the official board meeting. Anyway, we had an interesting discussion; she asked some good questions.

[That meeting was similar to] an executive session of a public board, but the difference is that a public university executive session has to be confined to the stated topics. When the board comes out of the executive session (this is certainly true now under the Virginia Freedom of Information Law) each member of the body is asked and must declare that only the authorized business was discussed during the executive session. So you tend to be pretty careful about sticking to the topics. Now, of course, if somebody says, "Gee, it's getting cold in here, I want to get up and close the window," you don't have to report that there was discussion about the temperature in the room, that that was not on the schedule. But anything else—[if somebody then said, "Are we ever going to do anything about this antiquated heating system?"]—at that point the chair of the meeting should absolutely stop it and say, "Now, I know how that came up, but that has to be discussed in open session." Which is not to say that either [circumstance] is good or bad, one better or worse than the other, but simply that they are different.

[About my decision to leave the Virginia presidency], I'd been doing this sort of thing for twenty years, and if I add the year and a half that I was executive assistant to the president at Buffalo to the four years at Cincinnati [as provost and executive vice president], five at Indiana, five at Wisconsin, five here, that's actually a little over twenty years. I also figured that [it was time to leave] if I were going to do anything else of substance. I'd seen lots of other people who remained in administrative office until they were sixty or older and found it very hard to get back into scholarship. Though I had always taught at least one course, and I had usually had a student research assistant, and I'd tried to keep up with the field, even so, there comes a stage in life where it gets awfully hard to go back into whatever your field is. There was also the founding of the Thomas Jefferson Center. In fact, the very first thing that the first member of the board of visitors who came to visit with me in Madison in November 1984 had said was, "You should know that a fellow member of the board of visitors just announced a very substantial gift to create a First Amendment center at the university. Does that sound like something that would be attractive to you?"

Of course, that was very appealing. So, it took five years. There was a major component coming from the *New York Times* and other pieces that had to get into place, and so when it came time actually to get the center up and running, the question was whether I would go out and recruit somebody else to take it over or whether that might not be an attractive alternative to me. I decided twenty years [of administration] in four institutions is quite long enough. While I can't say I felt worn down or burnt out or anything like that, I think that it was about long enough, and there was this very attractive alternative. The person within the donor's organization who was working on the structuring of the Thomas Jefferson Center came to spend a day or so with me in Madison in the spring of 1985 before I'd left there and said to me, "There seems to be some thought," (this is back in Charlottesville), "that it should be a think tank or just a research center and," he added, "my boss," (the donor), "doesn't see it that way. He thinks this ought to be an activist organization." I said, "Absolutely, that's exactly the way I would see it." The first thing I had done in California when I started teaching was to serve as an ACLU volunteer lawyer. The very first case I ever got involved in was trying to keep the California Department of Alcoholic Beverage Control from closing down a gay bar in San Francisco (this was 1962), where Melvin Belli and others went for lunch. It was a restaurant by day, but a gay bar by night. The city and county of San Francisco would never have closed them down even in the early 1960s, but this was the state ABC, and they got them; they [the owners] went three times [unsuccessfully] to the Supreme Court [seeking review] and finally closed. I did lots of other volunteer work for the northern California ACLU and I've done it ever since. So, my sense of the potential of a center of this kind converged precisely with what I felt [founding donor] Tom Worrell would like to see happen when the center finally did get up and running, and it was just a very attractive alternative that probably would not have been here [for me] by the time I would clearly have been prepared to leave office if we had gone out and recruited somebody else to be director.

[My so-called "lame-duck" period] was from October 1989 to August 1990. My sense these days is that's fairly normal [in the academy] as a time period within which to conduct a search and make sure that a successor can lead. In the corporate world, [it's quite different]. I've been chairman of the compensation committee of the James River Corporation, and we're now in the midst of a massive merger with Fort Howard; you assume that corporate CEOs may need a week to wrap things up, but basically in ten days they can turn a complete corner and be in a new role in a new company and sometimes even in a new industry. That's just unthinkable in the academic world [where] it takes at least six months to wrap things up, although I did have one [unusual] experience: I was simultaneously vice president/chancellor at Bloomington and president at Wisconsin in the spring of 1980. I commuted and held both jobs, but I had very able deputies in both places, and fortunately, that was a very quiet time for both places. If anything had really gone seriously wrong, then I think one board or the other or both would have decided they'd made a big mistake. But the two boards and the two board chairmen and everybody agreed that this was okay. The one place where [leaving has] been awkward was Wisconsin. I remained there full time until I left [to begin the Virginia presidency] because Frank Hereford was still full time [at UVA]. But I will never forget a regents' meeting in Milwaukee in May 1985. In the back of the room I could see a group of my chancellors who I knew were plotting some clandestine activity two months before I was to leave. I was supposedly still president, no one had been appointed as my successor (that didn't happen until September), but they were restive. That's one of the things about our campus/system structure. I don't know what they were up to, but I went to my executive vice president, S. Katharine Lyall, who has now been president there for years, and I said, "Katharine, should I get the regents to just tell them they've got to toe the party line?" and I think Katharine's judgment and that of the president of the Board of Regents was that it wasn't worth it, they'd speak to a few of them privately. But it was clear, something that was never the case here [at UVA]; I never felt any lack of authority or of either persuasive or dissuasive power in those transitional months here, and in Indiana it wasn't that long because I was essentially gone a few weeks after the appointment. But I sure did feel that way in Wisconsin. My appointment here was announced in January—January, February, March we got through okay, although things were a little chancy, but by May it was very difficult. So I think that may depend partly on structure. There was very little sense [at UVA] of people suddenly going off doing their own thing. No, everybody stayed pretty much on board. My successor was appointed in March, and one of my expectations was—and one of one's hypotheses would be—that from the moment the successor was appointed things would change. Didn't happen. I think it may have been that John Casteen (who was then still the president of the University of Connecticut and had plenty to do up there) let people know that they should continue to work with me until he got here. There were things that had to be done in transition, which he asked me to do. So, actually, it went very smoothly here, and we got quite a bit done that spring.

I resolved some issues—I had some just terribly messy sexual harassment cases on which I had to rule, and I think I felt freer to do the right thing there than I might have if I had been continuing. I went to meet with a gay and lesbian student group, which I thought was important to do—I would never have dared do that if I were still in office, I don't think. And several other things—I went and dealt with legislative committees and I told it like it was. I think people appreciated that candor. [I felt unfettered] and that may have been partly because it's the only time when I was not going on to another office somewhere else, so that if I really spoke my mind, let's say in Bloomington, somebody in Madison would hear about it, or if I said something in Madison that was outrageous, somebody in Charlottesville would hear about it. If I did that as I felt freer to do in the spring and summer of 1990, it wasn't going to have downstream impact on anything else.

If I take the three [executive] offices I have held, in each case I would say I knew my predecessor a bit, but got to know him (and they were all male) somewhat better afterwards. The one structured relationship [I had was with] Byrum Carter who was chancellor at IU-Bloomington [before me] and was really the first person to hold that office. I was essentially the second; a man named Snyder had held it for only a few months before Byrum, but practically speaking, Byrum was the first chancellor. He was a political scientist from Oklahoma and had spent most of his life at Bloomington. When I was appointed, he said, "I will be happy to talk with you for one hour about administration and then that's it." Now, we often went to the Carters' house, we had them to our house, we saw one another around the community (Bloomington's a fairly small place). Scrupulously did he observe [his dictum], and I felt that I had to as well, so that even if I had a pressing issue on which I figured Byrum had some experience, he had raised that wall and I respected it. In other situations, at Wisconsin, for example, my relationship with Ed Young, my predecessor as system head, was de facto almost the same as the de jure relationship that Byrum Carter's injunction had created, and here [at UVA] I'd have to say that my relationship with Frank Hereford has been in all cases cordial but distant. My relationships with both predecessors and successors have been uniformly cordial, and I hope they feel the same way; I have no reason to think they wouldn't. Ken Gros Louis, who is now finishing twenty years as my successor at Bloomington, has called me only once about an issue, and I think that was almost more to just let me know that he was still there. I don't think that in any of these roles I contacted my predecessor more than once or twice. It's an interesting question why that happens; I think it's probably a healthy sign. There is perhaps a feeling that your two situations aren't really comparable, and therefore you're not going to find out that much. Also, [there is] a feeling that you probably have to make your own judgments. But even so, I think it's surprising that there is so little reliance [on experienced hands] even when the relationship is entirely cordial. My successor at Wisconsin, Buzz Shaw, who's chancellor at Syracuse—we hadn't really known one another before he succeeded me, and I was gone from Madison by the time he got there. We did meet at AAU meetings—they seated people alphabetically. That's how I got to know Bart Giamatti; Wisconsin and Yale were seated next to one another, so my perspective on Bart is very much of someone sitting in the next chair waving his arms wildly.

Anyway, I don't know about other people's experiences—this is something on which I'm not sure I have ever compared notes. At least two of my successors, Buzz Shaw and John Casteen, are people who had held administrative positions elsewhere, and in Buzz's case went on to another place, and I'd be willing to bet that their experiences with both predecessors and successors have been very similar to mine. It's comforting to know that the person is there if you ever really needed to call on him, but in fact, you seldom do. Now, I have no idea what it's like if the relationship is contentious, or if the successor begins running down the predecessor, or if the successor has a difficult time and goes to the predecessor who says, "Well, we used to do it [differently]." And that happens. I've heard of people doing it. I think that's unconscionable. Even if you believe things were done better in your time or could be done better today, you don't say it. I recall an instance that is almost comical but it illustrates my point. A reporter called me one day during the transition here, in the summer of 1990, and said, "I don't believe what they're doing at Carr's Hill [the president's residence] to make over the master bathroom—they're putting in a Jacuzzi." I said, "Well, he has a bad back, for heaven's sake!" That absolutely stopped it right there. So, occasionally you can do something like that, little things, and I've had a couple of other such experiences. Even if I didn't know [about the bad back], I think I probably would have tried to put a stop to the story as a kind of comity between predecessor and successor. But I just don't have any feel for what I have certainly heard has happened at other places when the relationships on either end are contentious or difficult because mine have always been very cordial.

NOTES

1. The schools that made up Indiana University-Bloomington at that time were the college of arts and sciences and the graduate school; business; education; health, physical education, and recreation; law; library; music; nursing; public and environmental affairs; social service; optometry; journalism; and continuing education. The undergraduate/graduate-professional mix in 1974–1975 was 21,613/7,219; in 1979–1980 it was 23,084/6,794. Unusually, Indiana's medical school is not located on its Research I campus. E-mail correspondence with Thomas Malefetto, August 23 and 31, 1999, Indiana University Archives.

2. Jeff Browne, "A Tradition of Leadership at the University of Wisconsin—A Time of Retrenchment, *Change* 13, no. 4 (May/June 1981): 35–39; "Fall Enrollments Historical Table 1862–1986," *UW System Fact Book 1987*, p. 44, University of Wisconsin System, *Annual Report for the Year Ending June 30, 1981*, p. 8, internal publications provided by Archives, University of Wisconsin; "Fact-File: Endowment Funds of 176 Institutions Ranked by 1980 Market Value," *Chronicle of Higher Education*, March 23, 1981, p. A6, survey by the National Association of College and University Business Officers; "Fact-File: University Endowments Rise by Average of 25 Pct. in 1985," *Chronicle of Higher Education*, September 17, 1986, p. A36, survey by the National Association of College and University Business Officers; University of Wisconsin System, *Annual Financial Report 1985*, "1984–85 Expenditures," p. 15, Archives, University of Wisconsin; Scott Heller, "Plan to Boost Academic Salaries in Wisconsin Nears Passage After Year of Intense Lobbying," *Chronicle of Higher Education*, May 29, 1985, pp. 23, 25.

3. "Fall Head Count Enrollment by School, 1980–1989," source: University of Virginia Student Information System, "Rank of the Faculty by School/Activity, Fall 1984," source: University of Virginia Personnel/Payroll File, "Expenditures of the Academic Division, 1983–84 through 1992–93," source: University of Virginia Financial Analysis, all internal documents from University of Virginia Office of Institutional Assessment and Studies, fax from George

Stovall, August 18, 1998; "Fact-File: University Endowments Rise by Average of 25 Pct. in 1985," *Chronicle of Higher Education*, September 17, 1986, p. A36, survey by the National Association of College and University Business Officers; "College and University Endowments over $60-Million, 1990," *Chronicle of Higher Education*, August 28, 1991, p. A36, survey by the National Association of College and University Business Officers; Peter Baker, "U-Va. President Called More Scholar Than Doer," *Washington Post*, October 8, 1989, Final Edition, p. D1.

Benno Schmidt

Yale University 1986–1992

A recognized scholar of constitutional law, especially First Amendment issues, and a historian of the Supreme Court, Benno C. Schmidt, Jr. earned both the B.A. and J.D. at Yale University. After graduating in 1966, he clerked for one year for Chief Justice Earl Warren before going to the Office of Legal Counsel, U.S. Department of Justice, as a special assistant. In 1969, he became an assistant professor at Columbia University Law School, was promoted to full professor in 1973, and in 1983 became the Harlan Fiske Stone Professor of Constitutional Law. His appointment as dean of the law school followed shortly thereafter, and he took office July 1, 1984.

After a brief but successful deanship during which he raised a record-breaking $9 million for Columbia's law school, Schmidt accepted the presidency of Yale beginning July 1, 1986. He returned to an alma mater both smaller than and quite different from the university where he had become a professor. In 1986, Yale's student body was 10,569, with 5,147 in Yale College, 2,331 in the graduate school, and 3,091 in the various professional schools; its full-time teaching faculty numbered 1,382, swelling to 3,668 if research, clinical, and miscellaneous appointments were included. Yale's annual budget of half a billion dollars and impressive endowment of $1.7 billion were not enough to meet the institution's needs however, and money became a central theme in Benno Schmidt's turbulent presidency. By the time he resigned in May 1992 to head The Edison Project, he was widely acknowledged as the biggest fund-raiser in Yale's history, having launched a $1.5 billion campaign with more than a third of the total in hand. Yale's budget had expanded to more than $800 million and the endowment to $2.8 billion. In addition, Schmidt was lauded by trustees for salvaging labor and town-gown relations as well as "forc[ing] the university to come to grips with its fiscal future."[1]

Benno Schmidt's account of some aspects of his presidency is an edited transcript of his interviews with Leslie Banner at the Office of the Secretary of Cultural Resources, Raleigh, North Carolina, January 26, 1998 and at The Edison Project, New York City, April 2, 1998. The questions that prompted his comments have either been omitted or indicated with bracketed material to create a more readable narrative.

[The search process that brought me to Yale] was a smooth process, perhaps too smooth, and I'll say what I mean by that. I certainly was ambivalent about it, and I'll try to describe why, and I think that there was at least one issue which was resolved between me and the trustees—very well resolved—but which turned out to be an issue that was not well resolved as far as the broader Yale community was concerned, and that actually concerned my wife. I'll say a bit about each of those.

The search process, as I perceived it, was remarkably focused and expeditious, and I think if anything, too much so. I first heard about Yale's interest in the fall of 1985. I had heard rumors that I was one of the names Yale was thinking about in the previous spring, but they were only rumors and it was pretty late in the process that Cy Vance called me up and said that Yale was interested in talking to me about becoming president. He asked if I would be interested, and I said I would certainly be interested in talking about it. I had shortly before been named dean at Columbia Law School and that was a position I was very enthusiastic about. I had a clear set of ambitious objectives for what I wanted to accomplish there, and I felt very good about my chances of having a successful deanship as I was off to a terrific start. My first year as dean, for the first time in its history, Columbia raised more money than any other law school. We were having a lot of good fortune in faculty appointments—we had hired four senior people from Yale Law School, to name only one place. The alumni had rallied around, as the fund-raising record suggests, in a way that was incredibly enthusiastic, and I was very anxious for the Yale process not to derail that if they or I decided that the Yale position was not for me. So I insisted with Cy Vance on a very expedited procedure for the Yale Corporation's deciding whether they wanted me. I insisted that that procedure be closely held, that there be no publicity about it, that there be no public discussion. I didn't want anybody to think that I was looking for a different position. I wanted it to be very clear that I had not thrown my hat in the ring, as I had not, they called me. And I said to Mr. Vance that if Yale wanted me to consider being its president I would not do that as part of a short list of possible candidates. I would consider it if they told me I was the one they wanted, and I would give them a quick answer within forty-eight hours, but I was not going to enter into a process where I was one of several people, where I felt that the word would leak out. That if I was going to Yale I would say I was going to Yale and that would be it, but I would not [risk] indicating that I wanted to leave Columbia and then having it not happen. I thought that would have been very bad and demoralizing for Columbia, and I didn't want to hurt Columbia in any way, and that's the way it went.

There were a couple of aspects of that process which, looking back on it, were perhaps not ideal. It was in the nature of the process I insisted on that many members of the Yale Corporation had no chance to meet me at all. In fact, I met most members of the Yale Corporation on the day they actually decided formally to offer me the job. That meant the search committee of the Corporation was engaged with me over a period of some weeks and felt that they knew the person they were considering, but many members of the Corporation did not. I later learned that not all the members of the Corporation were necessarily of one mind about who should be the next president or indeed the type of person. Should it be someone from Yale or outside Yale? I was outside. Should it be someone from the arts and sciences as opposed to someone from a professional school? I was from a professional school. You know, there are lots of legitimate points of view about that, and some members of the Corporation, I think, felt less engaged and a bit less a part of the process. As I look back on it, that was partly due to my insistence that if the Corporation wanted me to consider [the presidency] they had to tell me I was the one, rather than engaging in a little bit more of a long-term process where I might have been one of several people in discussion with them. So, the expeditiousness of it was good in some ways for me but not good in that the entire board was not engaged, and some people felt the selection moved a little bit too quickly to a conclusion. I don't know that for sure, but I have the sense that that was the case. This did not pose any insuperable problem, but I think it might have been a little bit better for me had there been wider discussion, had the process taken a little more time.

[Later,] I generally enjoyed very stalwart support from the Corporation, but that was complicated by a couple of factors. One is that my presidency coincided with a very substantial turnover in the Corporation. Within two years a majority of those who were trustees when I was appointed had left, and new people came on in very large numbers. I think some who left, either partly because they left or partly because they had never had a chance to work with me or for a variety of reasons, felt separated from Yale and from me, felt some slight sense of alienation. I probably could have reached out a bit more to them. The new members coming on felt a great deal of institutional responsibility and pressure because I was telling them and, if you will, leading them, teaching them, that Yale needed to undertake some fairly fundamental changes in its financial governance, and that these changes were going to be difficult at best. They felt great pressure at having to deal with institutional change of a fairly basic and controversial character at the same time that they were newly arrived and in some cases relatively new to being trustees of a university. They always gave me unstinting support, but I also encouraged the trustees to speak their minds and their concerns, and given that I was prescribing (with their strong support I may say), a variety of actions that were difficult, it created more of a sense of institutional challenge, things not going along so much in a traditional way, and that, I think, was uncomfortable for all of us. You see, only a few years before [I became president], Yale had moved from a system of lifetime tenure for trustees to a system of trustee terms. When the Corporation made that change, they grandfathered the existing trustees who had been appointed on a lifetime basis, but many of them voluntarily elected to retire when they hit retirement age for the faculty, which at that point was seventy.

The upshot was that a corporation that had been marked over the centuries by a very high degree of continuity (with some members serving for decades and decades), went to being one governed by [trustees with] limited terms in office. At the same time the people changed: Those who had [served] for many years were moving off as they hit their voluntary retirement age, and the [new] term process started to turn other people over automatically. The result was a degree of turnover in the Corporation unprecedented in the history of the institution, coinciding with my appointment. At the same time I was saying to the Corporation and these new members, we really need to grapple with some realities about the university's financial and educational and institutional position, realities that really haven't been well understood or faced up to for many, many decades. I think I did not exaggerate the extent to which the institution had to change to put itself on a firm and promising foundation for the future. I don't think I exaggerated that, but it may be that my candid view was a little alarming to some of the new people.

Yale had only looked outside the university for a president once before. The other [outsider] was James Roland Angel, and I think some people on the campus thought, "It's time for another Angel!" Certainly not that I would qualify for that in either respect, but one of the beauties of Yale is that it is a university with a very strong family feeling. It has a very special sense of place and institutional identity, it feels that no one outside of it can quite appreciate fully its strength, its eccentric qualities, its place in which history is a powerful contemporary witness. To bring in an outsider is something that, were it Columbia, no one would bat an eye, that would not be odd; two of Columbia's last three presidents have been outsiders. But at Yale, bringing in an outsider was itself thought to be most unusual and was taken by the community, I think, as a sign, a harbinger of change in itself. [Although I am an alumnus,] from the faculty's point of view or from the students' [I was an outsider]. I didn't grow up in the institution as a professional, I left. As I was quickly persuaded that the university was faced with the need to make some difficult changes, all that, along with the great turnover in the Corporation, created a group that was tremendously supportive but finding its way to some extent, as was I.

There's no question that I was supremely happy at Columbia Law School, and it really would be hard to imagine being more enthusiastic about being dean and my prospects there. I think that the Yale presidency is almost certainly the only academic job of any kind in any university in the world that would have tempted me to leave. But I did feel that it was something of a call. I mean, sure, Henry Rosovsky turned it down when he was dean at Harvard, but he had nothing to do with Yale. I had two Yale degrees. In many ways I attributed almost everything that I had been able to do to Yale and particularly to Yale Law School, and I felt an immense sense of loyalty. I also feel that Yale is one of the places in American academic life where it's possible to stand for important educational principles and goals in ways that can have a very broad effect on society. One of the reasons that I was so happy at Columbia as a law professor and scholar and as dean, was the engagement in the real world of public policy and in the broader realms of public life, and I thought being president of Yale would, and indeed it did, enable me to participate even more fully in the public life of the country with respect to educational policy and related areas of public policy. I thought that that would be extremely interesting and valuable and satisfying, and I also had a sense of Yale—and this may well be somewhat parochial, speaking as a child of the place—that even more than some other universities that are perhaps Yale's equal, Yale uniquely in American life has stood for a particular set of educational values which I identify with the values of liberal education. I felt, I still feel, that American education since the Second World War at all levels has been corrupted by an excessive and often very crass utilitarianism that [is opposed to] the principles of liberal education—that knowledge is a good in itself, that education is for understanding, that it's about all of life not just one's career, and that, indeed, the best education for a career if it's a thoughtful, learned career, is an education for understanding, not for skill, not for just the job. And I felt that Yale uniquely had exemplified all that and that Yale's was the best bully pulpit from which to defend those principles so often lost in the shuffle.

I tried, in my public statements and with the trustees, to make it clear that I had a view of the university which I had learned at Yale, a view that I felt had been strongly reinforced by my experience, paradoxically, in a professional school where I had concluded that the best education for the profession of law was an education that stressed understanding and the ability to think and historical perspective and philosophical and moral perspective, and not so much a how-do-you-do-this-or-that complex legal transaction. I had become completely convinced that even in the world of education for the professions, liberal education is the best approach. I happen to believe it's also likely to be the only kind of education that maintains a democratic polity. So I have deep beliefs, and I thought that Yale would be a place in which I could try to live up to those principles, defend them as president, speak out in that almost unique public position. I felt pretty confident that I was well suited to defending and elaborating and exemplifying them. I found that very exciting and [felt that] the deanship of Columbia Law School or indeed any position in the legal academy, would carry only a very small fraction of that opportunity. So, yes, I was idealistic in the sense that I thought the most important aspect of being the president of a place like Yale was to bolster, defend, elaborate those ideals of what it is to be a university in the great tradition. I was pretty realistic about the strains, the difficulties in the 1980s, 1990s, realistic about the power of utilitarian ideas and the power of the notion that the university is or ought to be a political actor, a view that I reject. I think I was entirely realistic about the extent to which those ideas penetrated the universities, but I was certainly idealistic in my definition of what the job was and what the greatest opportunity in the position was, and I never changed that view.

I was genuinely surprised (and actually continue to be surprised) by the negative reaction many members of the Yale community had to the fact that my wife Helen felt she needed to be based in New York City to continue her career as a filmmaker. That had been very clearly understood in my discussions with the trustees, with Cy Vance, from the beginning. That was a view that I strongly supported, in fact, and a view that seemed to me both natural and right for Helen's career and for our relationship, and it seemed to be one that the Yale community, as a forward-looking and progressive community by and large, would understand and indeed, in many ways, celebrate. I thought Helen's career would be something that people at Yale would be excited that she was pursuing. In my naïveté, I thought that if there were to be problems about that view, they would come from the alumni, who might be hanging on to the idea of the traditional university president's wife presiding over teas and so forth. So I thought I might have some problems with the alumni or with the trustees, but I thought the faculty and the students would surely find the situation not only understandable, but forward-looking and good. And I guess it turned out to be exactly the opposite.

The trustees understood completely and found it perfectly acceptable. I didn't have much of a problem with the alumni, who were generally very supportive of me as president and many of them were enthusiastic about Helen's career. They'd see her films, read about her, and meet her on occasion. But the faculty and the students, at least in many quarters, felt that this reflected—I'm not sure what, and obviously one can't speak of "the faculty" and "the students"—but I had a very clear sense that with some faculty and with many of the students, the perennial issue arose of the president of a major university not being around all the time, or not being as accessible to everyone all the time as they might like. This was put into the perspective that because Helen was not in New Haven full time as her base and we kept a home in New York as well as the President's House in New Haven, that that somehow represented a lack of commitment by me to New Haven and to Yale. I think this attitude was also complicated by the view that New Haven has always had toward New York and that Yale has always had toward universities that are located in larger cities, and that was something that was very surprising to me. I was surprised when the most effective sign the prodivestment student protesters were carrying around campus was, "Where's Benno?" Helen and I talked about the way we were going to do this with a pride and openness that celebrated and protected her career as much as mine. I mean, I said with great pride I thought her career was every bit as important and worthy of respect in terms of family arrangements as mine was. Yet there were significant elements of both the faculty and the student community that really didn't like that.

Yale is not a place where criticism of this sort typically gets answered. It just doesn't. People are going about their business and no, there certainly was not strong [feminist support from the faculty]. There was a strong feminist view among the trustees—Deborah Rhode, Eleanor Holmes Norton, Maxine Singer, among others. Many of the male trustees, such as Cy Vance, were strongly feminist. Many of them had a reaction of surprise similar to my own. There were plenty of things to criticize me about because I was taking lots of controversial positions, but for [Helen's residence in New York] to have been a source of criticism and unhappiness was a big surprise. Still is, still is. I mean, we literally did not know anyone in our own social and professional circles in New York and elsewhere who thought that our living arrangements were even surprising. Even worth commenting on. But the newspapers picked it up, it became one of the strong symbolic features of my presidency, and I never would have predicted it, I never would have thought that. So, I don't want to make more of it than it was because it was not in any way a decisive [element, but] this is just one more example, I think, of the primacy of the symbolic over the real or empirically grounded views of a president. All presidents, many presidents, have to deal with the perception on campus that they're away all the time. Do you know the wonderful joke about Father Hesburgh that they used to tell at Notre Dame? What's the difference between God and Father Hesburgh? God is everywhere, including Notre Dame; Father Hesburgh is only everywhere. I love that. I think Ted told me that joke, actually. A university president, at least the Yale president when I was the Yale president, has to be on the road a lot. I had to raise a huge amount of money for the institution and a lot of what I had to do included taking a fairly strong role in Washington. Anyway, there was inevitably a fair amount of travel and because of that I actually took pains to have more lunches with students and more dinners and things like that with students, than any president had before. Notwithstanding, the perception was that I was away more, or as some people came to see it, a commuter president. And I think it was because most of the time people don't see the president, even when he's on campus. There are 25,000 people at Yale, students, faculty, staff—it's a pretty big place. Any president has a fairly hectic schedule so that these symbolic features of a presidency can assume much larger proportions than the reality would [warrant]. This was just one of those symbolic elements that took on a life of its own.

[Did I realize the financial strains on Yale, the maintenance problems when I accepted the job?] No. I saw the books—oh, I saw the books! It was not at all an issue of anything being hidden from me, not at all. I was given complete access and both the trustees and Bart Giamatti and his colleagues at Yale were absolutely open and very clear about the position of the university. I think the problem was that no one had tried systematically to assess Yale's financial position and I did that, or tried to do that, in my first year. The conclusions that I reached, which I thought then were right and I still think today are right, were new. I mean, they were genuinely new conclusions. Maybe a few people on the campus thought something like it, but to give you just one example: There had never been a complete engineering study of Yale's buildings, [a survey] so that people had a sense of what the problems were. There were very thoughtful people on the campus who could generalize about it, but no one, at least as far as I knew, did what I did in the first few months, which was to call in outside engineers and have them crawl through every building on the campus from the tiniest little house, the Chaplain's House, to the biggest, to the library, and go through the roofs and the basements and wiring and HVAC and [address every] structural issue and complete a big, thick, loose-leaf book on every building.

Yale had eleven million square feet of buildings, most of which were over fifty years old. When all of [the information] was assembled in one room and we had a chance to look at it systematically, it was shocking. Seeing it whole was a shock. Not that anybody was trying to hide anything, on the contrary. But it was shocking when put alongside some of our other emerging conclusions. I want to say "our" because I was not by any means developing these conclusions on my own; I was working with a lot of people on this process of trying to understand the university's situation. For example, Yale could not be a first-rate research university unless it was first-rate in the sciences and particularly in the life sciences. Yale had not created any new science facilities since the 1960s, and yet Yale was seeking to participate in the greatest intellectual revolution of our times (at least in my opinion), the revolution in the life sciences. If Yale was going to stake out an institutional mission of being one of the world's centers of great research in the life sciences, what that necessitates is being first-rate in all the basic sciences. I felt that Yale had this goal, this institutional mission and golden opportunity because of the wonderful quality of the medical school, but the facilities and the other capital investment necessary to be as great in the life sciences as in the humanities and the professional schools [were not there]. When you put that alongside the general condition of the physical infrastructure and address several other institutional necessities that called for redirecting the university's financial priorities and governance, the whole thing added up to a very substantial set of institutional challenges of the kind that the campus had not had to grapple with for many decades.

So you had a system of challenges that were beyond the memory of most trustees, even most members of the faculty, and obviously, of the students. A third of the books in the library were turning to dust and were unusable, and this in a library that had no air conditioning. I don't know any stacks with the precious contents of Yale's Sterling Memorial Library which not only had no climate control but the heating system was fifty years old and completely haywire most of the time. Only Harvard has similar responsibilities in the scope of its library collections, its natural history collections, its collections of art. Yale has the most extraordinary collections—historical musical instruments, second largest collection of dinosaurs in the world—and these were [at risk], not through anybody's fault, but just because as these collections were being built over the centuries, it was not realized that one needs to pay the same attention to issues of preservation and conservation as one pays to the issue of expansion. But that did not happen and had not for a long time. So when one looked at the special character and the special strengths of Yale, and one began to learn the lessons of modern custodianship with respect to conservation, and then one looked at a university that had in some respects not invested as fully in excellence in the sciences as it had in the humanities and some of the social sciences and professions and [therefore] needed to right that balance, and then one looked at the incredible architectural richness of a campus largely built over a half century before when maintenance and preservation had not been understood to be an issue and had been allowed to accumulate for decades and decades and decades—then you saw an institution that for all of its phenomenal strengths was living beyond its means and was consuming its future. And there is only one right answer in the context of a place like Yale, which is a university for the ages: It is not a debatable question whether Yale should be consuming its future; it should not. There is an ethical obligation as well as an obligation of institutional prudence that one try to operate in a balance between current needs and future needs, and my view was that Yale was way, way out of balance.

I remember this so well: After I was named president, I wanted to try to meet the faculty in a fairly personal way, so I sat up in the Sterling Library. I don't know if you know this, but the Sterling Library is a magnificent, cathedral-like structure in the middle of the Yale campus which contains an enormous volume of stacks rising up in a beautiful gothic mass. I didn't want to be in Bart's way (I moved up to Yale six months before I started), so I decided that getting a room in the library was the best place for me to meet the faculty. The librarian was kind enough to [arrange for me to use] a large room up in the stacks that held Yale's world-renowned collection of rare bookplates. So I sat in this bookplate room about twice the size of this [conference] room and had members of the faculty come see me every half an hour; it was brutal. I began to notice, sitting in this room, that some days (I started this process in January) I would be sitting there and my teeth would be chattering and I would be in my overcoat with my muffler around my neck. Other days it was just stiflingly hot, ninety degrees, having nothing to do with what the weather was outside. When I would get up and go down to find a men's room in the stacks, often I would have to walk through an inch of standing water. I remember asking about this and the librarian telling me that there had really been no work done on the library's heating system since it was built, and it still had the old plumbing system, and she was very much aware and people were very much aware of this, but again, not so much systematically. Then Henry Turner, a wonderful man, a great professor of German history and at that time the master of Davenport College, came for his appointment in the library. For masters I had allocated a bit more time because they had dual and in some cases triple roles as senior faculty, leaders of the residential colleges and the social life and fabric of the college, and sometimes other important roles as well. Henry came in, first time I'd ever met him, and said, "How much time do we have?" I said, "We have forty-five minutes." He said, "Well, I'd rather not use my forty-five minutes talking with you. I'd like to take you over to Davenport and show you the basement." We walked out of the library, I remember it well, a brilliant January day, very cold. Davenport is just down a short block or two and we walked in there and he said, "Come on down to the basement." Down we went. Standing water, exposed wires, pipes with all the insulation falling off. He would put his finger in the wall and pull off hunks of plaster. I'm not trying to be overly dramatic about it; Davenport College is one of the most beautiful colleges in the world, and the kids love it; the courtyard is magnificent and the dining room is one of the great places in New Haven. Not the kitchen—it was falling apart. But the heating didn't work well, the plumbing was a disaster. Then I started asking some of the other masters about the condition of their colleges and what was going on down in their basements. Again, this was not exactly news, everybody knew about these problems, but they just hadn't, for one reason or another, added it all up. My view of it was of an institution that had to go through some very difficult, even

gut-wrenching financial reallocations to get itself back in balance. This
was a view that was really forced on me by people like Henry Turner who
just said, "Look at it."

I'm afraid that understanding [of the situation] was not at all equally
distributed [among the faculty]. The scientists understood very well because their work depended to an important extent on the quality of their
facilities; most of Yale's science facilities were over fifty years old and
many of the scientists at Yale on the faculty of arts and sciences were
working in Dickensian conditions. Oddly enough, another group that understood this very well was the people in athletics where again, just as
with the scientists, they depend to some extent on the quality of the facilities. The crew coach knows what the condition of the rowing tank is
or of the swimming pool that would not hold water in the Whitney Gym
because it leaked so badly. So the faculty and others at Yale who had a
functional dependence on the facilities knew very well what the problems were. This was true also of the masters of the residential colleges
because they had to figure out what to do when the plumbing wouldn't
work or there was a flood in the basement or the electricity was out or
the roof fell in. But many of the faculty in the humanities and the social
sciences, who didn't depend on facilities directly for their empirical investigations or the work that their students did, knew that their office
ceilings were falling down or that their windows didn't work very well or
that it was cold, but quite understandably they thought some plastering
or a coat of paint [would suffice]. Yale, by the way, had no painting schedule, no [plan], no, "Okay, this kind of building we ought to paint every
ten years." So the faculty in other areas knew there was a facilities problem, but they really thought of it more as a problem of cosmetics. They
did know the library had a big problem, but—and I admit this—I was
not able to do anything, really, about the library. There are some problems that are almost too big to contemplate. The problem of preservation in the Yale library in terms of the numbers of volumes of books
seemed so much beyond the capacity of any single institution to address
that I took that problem to Washington. I told them, "Hey, this is true
at Columbia and Yale and Harvard, and for all I know it's true in the Library of Congress"—it *was* true in the Library of Congress—"and nothing short of a national preservation strategy can possibly deal with this,"
and some people, Congressman Yates (D-IL) especially [who supported
the NEH preservation program] understood all that very well. Others—
[I don't know]. But the library was such a massive problem, it was hard
to see that the solution could be an institutional rather than a national

one. I still believe that [it's] a national [one]; what are we going to do about our research libraries?

It definitely seemed that in some ways my presidency did take the character of a messenger with bad news, the first one who has to announce bad tidings, and I think that that was one of my failings, actually, because I was shocked by this and [therefore] thought that the university needed to share my sense of shock at the magnitude of the task. And so I went to the university and I went to the trustees and to the alumni with an unvarnished view of the situation, and what I failed to do adequately was to convey the incredibly exciting opportunities that were ours, that would be Yale's, if we dealt with the situation [effectively] because [that] would inevitably mean Yale was providing its faculty and students with vastly superior resources for their work. In the sciences and indeed in other areas, the opportunity was there to radically improve productivity for students and faculty. It was a message of sacrifice and institutional fiscal discipline without the equal and comparable message of immeasurable opportunities to enhance the quality of our work and our lives. The second thing that I think I did not convey adequately was that this was also a time [when] Yale's resources were in a period of unprecedented expansion. I didn't know [that] that was going to be the case for the first year or so, but after a year and a half to two years, I had a pretty good sense that the alumni were going to respond to this challenge at levels of generosity approached [only] once in Yale's history, in the 1920s, when thanks to a couple of special gifts from Harkness and Sterling the modern Yale was built. I started to feel, particularly in my second year, that the alumni and the larger financial community of foundations and others were prepared to support Yale to an extraordinary extent, with all of the tremendous opportunities for Yale's enhancement that that brought. In the meantime, our endowment was outperforming that of any other university in the country. I felt Yale had better prospects than any [other] university for the growth of its financial resources in those two respects, [which] turned out to be true and continued throughout my presidency and continues to this day. To some considerable extent, the momentum for that [growth] had been [created] by Bart Giamatti, during whose presidency alumni really began to support Yale enthusiastically and under whose presidency also an awful lot of discipline was imposed on the endowment, how it was managed, how much of it was spent. So there was this tremendous sense of the dramatic expansion of Yale's financial resources at the same time that I was conveying my view of the need for some difficult financial reallocations in the university. Although I certainly tried to make the good news clear and shout it from the rooftops, the message of constraint, that we've got to make up for decades [of neglect], that we've got to rebuild the place and it falls to this generation to sacrifice perhaps more than others—this message of constraint tended somehow to drown out, among the faculty especially, what I thought was the compensating good news about the tremendous expansion of Yale's resources.

Yale had some very dramatic large gifts, and we were able to do some things with those gifts that were enormously exciting, that enhanced the academic program of the university in tremendously exciting ways, ways that faculty members had dreamed of for decades: The two state-of-the-art facilities for molecular life sciences research at the medical school and on Science Hill; the first center for international studies at Yale, [a program] which had always felt like an orphan and had never had the proper facilities; major renewals of the Peabody Museum of Natural History; finally tackling the renovation of the college. All these things started to materialize and were tremendously exciting to certain segments of the community, but the overall message of fiscal constraint was interpreted by some [as] a greater concern for buildings than people. I blame myself for the fact that that rather dour and difficult message seemed to be a more basic theme in the minds of a lot of faculty and students than the fact of the expansion of the university's financial and therefore academic resources. It was very odd because even as the resources expanded and we had a lot of success and it became more and more clear that Yale could meet the challenges of rebuilding itself and providing for a really first-rate program in the sciences as well as in the humanities and social sciences—even as that was becoming more and more clear, somehow the sense of difficulty and institutional choices that were hard and controversial became ingrained. It's very interesting to wonder about why that was so, but it was definitely the case.

[You asked about my relationship with Bart Giamatti.] Bart was tremendously helpful to me in every way that he could be in the six months before I started. I developed in that time a tremendous regard for his intellect and his courage, both in his institutional character and personally. But at the same time, Bart had a very highly developed and precise view of what his proper relation to me was, and it was pretty much that the minute he stepped down and I became president, he was off to other responsibilities and what he owed me and the institution, he felt, was essentially withdrawal. I think Bart had felt to some extent in his own presidency that the shadow of Kingman Brewster had been a little more pronounced than it should have been, and so he took pains to withdraw. Not personally at all—we would see each other in a very friendly way, but he got away from the place, and many of his friends on the faculty would remark to me how much they missed him and how much they felt that he had really withdrawn as he went into baseball. Now, it has to be said because it's true, that Bart was a wonderful president, in many ways beloved, but he also had in many ways a very difficult time. The strike in 1984 was extremely difficult for him personally. He felt very badly about the way the faculty responded, very badly, and I think some of the faculty's response during the strike was irresponsible and was a betrayal. This was puzzling to me because Columbia had strikes, Columbia has many strikes! They just had one. When I started teaching at Columbia in 1969, Columbia was a rough place, believe me, much rougher than Yale ever was. But somehow at Columbia resentments didn't last, [whereas] the pain of that 1984 strike hung over Yale like a pall. It was extraordinary in a way that wouldn't [happen] at Columbia. Those are the only two universities I've been a part of, so I can't say which is unusual in that respect. But I think Bart was hurt by a sense of mistrust and a gulf that he felt existed between the faculty and the president and the administration. I mean, I was shocked when I arrived at Yale (this may have been quite naïve) and a number of faculty members told me, in a very clear way, that their attitude and the attitude of many, many members of the faculty, was that no administration was to be trusted, that the administration and faculty historically had a healthy sense of mutual skepticism if not downright antagonism, as a part of the institutional character of the place. I was just shocked at that. And yet I think in a way there was never any personal element in it as far as I was concerned because I had not been one of them. Bart had been a faculty member, and he found many of his old friends and colleagues approaching him, the administration, with distrust and an absence of institutional cohesion and harmony, particularly when things got difficult around the strike or around a few other tough issues. That troubled Bart, troubled him deeply. We talked about it; it's among the reasons that he thought the proper role for a president was to withdraw. And, by the way, I think there is a great deal of wisdom in that.

[I did have occasion to call on him for advice.] We would make sure that we had lunch or dinner at least three or four times during the course of the academic year. I did the same thing with Kingman, as a matter of fact, and that was also quite helpful and very, very pleasant and cordial. But I think they both had a sense from their own presidencies that once you're not in there, you're not in there. I mean, you can be a great source of advice and Bart was tremendously helpful about a lot of things, and there is obviously a continuity that they can speak to. But at the same time, they both had a sophisticated and circumspect view about the proper limits of their advisory function or capacity, and so, as time went on, the separation would increase. I don't have any sense of a growing separation or alienation or anything; I [just] mean on the day Bart left, he left. He [remained] friendly and helpful, but there was a clear sense of the crossing of a divide. I begged him to stay and teach, but fortunately or not for him—and indeed, this turned out to be the case for me—being president of Yale is something one does and then moves on, not back.

Kingman had coped very well with the financial exigencies of the late sixties and seventies; he decided everything should be subordinated to supporting the [academic] program and everything else could wait, because once the program was lost or diminished, it was relatively harder to rebuild or catch up. I think that was a reasonable choice and might well have been the one that I would have made. I think Kingman was very sophisticated about it, but at that time the science of endowment management was not nearly as well developed, and a lot of universities made terrible mistakes in the way they managed their endowments. Not through any fault, just because portfolio theory either had not progressed, or its progression hadn't reached the universities in ways that it did in the eighties and continues to now. So, I think Kingman and the earlier presidents grappled with financial issues that were in some ways as difficult [as our own] and certainly required a lot of sophistication, but the times were different. Today, the private universities are still facing some terrific challenges, but the resource base is dramatically expanded.

I certainly don't want to make any criticisms because I'm not sure I would have done anything differently. You also had a situation there for a while where the federal government was underwriting facilities, and when the federal government withdrew, it did so in a very precipitous way, in a very ill-advised way, at the same time that it was dramatically increasing programmatic support. So it's as if you had a federal government that for many years was making substantial capital contributions to save the infrastructure of the railroads, and then all of a sudden stopped making any capital contributions while tremendously increasing the amount of traffic over that infrastructure. That was what was happening in the sciences. The federal priorities were misconceived in my view, badly, and tremendously exacerbated this problem in the 1980s—and it's still the case. So there were many things that came together, but I think Yale faced a particularly, and I think uniquely, acute version of it through a combination of historical accidents, that is, when the previous great period of Yale building had [occurred, combined with] the crunch in the sciences [which] hit Yale very, very hard when the time for reckoning came.

[You asked about team building.] My effort was to try to maintain as much continuity as I could. After all, I was new from the outside, and so only where I felt that a change was required did I try to force change. Now, people were, as you said, moving along in a natural way, and so there were inevitably new positions to be filled, but where I could I tried to maintain continuity and I think that was the right thing to do. I was very lucky in that one of the things that was generally true about Bart was that he appointed, particularly in the deanships, some really extraordinarily able and good people. I tried to maintain that as much as I could. In effect, I maintained about half of the nonacademic, top administrative team and replaced the others either as they left or in one or two cases, [made changes] where I felt [they] really had to be made. [Among these] were a couple of personally difficult things, but there was no particular institutional angst about it.

[In regard to a honeymoon period,] it's natural for people to take a kind of wait-and-see attitude about a lot of things, but I'm not aware that there was any honeymoon. There was a period, a year or so perhaps, when people didn't know me at all, but certainly I had the sense of being thrown right away into the thick of things and having to deal with some very major institutional issues right away, because of the infrastructure problems, because of the politics of the campus—there was this terrific blowup about divestment, which started with Bart and continued over into my administration and caused a constant sense of frenetic upheaval—and also because the collective bargaining process was due to hit my second year and in the very strange character of Yale collective bargaining, the bitterness and the disputatiousness starts to warm up a full year ahead of time. [This was the collective bargaining with the clerical and service and maintenance workers unions;] they came up together and because the previous experience with the strike had been so horrendous, everybody was scared that there would be another one. There was tremendous controversy, there were faculty and students eager to have a melee, and the unions, for whatever reason, decided that their best strategy was to start to turn up the heat, and they were fueling the divestment protests in part to just raise the temperature. So I didn't have any sense of a quiet period at all. I mean, my own inauguration was one of the wildest public events in Yale's history. I enjoyed it; it reminded me a little of Columbia in the old days, with mounted police escorts. It was pretty wild. So, I don't think "honeymoon" is quite the way it felt, although I'm quite sure that if you ask most people at Yale they'd say, oh no, we didn't have any view of this guy one way or the other for the first year or two, or even longer.

[You asked whether I could identify a decision or series of decisions that created a defining moment in my presidency.] I am afraid I think there were quite a few of them. First, I had something of a reputation as a civil libertarian, which I think was right, and of course, Columbia *had* divested, right? And I was coming from the outside, and a lot of students in particular but also some faculty who saw eye-to-eye with them, thought that I might be coming to Yale with a sympathetic view toward divestment and toward the general notion that political agitation by students ought to cause the university to react sympathetically in all kinds of ways. In fact, I had a principled objection to divestment, but I had never been called upon to [express it publicly]. I had expressed it at Columbia; I told Mike Sovern it was a terrible idea when Columbia did it, that it was unprincipled, that it was not sound to take the position that if 3 percent of the student body started making a lot of noise you'd do what they said. I had an absolute view about freedom of speech on the campus, which necessitated my intervening early on in a disciplinary process that had punished a student for a rather puerile effort at satire which was antigay, and my view was that speech is sacrosanct. On a university campus freedom of expression is the paramount value, no ifs, ands, or buts. So I took that position and people were at that time, oddly enough, starting to identify as conservatives people who defended freedom of expression on university campuses (bizarre from a historical point of view) because it happened often that the speech that was being protected on the campus was unpopular, was politically incorrect. So when I resisted divestment, when I protected that kind of speech, when I made clear that Yale would have no speech codes, that there was not going to be any requirement that speech be nice in order to be protected, when I came out against what was being done on other campuses in a very clear and hard way, the students and a lot of the faculty perceived early on that I was a pretty uncompromising conservative. I plead guilty in part. I certainly was uncompromising. I am not sympathetic and I have never been sympathetic to the notion that universities ought to be explicit political actors in promoting a certain political agenda. I just don't believe that. Indeed, I think it's incompatible with the academic mission of the university in the long run. I was never sympathetic to the idea that universities should be the focal point for protests against the Vietnam War. I thought it was absurd. So this very, very deep, ingrained institutional habit of the university, of Yale especially in some ways, being the focal point for political agitation when something is wrong in the broader society—I was not sympathetic to that. And I'm afraid I made that clear. And that was viewed as a politically conservative point of view.

It had nothing to do with that. It had to do with my view of the university, my view that in its investment decisions the university had to bend over backward *not* to take a point of view about a controversial political issue so as not to convey to the university community that there was a "right answer" on a political question. My view that the university ought to generally act in accordance with principle, with a principled approach to things, to its governance decisions, meant that I was not sympathetic to divestment because there was no explanation of how the university should deal with other evils. I agreed that apartheid was terrible, but in what possible way does divesting from Coca-Cola, which was doing an awful lot in South Africa to help change apartheid and in particular to ameliorate its oppressions and its burdens, in what possible sense does having Yale sell its Coca-Cola shares, say "Coca-Cola, you're some sort of a moral pariah," in what possible sense does that help, does that forward a moral agenda? I couldn't get it. And nobody could explain that, much less explain why, if you are going to do it there, [then] what about the oppression of political and religious liberty in the Soviet Union and China? So, to the surprise and disappointment of a lot of people, who I think expected me to approach these issues differently, I conveyed right away that I'm sorry, [but] my view of the university is not that it should rush to ally itself with the latest cause that politically agitates a segment of the university population. Indeed, that it should resist [doing that].

The Corporation was divided and deeply divided [on the issue of divestment], but it did not cause me to lose any support in the Corporation. Indeed, the people who most vigorously disagreed with me in those various views I've just described turned out to be my biggest supporters— Paul Moore, Paul Tsongas, to take a couple of examples. Eleanor Holmes Norton bitterly disagreed with me but was a wonderful supporter of mine on the Corporation. So it didn't cause any problems with my relationships in the Corporation, not at all, but it caused some problems with the students and with certain of the faculty who were sympathetic to the idea that the university was a natural focal point for political agitation and moral indignation, and that was right away, as soon as I arrived. It was clear to me that I was deeply disappointing the very considerable segments of the Yale community who thought that the university's proper role was to take its place in the latest struggle for liberation. I just don't think that. I just don't think that. Some people I greatly respect and admire, like Vince Scully for example, for whom I have the greatest regard personally and intellectually, held that view of the university. But I was in a different place on that completely, and I think I greatly disappointed Vince on that account. He wanted the leader, the president of the university, to be a force for the cause of liberation and political progress, and I felt very strongly that that [shouldn't be] the case and took a pretty hard-nosed position. I think I alienated a lot of people in that process. I knew it, I was sorry about it, but I was pretty certain that I was right. I think there came to be a certain perception, which I'm afraid is probably not altogether unwarranted, of a rather uncompromising character who doesn't care too much about a lot of noise and agitation on these matters. I'm afraid that the style in which I conveyed [my feelings on] that issue, the uncompromising language of principle, was a style better suited to the law school setting where students are more adult by definition and are engaged in studying the relative roles of principle and politics and expediency and resolving different kinds of decisions. In that law school environment a certain rigorous clarity of position and expression is appreciated, and people who disagree can do so in no uncertain terms without losing their mutual respect and liking. But in a college setting I'm afraid that some of that came across as very austere, unsympathetic, and, among my most extreme critics, even authoritarian.

I don't think that last word is right at all because it never had anything to do with my having the answer or being unwilling to engage or participate in a full exchange of views and explain myself. It had nothing to do with an authoritarian streak, but it had a lot to do with my view of the university as a place that has to act in accordance with principle. One of my best friends at Yale, someone I admire greatly, came to me about divestment and said, "We really ought to divest." I said well, if we divest from companies that are active in South Africa, even if they are doing a lot of good, what do we do about companies that are active in China? "You don't have to think about that." I said, how can you not think about that? Doesn't it mean something, aren't you trying to behave in a way that's morally consistent? "Oh, don't worry about that." Well, why South Africa, why start with that? I mean, there are so many evils in the world. "Because the kids are making a lot of noise and you've got to give the kids something. They're upset, they want the university to listen." So, well, I agreed, it's better to listen, I *have* listened. But the fact that they're upset doesn't mean anything to me. Well, I shouldn't say it doesn't mean anything. It means I listen, but the mere fact that they're upset as a guide to action? No way. His view was, "Oh, no, absolutely. If you're a university leader, you gauge when they're upset, and you comply with what they want, try to calm things down, and get on with life." I suppose that's a reasonable point of view, but it's certainly not mine, and I made it very clear that it wasn't. In the process I think I may have conveyed an unbending view, which then was a negative when we got over into the totally different territory of, okay, granted we've got to rebuild the place and it's falling down, how quickly do we do it? I had people who thought, gee, this is a character who comes to what he thinks is right and then doesn't listen and doesn't bend much. I don't think that was right, but I think that was definitely the feeling that some people had.

[As to whether I thought about the risks I was taking when I made a decision,] I didn't think about it that way, but I think I should have thought about it that way. I didn't think of myself then so much as a risk taker as something a little different. When my brothers and I were kids, my father used to take us to a lot of baseball games, and he would say that the people who really count have the big slugging percentage. It's not the batting average, it's not how many hits. It's how many really big hits. It's how many home runs. It's what you *drive* in. I have always had the view in any job that focusing on the big issues, if they are given the right kind of attention and solved, will make a huge difference in the life of the institution, in whatever I'm trying to do. It is far more important than trying to focus on everything, trying to solve little issues because solving all the little issues means you're not going to deal with the big questions. On the big questions there'll be drift. I've always held that view. That was my view as dean, that was my view as a professor, and it was *definitely* my view at Yale. I think one of the biggest problems that all university presidents have is that the ceremonial aspects of the job are very important, and dealing with the abundance of little issues that are constantly bubbling up can take all your time if you don't, in a fairly disciplined and even ruthless way, say that you're not going to get [involved]. [Otherwise,] you will *not* deal with the really big issues that have the greatest consequences for the institution. I had a very strong view about that [at Yale], and it led me to take what turned out to be some significant risks. For example, to press forward with the radical financial restructuring of the place, to rebuild it. For example, to try to resolve the stalemate, the infighting that was paralyzing the school of management. For example, to try to figure out what on earth, after all these many decades, Yale was going to do about its philosophy department. For example, to raise such questions as, does it really make sense for Yale to have a school of nursing? Now, those are just a few of the issues that I felt it was important to tackle and focusing on them [made] a major and risky statement about the appropriate role of the president—[to take on these things] not because they are the big risks but because they are the big issues. But the reason they're the big issues is that people haven't tackled them before because they recognized the risk. Perhaps smarter. But my view was that if that's not what a president is for, what is a president for? Now, each one of those [issues I named] is its own complicated question, and on a couple of those my view of the necessity of tackling those questions and forcing the issue from the president's office was wrong because it raised big governance questions.

I did think nothing was happening [on some of those issues,] but there are ways to address that without the president being front and center as the driving force. There are a couple of other things that I felt deeply about and I think my views were correct but were risky positions to take. For example, it seemed to me clear that Yale couldn't be good at everything and it couldn't even be good at everything it was doing. The evidence for that was the great disparity in the quality and effectiveness of different departments and different schools. In most cases, these problems of quality and effectiveness were long-standing. On the other hand, there were areas of enormous excellence and energy and potential and creativity at Yale that had been starved for growth because of the very strong tendency of the institution, particularly in the faculty of arts and sciences, to pretty much take the status quo as given and view change in a very incremental, interstitial way. Now, I think that's the wrong view for a first-rate academic institution under any circumstances, but particularly under circumstances of financial stress and under circumstances where the *financial* status quo or the inertia of financial priorities, had gotten the institution deeply out of balance.

It seemed to me quite clear that a conscious and deliberate assessment of priorities would find that some areas and some departments and some schools should be given more resources, and some others should be reduced or eliminated. That seemed to me right, and I tried to push strongly in that direction. That turned out to be something that caused a very serious adverse reaction in the faculty of arts and sciences. Not elsewhere, but in the faculty of arts and sciences. Some of my friends warned me about that, and I can remember a couple of faculty members saying, look, you've laid out here a need to achieve a rather modest cutback in the faculty of arts and sciences budget. (I said it had to be 6 or 8 percent, and we could do that over several years.) They said, as long as you do that across the board, there will be grumbling about it, people won't be happy, but it will be doable. But if you say that you're going to do it selectively, with some departments having their budgets cut by 20 percent, 50 percent, other departments having their budgets increased—then that will be tremendously controversial. I disagreed, I still disagree, but it was

tremendously controversial. The initial response of the faculty was to resist strongly although that's what has in fact happened. It's not uncommon that the first time or two something is tried there's immense
resistance, and then eventually there is acceptance of the need to do
something.

[Was there ever a plateau period in my presidency, a period of relative
normalcy?] No. There were some real periods of satisfaction and achievement; I don't want to give you the sense that my answer to your question suggests the whole thing was constantly in a volatile state in a
negative way. That wasn't true. But no, I was never aware of a period of
calm. I'm sure in some sense perhaps there was a honeymoon, but I arrived at Yale in the middle of a fairly serious controversy about divestment. I mean, my inauguration was the wildest one in history, and I
hadn't had a chance to do anything. No one even knew me very well at
my inauguration. So it wasn't that that was a response to what I stood
for. No one had the least idea of what I stood for. And yet, it was only
mounted and motorcycle police that got me from the library to Woolsey
Hall. By the way, this didn't bother me. After all, I had started teaching
at Columbia in 1969 when that was the way things were all the time, so
it didn't bother me particularly. But there was that kind of fiercely agitated quality right from the beginning at Yale. I have already mentioned
the extraordinary power which labor relations and the threat of a strike
has in the Yale community to generate levels of anxiety and to encourage people to all kinds of theatrical displays. [Labor negotiations] came
up also very quickly, and I thought that when those two issues were more
or less resolved, things would calm down a bit, but by then my views
about the need for financial restructuring had been made very clear, and
I had had to face the need to restructure the school of management. So
one thing came pretty hard on the heels of another and created a sense
both among my supporters and my critics, of a presidency that was constantly dealing with things that riled people up. You know, all these were
issues where I had very strong support for what I was doing but also rather
strong opposition, and as is the case in a lot of collective and institutional life, opposition is louder than support. That's the way it is. It's
something that makes so many presidents so characteristically risk averse,
wanting to go by consensus.

[As to how I reached my decision to leave Yale,] I can tell you what I
thought at the time. I turned down heading The Edison Project in 1991
and thought that would be the end of it. I was quite interested, but I felt
in 1991 that there were two or three reasons why I could not leave Yale
at that time. One was this perennial shadow of collective bargaining. An-

other labor negotiation had to be dealt with in what turned out to be my last year, and I knew it was going to be a tough negotiation, a very bitter, controversial one, and I thought it would not be responsible not to try to conclude that. I also wanted to be the only Yale president in modern history who had never had a strike. Although there was an awful lot of agitation and static and noise, I *am* the only Yale president in modern times who never had a strike. I never would have thought this going up to Yale, there are strikes at Columbia all the time, but I actually concluded after I was at Yale and I saw how anxious and agitated the community was about labor relations, that if I could give Yale a period of labor peace and try to calm the thing down and make the process more professional and normal than this highly personalized, theatrical, hysterical process, that I would be doing the institution a great service. I think that. So I felt I could not leave when there was another round of collective bargaining coming up. I know that sounds odd against all of the issues and priorities of a great university, but labor bargaining at Yale, at least in this period of the last twenty or thirty years, has exercised a hold on the institution's sense of well-being that is really remarkable. So I felt I had to do that.

The other thing I felt I had to do was get Yale launched on this big campaign and raise the first half a billion dollars and make it clear that Yale was really going to play in the big leagues. Yale's last campaign had been a fairly unhappy experience. Nobody felt very good about the campaign; it had been difficult to conclude. It had raised over $300 million by the end of the 1970s, but it had been *very* difficult. Indeed, Kingman had had to leave before it was concluded, and there was a perception that Yale was not able—Yale had been the most successful fund-raising university of any in the first part of the century, but as we got toward the end of the century, there was a sense that places like Stanford and Harvard, and even to some extent Columbia, were outpacing [Yale], and I didn't think that was right. I felt that I had to launch this campaign in order to address some of the financial restructuring priorities that I had been insisting on, and that to do that credibly, I had to raise the first $500 million plus. We planned the campaign in the fourth year [of my presidency], then seriously developed it in the fifth year, launched it in the sixth but with half a billion dollars plus already in hand. Very important.

[Edison came to me the first time] when we were planning the campaign. We had the labor issue coming up at the end of the fall of 1991, so in the middle of the academic year 1991–1992, there were these two huge things, one potentially negative and disruptive (the financial side of the collective bargaining issue was not a small matter either) and the other, getting the foundation laid for a successful campaign. My opinion [about the length of a presidency] is that while institutions and people differ, something like ten years or maybe eleven or twelve years is the outside limit. I think complex institutions need new perspectives and indeed, need new energy, and I think presidents who do things tend to use up a lot of their capital. Doing controversial things in any political setting in the long run erodes your capital if you're doing things that are difficult because from a political point of view often the negatives or the adverse consequences of getting something done outweigh the positives in a political light. So, anyway, I had never had the view that I was at Yale for twenty years. No, it was my view that Edison was genuinely a once-in-a-lifetime opportunity to do something with respect to institutions of greater importance than any. That's what the public schools are. They were not working well and needed structural change of the kind that Edison could at least exemplify. So when Edison came back, to my surprise, in the late fall of 1991 and said, we would still like you to lead this effort, I started thinking about it seriously in November. It took me about four months to conclude that this was something I wanted to do.

I shared [my thinking] with Vern Loucks who was the senior fellow [of the Yale Corporation], the equivalent of a chair. (The Yale board doesn't have a chairman; the president's actually the chairman of the board, but the senior fellow in the Yale Corporation is the first among equals.) Vern Loucks was probably my closest confidant, supporter, and mentor on the Corporation. When I concluded that [leading The Edison Project] was something that I wanted to do, which was in April, I went to see Vern in Chicago and told him. I explained what Edison was and a little about why I wanted to do it, and Vern's view was, if you want to do it, you *should* do it; if Edison works, it will be a great thing and something like it is certainly needed. We then talked about what was the best way for Yale and for me to make the transition. Vern and I agreed in April (or it may have been March, I'm not sure, it was in the spring), that the best way to do it would be to say nothing until graduation so as not to disrupt the school year. But I should announce it right after graduation as soon as possible in order to give the Corporation the maximum amount of time to respond before the next school year started. Vern's advice was that I should not have a lame-duck period, that is, that once I decided there was a specific other job that I wanted to do, I should do it.

That was my preference, too. So, as Vern and I then turned to the question of exactly when should we announce it, we agreed that he and I both should talk to the whole Corporation face-to-face and we also thought that once that happened, the word would be out. So we looked at the question of when was the Corporation all together, and the answer was, over graduation weekend. Vern strongly thought that it was better to tell the Corporation then, rather than to wait a month and announce it at the end of June, because announcing it at graduation meant that the Corporation had a whole month followed by a regularly scheduled meeting at the end of June to figure out [what] steps [to take] with respect to an acting president and so on. So that's essentially why we picked the graduation weekend as the time to announce it, to make sure that it didn't get announced publicly until after commencement so that it wouldn't interfere with the seniors or with the full course of the university year. I did not really appreciate how big a national story that was going to be. I knew it would be controversial for me to leave Yale for Edison because I knew Edison was controversial; indeed, the very idea of competition and market forces having a role in public education was then a far more controversial idea than it is now. So I knew a lot was going to be controversial, but I didn't know—and here I think I just failed to understand how the publicity was going to appear—I didn't [realize] the way the timing of the announcement would make it look as if I had perhaps [tried to] maximize the [impact of] "Yale President Goes to The Edison Project" rather than Benno Schmidt goes to The Edison Project as his next thing.

I had quite a lot of ambivalence [about leaving Yale] because the question of going to Edison, despite the immense attraction that it held for me, was a very close question. I mean, that was not an easy decision, and as part of making that decision, I tried to think through very carefully what would happen if I did not go to Edison. Of course, no one can know, it's very speculative. What I thought was that, well, I knew the faculty of arts and sciences was quite upset about this internal restructuring that involved the effort to make decisions selectively about resource allocation and building excellence. There had been a real revolt against the notion that certain departments were to have their resources lessened on the basis of a qualitative judgment about where they were and what their prospects were, or what their importance was in Yale's future as an intellectual academic enterprise. There's no question that the faculty was upset about that and felt that the provost and the deans and the faculty committee members who had been appointed to lead that effort were not adequately reflecting all the views of the faculty. I expected trouble on that front—there was trouble through the spring of 1992 with faculty committees reporting their dismay at this whole process, and I expected that to continue into the next year. But on the other hand, I also had no thought of taking any actions until that process resolved itself one way or the other. I wanted to see how the reaction would play itself out because reality is constantly intruding on such reactions in the form of the university's financial situation, and in this particular reality, the fact is that Stanford, Columbia, and Harvard were all at the same time engaged in very similar efforts at budgetary restructuring, centering on the faculty of arts and sciences. There was a lot of turmoil; the reaction and where all that was going to come out was a much larger issue than just at Yale. It was playing out on a lot of campuses in a rather parallel way. So I thought that that situation was going to continue to be a source of resentment and resistance within the faculty of arts and sciences, but I had no need and did not want to make the situation worse by forcing decisions. I was prepared to wait. My thought was that if I waited, the faculty and I would continue to learn about the financial realities we were dealing with. Every year is different.

There were things happening at other institutions; this was more characteristic than not of most of the universities and even colleges then. Colleges in some ways were facing it in an even more severe form. I was very much aware that the turmoil about restructuring in the faculty of arts and sciences was not going to get worse, was likely to put itself into some perspective. I had been calling for Yale to work out a $16 million structural deficit. Well, Harvard and Columbia and Stanford were struggling with structural deficits that in their own estimation were three, four, five times that. So I thought that a lot of the faculty's initial reaction was likely to ameliorate over time. I had no need to force the issue. I also thought that some of the fairly positive things that were going on had a momentum of their own. I'd just solved the labor problem again, no strikes—sounds like I'm bragging about it but it's a fact. I had proven myself to be Yale's most successful fund-raiser by a huge dimension, I knew I had tremendous momentum there, and the results of that were beginning to be obvious in many ways programmatically and otherwise. I had just concluded an understanding with the mayor and the city of New Haven that gave Yale some benefits that it had been trying to get for half a century and more, first and foremost, the agreement by the city that it wouldn't challenge any of Yale's tax exemptions. Yale had been locked in litigation with the city of New Haven; [the university had taken a] very, very hostile and unfortunate adversary posture with the city about Yale's tax exemption and whether Yale was a good financial citizen of the city. I'd gotten the state to commit to the biggest urban development project in the history of Connecticut in downtown New Haven next to campus. The mayor had agreed to turn over several streets that went through the Yale campus, something that Yale presidents had been trying to get for sixty years. It doesn't sound like a big thing, but in terms of the cohesion of the campus [it] is highly visible. [We were able to] convert them from streets to campus walkways, and this had a huge aesthetic and cohesive and, in fact, safety impact. The alumni, not only through fund-raising but also [in many other ways], were really rallying around the university. The endowment had outperformed that of every university in the country, and on the other side, for all the controversies that I got into with respect to one thing and another, there had never been any issue of integrity or carelessness. This was when John Dingell was auditing every university president in the country and coming up with all kinds of miniscandals and accusations about how big was the flower bill in the president's mansion, or were there inappropriate expenses. It's the only time in my life that I've had every single one of my expenses audited by anybody. It was an amazing thing to have these federal guys combing, just looking for anything that they could come up with, and some university presidents got embarrassed in that process. Although I had my detractors, I was pretty sure that I had seized the high ground from a strategic as well as an ideological point of view in my defense of free speech. That's a good place to be for the long run, if you're a university president. So I thought those were very positive forces that were going to be at work and that would enable me to ride out this bit of a storm that had been created by the budget deficit and the call for restructuring and the call for a selective approach to resource allocation.

[At that time I still saw myself as part of the academy.] Oddly enough, I still do. Very much so. Some day I will get back into the classroom and the library and teach constitutional law again. In some ways I can't wait, although I'm having a great time trying to change public education in the meantime. But in any event, my calculation was that time was on my side. To be candid about it, there is no question that I had also developed a fairly high degree of disillusionment with certain aspects of the university. As I weighed the pros and cons of staying or leaving, there was no question that I felt there were certain aspects of the modern university presidency that were not a particularly good fit in terms of who I was and what I thought was important. I think the modern university has become a deeply conservative institution. I think there's a kind of visceral reaction against and resentment of the possibility of change. I think there's a tendency to avoid difficult realities if facing up to them requires tough choices. There's a tolerance of, or at least an acquiescence in, things that aren't working well because the process of coming to grips, of simply making a judgment that something is not working well, is [too difficult]. I mean, there had been a solid consensus at Yale, an absolute solid consensus, that the situation in the department of philosophy for many years was out of kilter with a place like Yale. The last rankings of departments had the Yale philosophy department ranked something like fortieth, [not the Yale way,] particularly where the history department, the English department, the law school are ranked number one, where the political science department and the economics department are ranked in the top three or four. That is to say, where *all* of the adjoining disciplines and departments in the humanities and social sciences are among the strongest in the world. There was no argument about the situation of the philosophy department on campus. But *nothing*, nothing decisive had ever been done about this situation, not for three decades. Now, I think I understand and appreciate the arguments for not doing something about that. Who wants to? Get on with your own work. It's an unpleasant kind of a thing to face. If you are going to deal with it decisively, it's going to take a lot of somebody's time. But I saw not only at Yale, or even particularly at Yale, that the modern university is very adverse to facing up to tough choices. Maybe that's good, maybe that's bad, but I actually wasn't comfortable with that even when I was a faculty member. I used to find it wrong, but especially as a dean or a president I felt my role was to try to actually do something. Not in a [unilateral way]—I think in the case of the school of management what I did was too unilateral and was a mistake. It certainly wasn't a mistake [that] something had to be done. But I'm not saying that the response [should be] some presidential edict—some ukase goes out from Woodbridge Hall. There has to be a process in the university and an appropriate one that engages the university [community], but if you wait for consensus about everything, including processes—the time to do it, how we do it, who should do it—nothing will happen. And I just didn't think that I fit very well; I was very impatient with that.

In the second place, just to repeat my previous point, I really am not in sympathy with the idea of the university as a place with a political agenda, an institution that it is appropriate to use symbolically and in other ways as a lever for political change. I'm not opposed to political change. I'm not opposed to agitation; I was actually a revolutionary about South Africa myself, but I feel very deeply that the politicized university we inherited from the 1960s has suffered a lot in terms of an atmosphere of relentless conformity when it comes to discussion of political issues. I also feel that the university of constant agitation and protests and chronic indignation about something or other is likely to be a university that is not spending enough energy defending its critical and unique mission, its academic mission, the predicate for which has got to be free inquiry. I also feel—and this sounds very old-fashioned, the students used to chuckle when I expressed this point of view—that in order to fulfill its mission, the university has to be, at least to some extent, a place of repose. A place of reflection. A place of—dare I use the word?—sobriety, or at least the sober second and third and fourth thought about things. The idea that the university in our society would take the place of the political reality, the labor management conflicts, the civil rights movement, that the university would become the focal point for the role of political protest—protest has a great role in American society and I go as far as anybody that I know to defend the right of protest and agitation, and in many respects, the value of it. But for the university to have become the center of that in our society seems to me to be deeply wrong. I have very little sympathy for that, and I made that quite clear. I hope I did so [while] constantly protecting the right of protest, but I was not sympathetic about it and I was out of sync with the modern university in that respect.

And third—well, it's really just stating the second point in a different way—I found so many of my colleagues at the university wanted to make prudential political choices about controversies facing the university, whether it was divestment or the right way to resolve the question of whether graduate students should form a union. My view was that for a university, the response to those questions had to be principled, had to be defended in terms of principle, that the implications of the response had to be viewed in a principled way for other issues. It's not ad hoc political questions, pick your position, and then go on to the next issue. That view of the university as needing to be more of a principled actor in those areas as part of its commitment to academic freedom was not the prevalent view. Not the prevalent view. I feel deeply [about that], and in that sense I think I'm quite out of sync. Now, there were a lot of faculty members who agreed with me about this, but it's not the prevalent view; in fact, it's viewed as kind of a minority and almost even a cranky position. So I had a feeling of some disillusionment, in particular with some of the faculty reaction to what I saw as necessary institutional steps to come to grips with reality and to face up to the need to make some difficult choices. But I also felt in some deeper way that these were strongly held views, not things that I felt it was appropriate for me to be shy about. I felt that a large segment of the university community really didn't share those views and didn't particularly want to have a president who embodied those views. Which is fair enough. I think they are wrong, but they have a perfect right to prefer a president who more nearly embodies perhaps what is the post-1960s institutional ethos of the place than I did. So while I was weighing the pros and cons of Edison or stay-ing at Yale, I had a generally positive view of what would happen had I stayed at Yale although I realized that I had this storm to ride out. But I think I had the wherewithal to ride it out.

Now, on the other side, I felt a very strong [attraction to] what I hoped The Edison Project could be. I know that to nine out of ten thoughtful people my view of The Edison Project's promise and potential might be seen as out of proportion or even grandiose. But The Edison Project did have a very deep appeal for me for all kinds of reasons and I did have the sense that the idea was right for where we were in history. I felt—actually, I still feel—that Edison has tremendous potential for good. I may be wrong about that, but the reason I felt that way back in 1992 and still feel that way is that I think public education generally in this country is in a very bad way. I'm on the more pessimistic side of the nation-at-risk debate, and I also agree with what has become the conventional view that nothing's more important in America than elementary and second-ary education. I mean, it *is* the key to opportunity. It's what immigration was, what the civil rights struggle was, it's literally what emancipation was. It's becoming more and more important all the time, and the prob-lems of inequality in it are becoming more and more serious. But beyond that, I feel that public schools are among the most literally anachronis-tic institutions we have. They haven't changed their calendar since this was an agrarian society; they make no serious use of modern information technology. They haven't changed their daily schedules since American mothers went to work. They are just incredibly resistant to change. In most respects they haven't even caught up with the industrial revolution, much less the information age. I thought that the reasons for that lay certainly not in the resources that are devoted to [public education], which have grown more rapidly than the resources devoted to anything in our economy including medical care over the last half century. [The reasons] had to do with the structure of it, the fact that it's a political, bureaucratic monopoly, and at the same time, it's a cottage industry. Schools aren't integrated and linked up. I thought that Edison offered a chance to bring in innovation and competition and to change schools from cottage industries to [parts] of an integrated system. There is *nothing* more powerful in its potential, mostly for good, but not exclusively, noth-ing that is more powerful than the change of some major activity from a monopoly structure to a competitive structure, and very few things more powerful than the change from a cottage industry to something that's in-tegrated. I think public schools are just waiting for that. I also thought the world was engaged in a revision of its political thinking that had to do with the fundamental reassessment of the power of bureaucratic political systems to deliver things as compared with markets. This reinventing government idea is revolutionizing Eastern Europe and [to a lesser extent] the United States, where public bodies are looking to competitive, private sector entities to deliver more and more public goods and services. [This seemed to me] an idea whose time had come, and it would probably have no more powerful expression in American life than in public education, although it's just beginning here and Edison is still, in a very small way, the main driver of [the movement].

I thought that Edison offered the opportunity to bring innovation into the most anachronistic sector of American society, to raise the level of performance of the most important sector of American society, to invent and create systems where cottage industry was the prevalent structure, and at the same time to focus all those changes on the poorest and most disadvantaged kids, which is what we're doing. And if that worked, it could be of historic importance. I still think that. I knew at the same time that it would be bitterly controversial among the people trying to defend the monopoly because no monopoly ever gives way to competition without tremendous resistance.

So, no, [it cannot be said that I went from a tough job to an easy one,] but it *can* be said that I went from a tough job in which taking action and deciding on things that are necessary is very difficult to achieve, to a job where it's very easy to take action and it's very easy to [make decisions]. Edison is a cohesive, entrepreneurial organization that acts. We may not get it right, but [our organization] is highly responsive, it's highly creative, it's necessarily highly entrepreneurial and risk taking—those are the [kinds of] people who are attracted to it. While the work of Edison is difficult, very challenging, and there's a lot of resistance [to it], within Edison itself the organization is tremendously focused and entrepreneurial and active. Whereas universities as institutions—I'm conservative about universities; they shouldn't be entrepreneurial and going after major risks and trying to figure out what's the greatest political hurdle that we can try to get across for the greatest good. That's not what universities are good at. But they've become so difficult internally to change and so adverse to decision making and priority setting, that Edison, for all its difficulty, is an enterprise I fit into much better than the administrative side of the modern university. The professorial side of a modern university obviously can be highly entrepreneurial; look at the medical schools. But the administrative levels, the governance structures, and the kind[s] of institutional habits that have developed have made university administration highly reactive and risk averse and anything *but* entrepreneurial.

Deanships are quite different in that respect [from central administration] because a dean can have a very clear sense of the collective consciousness of the faculty, whatever it is. The numbers are such that personal interaction with the faculty in shaping that collective consciousness is really possible. Indeed, it's inevitable. Deans have a degree of influence over all the things that really matter—budgets, appointments, promotions, standards of admission—whereas most university presidents have some limited degree of influence over budgets, have little or no influence over appointments even if they have a role in them (the president of Yale has no role in the process). Even where a president has a role in the appointment process it's only at the end. [Presidents have] very little role in the question of individual promotions, sometimes a blocking role, but that's not a shaping role. [Presidents] can, through budgets, have some degree of influence over the general evolution of departments, but not on the most critical matters of appointment and promotion, and in the Yale context very little. Very little [influence over] the standards of admission for students. But deans are in the thick of it, and with that influence and working with the faculty whom they know well and have a real personal connection with, it really is possible for deans to have a very powerful and very constructive shaping role, and the measure of what counts as a good dean reflects that. But for university presidents in most situations, the measure of what counts is raising money, being a good ceremonial head of the place, and avoiding trouble. Those are hard things to do, now; I'm not trying to make light of it, not at all, I have tremendous respect for people who can do it and do it well and do it for twenty-five years. But in my own case, the things that have given me a lot of satisfaction as a professor and as a dean and indeed, as head of The Edison Project, aren't really the things university presidents are expected to do. That's one of those statements of the obvious that some people don't like to say, but I say it with a deep sense of affection. I really loved the university in many ways and a lot of the people [there], and some day, when I've satisfied my entrepreneurial and radical proclivities with respect to public education, I plan to go back.

NOTE

1. Yale Development Office, *Facts about Yale 1986–87* (New Haven: Yale Unviersity, [1986]), 6–7, 12, 30–31; Yale Development Office, *Facts about Yale 1991/92* (New Haven: Yale University, [1991]), 31; Liz McMillen, "President

Quits Yale to Develop Network of Private Schools," *Chronicle of Higher Education*, June 3, 1992, p. A16. Yale's professional schools are architecture, art, divinity, drama, forestry and environmental studies, law, medicine (including epidemiology, public health, and physician associate programs), music, nursing, and organization and management.

Paul Hardin

University of North Carolina at Chapel Hill 1988–1995

A North Carolina native with A.B. (1952) and J.D. (1954) degrees from Duke University, Paul Hardin practiced law in Birmingham, Alabama, before returning to Duke in 1958, where he rose to full professor at the law school within five years. In 1968, Hardin began his administrative career, accepting first the presidency of Wofford College, a small, church-affiliated liberal arts institution in Spartanburg, South Carolina, and then in 1972, the presidency of Southern Methodist University. Asked to leave SMU in 1974 after exposing malfeasance in the football program, Paul Hardin gained a lasting national reputation for integrity in athletics that would later be cited as a factor in his selection to head the University of North Carolina at Chapel Hill. He was serving as president of Drew University (1975–1988) in New Jersey, another small baccalaureate institution with Methodist origins, when he was named to the UNC chancellorship.

In 1988, the Chapel Hill campus presented a dramatic contrast to the tiny Wofford and Drew and the somewhat larger SMU communities, with 23,579 students (7,888 graduate/professional), 2,008 faculty in thirteen schools, a budget of $593.3 million, and an endowment valued at $132.2 million.[1] In changing his academic arena from the independent sector to the public sector, Paul Hardin encountered the predictable culture shock of constraints imposed by state politics, system governance, and the cumbersome apparatus of legislature-controlled finances. Nevertheless, his vigorous fund-raising and consistent public challenges of the governor, the North Carolina General Assembly, and UNC System president C. D.

Spangler were generally successful, leaving the university, at his departure in June 1995, with not only a larger student body but also more faculty, a bigger budget, and an endowment that had more than doubled.[2]
Despite a spate of negative national publicity in 1992 and 1993 during
the contentious drive to establish a freestanding black cultural center,[3]
in retrospect Hardin was seen as having maintained his reputation for
"pushing racial diversity on campus" and was praised for completing
UNC's largest ever fund drive ($440 million), keeping the university's
athletic programs honest, and "successfully lobbying the 1991 General
Assembly to give the state's public universities more flexibility in managing budgets and personnel."[4] He capped his career in 1997 by serving
as interim president of the University of Alabama-Birmingham.

*Paul Hardin's account of some aspects of his chancellorship is an edited
transcript of his interview with Leslie Banner at the Office of the President Emeritus (Brodie), Duke University, October 17, 1997. The questions that prompted his comments have either been omitted or indicated
with bracketed material to create a more readable narrative.*

First of all, I was shocked and surprised when I was approached by the
consultant to the search committee because I did not even know that
the chancellorship at UNC-Chapel Hill was open, and my last suspicion
would have been that they would turn to a man with Duke degrees who
had taught at Duke for ten years. So I at first declined to send my résumé
because I was then president of Drew University and had been for a dozen
years or so, and I thought I would serve out my active administrative career at Drew. Thus, I twice declined to send my résumé. Then John
Phillips, who was the consultant to the search committee, called me from
Bermuda and said, "I'm on my way home tomorrow, and my first meeting tomorrow night will be with the UNC-Chapel Hill search committee. Now, you're embarrassing me because I told them you're the person
that they ought to come to, and you've never sent your résumé." I said,
"Okay, John, I don't want to embarrass you. I'll send it. But do you think
there's any serious likelihood that they will be interested in me? I don't
want to appear to be looking for a job because I'm very happy at Drew,
and I don't want to disturb the board of trustees, make them feel that
I'm restless." He said, "Paul, I think if you'll send your résumé you'll be
the chancellor." Intriguingly, Keith Brodie called me a few weeks later as
the search process unfolded and said, "Paul, my sources in Chapel Hill
say you're the man." So, only John Phillips and Keith Brodie suspected

that this would happen, as far as I can tell. I later learned that one of the reasons they were interested in me, of course, was the obvious one: As president of Wofford College, then Southern Methodist University, and Drew University, I had served three presidencies in the private, church-related sector. In addition, I was a North Carolinian with six hometowns in the state (because my father had been a Methodist minister), married to a preacher's daughter who had seven hometowns in this state, so we knew the territory and were known widely throughout North Carolina. But the other thing that appears to have had something to do with the search is that Dick Crum, the football coach at UNC, had recently been dismissed [with a contract buyout of $800,000]. That had been controversial among the faculty, and the Dean E. Smith Student Activities Center, which we now call the Dean Dome, had been built [at a cost of $35 million], and the faculty was uneasy, as faculties often are, about the apparent emphasis being placed on athletics.

As Bob Eubanks, chairman of the board of trustees at UNC and also chairman of the search committee, told me, they were looking for someone who had a track record of no nonsense in intercollegiate athletics, and I had had an encounter with the board of governors at SMU (the smaller body there, equivalent to the board of trustees in the North Carolina system) on the issue of integrity in athletics. I had lost my job on the issue but had maintained my sense of dignity; I had been informed about some cheating going on there that wasn't terribly big but it was very serious to me, and I uncovered it and self-reported it and disciplined the athletic director and the coach. And soon I was asked to leave. That was widely publicized around the country and as Phil Jensen, a professor of psychology at Drew University, put it to a *New York Times* reporter, "We hate to lose Paul, but isn't it nice that a man who lost a job fourteen years ago on an issue of principle, gains a better one now on the same issue?" I tell you that story because I'm proud of UNC, and I'm proud of the board of trustees for assigning that value such prominence in the search.

I met with the search committee for the first time in the boardroom of the Equitable Life Assurance Society in New York City because Richard Jenrette, then chairman and CFO of the Equitable, is a prominent alumnus of UNC and was on the search committee. So I had the confidential off-campus interview there with the full committee and then was invited to the campus for another interview with the full committee, at which point I also met President Spangler of the UNC system. Then there was a second visit to Chapel Hill which, as I learned when I got there, was the visit in which they hoped to make the offer and receive my acceptance. So that's a quick historical sketch of that search. Another aspect [is that] there had been a study of the UNC system by a committee chaired by James Fisher and a long report had been written, the so-called Fisher Report. I have known Jim Fisher [author of *The Effective College President* (1988), *The Power of the Presidency* (1984), and so forth] slightly for years, but I had nothing to do with that report and did not know of its existence until I was well into the search process. To be perfectly frank—and I think it is okay to disclose this because I won't choose sides—there was some tension between Bob Eubanks, chairman of the board of trustees on the campus, and Dick Spangler, president of the UNC system, because the report (which I read later) took a posture supportive of the flagship campus at Chapel Hill and a little negative with respect to the UNC system. It was fairly understandable that that would've made the system head uneasy; in fact, it made several people uneasy because the Fisher Report was hard-hitting. I remember it was critical in some respects of my distinguished predecessor, Chris Fordham, who is to this day a close, close personal friend of Bob Eubanks. I am absolutely certain that Bob would not have been behind any critical comments about Chris, and I don't think that Bob was personally behind any critical comments about the system. I think Jim Fisher was asked to come in and make the report, and he had a certain viewpoint about it that found its way into the report.

A good segue here may be to say that in the early months of my relationship with President Spangler I felt something less than full rapport. As I look back on it, I think it had to do with his fear that I had come there to advocate and execute the Fisher Report when the truth is I had come there because I'm a native North Carolinian and, I hope, a North Carolina patriot. I had had vast respect for UNC-Chapel Hill from the day I was able to understand what a university is, and I came because the search committee and the president asked me to come, and I came without an agenda. After I read the Fisher Report, two or three of its aspects appealed to me and others did not, so I formed my own agenda, in part by reference to that report, but it was by no means parallel to that report. I can give you one example. The most important, the most critical thing in the report from my standpoint was the lack of financial discretion, much less autonomy, [allowed the individual campuses and chancellors] in the system. As you probably remember, one of my early campaigns was to increase our fiscal responsibility, and that was finally granted by the legislature [with the budget flexibility bill of 1991]. There was some ill feeling for a while because that was not something that the president and perhaps many members of the board of governors wanted to be done. But it was done, and in the years following that my relationship with President Spangler became much better, I think in part because he discovered that fiscal autonomy worked well for all the campuses and was not just something that Chapel Hill needed—it was something all the chancellors wanted. When it came time for the General Assembly to consider the bill again (it had come into being with a sunset provision), it was approved with President Spangler's support, and so things were smoother after that. But I expect the search process had an underlying tension of which I was quite innocent, relating to the Fisher Report, which was contracted by the chairman of the board of trustees at UNC-Chapel Hill.

I knew I was beginning with a bit of a culture shock, which brings us to the second question in Keith's letter to me. Although I had not read the Fisher Report and did not know and do not know now for sure whether or not Mr. Spangler had another candidate in mind, I did know that I was coming from the private, tuition-dependent, church-related sector where I was responsible only to the board of trustees in the legal sense, although I've always felt the responsibility to students and faculty and other constituents. But I was the chief executive officer in an unambiguous way for twenty years, presiding over three privately supported schools. I knew that there was a system head here who was my boss, and I knew that state systems in general are fraught with bureaucracies and complexities that I had not had to deal with. So I did come in with my eyes open to the fact that I was entering a different culture, but I did not come in with any sense that I would be in conflict in personal ways with the president.

One other issue that I remember discussing with President Spangler was one that had been mentioned in that wonderful phone call from Keith: He didn't tell me only that I was going to be the choice; he said that he thought that President Spangler would not choose me if I made an issue of who attends AAU, of who has the UNC-Chapel Hill vote in the Association of American Universities. I felt then—told Mr. Spangler I felt then—and still feel now, that it's been a mistake for system heads to be the voting members of AAU when it was a single entity in the system that was the member and everybody knows that. I think, frankly, this is a legacy of Mr. Friday's vast prestige in the whole scene of American higher education. So Keith said, "Paul, Dick Spangler feels so strongly about that, that if you make a big issue of it, I think he will turn you down even though you are the best qualified person." In the course of my conversations with President Spangler I had decided on Keith's advice not to make this a do-or-die issue, but I didn't want to leave it silent.

After Mr. Spangler and I had several friendly conversations, I said, "Dick," (we'd become first name by then), "talk with me about AAU." "I'm going!" he said—got the hair up on the back of his neck. I said, "Well, let me ask you why?" He said, "Because I'm the Chief Executive Officer of the University of North Carolina." I said, "Well, yes, but I'm the Chief Executive Officer of UNC-Chapel Hill, and it is Chapel Hill that is the member, right?" He said, "Yes, but I'm your superior officer." I said, "Well, listen, let's not argue about that, but let me ask you something else. I happen to be now on the Federal Relations Advisory Committee of the American Council on Education, which means I go to Washington now and then and politic. Are you going to say you're my superior officer? Are you going to do that?" He said, "No." I said, "I'm on the Presidents Commission of NCAA, and I'm active in NCAA, and I think NCAA expects the campus chief to be in charge of that. Are you going to say you're my superior officer and go to NCAA meetings?" He said, "No." I said, "Well, I think you understand what I'm driving at. If you want to go to AAU, I will respectfully disagree with that, but I'll be quiet about it. I won't raise it as an issue. But I am just trying to determine that you really do want a chancellor," and he said, "No problem, Paul," and we never had another word about it. Interestingly, as we were planning for our bicentennial, I went to see the president on some other business and said, "By the way, Dick, don't you think it would be nice while we are having our bicentennial celebration for you to invite AAU to come here and meet during that time?" With some obvious embarrassment, he said, "Oh, I've already done that." It turned out that he and Nan Keohane (who had just been named president here at Duke) were going to cohost that meeting of AAU, and he had already made all the arrangements with our community relations people and our special events people. It passed through my mind that if he were going to host AAU at Appalachian State at the Broyhill Center, he would have talked with the chancellor of Appalachian, but that was typical. The system head feels so much at home in Chapel Hill that the relationship between the system head and this campus is quite different from the relationship between the system head and the other campuses. The denouement was that Nan and Duke were entertaining AAU the first night of the conference, and she graciously invited Barbara and me to come and we accepted, and a few days later, we got an invitation from President Spangler to come to the affair that he was to host the second night. You can see that AAU has been a very, very sensitive point with President Spangler and a point of irritation to me, although I didn't lie awake worrying about it.

On this business of coming into a different institutional culture, I take some responsibility for some of the early tensions because I had mentioned the AAU thing to Dick Spangler. I had told him as I became familiar with what was going on that I thought it was disgraceful that our budget was coming to us from the legislature with 405 line items instead of coming to me in a lump sum and letting us administer that budget like any other university would feel free to do. I had also disagreed with him privately on one other factor: his adamant support of low tuition. I looked at the average family income of North Carolinians and the average family income of UNC students, and our tuition at that time was unbelievably low. I made the suggestion that if I were given permission to raise our tuition just $500 a year for three years, or even $300 a year for five years, and keep that money on our campus, at the end of that time we would have a new plateau of income equivalent to about a five or six billion-dollar endowment. That did not impress the president. I also said I would be willing to set aside 40 percent of that for need-based aid so that we would not deprive anyone of an opportunity to have an education, but he conscientiously and relying (as he said) on the Constitution of the state of North Carolina, remained in favor of low or no tuition, the lowest tuition possible. His defense of that, in light of the fact that many wealthy parents send their children to Carolina, is that, well, those parents and those alumni will help us financially in our campaigns later on. So, we disagreed about that. Later, I abandoned my advocacy of higher tuition because I found out that the legislature has control over tuition which has to be appropriated to each campus; that is, it doesn't stay automatically on the campus where it was paid. Thus, for all I knew, our tuition increases were going to build prisons. My early years as chancellor were bad years in the state economically, and the state budget was under tight constraints, so I became, *ex necessite*, an opponent of using tuition increases as a substitute for tax revenue in our state because I understood that it wasn't in the cards that I would have discretion about how it's used and be able to keep it on the Chapel Hill campus. Incidentally, those battles continue now, and you will recall that President Broad had an early confrontation—it wasn't hostile but firm—with Dean Paul Fulton when he was seeking legislative approval of a substantial tuition increase in the Kenan Flagler School of Business to be expended on that campus. Even a little farther back, just as I was stepping down, my brand-new successor, Michael Hooker, and the board of trustees at UNC-Chapel Hill accepted an invitation by the General Assembly to add a tuition increase to be expended on the UNC campus, and that was over the public, strong opposition of Dick Spangler. So I never had the kind of public confrontation with President Spangler on tuition that our board of trustees later had. I never had the kind of public embarrassment that very likely flowed to President Broad and Dean Fulton when they had worked things through.

There has to be a system office and a system head in a complex situation like ours because you're so likely to get chaos, but you'll find that the chancellors of the flagship institutions—and in this state that's basically North Carolina State and Carolina and in some respects UNC-Greensboro as the original woman's college—you'll find them worried about the tendency to homogenize and to fund equally instead of equitably, and to fund to the lowest common denominator of success that a whole system can be brought to. Thus, I did find myself in subtle ways and in some direct ways, making sure that I protected the majesty and the incredible quality and reputation of UNC-Chapel Hill. That will be the driving life force in any chancellor of a major flagship public university, whereas chancellors of the newer up-and-coming institutions will be fighting for a stronger share and a system head has to mediate all of that. Just as President Spangler didn't always approve of my activity on behalf of the flagship, I didn't always agree with him on the way that he was dealing with the system, but I never failed to recognize, and I never failed to say when I was asked by the press, "Well, remember, he has a different constituency. My constituency is Chapel Hill, and his constituency is sixteen campuses of the University of North Carolina." So I tried not to make this a public dispute, and in our private conversations, with one or two exceptions when there were some pretty sharp words, it was not hostile.

[In regard to a defining moment,] let me quibble with Keith's definition. As you read his description of what he means by a defining moment, "the moment when you had to make a decision that would alienate some group, interest, or constituency," then the defining moment is bound to be a negative moment. I might prefer to say that the defining moment of my chancellorship was the achieving of the financial responsibility act. I might say the defining moment was the celebration of the successful conclusion of the bicentennial campaign that set out to raise $320 million and raised $444 million or whatever it was. I would not be tempted to say a defining moment was winning the NCAA basketball championship, but it was fun, and it was even more fun when the women did it less than a year later. So, I had a lot of defining moments in the sense of important moments for one reason or another, and I'm not going to take as defining moments the early alienation of some members of the board of governors and the tension with Dick Spangler because those moments were survived and we developed a good relationship. I think

President Spangler not only came to appreciate the appropriateness of the financial responsibility legislation but also came to appreciate his chancellors and learned to use them in a little bit more open way. He not only permitted us, but persuaded us, to go to Raleigh when we were trying to get the bond issue through for the UNC system. He had previously said, "Don't go to Raleigh, that's my job." He used us as his campaign chairmen, and we got the bond issue through. Toward the end of our relationship I found a lot to applaud in Dick Spangler's leadership, notably his insistence on gender equity, bringing two women chancellors into the system, and his staunch defense of free speech when the tobacco interests got mad because our school of public health was having a seminar on the health dangers of smoking and a couple of tobacco executives suggested that we were getting out of line. I obviously stood up for academic freedom and Dick Spangler backed me 100 percent. He backed me in some controversies with reference to the Sonja Haynes Stone Black Cultural Center, but I'll come to that in a minute. So I don't want to leave you with the notion that Dick Spangler and I never learned to work together. But in your chronology of my coming, I came as an innocent, unawares; early on I learned that I was in a new culture, and I had to take some risks with respect to my relationship to the president. Looking back on that, I would not change anything. If I had known more than I did, I would still have come because of my respect for this university, UNC-Chapel Hill, and my respect for the state.

I would have taken the risk, and I took some risks that I haven't told you about in conversations with Mr. Spangler. I wanted to bring a chief financial officer here from Arizona, Ben Tuchi, and I later did bring him, but he was making $113,000 in Arizona, and this position was capped in our system at $108,000. I asked Mr. Spangler for an increase in the cap just to make sure we could bring Mr. Tuchi here with what he was making, and the president wouldn't do it. He wouldn't let me take it to the board, he wouldn't take it to the board. He let me provide a car out of our UNC-Chapel Hill foundation for Ben Tuchi, which was a really poor second-choice way to lure a good man here, but we got him anyway. I thought that was just horribly shortsighted, and I said to Mr. Spangler, "You know, you are really presenting a problem which I don't think you ought to present to me." I think other chancellors than Paul Hardin had private conversations with President Spangler that involved risks taken. I'm sure of that because one thing I give him credit for is, he hired well; he hired good chancellors, and he hired chancellors that are not, by and large, obsequious. I expect that I did not have by any means the only confrontations with President Spangler. But I got over that, [and] we had a good respectful relationship. The last time we walked off the commencement platform at Carolina together, Dick said something that I really appreciated because we had been through a lot of wars. He said, "You have been a good chancellor. You have been a good chancellor." I appreciated that, and I can say, reciprocally, that he has been, on the whole, a good president for our system, and he was particularly a strong president in the second half of his tenure. Very positive.

On the other hand, there was a time when I knew President Spangler wanted me to resign. He didn't ask me to flat out, but after that financial responsibility thing went through, and there had been some tension with respect to tuition, I went to him one day after a board meeting when some issues had been resolved and said, "I think things are going well." He said, "Well, you may think so, but there are some members of this board that would like to hold my coat while I fire you." I said, "Well, Mr. President, I'm a survivor, and so are you. I remember you went to Pinehurst once with the board of governors and the rumor was out that they might be out to get you, and you're still here, so I think you and I better learn to work together." And we did. At that same season I told the chairman of the board of governors, "I'm going to tell you something that I won't say to Mr. Spangler because I don't want this to wave a red flag, but I think the president would like me to be out of the way, would like me to step aside. It won't happen. I'm too devoted to Carolina to resign in a temper on some short-term issue, and, frankly, if the president asks me to resign, I would respectfully decline and just see how it would work out in the board of governors." I don't know whether that message ever got to President Spangler or not, but I was never asked to resign, and in fact, the last four years or so, maybe even five, of my seven-year tenure were quite smooth in terms of my relationship with President Spangler. I think we set each other down and neither one blinked, and we decided to work together for the good of the state of North Carolina.

You know, in the public sector one of the things that we always get caught up in is that we have to campaign, we have to get the attention of the legislature. The faculty leadership would often say, we're going into severe decline, we're losing a lot of people, and so on. The fact is, we only lost a few, and we gained some, and Trudier Harris, who left, has come back bringing all kinds of people with her so that we've got the best African American literature program in America. We worried about the decline in the library when I came; I think our library was ranked nineteenth, and it ranked nineteenth when I left. It's now climbed back up to seventeenth or eighteenth, something like that. It's ranked a little bit ahead of Duke's, and I don't think we lost a lot of ground, but we

went through a lot of agony. One of the great stories I need to tell you—
and I don't think [Governor] Jim Martin would mind having this see the
light of day—in the early days of the [bicentennial] campaign I was out
at Dallas visiting Ross Perot, whom I had known when I was at SMU,
asking him for a million-dollar gift to buy a new telescope. He said, "I
want my million to be the last money, not the first money," and that now
is due because we've got the money from Congress for the telescope. But
anyway, I walked out of Ross's office, and his secretary told me to call my
office. I found out that while I was extracting a $1 million pledge from
Ross Perot, Jim Martin's budget proposal had lifted $12 million out of
our pockets at Chapel Hill. The year before, the legislature, in a tight
budget move, had raised the legislative share of our overhead receipts on
research contracts from 30 percent to 50 percent, but had promised that
the next year their share would go back down to 20 percent (it had been
on a 5-percent-a-year decline). But instead of bringing it down to 20 percent as promised, Jim Martin sent a budget to the legislature that continued to send 50 percent of our overhead research support to the state
of North Carolina. I called Nancy, Jim Martin's legislative assistant, from
Ross Perot's office and asked to speak to the governor. She said, "Tell me
what it is, Paul." I said, "I'm furious," and I laid it out. She said, "Well,
I know he would want to talk with you," and she indicated how much
control she had over the governor's time by telling me to call the mansion at nine o'clock the next morning and I would be able to speak to
the governor. I flew back to Chapel Hill, got on a plane early the next
morning with Dick McCormick [our provost who has since become president of the University of Washington] and a few other folks and went
to Washington where I was attending a meeting with Ernie Boyer. At
nine o'clock I called the mansion and a courteous highway patrolman
put me through. Jim Martin came on and said, "I understand you're mad."
I said, "Jim, you owe my wife and Dick McCormick a debt of gratitude."
He said, "Why?" and I said, "Because I have yelled and screamed at them
for the last twenty-four hours, hoping that I would be reasonably civil
when I talked to you." He said, "You are mad, aren't you?" I said, "Jim, I
have never been as upset in my life." He said, "Well, calm down because
after I talked with Nancy, I checked. I did not know when I did that
what the legislature had promised the year before, and I did not know
that UNC-Chapel Hill accounts for 77 percent of that money or whatever it is, and I'm going to make a supplemental budget proposal, but if
I'm going to do that I need you to stay on my case." We talked about
practical politics, and I called Larry Monteith [chancellor of North Carolina State University], and the next day we had the first and only joint

press conference ever held between the chancellors of the two flagships
in North Carolina. We excoriated Jim Martin and everybody must have
thought we were very bold, but we were doing it at Jim Martin's request,
which I think is one of the great political stories of all time. I'm a Democrat, but I got along very well with Republican Jim Martin. I later had
conflict with [Democratic governor] Jim Hunt when one of his budget
proposals threatened the very life of our graduate program. I was in his
office chewing him up and he changed that in our favor. So, I not only
had to confront our president, but I had to confront Republican and
Democratic governors alike without fear or favor, and both of those confrontations came out okay. But you just have to be alert because somebody is going to do you in if you're head of a public institution.

   I think that the defining moments probably ought to be—at least those
that had thoroughly positive consequences—those moments that were
private then, can be discussed now, of standing up for Carolina at some
risk, both with respect to the president of the system and to the two governors. But I think that the person on the street, so to speak, would see
the black cultural center controversy as the defining moment because
through that long, arduous experience I suffered more wear and tear than
I ever have. I don't think I showed it, I've got a lot of stamina, but that
hurt me a lot. That was a defining moment because I ended up having
to offend both sides of that equation. Initially, as you'll recall, the advocates of an expanded black cultural center (which existed then and still
does in the student center in inadequate space) wanted to take over Howell Hall, where the school of journalism and mass communication was
housed, but that was an inappropriate part of campus for a student activity. As you know, the great quadrangle that fronts Franklin Street is
an academic quadrangle while student life is centered around "The Pit."
So I didn't want to recommend Howell Hall, and I said something that
I still believe but that became an inflammatory comment: that we want
for the black cultural center a forum, not a fortress. That if you have a
freestanding building, it is likely to be seen as a fortress. Let's make sure
that we're talking about a facility and a program that are not exclusive,
that are open and affirming and educational. But it suited the proponents, the student activists, and the woman who then was in charge of
the black cultural center, to treat that as a confrontation[al] [statement].
And so I became for a moment a reluctant hero with the conservatives
who did not like the whole idea of a black cultural center and an enemy
[among supporters of the BCC] which I think was an artificial construct
and very hurtful. I had always championed diversity and had taken steps
to establish diversity on this campus and had said that if you satisfy me

that you're establishing an institution that would be open and that will be constructive, I will support it to the hilt. Later, when I had Provost Dick McCormick chair a committee to make recommendations to me, Dick tried to enlist those student activists on the committee, and they refused to cooperate just to show they were more interested in the issue than they were in a solution. Dick McCormick made the best of it without the students, and his committee recommended that the freestanding black cultural center go forward and be constructed on an appropriate site, that it be open programmatically to everyone regardless of race, and that it be an educational facility and not a segregated black student union. At which point I endorsed it and incurred the wrath of the conservatives. I think the true liberals were more or less people who think as I do about these things, who have an open mind and really want the races to work together, who believe in integration. I think we were all just kind of baffled about how these things got out of control. [The BCC controversy] had an interesting denouement in that I did support it and Dick Spangler supported me. I think he was brought into that discussion by some members of the press, and he responded that the chancellor was handling the BCC and handling it well, and he supported my decision to support the freestanding center. I made the first financial pledge that was made to the Sonja Haynes Stone Black Cultural Center, the only one out there for a while.

Of course, we had a confrontation at that time over where it was going to be built. The students wanted the site that for years has been on our campus plan as a kind of preserve for the natural sciences. I decided instead to recommend to the board that we use the site across the street near the bell tower, which had not been on anybody's plans for academic expansion. With the chemistry towers where they are and the surrounding science-intensive disciplines there, I still think that was the right decision, to preserve that plot in the shadow of Wilson Library for the sciences. So, the BCC was a defining moment in the sense that I had to pick my way through my personal feelings and what I thought was best for the university, and I had to do it simply without regard to public opinion because it was a lose-lose situation. There was no way I could approach that problem in terms of what's going to make people happy. Absolutely no way.

And then the press! Particularly ABC television newsman Peter Jennings. I've boycotted him personally—I don't watch his news program—because of what he did. I was home in bed with flu, and [my assistant] Brenda Kirby called me and said, "You might want to come over here; there's an ABC network reporter here, a camera crew, and they're interviewing the student athletes who have become active advocates of the center. I think they are taking the position with those athletes that they've forced your hand, that you have approved the center because of them." I said, "Oh, my word! If I were half-dead, I'd come," and I went over there and said, "You know, the reason I came over here to talk with you is that [your interpretation] is so far from the truth. Let me illustrate it by saying that the most publicly noticed thing I've done in my entire career was to stand up to athletics [at SMU] in a situation which confronted the values I hold dear. When these young men came to see me and said, 'If you don't approve this black cultural center we plan to boycott and not play football,' my exact response was, 'That is the most underwhelming threat I have ever heard in my life. You think that I have nothing to do on Saturday afternoon but go to a ballgame? I love golf, I have seven grandchildren'—nine now—'You know, the only thing that is going to get hurt is football. You are not going to hurt anything except what you love so much.'" The reporter, a woman, said, "I'm so glad you came over here because I had a different impression," and I know she reported faithfully what I said, and Peter Jennings went on the air and said that I had changed my mind after I was confronted by the student athletes. I never watched one minute of Peter Jennings from that time. I had a friend who was a vice president of ABC, we served on the Carnegie Foundation for the Advancement of Teaching together, and I told him about this. He said, "Write Peter Jennings and send me a copy, a shown copy [of your letter]," and I did that, and I heard from the vice president, who's a friend, never heard from Peter Jennings or anyone speaking for Peter Jennings. I said, "You know, you have committed agenda journalism; your reporter was sent down with an agenda, she came back with a straight story—I know because we had a good, positive interview, and you got on the air as if she had never come down here." So, when people tell me how much they admire Peter Jennings, I demur.

I would say that the competition for defining moments would be close in the public eye. When all the facts are on the table, I would choose that aggregation of confrontations with my president and with my two governors that had positive outcomes, protecting and strengthening the university. The confrontation about financial responsibility clearly strengthened Chapel Hill, and it would not have taken place if I hadn't taken some risks. The confrontations with two governors resulted in budget turnarounds that you can't say greatly strengthened the university, but they avoided weakening it. The loss of strength would have been obvious. Incidentally, another way in which that victory over Jim Martin paid off: I left something for Michael Hooker and all of his successors that

is very important and not well known. When that $12 million in over-
head recovery that the university had not counted on having that year
came back into the university coffers, with the full knowledge that more
would be coming as the legislature's share declined from 20 percent to 15
to 10 to 5, and now we're home free—I captured $5 million of it to cre-
ate a discretionary fund for the chancellor at UNC, to use for the important initiatives, the priming, the encouraging or challenging that you want
to do. I set up a committee chaired by Dick McCormick to advise me on
how to spend that money. The committee recommended also that we take
a percentage of all the state appropriations to the university [to add to the
fund]. We ended up taking about eight-tenths of 1 percent from the academic appropriation and 1.5 percent from the administrative program, and
we created what amounts to something like a $7 or 8 million discretionary
fund that the chancellor uses in consultation with the committee. I don't
know how Michael Hooker's using it, whether he's using the same committee or what. That seems like a lot of money, but in an annual budget
now approaching $1 billion, $8 million is not too much—to set up prizes
for good teaching, to support a promising scholar whose grant has expired,
to support the Playmakers Theatre. You just have to have money like that.
I was able to ensure that the departments that generated the overhead
money got more than they ever had before but that there was also a little
that came in for the chancellor. Incidentally, I followed that practice any
time I had a discretionary fund to administer—even though it's legally
been at my discretion—I appointed committees. I did that at UAB when
I got to the University of Alabama at Birmingham as interim president a
year ago. I found that there were two funds the president administers
there, much larger funds than I had had at Carolina, and there was some
unrest as to how they were being administered. I appointed two committees, one for one fund and one for the other, to make public recommendations to me on the expenditure of that money, and campus morale just
soared after that. Now, other people who have discretionary money don't
do that, but I think the chief executive officer can well sacrifice a little
bit of autocratic authority in the interest of campus morale. [Because of
those committees,] I'm sure I made better decisions about how to use that
money. Usually, I approved its use for things that I had not even known
about, but the presence of the committee brought those things to my attention, and when the reports came in I accepted every one of them, just
as they came in.

    Another defining moment [at Chapel Hill] that I think was educa-
tional for the whole campus—and I had a good time with it, I really had
a good time with it—was when one of the graduating classes made a gift

of statuary [to the campus]. It was entitled "The Student Body" and was actually seven statues depicting a variety of students. A committee, which advises on where public art should be placed on campus, had recommended [that "The Student Body" be placed in] an absolutely beautiful brick planter in front of Davis Library where the students would see it every day, and I had approved that. When the statues were delivered, they soon became highly controversial. One of the figures represented Michael Jordan: he had a book under his arm and [was spinning] a basketball over his head. There was another statue of an African American woman who (and I think this showed really poor judgment on the part of the sculptor, but I didn't see the thing until it was already in place) carried a book on her head as African women carry objects or loads on their heads—a beautiful, stately woman, balancing a book. If you look at it with a positive eye, it's a beautiful thing, has the dignity of the woman representing her African culture where they carry burdens on their heads, but the burden she elects to carry here is an intellectual burden. But there were a lot of African Americans on campus and some liberal sympathizers who were offended by the statue, and so it was demanded that it be moved or taken down. Don Boulton, vice-chancellor for student affairs, and I fretted over that, and I said early on—I just made a decision—I will move that sculpture one time because I am impressed by the argument of the dissidents that they are a captive audience—every day they have to go to Davis Library they will be confronted by the sculpture and it offends them. However, it is a public work of art, and my interest in free expression is so strong that the condition is that where it goes must be a public place. I also wanted the recommendation of a new site to come with the agreement of all sides to the dispute. Well, the committee made two or three recommendations, none of which suited the dissidents who had wanted it moved. So Don Boulton and I stepped in. Don told me about this beautiful little place behind Hamilton Hall, a little garden. He showed it to me, said, "That looks like a frame without a picture. That's the perfect place for it." We talked to some student leaders who were resentful of the other place and they agreed and I moved it. Now, people who want to find me insufficiently attentive to free expression can find fault with that, wanting me to leave it right where it was. People who think I'm too sensitive to African American concerns and so forth can find fault with it. On the other hand, the African Americans can say, I'm still insulted by it, and it's still in a public spot and I have to see it every day. There, I had to make a decision that to me balanced two tremendously valuable objectives: on one hand, the hope that everybody feels comfortable on our campus—if we admit people, we want them to feel comfortable. On the other hand, we don't want to sacrifice our support for freedom of expression. So that was a little microdefining moment. A lot of people felt sorry for me, but I was exhilarated by it because legal training consists of cases that come to court and are tried on appeal and find their way into the court reports and are close cases by definition. So lawyers learn to look at competing values that are pretty well matched and make a decision, or help judges make decisions. I felt like I was back at home, balancing equity, balancing values, and I'm trained to do that. I find that stimulating, and I feel we made a really good decision that was a risky decision, to a certain extent.

[My legal education has been useful] everywhere I've been. It was extremely useful at Wofford because when I went to Wofford College, my first presidency, I had been on the law faculty at Duke for ten years, and I was steeped in the whole [academic] process. The reason I was elected president of Wofford was that a lot of colleges and universities were turning to lawyers in those days, particularly academic lawyers. You see, our writings gave us credibility with faculties. Boards of trustees were looking for people with some experience in dispute settlement as this was the day of activism and campus unrest; they wanted someone who could stand between the student activists and the reactionary constituents. That didn't scare me, and so I took that training to work every day at Wofford College. I took that little school through all that period, and we had the trustees approve the first absolutely open-speaker policy of any institution in South Carolina. We were ahead of the public institutions. That meant yes, a card-carrying Communist could come and speak. There were only a few limitations: One, whoever sponsors the speaker has to be a member of the Wofford community, whether an organization or an individual; two, you have to make arrangements so that a place is available and the date doesn't conflict with some other speech or event; and three, any speaker has to submit to questions [from the audience]. I got that approved, and the test case was Dick Gregory, who had been invited by our activist chaplain to come and speak. When I had brought the open policy proposal to the board, the most conservative member of my board, Roger Milliken (he used to send the *National Review* to every member of the faculty; when he asked me if I would be offended if he sent it to me, I said, no, if you won't be offended if I don't always read it), as I expected, was the one who asked a penetrating question. "Paul, I trust that you must have a good reason for this, so tell me what it is." I said, "Okay, for the liberals among you (and I was giving you the benefit of the doubt), I believe in free speech, and I'm a John Stuart Mill advocate, and in his essay on freedom of thought and expression, he says,

'I may hold the truth, but I hold it by accident if I haven't heard it challenged by someone who passionately disagrees with me.'" (That's a paraphrase.) "So that's the liberal argument. The conservative argument is, Roger, if we don't have an open speaker policy, the alternative is what? A committee or person to say yes or no to every speaker proposal? Let's take Dick Gregory as an example. If you don't approve this proposal so that Dick Gregory can come here under our open-speaker policy, which is a policy we adopt as a matter of principle, then one of two things happens: a committee of this board will say, 'Turn down Dick Gregory,' and incur the wrath of liberal faculty and students, or a committee of the board of trustees accepts Dick Gregory, and it could rightfully be said in the community, 'This must represent Wofford's point of view, the trustees have approved his coming.' Wouldn't you rather just have a policy so that every speaker who comes is coming to neutral territory?" He said, "I move the question, I call the question!" I used my legal training. Outsmarting smart people, helping smart people be smarter, is a lifetime commitment, and I wouldn't have been equipped to do that with the comfort that I've had without legal training, although I think other kinds of training are similarly useful.

[You ask whether fatigue was a factor when I decided to step down.] If I was tired, I didn't know it. I'd always had a feeling that if I didn't take the steps two at a time on the way to work, it would be time for me to step down. I had times when I was tired, but I don't think I was seriously discouraged at any time. You get tired because you lose sleep. Now, I did feel the weight of that black cultural center debate, and maybe one reason I didn't get beat down by it was, I was open about that. I said to the press, "This is the hardest thing I've ever confronted, and this is very wearing because I'm being caricatured by both sides of the argument. When I want to sit down and talk with the student leaders and I invite them to talk, they have a prearranged signal when they walk out. I'm not comfortable with that kind of conversation. That's a confrontation, that isn't a conversation. And you know, this is really tough." Now, I will have to admit that I wasn't as fresh on the day that I made my decision to announce my eventual retirement as I was when I first came to the job because I was six years older and I had not had a smooth, tranquil, totally positive experience.

Let me tell you how I came to step down. This almost goes back to my continuing, albeit friendlier competition with the system. President Spangler had made it clear that he wanted every chancellor to step down at age sixty-five, without any question. Now, that may not be legal, to demand that, but that was his decision. Incidentally, when he stepped down at sixty-five he didn't want to, but he had gotten himself into a corner by imposing that absolute edict on all the chancellors. I knew a couple of chancellors who wanted just one additional year to complete something, and he said, no, sixty-five is it. Well, I began to compute, and I was to turn sixty-five on June 11, 1996, about a month after commencement and just before the end of the fiscal year. I would have been required to step down then, willy-nilly. I've always wanted to step down when more people would say, why so soon? than would say, it's about time! I've always wanted to step down on my own timetable, and, too, I had a sneaky motive: I knew that on June 30, 1995, the month that I would turn sixty-four, we would conclude the Bicentennial Campaign for Carolina, and I would be guaranteed to go out on a high note. Now, if tired was a factor, it was the fourth factor in there, and along with being a little tired, I am very happily married and the father of three fantastic kids, all of whom have married wonderful people and in turn have three children each. So, all those things came together, and it was easy for me to make the decision to step down. I didn't need the job as some kind of a psychological support, I had no idea that I would have other opportunities such as the one at UAB. That's been exhilarating; the best tenure in the world is one that's planned to be interim from the very beginning so that the honeymoon lasts as long as the tenure. That's what I had at Birmingham. Anyway, all those things came together. That does bring me, though, to the lame-duck situation.

My board of trustees, whether they approved of President Spangler's policy or disapproved of it, were very aware of it. Now, why did I announce it a year and a half in advance? I felt, although I didn't feel worn-out or defeated, that I didn't have the same automatic, full-hearted, positive response of my board when I made various proposals as I had enjoyed in the early phase. That's just a natural human process, [but] I felt like it might be time to let them know that I wanted to renew our mutual commitment and get going. So I wrote out by hand, longhand, a careful retirement statement that I had rehearsed only with the board chairman and made it at a board meeting with the press present. They had no idea it was coming. This was almost exactly a year and a half prior to the end of the campaign, at the January board meeting in 1993. I told them that I would step down in June of 1995 at the end of the campaign, that there would be a success there, and I would not be able to stay in office long enough under the age sixty-five expectation to preside over the new surge of energy that the campaign would be bound to give to the university. I wanted to bequeath that to a successor. So in order for the trustees to absorb that and to make plans for a smooth succession, I was announcing right then that I would retire at the end of June 1995, and I asked the trustees to launch the search process in a timely fashion so that there could be a smooth transition. Then I said, "I'm not tired, I'm exhilarated about working with you to complete this campaign and to do all the other things a chancellor does. So, let's not make much over this announcement, let's go back to work." One board member, I later learned, was sort of a General Bullmoose character who thought that once a CEO announces his intentions to step down sometime later, he might just as well get out of the way right now. That's true if he's being forced out. If a man is being forced out, or a woman, he or she ought to get on out of the way; if it's a violation of the contract, the board ought to pay off the person because it's not a good working relationship. But I did this at a time when we did have a good working relationship, and the full board, if they discussed this in executive session, obviously decided to accept my timetable. I took a calculated risk that instead of having a negative lame-duck period, I might have a reenergizing, and that's what happened.

I think I put the same phenomenon to work at Alabama. When people you are serving realize that you are not making decisions for your own long-term or short-term advantage, they are likely to follow your leadership very well. My going to Birmingham was under an avowed disclaimer of any interest in the permanent position. In December of 1996, before I went to work in January 1997 at UAB, somebody in the press asked me if I was a candidate for the permanent position and I said, "No. If I were fifty-five or forty-five instead of sixty-five, I would say yes, cancel any idea of a search, you've got your person. This is a great, promising place, but I am definitely not interested, and in fact, I would judge the success of my tenure in part by its brevity." They laughed and wrote that down, and it appeared in the papers. I kept prodding the chairman of the board of trustees at Alabama to get that search underway; I didn't sign up for a year, I signed up month-to-month, and in fact left in the middle of the month when they had a successor. So at Carolina, while I didn't have the Birmingham experience to draw on, I had my own instinct that my administration might benefit, might to a certain extent be recharged or reenergized, by my making a completely unexpected announcement. I knew when I would step down, and I wanted them to know so they could make their plans. I think the majority of the board appreciated that, and I found no signs that cooperation between the board and me suffered. In fact, we had not had division on the board. Among the difficulties I experienced as chancellor, I never felt I had to go back and forth among board factions, and I never felt that I had trouble with the faculty. I mean,

I had faculty with great enthusiasm for my leadership, and I had faculty with less-than-great enthusiasm, I had faculty who were basically agnostic about my leadership because they were too busy doing their own work, which is fine. But I always felt supported by the faculty governance body. It was a wonderful experience, presiding, being in that faculty senate for seven years, just terrific. Students are always divided and to some extent antagonistic toward the flagpole, so that wasn't always perfect, but looking back on all my presidencies, I feel most consistently affirmed by faculty first, and then trustees, and then students. I came from the faculty and not just a quick and dirty experience on faculty, but ten years climbing through the ranks of a good faculty, having no administrative responsibilities. I never had a deanship or a department chair, I was assistant professor, associate professor, professor of law at Duke University writing my books and articles to get promoted, teaching with enthusiasm and joy, never thinking I would do anything else and then suddenly, bang, I'm a college president at Wofford, unspoiled by any administrative experience. I never had one day of confusion as an administrator about the center of gravity of a college or university; that's the teaching/learning enterprise, the interaction between students and faculty, and they are the prime players. I hope that conviction was apparent in every gesture and every decision and every comment that I ever made. One of the real problems I found at UAB, the essential problem I found there, was that the previous president and especially the previous provost had absolutely no experience with the undergraduate liberal arts environment and little experience teaching. The provost had never even had teaching experience and was appointed by the president without a search and the faculty had never felt comfortable with that administrative team. They did not use committees to advise them on how to spend discretionary money; they weren't sensitive to faculty concerns. The provost would call faculty together and say, now here's the agenda for our discussion, is there any objection? and the faculty would not say anything and he would consider that an affirmation. Just insensitivity to faculty.

[UAB had a faculty senate] with very limited powers and just before I got there, they voted more power in their faculty council, as they call it. But they were not used to having the president come to the meetings of the executive committee and stay as long as the executive committee wanted him to stay, let his hair down figuratively, and talk about anything they wanted to talk about. They had never had any experience of fully open, very frank discussion with a top administrator. They didn't feel involved in the policy decisions, although they had the body established. But my habit of dealing with faculty bodies in a candid, open way sold well at UAB, and letters I've gotten from faculty colleagues there since I left are among my treasured papers because it just clicked. I don't want to make that sound like it was a more important job in my career than UNC; nothing was more important in my career than the chancellorship at UNC. But some things were more fun from time to time.

Coda is a good word [for my UAB experience]. I can't tell you how comfortably all of my previous experiences fit the needs of UAB when I got there. You combine that fit with my being above suspicion in terms of being a candidate, and it was going so well that the chairman of the board came to me and said, "Please give us three years. We won't ask you to make a long commitment, just please give us three years." I said, "I'm flattered, but listen, you just don't understand. Eighty percent of this rapport that you are celebrating by asking me to stay is based on the absolute assurance that I will not. As soon as I say, okay, I'll stay just three years, all across the campus, I know, faculty will be saying, uh huh, uh huh, we knew we knew, we knew! And the magic is gone. I'm getting out of here as soon as you have a successor, and I'm going to put the whip to you to get that done soon. Not because I don't love it here; you can tell I love it. Barbara and I started our life together here in 1954, and I practiced law with the greatest firm in the Southeast, and I'm telling you, my exploits as a lawyer have been magnified by my long absence from Birmingham!" It was everything Barbara and I hoped it would be—a homecoming and an adventure in a place that we loved when it wasn't very lovable. Birmingham used to have awful image problems and the image was earned. Police dogs and fire hoses in the 1960s after we had left gave Birmingham an image that it has retained to a certain extent today, even though a great healing institution, UAB, has now replaced steel as the engine driving the economy in Birmingham. As I said in all of my speeches around town, what I covet is for this healing institution to be healing not only in the sense that it can strengthen the economy of Birmingham and of Alabama—and it has helped to clean up the air so that now we don't have dirty cuffs before noon—but in the sense that it needs to be a prophetic presence in a city that has only a few short steps to take to rid itself of that image that it earned in the 1960s. Carolina was the culmination of my career, and I would have been happy with my career without Birmingham, but Birmingham was the exclamation point to my career, [the experience was] so affirming. But it's not fair to compare that, which had success almost built-in, with North Carolina, that had risks both known and unknown and complexities known and unknown.

[UAB] wasn't just a passive, hold-on-for-dear-life deal; we made some serious decisions there. I felt like a consultant with power to act because everyone wanted to know, what do you think we need to do? One thing that is going to come out of that, I think, is a merger of three schools into one. Where we at Carolina have a college of arts and sciences, they have a school of arts and humanities, a school of social and behavioral sciences, and a school of natural science and mathematics—three deans where we have one dean and therefore no "super school" on the west side of campus to counterbalance the medical school. Any problem we had at Carolina I could solve by having both Stuart Bondurant [dean of the medical school] and Steve Birdsall [dean of the college of arts and sciences] in the key consultation. Just as the other schools on the medical side of the campus were content to have Stuart represent them, the schools on the other side were content to have Steve Birdsall. There at Birmingham, where medicine is even more dominant than it is here, there is no even partially counterbalancing powerful school representing the essence of nonmedical education. I think that's going to be changed. I gave them the assurance that I thought it was the thing to do, and as I left, those three deans said, I guarantee you the faculty will vote for it, and we will all support it. Now two of those three are going to have to lose their jobs.

We did some things on the medical side. We bought a $20 million eye hospital instead of waiting for my successor; it was a now-or-never deal. If we didn't buy that hospital somebody else would, and this is a tough, managed-care environment right now. So I wrote my name on an authorization to spend $20 million on the hospital and I approved the $30 million Howell Heflin Center for Human Genetics because we had an opportunity to seize the moment in Congress with the retiring Senator Heflin's friends. Now, I guess I made decision after decision that was monumental and did it without losing any sleep because these were so obviously the things to do, and nobody was saying, "Now, wait for the new president." That's a gung-ho, entrepreneurial, get-up-and-do-things outfit down there. [UAB is] barely thirty years old, and counting the whole health side, it has a one and a half billion dollar annual budget, a little bit bigger than ours in Chapel Hill.

[Their board of trustees said to me,] "We need leadership and that is not just hold-the-line and mark time. There are some decisions that have to be made, and we brought you down here to help make them." It is an object lesson, particularly in health fields where a revolution is in process. A strongly health-oriented university can't mark time, can't afford a long period with a lame-duck crippled leader, or a long interim where you are waiting for the savior to arrive. If things are broken down, you need to get somebody in there who has no personal ambition, but who has some experience at making decisions and will sit down and listen. First thing when I got there, they said, "How do you want to get acquainted?" I said I wanted to visit every school on its turf, see the physical plant, have a private consultation with the dean and the department chairs and also have a chance to hear what the faculty think the needs of the university are in an open forum. I did that in all of the twelve schools, and by the time I got through (it took about three or four weeks) I knew what they thought needed doing. When I made these decisions, it wasn't like they came out of the blue. In fact, before my scheduled visit with the medical faculty, I had a proposal to make that was an important structural proposal for the health system, and I asked for an audience with the department chairs before I had even met them. I made a proposal that they didn't want, and I said well, when I committed to ask your opinion, I committed to take it seriously, and so I'm not going to pursue this proposal. At which point, I could never have done anything wrong because they had never had anybody consult with them and do what they suggested. I let them persuade me, I didn't just consult, and after that when we made important decisions, the faculty knew that I must have thought these were extremely important, right decisions because they had seen me back away from a decision that I had proposed to make.

[To return to the question of risk taking at UNC,] I felt like it subsided just a bit because of the resolution of the black cultural center. It wasn't cured, but it was resolved in the sense that the decision was made by me to recommend to the board, and by the board to approve, the establishment of the free-standing black cultural center once it was determined that the nature of the institution was appropriate to the mores and the values of the university. It's still going to be a good while before that's funded, but at least I wasn't in the middle of a storm for the last couple of years. I'm trying to think, the risk taking diminished a bit but I like to think it's because the most important parts of my agenda were accomplished. Incidentally, the single imposition of an agenda item that was most apparent when I came here was that I would be a fund-raiser, which was not my most idealized self-image. I've always thought of myself as a teacher/scholar and a promoter of the values of the academy, and fund-raising came along because it's necessary. I did find that it's not arduous for me to ask people to support things that I believe in. The university was facing the bicentennial era, which would have two parts: the campaign and a celebration. The previous administration had already had a needs assessment going on under Dean Richard Cole and a campuswide committee, so it was clear that there would be, in conjunction with the bicentennial observance, a bicentennial campaign, and that the trustees were looking for someone with the energy and the experience to lead it. So that was imposed on me, and I accepted it perfectly willingly, and it proved not to be arduous. It really went well. We had never had a campaign for more than $35 million—that was the arts and sciences amount in the 1970s, it was the Smith Center and Koury Natatorium amount in the 1980s. Then we came along in the 1990s and had a comprehensive financial campaign excluding any athletic capital, and after hopefully, prayerfully, setting a $320 million goal, blew by that in the first three years of the campaign and had to raise it to $400 million, and then passed that (ultimately raising more than $440 million). So, that was an imposed agenda in which I cheerfully acquiesced and that went well. It was bound for success.

During my chancellorship a strong start had been made on improving our relationship with the board of governors, the president, the legislature, and so much more—I don't know how many scores of millions of dollars in campus improvements had been approved and were in process when I stepped down, but I'm being invited constantly to building dedications. A lot had gotten done, and I don't think there was a specific controversy on the table. That could be a subjective response to a twenty-eight-year career as a university president or chancellor, in all of which time I was willing to take risks when it appeared to be necessary. Maybe I lost my ability to discern situations in which risks powerfully were needed. I don't think so. I think my rhythm in this chancellorship was not a crescendo of problems resulting in fatigue; my rhythm was inheriting some risks, some of which I knew about, some of which I did not, confronting them, having a culminating crisis or a top-of-the-chart crisis in racial conflict midway through, but then not a continuing increase of tension but rather a decline in tension, maybe because the bicentennial observance and the bicentennial campaign went so well. Just during the observance, our faculty set new records every year in sponsored research; our athletic program for that period of the bicentennial was no longer a source of constant friction with the faculty because we had lived down the Crum firing and the building of the Smith Center, which had been done before I came. I supported the Doris Betts committee's recommendations about athletic reform and took those to the NCAA Presidents Commission, and the insiders on the faculty knew that I was of one mind with them on athletic reform. I asked the Educational Foundation [UNC's athletics booster organization] not to raise any capital money for the whole seven-year period of the bicentennial campaign (including the planning phase), and they not only acquiesced and forbore to raise any capital money, but they helped us with the bicentennial campaign itself. In a letter to the editor of the [Raleigh, NC] *News and Observer* not long ago, I reminded the readers that we had abstained totally from capital fund-raising in the athletic realm for the entire seven-year period of my administration, and the members of the Educational Foundation, counting only gifts of $100,000 or more, gave $87 million, 20 percent of the total campaign.

As long as we're speaking of athletics—this whole conversation has been maybe 2 percent athletics—how lucky can a chancellor get, to have in his administration a restoration of confidence between the faculty and athletics? We lived down the Crum affair, we lived down the Smith Center. We were successful in the moratorium on athletic fund-raising. You know, while I was chancellor, we won the first-ever Sears Directors' Cup for the best all-round athletics program in the entire United States of America. Stanford, second; the next year, Stanford first and Carolina second. In the bicentennial year, 1994, the men's basketball team went in as NCAA basketball champions and the women came out wearing the crown. I'm the only chancellor in history whose school won both men's and women's basketball championships while he or she was in office, and mine came in the bicentennial year that was otherwise nonathletically focused and wonderfully successful academically. So partly because I took the risk of a lame-duck thing, and partly because I just got lucky beyond all bounds and expectations, I did not wear out in a crescendo of crisis. I stepped out on my terms, on a high, and can feel really, really good about that eighteen months. I have a hunch that people who might have challenged me if I had not announced my intention to retire, decided to wait and challenge somebody else. Maybe because they had seen me face challenges and not blink, maybe because there just wasn't anything sufficiently negative to counterbalance the good feelings about the bicentennial. I consider that I had some tough times; I lost a lot of sleep at Carolina, but I think that by some accident or some intuition and by a lot of luck, my resignation was appropriately motivated and somehow rather fortuitously smooth.

[As for dealing with the legislature,] in the last analysis, what happens there doesn't depend upon the newspaper coverage, doesn't depend upon taking a strong stance on alcohol, doesn't depend on anything but quiet, behind-the-scenes, good hard work by the [system's] general administration and by the chancellors who, with or without the approval of the boss, really, really work hard with government and legislators and faculty leadership. I paid so much attention to the faculty that the faculty officially became my strong ally in politics. I went to a meeting of the American Council on Education while I was chancellor, and the president of the National Association of Independent Colleges and Universities (of which I used to be a member) made a speech about changes in the environment in higher education, and talked about the age of accountability and how we were being held accountable more and more by parents, by students, by legislators. "But," he said, "I think what's going to happen here as we circle the wagons and defend ourselves against all these attacks, is that faculties will be less critical of administrators and more our partners." He was describing what had already happened at Carolina.

NOTES

1. Office of Institutional Research, University of North Carolina at Chapel Hill; "The Nation: Resources: College and University Endowments Over $100-Million, 1988," *Chronicle of Higher Education Almanac*, September 6, 1989, p. 22, study by the National Association of College and University Business Officers. In 1988, the schools of the University of North Carolina at Chapel Hill were arts and sciences, business administration, dentistry, education, evening college, information and library science, journalism, law, medicine, nursing, pharmacy, public health, and social work; in 1995, the number of schools remained the same with two nomenclature changes: "journalism" became "journalism and mass communication" and "evening college" was replaced with "continuing/off-campus studies."

2. In 1995, UNC-CH had 24,463 students (8,568 graduate/professional), 2,328 full-time permanent faculty, a budget of $918.4 million, and $264.6 million in endowment (Office of Institutional Research, University of North Carolina at Chapel Hill; "Fact File: 460 College and University Endowments," *Chronicle of Higher Education*, February 16, 1996, p. A33, study by the National Association of College and University Business Officers).

3. See, for example, in 1992 the September 11, Late Edition, *New York Times*, "At Chapel Hill, Athletes Suddenly Turn into Activists," pp. B9, B11, the September 23, National Public Radio, *Morning Edition*, "Black Cultural Center Wanted by UNC Students," the October 11 *Los Angeles Times*, Home Edition, "A Place to Celebrate Black Culture Racially Divides a Campus," p. M5, the October 12 *Newsweek*, United States Edition, "A Place to Call Their Own," p. 92, among others; and in 1993, the April 12 *Washington Times*, Final Edition, "Jackson to Visit Protesting Students," p. B5, the April 17, *Orlando Sentinel Tribune*, Central Florida Edition, "Jackson Urges Students to Stand Firm on Demands," p. A12, and the April 21, *New York Times*, Late Edition, "Dispute over Black Center Tears U. of North Carolina," p. B11, among others.

4. Deidra Jackson, "Hardin Takes Job at UAB," *Raleigh (NC) News and Observer*, November 14, 1996, Final Edition, p. B5.

Vartan Gregorian

Brown University 1988/89–1997

Born in Tabriz, Iran, in 1934, Vartan Gregorian came to the United States in 1956 to attend Stanford University where he earned a B.A. (1958) and a Ph.D. in history (1964). A dedicated teacher at San Francisco State College (1962–1968), UCLA (1968), and the University of Texas (1968–1972), he began his extraordinary administrative career at the University of Pennsylvania, where in 1972, he was named professor of history, Tarzian Professor of Armenian and Caucasian History, and professor of South Asian history, and two years later became the first dean of the faculty of arts and sciences. In 1978, he accepted the provostship and became, by all accounts, the faculty's favored candidate for president. When he was passed over by Penn's board of trustees, Gregorian resigned, and the following year agreed to head the struggling New York Public Library. As president (1981–1989) he revealed a genius for fund-raising, public relations, and administrative leadership and was credited with having "restored the fading [library] to its place at the heart of American intellectual life."[1]

Vartan Gregorian's departure to become Brown University's sixteenth president was motivated, he said, by a desire to return to the academic life, but the appealingly small size of the university[2] was matched by a less appealingly small endowment (compared with its peers in the Ivy League). Fund-raising thus played a larger and more important role in his presidency than Gregorian had foreseen. During his nine-year tenure he kept Brown's enrollment (7,243/7,309) and faculty (532/548) numbers stable and its budget growth restrained ($212.1 million/$297.9 million), while building the university's endowment from $398.1 million in 1989 to $1.05 billion in 1997.[3] Increased financial security, however, was not the only measure of Gregorian's presidency; in addition to strengthening Brown's academic reputation, he improved its public image through high-profile public service commitments, including the establishment of the Annenberg Institute for School Reform to address the plight of the nation's public schools. When Gregorian was named to head Carnegie Corporation of New York in January 1997, the chairman of Brown's board of trustees described him as having created for the university "a time of tremendous rejuvenation" during which Brown had become "one of the most important institutions in American higher education."[4]

Vartan Gregorian's account of some aspects of his presidency is an edited transcript of his interview with Leslie Banner at Carnegie Corporation of New York, October 24, 1998. The questions that prompted his comments have either been omitted or indicated with bracketed material to create a more readable narrative.

As you may or may not know, in August 1988 I faced three choices of institutions [to serve as president]: one was the University of Michigan, the second was Brown, and the third was the MacArthur Foundation. I spent a lot of time analyzing the strengths and weaknesses, the possibilities and limitations of each of these institutions. In the case of Brown, because I knew Richard Salomon who was chancellor then, my interview with the committee took on a more personal character. There were certain things that were not volunteered and I did not ask, things that did not occur to me to ask. I had not done an exhaustive study; I had not done a great deal of homework. I did not know that Brown was operating under a consent decree as a result of a sex discrimination case. The Lamphere decree governed Brown's entire hiring system; a federal judge had to approve each outside hire. The first inkling I had of that fact—I thought it was a joke until later I discovered it was not—was when I said, well, I would like to be a member of the faculty, I always have been, and [the response was,] "Well, we'll see what the judge will say about that." So, anyway, that was one surprise. The second surprise was again my fault, not theirs; this was the issue of (and something that I recommend every incoming president ask about) the last accrediting committee report. [Brown had just been visited by] an accrediting committee in 1987–1988, and I was not given a copy [of the report]. It was a year later, after I had come, that I stumbled onto it. That report had analyzed several strengths and weaknesses of Brown which I should have known about. So, in terms of the search, the committee did not volunteer [this information], it might not have occurred to them [to do so], and it did not occur to me to ask during the search process. Also, I did not know that one of my friends, who happened to be a member of the board of trustees at Brown, was a candidate. It was only later that I discovered this. Otherwise, the search was a lengthy one and a thorough one and a professional one. It would have been nicer to be able to touch base with [my friend], but you can't touch all the bases; it's a very hard period because you're studying your own transfer, your own dislocation, your own uprooting, and more attention sometimes is paid to how you're going to extricate yourself from your current obligations than to what kind of new ones you're going to have [to take on].

One of the things that I asked to be written into my letter of appointment as president of Brown was that I was not going to be the chief fund-raiser for the university, and that shows how naïve I was. Maybe it was wishful thinking, or wistful, but that was included in the letter. One of the reasons I chose Brown was that it is small, private, and manageable, and I wanted to do a lot more in terms of intellectual and academic and educational issues, to deal with these rather than with financial issues. But, I tell you, that was unrealistic in retrospect. Because the moment you, as president, discover the financial situation, you have to do something about it. You have to start fund-raising. You can always have a balanced budget through deferred maintenance, but deferred maintenance, unless you have plans for it, becomes planned neglect. So I'm never impressed by balanced budgets alone. First, you have to see what kind of shape the campus is in, [what the situation is with] financial aid, all kinds of things. I did not know what Brown's aspirations and needs were. So anytime you have a [potential] president being interviewed, he or she will need not just to see whether the books are balanced, but to see [that] the books aren't balanced at the expense of something important. Second, you have to understand the aspirations of the campus. Discussion of these issues is often deferred until [the campus] gets a new president.

[While] Brown and the New York Public Library are different cultures, my adjustment [to Brown] was not bad because of my experiences as provost of Penn—there was a lesser adjustment issue than I would have had to face [otherwise] because you have practically the same vocabulary, you have the same issues. Everybody knows what the issues of universities are—the issue of access, the issue of aging faculty, the issue of deferred maintenance, the issue of voluminous rules and regulations, federal, state, city, and so forth; how to cope with alumni; the issue of drinking on campus, the issue of athletics—these are all universal issues. They [only] vary [somewhat] from one campus to another. These are common challenges. The real issues concern what solutions you bring to those problems or those challenges. That is what is hard.

There are two ways you can work with trustees. One is to finesse them, flatter them, please them. The other is to involve them, to give them a sense of ownership not only of the general vision, but also an understanding of the intricacies. I have always chosen the latter approach. Recently, Peter Drucker wrote an article that appeared in *Forbes* [October 5, 1998] [saying] that nonprofits are as complex as, if not more complex than, businesses [because they serve so] many constituencies. So the issue is, first, how to involve the trustees in the process of understanding the complexity [of the university], not finessing them, but involving them. Second, is how to understand and appreciate the faculty and its aspirations. And third, is [how to] truly deal with student needs up-front. If you cannot cope with some of the problems because they are not soluble, you have to tell [people] right away rather than [say,] "We're working on it." Those initial pronouncements are very important and set the tone of an administration. My style always has been to involve the trustees in my thinking, to keep them abreast of things, and I was very fortunate at the New York Public Library and at Brown—I've had good chancellors and good board chairmen. And that makes all the difference because the board, instead of becoming an overseer, an obstacle, becomes your ally. You develop a common vision, a common strategy. (There are people who confuse tactics and strategy and mission. They are not the same. The mission is the goal, the strategy is what kind of options you intend to apply to get there, the tactics can vary in the process—retreat or advance or so forth according to given conditions.) At Brown I had the full support of the trustees. I met with every trustee, individually.

Brown is run in a very peculiar, original fashion. You have the fellows, twelve of them, and then you have thirty-six trustees. The fellows grant the degrees, approve the formation of academic departments, maintain the charter, and so forth. The president is the president of the fellows. He is one of the fellows, as at Harvard. The trustees are headed by the chancellor. The trustees and the fellows together constitute the corporation. I met with every one of them so that there would be no misunderstanding as to my public statements and my actions. Every decision I took, even unpopular ones, had the full backing of the trustees and their understanding as to why I was doing what I was doing. So, my conflicts with trustees were practically nil, I hate to tell you! Practically nil. The entire nine years I was at Brown, there were only two votes forced that questioned my judgment, both by one individual trustee. Only two. I was up front with them. Also, Brown has a system, which started in the 1960s, [in which] a committee of trustees deals with the relations between the faculty and the president. Once a year that committee meets with the faculty leadership. [They meet] in the president's absence, the faculty chairs and the trustees in charge of liaison with the faculty, to hear about their complaints or their satisfactions—"The faculty has not been hearing from you," and so forth, whatever is bothering the collective faculty. So, in a sense, it's a review of the president, a review without saying it's your review. But it's still there as a safety valve so that issues don't get out of hand, so that you have indications where there are problems. Faculty members would bring some issues [to those meetings with trustees] and [my response would be], "Well, if they're complaining, how come I don't know about these issues that they have never raised with me?" Or, "You're absolutely right; we'll see what we can do about this." I only accepted recommendations [from the trustees] if there had been promises made by my administrators which were not delivered, or if senior administrators had been inaccessible to faculty members, issues of that sort. But [the meetings were] not for adjudication; they were just to say, this is what the faculty is worried or pleased about. [The faculty could communicate] only in a structured way with the trustees, once a year, through their faculty leaders and representatives of the trustees. It was not just pick up the phone, call, say, "Let me tell you—." It was in a structured way.

It's a very surprising thing, [but] the only time a vote was forced in the executive committee of the trustees [was when] a person disagreed [with me about] whether I should buy this [certain] building. I was determined to do it because it was a unique opportunity for the university. Naturally, I did not want that to happen again because I did not want this trustee to lose the vote; it [begins to appear] that you don't pay attention to his opinion. So, that's where a good administrator has to be able to know what is going on, and what's the position of people on various issues, so you don't get surprised. I've never had problems with my boards. None. [I have had] good boards and good chancellors—that makes all the difference. At the New York Public Library and at Brown, I had board chairmen (or "chancellors" at Brown) who were former chief executive officers and former presidents of their own organizations. So they knew the difference between setting policy and micromanaging. Andrew Heiskell at the Library had been chief executive of Time, Inc., and Alva O. Way, chancellor of Brown, had been chief financial officer of American Express and General Electric and head of I.B.J. Schroeder Bank. Also, I never allowed the trustees to be surprised. That's the key issue. Conflict comes with a surprise, when there is lack of knowledge, when there is lack of context, and also when they don't understand your vision or your plans or your strategy.

Right after I arrived, the trustees said, "We're ready for a [fund-raising] campaign," and then, having seen the university's needs, I had no choice but to deal with those needs. Once you agree, you cannot be a distant observer or inactive. So I had to give all my efforts to the campaign. The former chancellor joked that he put a PS in his letter of appointment, in [his] handwriting, "You will try to do your best." It was unrealistic for me to expect that I would fulfill aspirations without money. [My original agreement about fund-raising did not actually become a conflict] because of my relationship with the board; they worked very hard. If the board had said, "We hired you, it's up to you now, we are not involved," then it would have caused conflict.

[Faculty governance at Brown] was completely different [from that] at Penn [where] you have both an elected faculty senate and a university council that represents the whole university—its members include staff, administrators, faculty, students. That was different from Brown. At Brown, an executive committee represented the faculty, with members elected from the various disciplines. But they were not authorized to decide matters on behalf of the faculty—they had to go back to the faculty for a vote by mail ballots. And they met once a month at faculty meetings, which were presided over by the president. I would give a report, and there was a question-and-answer time, and then if there were other questions, they were passed anonymously to the faculty executive committee who then sent them to me, [to be answered at the] next faculty meeting. That did not mean that faculty would not ask a lot of questions during the meeting, but again, I had very good relations with the faculty. My notion of [being] a president always has been that I am there to serve the faculty and students, for they constitute the university. [They are the] heart of the university. So, I take "service" as my main motto. I serve them, they don't serve me. By serving them, I lead them. That was my strategy and my mode of behavior at Penn, the same as it was at Brown. As a result, I got to know most of the members of my faculty at Brown and almost all of them at Penn. I knew about their work, their problems, their aspirations, so that they were not faces and parts in a machine. They were individuals, scholars, teachers. I've always believed that universities are places to create knowledge and to educate and that budgets and everything else are there to facilitate that. [When the budget can't deliver what the faculty want,] you have to explain to the faculty why not, not dictate to the faculty. Basically, I found 90 percent of the time that that's fine with them, as long as they understand that you have the right priorities, you work hard, and that any amount of money you get is being spent primarily on the educational mission of the university.

Brown has a mandate that we cannot have a deficit. Therefore, first of all, we must have a balanced budget. So for eighteen years Brown has had balanced budgets. So that issue is settled: If you don't have money, you cannot spend. Then the second thing is, in the case of Brown, faculty salaries were the most debated issue. Brown was very competitive at the assistant professor level and the associate professor level, but at the level of full professor, salaries were 10 percent below those at other Ivies. Now, that does not take into account the cost of living in Rhode Island, which is not an expensive state, but even if you take that into consideration, you will still find [considerable] disparity in Brown's salaries. That was one item that always would come up with the faculty. So when there would be a budget surplus, you might want it to go to faculty salaries. During the first year of my presidency, I raised faculty salaries by over 8.5 percent. But then, as a result, I found I had a deficit. So then the next year, I did not do the same thing. It was all an open dialogue, open discussion, without stacking committees to recommend [cuts] so that you could go through the motions. You have to understand that Brown also has a budget council consisting of graduate students, undergraduates, faculty and administrators, an elected group that deals with the budget. They recommend to the president the percentage of salary hikes for faculty and the staff (for example, how much salaries should be next year). They calculate revenues and they calculate expenditures. Within that framework they recommend not only salary levels, but other expenditures and priorities as well, including tuition. They are advisory to the president. That committee [functions as a] shock absorber in many ways. If the committee recommended a 4 percent salary raise, it was up to me to see whether we could afford it or not, and I would usually deviate just a half percent or so. That was all negotiated; it did not just come out of the blue. I would ask that all the budget facts be available to that group so that there would be no secrets. They knew how much development was bringing in, what the annual fund was doing, what the yield of federal research contracts was, what their overhead was, and what the draw of the endowment was. In a sense, then, they knew what the amount of money was coming in and what the expenses were going out—there were no secrets. After you take care of union and faculty and staff salaries, how much was left to do what? So that was one issue that always [created] tension; that was normal.

The second issue throughout [my presidency] was the extent to which Brown could become a need-blind institution. Well, there I insisted that honesty required us to admit that we were not 100 percent need blind. Of the students admitted to Brown in a given year, fifty to one hundred of them who needed it did not receive a full financial aid package. I was advised not to acknowledge that because it would be bad for our reputation. I said, no, we will publicly acknowledge that we are not 100 percent need blind. But in order not to have any [further] erosion of our financial aid funds, I asked the trustees to approve indexing financial aid so that every year, as we raised tuition and fees, financial aid would go up the same amount, and any new gift that was earmarked for financial aid would be incremental, add-on. Many faculty members did not like that because it was tying most of our unrestricted income to financial aid, [rather than spending those dollars] on faculty salaries, the library, and so forth. You have to choose a priority and defend it, so I chose that. We had financial aid in order to get the best students. [There were times of questioning between the faculty and me,] but they did not go beyond questioning to censure or expressing displeasure. The faculty only once decided to express a vote of confidence and support in me. I said no, I don't need a vote of confidence, I already have that. So, I hate to be disappointing, but I had excellent and honest relations with faculty both at Penn and at Brown.

So what happened then, when I left Brown? The faculty honored me with their medal, the Rosenberger Medal. It was only the third time in this century that the medal was awarded to the president of Brown. It was their testament that my values were the right values, that I was not there to build some palace for myself or some edifice to posterity, but rather that my priorities were theirs also: Number one, the faculty; number two, the students; number three, the library. They knew that if I had more money, I would put more into those priorities. They knew that we tripled the endowment, and that in five years we more than doubled what Brown had raised for financial aid in two centuries. But again, the students were not happy because they wanted need-blind admissions *now*. And the staff was not left out—[we established] the first day care center, the first maternity-leave policy; we created same-sex partner benefits. Some of these benefits were awarded to the staff. They did not have to ask for them. When I was advised, "Bargain with the union, don't give in to them," I said no, this will be available for everyone, no trade-offs were needed. They were all part of one community.

These factors are some of the reasons why the [faculty] trusted [me]—it all comes back to the trust issue. If they know you live your values and you mean what you say and you say what you mean and you act accordingly, they forgive you your human shortcomings. But if they know you have [more than one] version of what you say, one for the students, one for the trustees (you say how tough you are going to be, how you are "holding the line against the faculty"), and one for the faculty ("My God, the trustees are breathing down my neck"), then, when all three come together, you're finished—they know that you've been playing one against the other. In my case, everything I told the faculty was the same thing [the trustees and students heard] from me. I did not have dual positions: one private and one public. I also had very good relations with the staff, notwithstanding two strikes, one strike by the library workers before I came and one by plant operation workers over whether or not they would [have to have a] co-pay on their health plan. They demonstrated in front of my house and other locations chanting, "Hey hey, ho ho, co-payment has to go!" At the end, they agreed to [a] co-pay, yet they claimed victory. That was fine with me. You don't have to show the faculty and staff how tough you are, you don't have to boast that you wrested concessions or draw attention to your bravura.

One of the major problems for university presidents is they must cultivate two different cultures. One is the traditional scholarly culture which has been with us since the eleventh century, and the other [is the] current corporate culture. Since most trustees come from the corporate culture, presidents are forced to develop a schizoid language; they defend their [policies] to the trustees in corporate language and to the faculty and students in academic language. Sometimes, therefore, they become victims of their rhetoric with the corporate culture, even though the trustees have elected them not as corporate [executives] but as academics. I am sure if the [trustees] wanted a business [leader] they would have retained an accountant or a business manager or leader to run the university. It's hard to understand and master the corporate language without succumbing to it because otherwise the trustees would say, "Well, you don't understand the current ratio of this," or (especially if you are not an economist), "We'll send some assistants to help you with that." Presidents cannot go and tell the faculty, "The trustees have decided, guess what, to implement the following Wall Street management tools." That does not go [down] well with faculty. It's hard to keep the two cultures talking without telling two different things to the inhabitants of those two cultures. That's the most difficult task for a college president. In the 1960s, we saw many instances when university presidents fell as a result of the clash of these two languages and cultures by promising two contradictory policies, one to the trustees and one to the faculty. The trustees, in general, want a well run and [well] managed university, but they also want it to be academically good. So then the issue is, how do you explain efficiency and excellence without constantly resorting to bottom-line analysis? You can show academic excellence in Egyptology, for example, but you cannot show a successful cost-benefit analysis of Egyptology when you have only a handful of students studying it. How are you going to explain that to the trustees? You have to explain the university culture to the trustees, its complexity, the fact that it's a 900-year-old academic culture that has evolved, and that you're heading this, gradually changing it, managing it, leading it, but it's not a uniform corporate culture. There's no clear vertical integration and horizontal integration in this business. All tenured professors are equal, not only in their departments but also in the university as a whole. Their salaries may not be equal, their stations may not be equal, the Wharton Professor of Finance and the classics professor may not drive the same cars or have the same lifestyle, but they all believe, "I have one vote and you have one vote and [we are both] members of this corporate academic body called the faculty." That's what gets leaders into trouble, how to talk one language with which you bring both parties to appreciate the academic culture despite its inane rules and its perceived inertia and seeming opposition to change.

The faculty knew I was honest. I was dean and provost at Penn for eight years, and president at Brown for nine years, and was a professor at Texas for four years. With the exception of the Title IX case,[5] in all those years nobody had sued me on any substantive issue. To the contrary, when I came to Brown, women faculty joined me in asking a federal judge to vacate the Lamphere consent decree because they trusted me, [knowing my reputation at Penn.] When I came, after one year they went to the judge and said, "We will work it out. We don't want to be in receivership. We will work it out with the president." At Penn I was [known as a] fair administrator and a trustworthy "closet" feminist. I never advertised what I did for women or for minorities. That's another thing—you must do what is right, not what is expedient. When I left, there were more women professors at Penn than at any of the Ivies. But I never advertised nor did I boast, "Let me tell you what I'm doing today; today is Tuesday, I've hired another minority faculty member." The only thing I said was, "If you trust me, you have to trust that I will do my best within the rules and priorities of the university. Give me time to do it my own way. If you don't want the trustees to micromanage, you don't micromanage me. Just see what the results are." So, the Brown faculty knew about my reputation at Penn. According to the press, one of the reasons I was not named president of Penn in 1980, when I declined to be chancellor of UC-Berkeley, was that some trustees believed I would be the "faculty's man" as president. The controversy at Penn culminated in a general faculty meeting that voted two-to-one to put my name forward as their president, even after the search committee had made their recommendation. I told the faculty I was not interested. So the Brown faculty knew that I had principles; if I said something, I meant it. I was not trying to win favors; they knew that I meant it because I value my word and my commitment and, therefore, if I said that I will work at something, even if I fail, then my failure will be a public failure. Having tried and having failed for a worthy cause and assuming responsibility for it is better than to rationalize, mislead, or pass the buck. To disarm their critics, some university presidents fake sincerity. That will always get them into trouble. The faculty are like sensitive children in many ways: they can see through you, they will detect whether yours is pro forma kindness or ritualized politeness, or whether you genuinely like them.

The faculty [at Brown] were 100 percent behind me during the Title IX lawsuit, including the female faculty members. So were the student government and the Brown student newspaper. The staff were behind me. After two strikes, one of the union organizers one day told me, "We have a problem with you, Mr. President. You don't act like a president. Therefore, we cannot organize." Why? Because they thought I had a master plan to finesse them. They thought all my actions were politically motivated. They too soon realized that I mean what I say and, indeed, I do what I say. They were surprised that sometimes I followed the union's advice. Right after I came to Brown, I asked one of the union stewards, Mr. Bill Bell, a simple question. I asked, "How are your families?" He said, "Funny you should ask—our families have never been on campus; the only time they have come on campus is when they have walked the picket line with us." I said, "What would you do if you were me?" He said, "I would give a big annual party for the families of all the workers." I said, "That's a brilliant idea!" So I gave, every year, a campuswide holiday party for two days, inviting the staff, faculty, and students. Eight or ten thousand people came. That is an annual event now. There's skating, the students singing, our bands playing, and I owed this all to Mr. Bell. This was not my original idea. Well, unfortunately, the first year when I did this, the union was on strike so they did not cross the line to come to their party! However, when I left Brown, the staff rented a crane to have their collective picture taken, and they had a skit show for me, and they did it on their own time. They were wonderful, so I can't complain. But it takes lots of time, lots of attention, lots of effort. You must set an example for the rest of your staff because some of them don't agree with you that all of these people are part of an institution which is horizontal and not vertically integrated. The biggest problem of all at universities in the United States is that even though they are vertically integrated organizations, they are set to act as if they were horizontal. The outside world thinks the university is a vertical organization, and that's where some of the problems lie, leading to misleading perceptions.

In the context of faculty and students, I also taught a course every year—one freshman seminar, one senior seminar. I corrected my own exams so that nobody would say, "It's easy for you, we are in the trenches, you are presidential." So I set an example. At that time, for Brown, my priorities did not include securing a car for myself. When needed, I rode in the police car back and forth. To save money for the university, I took the Bonanza bus from Providence to the Boston Airport because it was only $11.50. I did this to the great horror and dismay of my staff and my wife; yet, I did it to highlight the priorities of the university.

[How I created my administrative team] is the most difficult question that has been asked of me in this interview so far. As a rule, when I move to a new institution, I do not take anyone with me. I only did it once; an assistant, who was in charge of my schedule at the New York Public Library, accompanied me to Brown. Why such a rule? First, for the sake of the institution, I've always tried to see that local talent is given the first priority. Second, it's very hard to know what you need until after you have been there for a while and analyzed it. That creates problems. If you don't move fast, within the first six months, to build your own team, your decisions appear to be whimsical. If you do it within six months, it's impersonal, no hard feelings, "He always brings his own team," and when displaced people apply for jobs elsewhere, they say, "He's bringing his own team. Nothing is wrong with us." But after six, seven months, if you let people go, they know they did not meet your expectations. That's the biggest problem. So when you build a team, you must first of all give insiders a chance, and then try and see where their weaknesses and strengths are. But this takes a lot of time. In nine years I made some mistakes in my appointments. I followed the recommendations of the faculty-student advisory committees. What search committees sometimes saw as strengths, I saw instead as indecisiveness. People they saw as tough individuals, I sometimes saw as not necessarily tough or knowledgeable. And sometimes their notions about the positions and perceived priorities were not the same as mine. Some of them did not share my notion that administration's role is only to serve faculty and students as well as to help them. Members often saw the university as a strict hierarchy: They were determined to exercise their authority and power, rather than deal with the principle that, "We've been entrusted with the fate of this institution and who is strong enough to lead." There are two different approaches, and if you, as president, are very busy the entire time, fundraising and so forth, you don't necessarily realize this subtle attitude of your colleagues and the consequences of their recommendations.

You always have university-wide search committees for vice presidents and provosts and deans and so forth, and then you try to get the best possible one from that list. That was difficult, putting the administration together. I would say I made four, five big mistakes during my nine years in terms of judging character, and once you make a mistake, you have to realize [you should] cut your losses. Most presidents don't do that; I did not even do it in one or two instances. Yes, [it's very hard to let someone go,] but then you compound the situation by not dealing with it effectively and immediately because you don't want people to think you cannot keep [administrators], or you're indecisive, or you haven't the capacity to judge who's the best person. But by delaying you hurt the institution and yourself, [and] the person, too. It's not the person's fault because that role was thrust on him or her on the basis of interviews. So, if you interview somebody and you're not a good judge of character, you can't blame the person. He did not say, or she did not say, "I'm the greatest." You thought they were. You chose them.

There's another thing I should mention along this line. I've always surrounded myself with strong people, tough persons, independent minded, whether at Penn, at the New York Public Library, or at Brown. This also is a very tricky business because while I appreciate strength, outsiders may perceive a vice president or provost or dean as being stronger than you are. That's all right for me, as long as the vice president and others don't think they're leading you rather than serving you, or expect that you must do what they say. The important thing is that you develop an effective team. Otherwise, your administration will be divided into "Mr. or Mrs. No or Yes," the soft ones and the hard ones. [People will see] if they want something, they will go to the soft ones. They have to be part of one administration. So, [the question is,] how to gather strong people around you for a common mission rather than strong people around you who may be divisive, or who put their personal agendas and ambitions first, trying to impress the trustees—"We're running the show while the president is traveling," or sigh and say, "Oh my God, you should see what I am doing, and he is opposing me." That's where you make some big mistakes, by tolerating them. Strong people sometimes undercut each other. If you bring weak people, they don't serve you well. So how you put the right team together is a major challenge. It worked for me very well at Penn, but I would say at Brown it was not a spectacular success because I had some appointees who saw each other as rivals rather than as team players. That's a very important point.

You make your decisions on the basis of experience, judgment, discretion. For people I work with, we always check their credentials on paper, but sometimes we don't check their behavior on the job, although we would like to. I can't know, for example, about a woman who has accomplished a lot but does not like other women who are younger, who are climbing faster, or something like that. I learned this the hard way. With some candidates, I can see their attitude right away. It's hard, however, to come to know the complete circumstance, psychology, or behavior of candidates and to select people who have the same value system and ability. There is nothing wrong with ambition as long as that ambition is not harmful to the institution or to colleagues. That's very difficult to handle, especially when you inherit a staff and you're making changes incrementally rather than wholesale. And, further, if you enter an institution and make changes wholesale, it may imply that your predecessor did not have good judgment. So, your predecessor naturally does not like that, people who have been with this president [don't like it], trustees won't like it because they will have been in charge for the past eight, ten, twelve years and you're passing judgment on them also. So, how to make those changes in a way that is not judgmental? You have always to say that you are looking to the future rather than to the past, and you're trying to tailor an administration to fit the mission you have articulated. And even that is easier said than done.

[Now, on the subject of risk taking.] First of all, there are two types of presidents: people who have served public universities and people who have served private universities. Public university leaders who go to private universities get paralyzed for the first year or two. Even though they are intoxicated with the freedom they're inheriting, they get paralyzed. After all, they have spent most of their time in the public university trying to legitimize their potential actions—touching base with a regent here, with a legislator, with the city there, with the tax assessor or whatever. At the private university, you don't have that constraint, but you're under the impression that you still do, so much so that you delay your actions because you think somebody may object to what you intend to do.

So, having put that in the background, I had no honeymoon. My first day [as president], there was already a sit-in in my office. I went and sat with them and talked to them. It was about ethnic studies—[the students] had a thousand signatures [on a petition] they'd been waiting [to give me]. Then in the first year came the library strike. So there was no honeymoon in that sense. But I was not held responsible for those. The first thing, therefore, I had to do was the articulation of the mission of the university—what are we going to do and how are we going to do it? What is going to be my modus operandi? I said up front, the first day, I don't accept demands. Student demands, staff demands, no demands. I only accept petitions, letters, complaints, suggestions, but no demands. The second thing during the honeymoon period is how you communicate to your constituencies; how you behave stamps the mark of your presidency. You must set your imprint within two or three months. Perceptions are important because they assume a reality of their own. For example, within three or four months of my presidency—it may have been less than that—there was a racial incident. Somebody had written racist graffiti. I immediately went to the dormitory where this happened because I knew that this would be used by some for different ends. So I became the main speaker. I asked students to join me, denouncing anti-Semitism and racist slurs against blacks. I even got myself into trouble by saying if I found those who were doing [these things], I would expel them immediately. But the ACLU said, no, you cannot do that, you have to judge, you have to go through a process, who do you think you are? That said, the students were testing me, they were already determining who I was. I said there are many outlets for racism in this nation; Brown is not going to be one of them. Period. No ifs and buts. We'll see what we can do, let us unite, and let us reason together.

[As a rule, I didn't use a spokesperson.] I spoke for myself. I wanted people to hear where I [stood]. Presidents have to have their own style; there is no formula for what presidents should [do]. Circumstances require different solutions and stances. For example, the students collected signatures every year [on a petition] not to allow armed forces representatives to come to campus to recruit because they were seen as violating laws concerning sexual orientation and discrimination. The [students] said we must ban the recruiters. I decided to issue a statement. I wrote an eight-to-ten-page letter after studying the problem, and I found out that all Communist countries (China, Cuba, Vietnam, and so forth) had antigay legislation. I found that all the Muslim countries had antigay laws. I found also that Israel has such laws. So I said, now, are you telling me that I have to ban the nationals and officials of all these countries from our campus? Should Brown's rules supersede the laws of the nation? I wrote similar letters about controversial issues every time such a situation arose. I did not conceal [where I stood] if a member of the Brown faculty was raising an issue that was important for the entire Brown community. I sent my response letter to every faculty member and every student. The letter read, "Dear Members of the Brown Community." Ten thousand letters conveying where I stood on any major issue. Everybody got it in their mailboxes. Arming campus police? I said no. The police union wanted me to arm them. The students did not want to arm them. The staff wanted to arm them for protection. The decision always came to me. I issued a statement as to why not. On important issues, I did not keep myself [away] and then disown the university spokesman or decision makers. I spoke up. University presidents have to speak out on major academic, moral, and political issues, but many people don't. I don't know why—maybe because they are afraid to displease some trustees or some faculty. But in my case, I thought my role as an educator extended also to dealing with conflicts. I saw that conflicts gave opportunities to deal with crucial issues confronting the campus community. So I wrote to the Brown community about freedom of speech, about tolerance, about all kinds of issues. In my farewell [speech], written before my successor came, I discussed religious freedom and tolerance because there had been indirect criticism on campus by some about having a Mormon as my successor. I discussed religious freedom, academic freedom, [I spoke] against political correctness. Perhaps I'm the only president from the Ivy League who has spoken against political correctness. In the *Rolling Stone* interview, I said it's intellectually dishonest because linguistic niceties are no substitute for dealing with some of the important issues confronting us. Indeed, they may even divert us.

[Was I taking risks but not even thinking of them in that way?] All the time. All the time. I invited the Aga Khan, the spiritual leader of Ismaili Muslims to be the first Muslim to give a baccalaureate address at any American higher education [institution]. I brought him to the Baptist meetinghouse where he spoke; it was televised. To the best of my knowledge, during my presidency Brown was the only university where, in addition to the Talmud and the Bible, there were readings from the Koran, and the "Call to Prayer" was done as a Muslim minaret call. I did not ask the faculty, do you think it's a nice idea? It was the right thing to do because all three faiths—Judaism, Christianity, and Islam—are Abrahamic faiths. They are all prophetic faiths. Similarly, another initiative I took for which I've gotten more credit than anything I've done was something very simple: Every parent, grandparent, uncle, brother, sister, relative who was a kindergarten teacher, elementary school teacher, high school teacher, university professor—if their child or relative was graduating from Brown—was invited to march with our faculty in academic regalia. Every year we do this. Now it has become a tradition and it is very popular. I thought it was the right thing to do, to honor all the teachers. Do you think this would have gotten done if I had taken it to the faculty and said, "What do you think?" "Define teacher," they would say. And they did! But I did it in the name of the faculty and the faculty liked it. After it was done, I said, "This is what I am doing; I actually want to respect the teaching profession." They did not [react badly] because again, they know the overall thing, that you're trying to highlight nationally the importance of teaching. Brown could not be the site of educational reform if we didn't respect teachers whose children are graduating.

Another independent action of mine involved the state of Rhode Island. The governor asked me to chair an investigation of the entire collapse of the Rhode Island Savings and Loan banking system. I was crazy to do that but I had to because it affected—among others—at least a thousand of our employees, many of them poor people whose savings were in danger. Members of our union, community, and others were affected. Some faculty members called me and said, "Don't do it, it's a very dangerous thing, the mob may be involved in this," whatever. But I had to do it because it was the right thing to do. [I did not discuss it with my trustees.] I told them I was invited by the governor and I intend to do it. And I took one or two months off to do it. I [came in to] my office, [but] I was dealing with some of these issues. I am glad I did because respect for Brown on the part of the people of Rhode Island went up because my report, which attacked both Republicans and Democrats, the whole machine, as an incestuous system, was considered to be thorough, objective, and instructive. The governor [had been] astute, but I don't know in retrospect [whether] he thought it was possible to come up with a thorough analysis of the whole system in two or three months, or whether whatever [we] came up with, [we would] just say, we are still studying it. The state spent four million dollars in a subsequent investigation and, according to the governor, did not add a single point to what was in our report. Everybody who worked on the report did it on a pro bono basis, including the stenographers union. And I was happy because almost everybody recovered their money. [Brown gave interest-free loans to employees, a somewhat financially risky decision I took alone.] [The trustees] could have gotten angry, but again, they knew why I was doing it, they knew the savings banks were very important. When the recession came, I had to find two million dollars to help parents who had lost their jobs, whose children were at Brown but they could not pay. We did not tell the children, "Leave school." We can't do that.

[Some of the board members had ties to Rhode Island,] not all of them. But many, yes. Ten, twenty; the rest of them were national. But again, I did not confront this issue [with the trustees] because in my opinion when they hired [me], they hired [me] as a leader rather than as a manager. Leaders can always hire managers. Managers never hire leaders. I did not just present the trustees with a fait accompli. I told them, we discussed it. But as president of Brown, I was also the chair of the executive committee of the board and therefore met with the chancellor regularly, every month. So there was opportunity to communicate all of these problems. The result was, we got tremendous positive reaction about the report of our commission, with gratitude that this was the best thing Brown had done for the community.

We also formed HELP [Health and Education Leadership for Providence], getting the hospitals and educational institutions of Providence together to help the city. Six hospitals and four colleges in Providence got together. In addition to everything we were doing in-kind for Providence, we put in $1.5 million annually to help get rid of lead poisoning in houses, to inoculate children, to train the teachers of Providence, and to provide dental care. [I was directly involved in getting these institutions to combine.] Each one had to pay, and they paid, and it's still functioning. All of these—the Providence plan, the governor's economic council, and so forth—were extra work for me. But you have to do it because you have to show what you're doing, [what the university is doing], for the community in which you live. Not paying lip service, but trying to help, because if the community collapses they drag you with it. That is why I marched with the students in "Take Our Streets Back," with a candle. I rode in a police car in the evenings when there had been some racially motivated off-campus beatings. I visited all the dormitories so they would know that I'm not relying on my dean of students to call me if there is trouble. You can afford that only in a small place like Brown, this kind of visitation.

[Was there a defining moment?] The defining moment to me always has been, in any job I've had, when you're afraid that you may lose your enthusiasm, your curiosity, your sense of mission and direction, and when you know the routine is taking over. And then you get apprehensive that maybe you are beginning to love the routine and sit back. That's when I leave. Right before we finished the campaign, in the midst of it actually, my defining moment was when Columbia University offered me the presidency of the university. I said, if you wait a year I may accept. For the moment, I knew that I could not leave Brown in the middle of its fund-raising campaign, which was called the Campaign for the Rising Generation. Subsequently, though, I asked myself, do I really want to continue as president of another university, or have I done the presidency? I concluded that I had done the presidency. I wanted to move on. So my defining moment was actually one year before Brown's campaign ended. Once a campaign has ended, then something sets in with the president. You start competing against yourself, and you believe your own rhetoric and in people who say you can do more, you can do anything. You start acting; you become a caricature of yourself. And that's where you have to split, when you know you already have succeeded, you've accomplished the goals you've set for yourself, for the institution. The institution then needs new blood, needs to bring another wave of energy, vision, imagination, and challenge. Change does not come naturally. I calculated that I had hired 50 percent of Brown's faculty during my tenure, educated almost 20,000 students—more than one-fourth of the alumni are my alumni—strengthened links to the community, strengthened the academic foundations, and the mission of Brown and the Brown community. When I resigned from Brown, that was a defining moment for me because I had not anticipated what people's reaction would be. My wife was given an honorary degree by the trustees, a great surprise. I was given the faculty's Rosenberger Medal. The trustees named a quad after me—Thayer Quad is now Gregorian Quad. The community of Fox Point had fought Brown since 1968 because Brown was displacing families, they said, [through] gentrification—it's a very poor, immigrant neighborhood. The mayor and city council, with the support of the community, named the Fox Point Elementary School, "Vartan Gregorian" Elementary School. I am the second president in the history of Brown to have a school named after him. That really touched me the most. Then the graduate students gave me their first medal, and the undergraduates came, among others, those who were arrested two or three years before at a strike, to thank me and apologize for any trouble they'd caused me. So I said, this is crazy. Nobody can have the confidence of all these people. I have on a shelf in my office, thirteen volumes of their farewell letters which I still have not read even though I thanked the writers because if I read them, they will go to my head. These are all the faculty and friends who have written to me, thanking me. I say, one day when I retire, I'll have a chance to read them, so I left them untouched.

I left Brown in great form, in hindsight. People did not say, "When is he retiring?" We have used a lot of "I" today because the questions here are addressed to me, personally. However, I must stress that everything I have done, I have done in the name of the trustees, faculty, students, and staff, not in my name. If you share credit, you can get lots of mileage and lots of cooperation. Some presidents never realize that. They are either insecure or not smart, because they think they did it. You can't do it without a team. The greatest orchestra conductor cannot conduct without an orchestra, and the greatest orchestra without a music score known by all, cannot play. If a conductor has no musicians, no score, no audience, it's hard to tie all of those things together.

[Now, about becoming a "lame duck."] You become a lame duck—it doesn't matter when you step down—if your stepping down coincides with a budget cycle. As long as you are in control of the budget, you are not a lame duck. So my advice to any president is not to resign July 1 for the new fiscal year; otherwise, everybody [looks to] your successor [and] second in command for decisions. So I stepped down from Brown, formally, in September. That was learned from Martin Myerson's experience at Penn and from others as well. When you announce your resignation or retirement, they always like [for it] to coincide with the academic year and, therefore, nobody feels compelled to call on you. But if you are controlling the next year's budget, it doesn't matter what you call yourself, lame duck or not lame duck, you are still in charge. I made lots of decisions in the last three months when I was quote unquote the lame duck. Important decisions. Up to the very last day. I learned it the hard way. So "lame duck" is "budget duck"!

NOTES

1. Joseph Berger, "Gregorian Is Chosen as President of Brown University," *New York Times Biographical Service*, September 1, 1988, p. 971. See also Philip Hamburger, "Profiles: Searching for Gregorian," parts I and II, *New Yorker*, April 14, 1986, pp. 45–61, and April 21, 1986, pp. 53–68.

2. Though a Research I institution, Brown has only one professional school—the school of medicine—in addition to the undergraduate college and graduate school.

3. In 1989, Brown had 5,619 undergraduates and 1,624 graduate and medical students; in 1997 undergraduates totaled 5,697 and graduate and medical students had dropped slightly to 1,612 ("Review of Brown," in *Brown University Financial Report 1988–1989*, p. 23; "Selected Statistics," in *Brown 1996–1997: Brown University Financial Report*, p. 14). Faculty numbers for 1989 and 1997 come from the Office of the President, Brown University; budget figures are found in "Total Expenditures and Mandatory Transfers," in "Statement of Cur-

rent Funds Revenues Expenditures and Transfers," in *Brown University Financial Report 1988–1989*, p. 16, and "Statement of Expenses by Function," in *Brown 1996–1997: Brown University Financial Report*, p. 26. Endowment totals are reported in "The Nation: Resources: College and University Endowments Over $100-Million, 1989," *Chronicle of Higher Education Almanac*, September 5, 1990, p. 26, study by the National Association of College and University Business Officers, and Vartan Gregorian, President Emeritus, *In the Service of Brown University: A Report on Nine Years, August 31, 1988, Through September 30, 1997*, (New York: Carnegie Corporation of New York, 2003), p. 39.

4. "Statement by Alva O. Way, Chancellor," Brown University News Bureau, January 7, 1997.

5. In *Cohen v. Brown* (1992), members of Brown's women's volleyball and gymnastics teams, which had had their status changed by the university from varsity to club, filed suit under Title IX, arguing that even though two men's teams had also experienced the same change in status, women were underrepresented in athletics at the university. A settlement was approved in 1998, when the suit was described as "the most important litigation to date on sex discrimination in intercollegiate athletics," at least partly because the concept of "substantial proportionality" was further defined. Vartan Gregorian, email communication of August 16, 2004 to Leslie Banner; Jim Naughton, "Judge Approves Plan to Settle Lingering Claims in Title IX Suit Against Brown U.," *Chronicle of Higher Education*, June 24, 1998, http://chronicle.com/daily/98/06/98062405n.shtml.

INDEX

131, 132, 327–28; risk taking by,
48, 49–51, 126, 322, 324–26;
Rolling Stone interview, 49; Rosenberger award, 316, 327; search
committees under, 321; on service,
314; at Stanford, 309; teaching career, 309, 320; on team building,
124; team building by, 22–24,
320–22; at University of Pennsylvania, 309, 314, 316, 318–19, 321;
at University of Texas, 309, 318
Gregory, Dick, 297, 298
Gulf War, 89, 238
Gutmann, Amy, xviin4

Hardin, Barbara, 286, 302
Hardin, Paul, xiv; academic career of,
95; agenda setting by, 27, 125, 284;
on American Council on Education, 286, 307; attendance at
AAU, 19, 285–87; and black cultural center controversy, 44, 70–72,
282, 289, 292–94, 298, 304; on
boards of trustees, 297; and Brodie,
19, 282, 285; and C. D. Spangler,
19–20, 44, 49, 86, 129, 282,
284–90; candidacy at UNC-Chapel
Hill, 5, 6, 124, 282–84; career path
of, 95, 103; commitment to UNC-
Chapel Hill, 20; defining moments
for, 43, 44, 126, 288–89, 292,
294–96; Drew presidency, 281,
282; at Duke, 297; on freedom of
expression, 296–98; fund raising by,
288, 304–6; and James Hunt, 44,
88, 292; and James Martin, 44,
87–88, 291–92, 294; lame duck period of, 110–12, 132, 299–300,
306; law practice of, 281; lobbying
of legislature, 86, 281, 289, 306;
preparation for UNC-Chapel Hill,
18–20; relations with UNC-Chapel
Hill faculty, 300–301, 306–7; relations with UNC-Chapel Hill

trustees, 28, 111, 128, 129, 283,
300, 304; resignation of, 94–95,
130, 132, 134, 298–300; retirement
statement of, 111; on risk taking,
45; risk taking by, 49, 126, 289,
304, 305; SMU presidency, 281,
294; and student activists, 66, 127,
128, 292–93, 301; successor of,
111, 287, 294; on tuition, 287; at
UAB, 295, 299, 300, 301–4; and
UAB faculty, 302; and UAB
trustees, 303; and UNC board of
governors, 290; and UNC-CH fiscal autonomy, 44, 86, 284–85, 290,
294; and UNC governance structure, 85–88; on value of legal
training, 297; Wofford presidency,
281, 283, 297–98
Harris, Trudier, 290
Harvard University: admission of
women, 235; budgetary restructuring at, 59; *versus* Dartmouth,
14–15, 211, 212; undergraduate education at, 235–36
Heiskell, Andrew, 313
HELP (Health and Education Leader-
ship for Providence), 50, 326
Hereford, Frank, 70, 117, 122n24,
241; and Farmington controversy,
228–29
Hesburgh, Father Theodore, 67, 254
Heyman, Mike, 38, 227–28
Higginbottom, Sam, 189
Hiring decisions, backing out of, 24
Hockfield, Susan, xviin4
Hofstadter, Richard, 181
Holbrook, Karen A., xviin4
Holloway, John, 237
Holmgren, Janet, 171
Honeymoon phase (in university
presidencies), xiii, xiv, 31–39, 125,
126. *See also individual presidents*
Hooker, Michael, 287, 294
Hoover Institution (Stanford Univer-

About the Authors

H. KEITH H. BRODIE is President Emeritus, Duke University, and James B. Duke Professor of Psychiatry, Professor of Law, and Professor of Psychology. Prior to his eight-year presidency, Brodie served as both Chancellor and Acting Provost. His medical career has been focused on research on the biochemistry of mental illness. He is author or co-editor of thirteen books.

LESLIE BANNER is a writer, editor, and higher education research specialist at Duke University, where she also served as Special Assistant for University Affairs during Dr. Brodie's presidency. She is author of *A Passionate Preference: The Story of the North Carolina School of the Arts* (1991).